MW00353809

TAPES FROM CALIFORNIA

TEENAGE ROAD TRIPPING, 1976

Tapes from California: Teenage Road Tripping, 1976
© 2018 Jill C. Nelson. All Rights Reserved.

No part of this book may be reproduced in any form or by any means, electronic, mechanical, digital, photocopying or recording, except for the inclusion in a review, without permission in writing from the publisher.

Published in the USA by:
BearManor Media
PO Box 71426
Albany, Georgia 31708
www.bearmanormedia.com

Hardcover: ISBN 978-1-62933-210-9
Paperback: ISBN 978-1-62933-209-3

Printed in the United States of America.
Cover by JSV Designs.
Book design by Brian Pearce | Red Jacket Press.

TAPES FROM CALIFORNIA

TEENAGE ROAD TRIPPING, 1976

Jill C. Nelson

Foreword

Have you ever wished you had a time machine so you could go back and visit a special time in our history, say the mid-1970s when hippies roamed the landscape and the Counter Culture was still going full bore? Well, you do have one: this book. What Jill Nelson has created is not merely another memoir; it's a guided trip back to another time, a magical time so different from the 2010s in fundamental ways that it might as well be a hundred years ago. If you are too young to have lived through those days yourself, or too old to remember them clearly even though you were there, Jill's highly personal, skillfully crafted narrative will make that age live in your mind.

Come smell the air of 1976. Take a ride down the open road with one of your best friends beside you and a questionable character you just met behind the wheel. Bunk down in a seedy, bug-infested youth hostel for the night, wondering where you will be tomorrow; and the day after that.

What was it like to explore the world beyond your hometown in the mid-1970s before GPS, smartphones, Google Maps, or any other technology that could keep you connected 24/7 existed? Relying only on a battered travel guide, pay phones that took dimes, and the few dollars they had saved from their last job in their pocket, teenagers Jill and Jan set out to see the world, or at least the West Coast of Canada and the U.S., guided by a keen curiosity about life, a healthy caution towards the evil in men's souls, a youthful optimism, and hearts that were brave and wise beyond their years. They had no set plans. They would know where they were going when they got there, and once they had learned what they could from the people they met and the places they visited, they would move on to the next adventure.

Join them on this remarkable trip. I promise you the time will fly by. Jill Nelson writes with uncommon clarity and intelligence, creating a vivid sensory record of the things she saw, the ideas she entertained — accepting some, rejecting others — and the wide range of feelings she lived through as she found her way in this world. As a writer who lived through those times and experienced firsthand the hopeful blossoming and eventual collapse of the 1960s-70s Cultural Revolution, I can vouch for the fact that Jill got it right. I haven't read anything that so faithfully captures what it was like to be young and free and alive in those days, not only witnessing the enormous social, political, and spiritual changes taking place in our world, but also playing a small role in that larger change. My teens and twenties were spent in Southern California, where much of Jill's narrative takes place, and I can attest that she evokes that time and place with dead-on accuracy. Her depiction of life in a communal environment graced with New Age trimmings rings especially true for me. I knew people who were exactly like the cult leaders she writes of: charismatic charmers who were intensely sincere visionaries on the one hand, and smoothly persuasive manipulators on the other hand. Jill held her own against these powerful individuals, learned from them what they had to teach her, and then decisively moved on when it felt like it was time to go.

I doubt I would have had the courage that Jill and Jan displayed when they set out on their journey with no established destination and very limited resources. To my mind, they were bold pioneers, pluckily finding a path through a wilderness of far-flung towns and cities, off the grid spiritual centers, long winding highways, and a wild cast of dodgy characters. And their courage paid off in riches that they hold to this day: the odd, miraculous memories of life lived to the fullest while working days as chamber maids in a downtown hotel, or enjoying the warmth of the desert sun on their shoulders at impromptu potluck feasts, or spending a sleepless night in the backseat of a troubled man's car somewhere near Mount Shasta. It's a journey few of us have taken, a leap of faith, and you can join them in the pages of this book.

I've known Jill for several years and I consider her one of the brightest, most sincere human beings I've ever met. She has a natural gift for storytelling, and I'm very glad she has chosen to tell this story, because it's one that only she can tell, and it's a story that wants to be told. A tale of two young women who desired to better know their world, and went out one fine day to see what they could see. And now it's your story too, because when a writer is really doing their job, as Jill has done here, you live their story and take it on as your own. This is a story that will linger in your mind and heart long after you've read the last page. And that, to me, defines good writing and good storytelling.

DAVID BARKER
Author of In the Gulfs of Dream *(with W. H. Pugmire)*
Salem, Oregon
May 2015

Overture

On February 19, 1976, after flying 3000 miles west from Toronto, my friend Jan and I arrived at the YWCA in downtown Vancouver, our temporary new home. At seventeen and eighteen years old, knapsacks secured on our backs, this was the beginning of what would be six-months of work and travel. Having grown up in an era of independence and free-range parenting, other than giving us their blessings, our parents didn't factor into the equation.

Completing six weeks working as chambermaids at Hotel Vancouver, the duration of our journey, we explored big and small cities and landscapes of Victoria, San Francisco, Santa Cruz, Big Sur, Los Angeles, San Diego, Hemet, Yosemite, Hope, Banff, Jasper, Edmonton, Calgary, Saskatoon and Regina. In exchange for gas money and companionship, fellow travellers often transported us to our next destination. Other times we took public transit. Mostly, we hitchhiked. In 1976, hitchhiking was far more commonplace, enabling the young and the curious to access far more for less. Returning home in August, utilizing our thumbs, Jan and I'd logged approximately 3000 miles of an 8000-mile journey.

It was the latter half of the 1970s; the final vestiges of the hippie counter culture fostered a decade before that saw bright-eyed youths from far and wide strike off to parts unknown in an attempt to explore the world and find their own truth along the way. Mid-way through my teen years, I wanted to latch on to that experience. Jan and I studied road maps, scrutinized hostel guidebooks, relied upon letter writing. Because of expense, long distance phone calls home were few and far between. Learning to trust and look out for one another, we felt indestructible, shielded from harm.

Employing my journal, Jan's immaculately recorded diary, our memories, letters sent and received during our six-month absence, HOOM's bible: *The Holy Order of MANS* (published in 1967), and *The Meadowlark Cookbook* (published in 1978), combining an eighteen-year-old's perspective with late-50's insight, faithfully and chronologically, I have reconstructed our timeline, surroundings, adventures and impressions; the people and friends we had known. This memoir includes photographs, illustrations, allusions of influential songwriters of the period, mementos, and pictures that represent an event or memory and provide context for our journey. Unless otherwise noted, all photos that appear in the book were shot during our sojourn. Portions of the vernacular chronicled in our diaries reflecting the simplicity of those years has been shaped into this account. Canada was in the process of phasing in metrification (1970-1977) when this story took place. *Tapes from California* utilizes the commonly used Imperial measurement system to track distances, calculate units of food, and compute values for gas. The Fahrenheit scale is applied for measuring temperature.

Tapes from California is written in Canadian English. For the provision of privacy, pseudonyms have been used for many of the people introduced in this memoir.

Some claim it took nerve to do what Jan and I did — striking off without clarity or compromise. Others believe that we were young, gullible, too trusting. Since our travels began forty years ago, the planet has changed exponentially. With the advent of social media, social engineering, legal regulations, and new technologies breaking ground every day, in the contemporary world, adventures such as ours have taken on a different focus and meaning.

Greek philosopher Heraclitus is alleged to have written, "No man ever steps in the same river twice." Like a riverbed, our memories surge through the channels of time.

JILL C. NELSON

Initiatives emerge after a period of longing, for direction, for change. Melancholy is deflected by hope; infectious gloom adjusts to twinkling eyes. Prophetic words compel time to listen.

JILL C. NELSON, JANUARY 1976

*This book is dedicated
To young wanderlusts everywhere,
in body and in mind.
And especially to
Howard, Corey, and Andrea*

The YWCA, Downtown Vancouver, February 1976.

CHAPTER 1

I Get Up; I Get Down

"Find the crossroad leading in every direction."
JILL C. NELSON, *February 1976*

Shortly after sunrise, I said so long to my parents.

Knapsack and sleeping bag fastened snugly to my lime green ski jacket, yellow canvas satchel slung over my shoulder, having tepid misgivings, I tramped out of our suburban split-level house, down the front porch steps and onto the snow-coated driveway. In the dark, my friend and travelling companion, Jan, waited excitedly with her father, warm and dry inside of his light blue Oldsmobile. A Toronto attorney, Jan's dad had offered to drop us at Southern Ontario's Pearson International Airport on his way downtown. It was Thursday morning, February 19. Our direct Air Canada flight to Vancouver was scheduled for a 9 am departure. With the newly fallen snow and probable slick roads, we didn't want to run the risk of being late. Backing over a thick ridge of white stuff left along the foot of our driveway by the city's snow removal truck, the Oldsmobile pointed east onto the crescent. From the living-room window, wearing faded terry dressing gowns, Mom and Dad waved in accord.

The winter morning was viciously cold. Draped heavily around fir trees and covering the otherwise naked branches of maples, elms and oaks like a cloak, snow and ice, plenteous and steadfast, created deep ruts along the highway where three-foot drifts had spiraled, clutching onto the shoulder of the road, asserting a new home until the spring thaw. By the time wintery mornings in Southern Ontario were replaced by dewdrops heralding the return of magnolia and cherry blossoms and birds flitting about preparing nests to groom their young, Jan and I would be thousands of miles away. Hopefully, far south of the border.

Amid snow squalls, driving along the Queen Elizabeth Way, 35 miles between Burlington and Toronto, can be tricky and treacherous. Native to the area, and accustomed to unstable weather, Jan's father was comfortable in the role of designated driver. After many years going to and fro, regardless of what the forecast had in store, Mr. M. could practically freewheel between the two cities with one eye closed.

The day of our departure, Jan was one month beyond her seventeenth birthday. The previous autumn, I'd turned eighteen. One month before setting out, my friend and I graduated Grade 13. One of the first in our school to have completed secondary school at sixteen, boasting a coveted grade point average hovering in the low 80s, Jan's accomplishment was most impressive in a learning establishment in which the semester system (five 80-minute periods) had been introduced only two years earlier. Due to my own undoing, I'd managed to scrape together a mediocre 67 percent overall. In those days, second-rate marks could still guarantee acceptance at a respectable Ontario university. College, a close second, was a shoe-in. To keep my parents at bay, as a backup measure, I'd applied at a couple of colleges between Oakville and Kingston, though had no serious interest in attending come September. Final marks were insignificant numbers — a one-way ticket to emancipation — so I thought. Post-secondary education was the furthest target on the sensor.

As a blossoming teen, I'd begun to question the logistics of following expectations and obligations plainly laid out by parents, teachers, and fellow students. In the process of choosing more school or entering the work force full time, it seemed to me, kids were impatient to assimilate into adulthood.

In one form or another, the West Coast trip had been in the works for the better part of a year. Discussion of travel often cropped up amongst our close group of friends. The thrill of spinning the atlas, imagining flying somewhere thousands of miles away, was an abiding draw. At one stage, one of my closest friends, May, and I had talked about travelling to England together. Take in the sites of Liverpool, London, and Manchester — birthplaces of the Beatles and other seminal British bands we all adored. Supplementary, unfinished proposals were also put on the table, and eventually displaced when other objectives and interests intervened. Remaining true to myself, acuity regarding post-secondary goals encouraged me to move forward. Working part-time, I realized I could bank enough money the final year-and-a-half of school to purchase a one-way ticket somewhere in Canada. The West felt lucky in those days. I had relatives living in British Columbia and California. Seeking employment, other teens from our town had already migrated to Alberta and British Columbia.

Unveiling my emerging scheme to another school friend with whom I'd shared a number of hours listening to records, drinking draught beer, and occasionally getting high, Jan was cautiously excited. Presuming we'd make simpatico travel companions, given the situation, she and I could both lead and follow — a seamless partnership. July of 1975, during a quasi-semi-trial run, the pair of us had ventured on a two-week vacation to Barbados, where our compatibility was put to the test.

The experiment was a success.

Returning home that summer, we forged a pact. Following several months anticipating details, overcoming occasional doubts, our mission, to fly to the West, and subsequently, wind our way to Southern California, began to coalesce. Final touches crystallized. Once we were emotionally set, chips fell into place. Momentum caught fire. We announced our news to friends first, our parents last. Once the plan was out in the open, it became a promise that would not be renounced.

In the months leading to our leaving, developing a list of destination points made high school endurable. The tentative strategy: land in Vancouver, find temporary jobs, and then travel south of the border in spring, our approach was to stay mostly in youth hostels, do some camping, and return home in August through Western Canada. After that, we would see about post-secondary. Maybe I'd meet a male companion and dump school altogether. United in our quest, we'd prolong travel. Never touch ground.

Equipped with Canada and United States roadmaps, birth certificates, and an International Youth Hostel manual, following one plane change and a three-hour delay on a god-forsaken glacial February afternoon, Jan and I boarded an Air Canada DC-9 jet aircraft westbound for Vancouver. Exactly one hour after the plane's ascent, through the intercom, our pilot's muffled voice interrupted cabin activity, informing all passengers to expect changeable weather ahead. Typically, we would be flying against prevailing winds.

Skipper didn't say how long we might expect turbulence.

Hotel Vancouver, winter 1976.

CHAPTER 2

YWCA &
Hotel Vancouver

*"The world is a looking glass and gives back to every man
the reflection of his own face."*
WILLIAM MAKEPEACE THACKERAY

Touching down at 1:45 pm Pacific Time after a five-and-a half-hour flight, feeling like two adolescent girls unchained in a capacious world, Jan and I hustled into the bustling Vancouver airport located in Richmond. Collecting our packs from the luggage conveyer, we joined travellers and commuters on the airport bus for the short ride downtown.

Vancouver is a major west coastal Canadian city situated on the Burrard Peninsula between the Burrard Inlet to the north and the Fraser River to the south. Guarded by the beauteous Rocky Mountain range, British Columbia's mainland leads out to the Pacific Ocean. Possessing one of Canada's warmest climates in winter months, Vancouver is also one of the wettest. Some have asserted the damp, populated seaport has one of the highest suicide rates in the country. Rainy as expected, Vancouver's moderate temperature was a reprieve from the bone chilling days leading up to our leaving. By comparison, the seaside city felt tropical.

Our first stopover, the YWCA on Beatty Street, a $10 per night (or $100 per month — weekly rates were not offered) temporary accommodation for women and girls would enable us to acclimate to the city while seeking work. Our hostel guidebook indicated that individuals couldn't stay anywhere longer than a few days rendering the Y the only semi-affordable game in town. Deciding to sign up for 30 days rather than paying the nightly rate, a gruff female manager assigned Jan and me to a no frills, semi-private room with two cots. One of the newer tenants had tipped us off. Even if we didn't plan to stay the full month, paying the less expensive 30-day fee was the best way to go, at least for the short term.

Registration completed, standing in the lobby looking out the front window toward slick two-lane charcoal streets where rain had turned to hail, we watched a police cruiser smash absently into a blue van parked next to a meter.

I wondered if the slipshod incident had meant anything.

Situated in downtown Vancouver in the north-central part of the city, the YWCA's apartment-sized complex was within proximity of primarily everything and anything two teenage girls might have desired back in 1976. There was the constant rush of activity, a throbbing pulse of purpose and excitement. Buses, pigeons, people, and rain were plentiful. From first impressions, so were junkies, hookers, and the odd, conspicuous derelict building, reminiscent of Queen Street, in Toronto's downtown core. Hoping to eventually become incisive observers of our foreign surroundings, in the interim, Jan and I fell in unnoticeable to long-time denizens of the city.

Immediate needs consisted of a short list. Apart from finding employment and anticipating travel, we were interested in meeting likeminded youths (boys *and* girls). Required, was an address wherein we could unload our backpacks (check), have a roof over our heads (double-check), and a place to rustle up a meager breakfast.

My own pack, a sizable hunter-green canvas army knapsack, was fitted with handles that doubled as anchors for my arms to hook through. Less cumbersome to tote than mine, Jan's red nylon apple shaped pack offered sufficient room for storage. We carried $200 each — a respectable amount of seed money to help get us situated, nothing more. Half of it was already gone and we'd barely touched ground. Job-hunting would have to begin tout suite. Not a trial during those days, but we couldn't afford to be finicky. With limited cash and expectations, options were either A or B, though this was not a deterrent. Having too many choices presents problems. We didn't anticipate problems.

This was my second visit to Vancouver within an eight-year span. Along with my parents and Brother Steve, in 1970 I'd vacationed at a few of Canada's western cities, including a three-day layover in Vancouver. We toured Stanley Park, rode to the top of Grouse Mountain Ski Resort in a cable car, scampered along the narrow, death defying (we believed)

Capilano Suspension Bridge poised several feet above a forest of Douglas firs in North Vancouver, and watched seals sun themselves on the flat rocks in Vancouver harbour. The highpoints of our trip my dad had filmed with a little home movie camera he purchased the previous spring. Holding affectionate memories of that summer, and particularly Vancouver, there was the desire to return.

During our first few days in the city, Jan and I expected to do a little sightseeing. No longer living in the comfort of our parents' houses, priorities were about to be realigned.

Necessities were simple and sensible. We were quick to learn that crackers, cottage cheese, bread, milk, sesame snaps, and fruit could sustain us for days. Dried salad in a bag cost 50 cents. Meat was a luxury. Forgetting to pack them, I made a mental note to request Dynomints (as in the commercial, "I'd do anything for a *Dynomint!*"), a favourite breath mint, to be sent from home.

Music had always been a great source of happiness and commonality shared amongst our group of tightly knit friends that consisted of me, May, Liz, Jen, Dee, Kelly, — and Jan. Routinely, we'd analyze, characterize, scrutinize and grade the latest blue-chip offerings from our favourite bands. From grade ten until the end of high school, junkies for rock, pop, and progressive rock, the gang of us regularly attended concerts at Maple Leaf Gardens in Toronto. Taking the Go-Train home in the early hours of the morning (usually) on a school night — dead tired, half deaf, ears buzzing like locusts, we'd be blissfully happy.

The tape recorder and audio tapes Jan wisely thought to cart along provided cheap entertainment, enabling us to revel in the company of The Beatles, The Who, Yes, Genesis, Roxy Music, Jackson Browne, Bowie, Neil Young, Bob Dylan, James Taylor, Gilbert O'Sullivan, Elton John, Jethro Tull, Cat Stevens, Procol Harum, Joni Mitchell, Deep Purple, Edgar Winter, Carole King, Bryan Ferry — rock, pop, and folk heroes who would help sculpt the canvas for experiences yet to unfold.

Shortly after our arrival in Vancouver, Jan and I filled out job applications at various local eating establishments (White Spot and Mickey D's, specifically), and at surrounding hotels. There were several postings at the Y for dancers (it took a week to realize that "dancing" holds different connotations). In the event we weren't hired straight off, we were advised to apply for "pogey" (Unemployment Insurance) — AKA cash that does not have to be repaid. Arriving at administration offices located at 535 Homer

Street West, we were instructed by pogey officials that when taking leave from previous employment, before one can apply for benefits there is a two-week cooling-off period.

Returning to our temporary home optimistic, we were redirected to another room on the fifth floor, sporting three single beds. Containing three night stands and three closets, our new room had an adjoining bathroom bog shared with Cheyenne (Dallas Cheyenne Mercereau), a native girl from Northern Ontario. The sole inhabitant of a highly coveted single on the other side of the latrine, apart from a money bribe — something neither of us had, Cheyenne wasn't about give up her prize. Additionally, Jan and I acquired a bright new roommate, 22-year-old Debbie from Chilliwack. Having resided in the L-shaped space for a few months, Deb's bed was the one closest to the window.

From the onset, our new roomie was a real firecracker — bubbly, vivacious — funny and fun. In the capacity of unfamiliar roommates, Jan and I could have done a lot worse. Employed full-time as a bank teller, Deb woke up every morning bright and early. In other words, she was responsible. There was only one liability. Deb insisted our bedroom window be open halfway every night for "fresh" air to clear out the lingering stench from her du Mauriers. I don't care how balmy Vancouver is during winter, the middle of the night in February is damn cold.

Common-area lounges located throughout the building provided space to gossip, watch television, and smoke. A conglomeration of working girls, cadets, travellers, and lesbians seeking hookups, the Y also had its share of druggies and hookers. Many of the girls were decent human beings; others were downright freaks and hard-bitten individuals who, either by choice or otherwise, had nose-dived into the darker side of life, made evident by how they terrorized other residents verbally, even physically. There was tension. There was fear. There was rage. Commonly found in facilities housing people of the same gender, a hierarchy existed. "Lifers," girls and young women residing at the Y longest, took liberties that other, less savvy girls wouldn't dare. For the purpose of self-protection, proaction was exercised. Jan and I made it our practice to keep our traps shut and noses clean.

Preservation came with a caveat. Surly girls took delight preying on fresh meat and were skilled at winning over unsuspecting tenants using tricks and strong-arm tactics. The rotten apples led me to conclude the Young Women's Christian Association is the antithesis of its name. No doubt, intentions of the founders of the Y, whose motto, "Save souls and succor the poor and needy," were principled and praiseworthy. In

our experience however, many of the people hired to carry out manage-
rial duties could be equally devious and dishonest as those in need of
services.

Whether escaping the streets, compromising family situations, bad
boyfriends, sinking grades, or in the market for work, nice or nasty, a good
number of us were there for the excitement of gaining independence and
freedom from establishment and parental constraints. Thanks to Deb,
with relative ease, Jan and I became acquainted with several girls on our
floor and other floors, of neutral variety.

Girls such as Lois, Cathy Henry, Leslie, Sarah, and Wendy.

Less than one week after our arrival, I had a brush with authorities of
the premises. Unwisely, I'd made a half-witted attempt to help a homeless girl by pinching (I was merely *borrowing* to later be replaced once an
opportunity arose) a few stray pizzas from a local store while the owners
took a break in the back room. The leftover pizzas were from an order that
wasn't picked up (so I was told), and about to be thrown away. Figuring
no harm, no foul, this was an opportunity wherein I was robbing from
Pete so that Paul could have something to eat. Apart from sneaking a
couple of chocolate bars from the corner store when I was a kid, stealing
was not part of my repertoire.

The ploy backfired. I wasn't apprehended by the storeowners. Rather,
I was caught red-handed by the don (middle-aged hall monitor) on our
floor. I'm not sure which was worse. Following my lame attempt at uncon-
vincing double-talk, using language that would have gotten my mouth
washed out with soap when I was a kid, the don tore a strip off me.
Concluding her little tirade, I was sent directly to bed without any pizza.

Somebody had snitched. I didn't doubt that for a minute. Girls got
off on opening their flaps in expectation of favours down the road. In the
end, it was no big deal, though being barred from lending a hand was a
disappointment.

I would know better next time.

The best way to become acquainted with the guts of any city is on
foot. Carrying a street map at all times, it didn't take long to become
familiarized with Vancouver's topography, attractively accentuated by
an assemblage of Edwardian buildings, conifer trees, alders, and maples.
Lined along the sidewalks in abundance beneath the tree's umbrellas
were azalea bushes, snowdrops, and flowering exotics. Rhododendrons
dominated along the North Shore Mountains like wild sage.

During daily walks, Jan and I visited Gastown, Bloedel's Conservatory, Robson Square, the Art Gallery, and Stanley Park. The first couple of Sundays, we attended church at two different venues hosting contrasting faiths. Usually preferring to access the Burrard Street Bridge, for inexpensive lunches, we walked 2 ½ miles from downtown Vancouver to Kitsilano. When feeling the urge to change the scenery, we'd take the Granville Bridge.

People and experiences continually varied. Walking along West 4th Avenue one afternoon, a sniper was arrested by a SWAT team, inducing us to return to the Y via an alternate route. Enthusiastic to explore some of the sketchy areas of town, Jan and I often ventured to East Hastings Street, unofficially known as "Skid Row." Home to many of the city's heroin users and rummies, East Hastings was unlike anything I'd ever witnessed. Emaciated youths, prematurely aged due to drug addiction, displayed gaping bald spots where hair should have been. Open spotty sores revealed ravaged, scaly skin. Sadly, it seemed that Hastings had become the Canadian counterpart to San Francisco's decaying drug infested Haight Ashbury, once a Mecca for the bohemian and hippie movements of the 1950s and 60s.

On East Hastings, there is no such thing as discretion. Using openly, junkies aggressively solicited passersby for money, drugs, or offered sex for drugs. I had a healthy fear of amphetamines, opiates, and anything else along those lines. Witnessing the deterioration of people reinforced instincts to steer clear of synthetic substances.

One week after landing in the city, Jan and I were hired by Mrs. Ferguson, the housekeeping manager at Hotel Vancouver (known today as Fairmont Hotel Vancouver) to begin work as chambermaids. Located at 900 West Georgia and Burrard Streets, the gothic, multi-tiered building is one of the oldest, most prominent fixtures in the city. In those days, the average fee for a room was a whopping $143 per night.

At $4.26 per hour, Mrs. Ferguson informed us our wages would be appropriate for our services.

We would be on call.

Supplied with bright, short-sleeved, pumpkin-orange uniforms, crisp white aprons, and two pairs of panty hose apiece, upon our hiring, our new boss asked that we apply for replacements for our social security cards, which we did. Following our hiring, Jan and I agreed, we would work at Hotel Vancouver for one month. Take it from there.

On call from one day to the next, we never knew if we'd be working. Hotel management didn't know until morning when somebody called in sick. In the event we *were* called into work, it was tough making concrete plans. We stuck it out. Averaging potentially thirty hours a week, part-time work could earn us close to $500 a month. It was enough money to eventually leave the city and head across the border through Washington and Oregon, reach California by April — our designated spring destination.

Most mornings it turned out, the house phone rang in the hallway on our floor. Because our room was down the corridor and therefore out of range from the shared telephone, the first girl to respond usually wasn't Jan or me. Following an annoying *Blat, Blat*, inevitably, someone would pound loudly on our door — usually whichever girl was the first to be awakened from deep sleep by the incessant ringing. In the bed closest to the door to our room, poor Deb often had to get up to answer it. It would be the hotel calling Jan, or me in to work for 7 am. On day shifts, this was the general routine for the duration of our employment.

Hotel Vancouver's clientele consisted primarily of business executives, sightseers, pilots, flight attendants, professional escorts, and second-string prostitutes. To the naked eye, the mature, castle-like brick monstrosity containing 55,000 square feet of luxury and elegance, each spacious room characterized by plush draperies, mahogany headboards, heavy desks, bureaus and armoires delineated by handsome woven broadloom, was most effecting. Underlying nebulous activities that took place within the eminent structure, a host to musty corridor odours and bacteria, told a different story.

Though Jan and I slogged hard, we never did become proficient at our duties. Assigned between twelve to fourteen single and double rooms to clean and make-up daily, it was no small feat for two teenaged novices. Often faced with sexual remnants lingering from a quick morning screw or a marathon make-out session the night before, spattered across 400-thread count cotton sheets was the undeniable smoking gun: dried shot spots. On top of that, residue: clay-like foundation thick as cement lined the top of the soaker tubs — typical grime left behind by female Asian airline attendants with an affinity for heavy cake make-up.

Draped in weighty satin spreads, the majority of beds in the single and double rooms were queen and king-sized. Neither of us had seen beds *that* ginormous before, nor knew they existed. To make the rooms up precisely, between dusting, vacuuming, cleaning bathrooms, mopping floors, restocking bath towels, soaps, toilet paper, and shampoo — stripping and remaking the beds fabricating tight, hospital cornered sheets required pristine effort. Unsuspecting of what I might find every time I turned the key in a door and cried out "Maid," I'd recall my mother, who got furious whenever we messed up the house immediately after she'd cleaned — a misdemeanor compared to these hideous offenses.

On a good day, during an eight-hour shift I was able to get ten rooms finished and felt as if I'd won a triathlon. Our co-workers, a plucky group of Portuguese women under the hotel's employ for several years, usually had to complete what Jan and I weren't able to do. In return, we were afforded some form or another of comic relief. Coordinating our room assignments so that we could meet for lunch, breaks consisted of chewing on stale sandwiches in the ladies' locker room, clustered together with eight to ten of the Portuguese clique, communicating freely in their native language. Each shift, the women ate up much of the half hour ogling *Hustler*, *Lesbian Lover*, and *Playboy* — magazines they'd swiped from the rooms, and made a game out of pointing out nudie center-fold pages depicting spread beavers and well-endowed men. For kicks, one or another would attempt to simulate the explicit oral action illustrated inside by licking the pages of the magazine. Then they'd all bust up laughing.

Jan and I did not participate.

One morning, after repeatedly knocking and calling "Maid" and getting no response, Jan encountered a hotel guest buck-naked. To save himself (and Jan) from embarrassment, the flabby, mid-sixties club owner spent the extent of her hour in his room concealing his gun and holster behind the television set. Hurriedly, Jan dusted, changed sheets, and scrubbed the man's shower and toilet. For her trouble, the man gave her a ten spot.

One afternoon, I surprised a call girl (a Dolly Parton clone) when I arrived to make-up the room as she was about to get down and dirty with a john. Fortunately, for me, Dolly was sweet about my intrusion, sending me on my way without having so much as to wipe my white duster across a night table or scrape her toilet bowl — a real bonus. The following day, Dolly wisely hung the "Occupied" sign outside her door.

Some days, people were generous and tipped us for trying hard. The best part was comparing notes at the end of each shift to see who was rewarded for going the extra mile.

We added the cash to our stash.

At the end of the day, there were checks and balances. Our commander in chief, Kathleen, a muscle-bound, bottled-blonde, East European drill sergeant, stayed untiringly on our tails to ensure we'd met job requirements.

One time, Kathleen accused me of cutting corners by taking a soiled bottom sheet slept on by a guest, and using it as a top sheet for the next guest rather than retrieving a fresh top sheet from my cart parked in the hallway. Confessing my guilt, I was chastised with the threat that Kathleen would report me to the hotel manager if I attempted the dirty trick again. No doubt, a trio of dark pubic hairs clinging obstinately to the fitted sheet had been the dead give-away.

Jan's sin was the habit of leaving too much "sheet" in the toilets. She was never certain if Kathleen was talking about a clean *shit* or clean *sheet*. To ensure the mistake was not repeated, our supervisor taught Jan how to dexterously scrub and scour (no gloves were provided) until her fingers were raw. Sparkling clean toilet bowls resulted. Further confrontations were avoided.

After a period of grooming to masterly polish away skid marks, we (sort of) got the hang of our new jobs. In due course, a short-lived slow down at the hotel granted us a few days off.

One Sunday morning in late February, we headed over to the Coin Laundry on Carrall Street off Hastings to wash everything we'd worn until that point. The sign on the wall next to the dryers made no bones about it: "No booze or drugs allowed." Another, smaller sign read, "Showers: $1." The last three years of high school, I worked in a laundromat and dry-cleaners combined. A shower, I thought, was something you took at home.

In the afternoon we walked down to the bay, caught a bus over the Lion's Gate Bridge through North Vancouver to West Van, a picturesque residential district on the northern side of English Bay. Invited to spend a few days with my cousin Betsy (on my father's side) and her family, Jan and I arrived at Mather's Avenue late in the day. Located in a quiet, mature neighbourhood with peek-a-boo water views, the area reminded me a little of home. Jan and I tracked down the key my cousin had stealthily concealed in a shrub behind the mailbox. Away on a ski trip at Sunshine Valley, Betsy, her husband Tim, and their two boys wouldn't be returning home until the following day. My cousin had left a note, inviting us to help ourselves to the fridge and treat their home as if it were our own. Considering I hadn't seen Betsy since I was a little kid, this was a big-hearted overture.

Jan and I cooked up scrambled eggs for dinner and shovelled the driveway. Sitting on the elevated backyard verandah at dusk looking out at snow-covered mountains and cypress trees touching down on the shoreline contrasted by a cherry coloured sky, Jan remarked the poignant setting was similar to photographs she'd seen of Northern Ontario.

Following a walk down to the water the next morning, we returned to Mather's Avenue about the time my cousin and her family landed home. Not having seen Betsy since I was ten, the familiarity of her warmth and likability immediately returned. A part-time RN, loving wife and mother to her two sons, my cousin was also a fine chef.

Like Betsy, Tim was welcoming and seemed genuinely pleased to have our company for the few days we were there. Our best chats took place outside on the back verandah surrounded by woods, numerous birds, and other forms of wildlife. A short walk from Vancouver's inner harbour, Betsy and Tim's backyard property was a quelling sanctuary — the perfect setting to fuse generations.

One afternoon, Betsy drove us out to North Vancouver, a beautiful domiciliary area located directly across from Vancouver on Burrard Inlet's north shore. Another cousin on my father's side whom I'd never met, a professor of history at Simon Fraser University, Drew and his wife Carrie lived in North Van with their three young daughters. Setting foot on the front porch of the attractive contemporary home, my attention was tweaked by what appeared to be cannabis seedlings sprouting up from various terra cotta clay pots decorating the windowsill.

A salutation, I thought. Perhaps there was a chance of sampling something harvested inside? (Later I learned it wasn't grass but Chaste tree seedlings.)

Betsy, Drew, and I are all offspring of siblings. Drew had not seen a photo of me before, prompting Betsy to play a little game asking him to guess which one of us was his cousin. Mulling over Betsy's challenge, glancing first at me, then Jan, and back at me again, carefully studying our faces, Drew finally decided on Jan. Sharing many physical traits consistent with our lineage: fair skin, dark blonde hair, light freckles, and blue eyes, it was interesting Drew didn't get it right. Throughout the course of our visit, I learned that my relative's interests: history, art, and writing, also aligned with my father's side of the family.

The personification of modern day, middle-aged hippies, Drew and Carrie impressed me as intellectuals, conversationalists, and conservationists. Having taken an eight-month sabbatical to pen a historical journal, Drew helped raise their three daughters. Carrie, a gifted artist experimenting primarily in oils upon liberal-sized canvases, had recently sold some of her works for a tidy sum. As many artists are inclined to become fixated on a specific theme or premise, Carrie was preoccupied painting a collection of male rock musicians. Stark evidence of her talent indicative of her muse swathed the walls of the couple's living room and den. Specifically, Carrie created an exposé of hard-bodied guitar men working arduously at their craft. Most transfixing about her technique was the symmetry between instrument and human form, distinguished by an exaggerated display of hues and textures.

In short, Carrie's work was spicy hot.

Rekindling relationships with Cousin Betsy had been rewarding. I was ever pleased to become acquainted with these brand new relations — in my youthful mind, talented, bright stars. In particular, Jan and I were enamoured with Carrie, who didn't allow her principal responsibilities as spouse and mother to deter from her craft, or her 'professional' attraction to muscle bound guitar studs with long, tangled hair.

Cousin Drew's partner could easily have been the gold standard for all women.

Pied Pumpkin program cover.

CHAPTER 3

Break the Law Day

"We can't return. We can only look behind from where we came."
EUGENE MCNAMARA

Early March, it was officially time to apply for pogey. Returning early to the unemployment offices at Homer Street, keeping time with the juicers and speed freaks, Jan and I waited outside until the building opened. Standing against the red brick building, a girl about sixteen passed fat white joints to men with exposed raw skin revealing bloody cuts. All of them looked older than their probable years. Next to a garbage can, some poor bugger nodded off long enough to miss his appointment with a counsellor, forfeiting his opportunity for cash.

Once inside, sitting opposite a woman who created my case file, I filled out the required paperwork. Whatever I scribbled down on my application was the information they were looking for. I was to receive two cheques totalling $350. The first would be ready the following day.

Not a bad score for having worked part-time during the last three years of high school — though part of me felt guilty. After all, I *had* secured a job in the city practically right out of the gate. Technically, I was no longer entitled to the money. My shameless alter ego somehow convinced me I had the right to funds — for insurance. Plus, I'd made regular contributions to Unemployment Insurance while working in Ontario. To ease my conflicted conscience, I would split the cash with Jan — who equitably, had opted out of applying for pogey.

Leaving the unemployment offices, Jan and I walked over to National Trust and opened up new savings accounts.

Believing we'd be leaving Vancouver within a couple of weeks, we rode the double decker bus across the Lion's Gate Bridge to Mather's Avenue to join Betsy and Tim for dinner. A dramatic change from our earlier visit, that evening Tim was in a foul mood. Noting the ruddy face and bloodshot eyes — clues that I'd neglected to pick up on before, I wondered if Tim might be a drinker.

The following morning, a chain of events involving our funds transpired. Returning to the unemployment office, I picked up my first cheque ($175) and withdrew money from my new savings account at National Trust. As the holder of a primary account at Bank of Commerce, on my behalf, Jan opened a second account. Depositing the money I'd withdrawn from National Trust, I cashed my pogey cheque at the Royal Bank (where I usually banked). At that point, we divided up the money.

Three banks. Three transactions. Confusing, I know. This was to safeguard against being tracked by Unemployment Insurance. Between what I had left from paying my share of the month's rent, including my new financial acquisition, not counting my forthcoming paycheck from the hotel, I'd soon have a grand total of $234 in savings. Feeling rich, we took the transit to Gastown, Vancouver's heritage district (known for marijuana riots between hippies and cops in the early seventies), and whooped it up. Entering Breadline, a 1920's natural food emporium where senior citizens served customers, we were the beneficiaries of a delicious, inexpensive meal.

On our way back to the Y early evening, a film crew had set up down Burrard Street. Asking around, we discovered they were shooting a scene with Chief Dan George, actor and Chief of the Canadian Tsleil-Waututh nation, whose reserve is located on the Burrard Inlet in the district of North Vancouver. Dan George, also a poet and author, had garnered fame for his appearance in the 1970 feature film *Little Big Man* starring Dustin Hoffman, and had made several TV appearances. Crossing the street to get a closer look, by a hair, we missed an opportunity to be walk-ons.

Cordoned off by yellow tape, buoyed by the prospect of catching a glimpse of George, for more than an hour bundled against onlookers, Jan and I remained on alert. Upon learning the crew was shooting wraparound scenes and the actor wasn't expected on set until late that evening, we finally called it quits, hustled to the lobby of the Y, and rode the elevator to our room.

Anne, a friend back home, would soon be celebrating her 19th birthday. Deciding to mail her the complementary bottle of red wine provided during our flight, Jan wrapped it in tissue paper, slid it into a cardboard box and taped it up.

We would ship it next day.

Another of the semi-regulars, Gillian, had scored an enormous bag of weed and offered to smoke us up out front of the building. Our first chance to smoke pot since leaving home (in 1976, it was a criminal offence to possess or sell marijuana in Canada and the United States), with the windfall pogey cheque and free dope, jokingly, Jan referred to these two events as our "break the law day."

Comfortably high, the three of us headed to the third floor lounge to chat and goof off. A couple of girls from Prince Rupert and Northern California provided tips on what to expect once we started moving south. Soaking up the data like Malibu sunshine, we were eager to wrap up employment at the hotel.

After work, many of the girls generally congregated in the lounges. Others, with nothing better to do, hung out, or got into trouble. Providing cheap entertainment, spending time in the third and fourth floor dens in the evenings became part of the daily routine. One night in mid-March, I encountered Yvonne, a recent addition to the Y. The eighteen-year-old street-fighting dyke (her own description) was reputed to have whooped the asses of a few foes during conquests in and around the city. Observing the powerfully built girl — tall, hard-shelled, juxtaposed by an oddly pretty face — from the doorway, I didn't doubt the validity of these accounts. For a split second, I debated turning around and walking out the door.

Despite my misgivings, the lounge was for everybody's use. So I approached with caution.

When provoked, or if she didn't like the looks of somebody, it was rumoured Yvonne could turn attack-dog. It was wise to err on the side of caution. In time, I would learn that carefully structured conversations belied Yvonne's propensity to strike. The girl could be personable, even mellow when she wanted to be, and devious to a fault. Discernible through her tough exterior lived a shy, albeit resilient introvert.

Careful not to get too close, that first night I selected a chrome framed two-seater sofa, a good five feet from Yvonne, and sat down while Gary Wright's "Dream Weaver" filtered through the corridor from someone's portable record player and into the lounge. Talking about how much we both loved the song, Yvonne and I treaded into cagey chatter. Because I didn't want to end up splattered across the carpet with a fist in my face, I was certain not to make a false move by saying or doing the wrong thing. Well versed at keeping people at arm's length, Yvonne was reluctant to reveal much behind the well-merited façade. I guessed my new acquaintance played her cards close to her chest, partly out of habit, mostly out of desperation. Accustomed to taking people down in a physical way to exert dominance and maintain control of her environment, Yvonne admitted as much. At times, I attempted to be stronger too, and confided this information. Surprisingly, Yvonne didn't call me out. Instead, she gave me an approving nod.

It is a fearsome thing to reveal weakness. Moreover, I didn't want to appear vulnerable facing somebody of Yvonne's notoriety. Putting her trust in saints, Yvonne said she believed the hallowed spirits were omnipresent. It is from Yvonne I learned that everybody is capable of being a saint and a sinner.

Another evening, a willowy speed freak rumoured to have been a ballet dancer in another life entered the fourth floor lounge clutching a paper bag as if it was her security blanket. Out of range of our conversation, the girl sat down on a stool. Jan and I had seen the kid before. Yvonne said she found the girl attractive.

Despite her pleasant face, the teenager's arms and legs were frightfully thin. On one side of her head, a bald patch displaced where frizzy, strawberry-blonde hair should have been. Watching the girl from our corner of the room, for the duration of her time in the lounge, not once did she look over or make motion to speak. Peering out from behind glazed-over eyes, compulsively, the girl dipped her hand inside of her scrunched up sack. Without ever removing the item from the bag, every so often, she'd look up, smiling blissfully.

It was hard to know what to make of this gesture. Most likely, the girl was tripping. She could have been a psych case. Maybe it was a little of both, I wasn't certain. Folks suffer from a myriad of problems. Some are transparent, some not. With few exceptions, girls of the Y deserved the benefit of a doubt. Despite fundamental differences, Yvonne and I saw eye to eye on one verity. The YWCA served as refuge for some weird creatures. Ironically, she extricated herself from the hard luck cases.

One day a surprise arrived in the gift of a twelve-page letter from Liz. Having had periods of homesickness for family and friends back in Ontario, the lengthy correspondence was a welcome friend.

The following day, a package appeared in the mail. It was from May who had sent photos taken at our 'last supper' prior to mine and Jan's trip. Partly to avoid our high school graduation dance, our expanding group of friends, which included 84-year-old Herb from the plaza where May and I'd worked, a 43-year-old customer and his fourteen-year-old son, gathered for an Italian feast at a local eating establishment. The past year, our ragtag gang had gone out semi-regularly for dinner and beers — good times. On the last outing, we'd taken photos commemorating the occasion.

Sifting through the pictures, I fought back tears. Travelling 3000 miles from home and being free to call your own shots had its perks. It also had its disadvantages.

Friday nights in Vancouver frequently involved hitting the bars with various girls from our residence who looked to meet, party with, or conceivably sleep with good-looking, eligible men that weren't total grebes. A tall order, maybe. It was fun trying. Money being an issue for most of us working odd hours for minimal pay, there were ways around that — if you could manipulate men to buy your drinks.

I very much liked the opposite sex, and had had devastating crushes on classmates (and a couple of teachers) as any other hormone-fueled female did. So far, personal experience with guys was limited. Due to lack of confidence and self-esteem, it wasn't until my final two years of school I formed friendships with several boys with whom I felt I had something of value to offer. Not considered pretty in a traditional way, I wasn't completely unattractive either. Interactions usually took place in neutral territory — at a local downtown pub. Over rounds of beer and the occasional joint, conversations entailed bogus intellectual babble about books, contemporary films, and latest trends in music.

Marvelling at girls who could interact freely with boys without showing an inkling of insecurity, I'd even grown to resent some of them, not realizing for the longest time that I was the one with self-confidence issues. Even more excruciating, I was embarrassed to admit I was still a member of the 'V' club. This was not a limited membership at my school by any stretch, and it wasn't my goal to become a slut. Far from it — but I sensed the proverbial clock ticking. And I was curious. Enviably, within the last year of high school, two of our closest friends, May and Jen, had snagged above-average boyfriends. I hoped good fortune would soon rub off on me.

Jan also had affection for boys, though mostly from afar. Certain that her relationships with males were pretty much on par with mine, interestingly, we didn't often discuss the intimacies of our private lives beyond declaring our attraction to various members of the opposite sex, or anything else we were willing to admit openly to. A lot of information in those days was taboo, even between good friends.

That winter, my everyday attire comprised mainly of jeans. In particular, I preferred one dodgy pair that sported several holes and the odd patch.

Filling out the balance of my wardrobe mostly with plaid flannel shirts and work boots, I also owned a couple of ratty sweaters (one auburn cardigan, and one grey, black and white V-neck); hand-me-downs from my mom. The Christmas before we left, Ina, our boss at the dry-cleaners, had kindly knitted me a (too big) bulky, cream-coloured sweater-coat with round wood buttons. (She'd also knitted May a pullover.) Though my top-heavy figure had a way of offsetting the basic attire, my clothes weren't considered typically feminine. Wearing my thick, dark-blonde hair long, occasionally I'd part it down the middle, pull the front strands back and fasten it into a barrette.

In my eyes, I was a hippie girl through and through.

One spring-like afternoon, Jan and I passed a clothing rack outside of a funky dress shop on Granville advertising marked-down items. For $4, I purchased a sandstone wrap-around cotton skirt that became part of my growing collection of gypsy clothes. Adding the skirt to my small inventory of mix and match was an opportunity to break up the boredom. The best part: it had an adjustable belt allowing for weight loss and gain. Due to inconsistent eating habits, this was a frequent occurrence.

One night, our roommate Debbie had a brainstorm. If Jan and I disguised our ages wearing grown-up clothes to go out clubbing, chances of meeting men willing to buy drinks would improve. Since neither one of us owned garments denoting sophistication, Debbie was happy to loan us choice picks from her own closet, a selection that vacillated between business casual and cocktail. Following a costume transformation, I, complete with ruby lips, carefully applied mascara (by Debbie), eyeliner, hair swept back, a tailored skirt, long navy sweater, and four-inch heels; and Jan, fully ensconced in a chic, black fur coat and leather boots, flanked Debbie as we entered the foyer of Charlie Brown's, a popular Vancouver nightspot. Settled conspicuously into a booth inside the stylish, low-key, black and gold dungeon, following Debbie's lead, we proceeded to order precisely what she'd instructed us to do beforehand: Strawberry Daiquiris and Sex on a Beach — a far cry from our usual diet of draught beer and Blue. I had absolutely no clue what was in the drinks, nor did I care. Sweet to the palette, the booze got you smashed in a hurry.

In 1976, the legal drinking age in British Columbia was nineteen years of age. I was six months shy of being deemed legal. Still a babe at seventeen, prior to her transfiguration, Jan's pixie face and brown freckles gave cause for concern. In less than thirty minutes, Debbie had masterfully converted two Cinderellas to acceptable cosmopolitan women, enabling us to camouflage neatly into the scenery without being asked for ID.

A seasoned business girl, Deb had enjoyed more than her share of nights on the town. A flawless role model, casually, she showed us the ropes, demonstrating how to behave in a high-class club, and explained the art of patience and poise — foreign attributes to me. Composed and cool, our roomie taught us etiquette — key physical characteristics such as holding good posture, crossing one leg over the other, nodding and smiling world wearily as if we'd done it a hundred times. Fidgeting with clothes and giggling moronically was out of the question. This was a serious game called flirting — being an opportunist — the art of negotiating free drinks without putting out.

Sure enough, several minutes after we sat down a round of complementary beverages miraculously arrived at our table. Casting baby blue eyes across her right shoulder, Debbie subtly acknowledged an intoxicated group of men, likely co-workers, grinning blotto in our direction, hoping to get laid no doubt.

Turning to get a better look, not more than ten feet away, I noticed a group of covetous businessmen at the bar, ready to pounce.

Debbie was good. Not once did she defer to their horn-dog eyes. Instead, wedged between us, slyly, she began swirling her curved neon straw that stood upright in her glass. Taking slow sips, Deb played coy, as if she had no special place to be. Other than an imperceptible *thank you*, our roommate didn't give the men an ounce of attention.

Now, I like free booze as much as the next person. Pretending to find some lusty drunk more than twice my age attractive is not my idea of a model evening. Without a doubt, *I* wasn't having sex with *any* of the men.

Thank god, we didn't have to make believe. Once Debbie gave us the cue, finishing our drinks quickly as the girly straws would allow, we exited Charlie Brown's to meet up with friends at Denny's for a midnight snack.

Debbie had taught us an invaluable lesson. Drink up and get the hell out.

March 14, Jan and I caught wind about an upcoming show. Pied Pumpkin, a local three-piece band, was scheduled to perform at Queen Elizabeth Playhouse, a small music hall in the city. Though unfamiliar with their music, based upon the band's rapidly growing reputation in the Vancouver area, for $7 we purchased two tickets.

Disappointed, we were not.

Throughout the show, flautist and lead singer Shari Ulrich wove a remarkable tapestry of showmanship and storytelling, particularly during the debut of what would become Pied Pumpkin's towering signature piece, "Fear of Flying." Through phrasing, melody, stylization, and audience interaction, the group's performance moved spectators in a profound way. Resonating with her encore cover piece, "Bicycle Built for Two," Ulrich's rich vocals pierced the hall to the core. In a fitting end, Shari's black lab, Moose, bounded onto the stage to join in celebration.

Pied Pumpkin's magic and synergy remained for several days. As winter dissolved into spring, our experience at the Queen Elizabeth Playhouse would set the bar for future impromptu performances.

One weekend, Debbie's hometown friend also named Debbie, came for a visit. Following dinner at Lifestream restaurant, a natural food store and eatery located on West 4th Avenue in Kitsilano, a group of us went for drinks at the Ritz Carleton. Thanks to Deb's careful grooming, Jan and I'd gotten smarter exploiting our budding instincts to entice male patrons to purchase our drinks.

The Carleton, an upscale establishment, proved more than we'd bargained. Worried about being asked for identification, for back up I'd tucked an expired driver's license depicting the name *and image* of our friend Jen's older sister Kim, into my wallet. Required to produce my credentials, the waitress glanced at the photo and skimmed the date of birth (1955). Satisfied, she handed it back to me. Now, I don't resemble Kim in any way, but as long as I carried identification, it was good enough for the club. Cheyenne, our bog mate, was kind enough to loan Jan her birth certificate.

It didn't have a photo.

Fudging our way through the evening, Jan and I managed to get smashed. As fools tend to do after surviving a chaser of vomiting and the craps, a couple days later I was raring to go again.

At this stage, some of the girls at the Y began to leave the nest for greener pastures in the way of schooling, travel, better job security — even marriage. Others weren't so lucky. One morning we learned that Yvonne, unquestionably the toughest kid on the block, was evicted and arrested after beating up the lobby security guard, Winnie — a kindly person. When I heard the news, I felt awful, not only for Winnie, but also for Yvonne. A troubled girl with a complicated past, there was no question. Yet, even as a naïve kid, I identified Yvonne salvageable and worried where she might end up.

On St. Patty's day, someone within the tribe recommended The Blarney Stone, an authentic Irish pub in Gastown. Dressed in inventive assortments of green to pay homage to the holiday, our boisterous group, totalling twelve in all, plopped down at two adjoining tables and ordered up assorted pizzas and several pitchers of green beer. Blissfully, we drank and danced to the house band until closing time.

The evening was capped off by a memorable off-the-wall sexual twist. The eldest in our group, Denna, a 23-year-old, chain-smoking, tarot card reading black witch, had a 'tryst' with one of the pub bartenders. There was no coercion on part of the man. It was Denna all the way.

Beginning with an ambitious oral effort courtesy of Denna (exhibiting zero discretion after downing multiple tequila shots), the burly, bearded fellow shucked his pants and jockey shorts partway to his thighs. Disregarding the wildly appreciative audience, Denna proceeded to provide concentrated attention on the man's member. With only the back of Denna's head and the bartender visible from the bar level up, Denna's action was blatantly obvious. Egged on by zealots chanting the bartender's name, still covertly concealed by the bar, the man finally reached down to pull up his pants.

The show was over.

Vancouver's nightlife after last call took on all shapes and sizes.

With Gillian and Lorraine, YWCA fourth floor lounge.

CHAPTER 4

8 to 5 Girls

"It's better to be free boys, beneath a wide blue sky.
And livin' by the sea, boys, where the ships go sailing by."
SAILOR'S LAMENT

Apart from letting them know we'd arrived in Vancouver safely, I hadn't spoken to my folks since our departure. Collect calls were expensive and reserved for emergencies only. Jan and I continued to remain in contact with our families and friends through the exchange of letters — our lifeline to reality.

Business at Hotel Vancouver started to pick up. We were called in to work five days straight. One afternoon the hotel held a used clothing sale on the twelfth floor. Anticipating spring and summer just ahead, I purchased a second-hand pair of Roots sling-back earth shoe sandals, a half size too small, and a non-fiction book about Steven Truscott, an Ontario boy wrongly accused of murder. When payday arrived, we were rewarded $300 cash.

It was a good week.

The first Saturday off following a straight week of steady work, Jan and I set out on a five-mile hike along the dirt trail in picturesque Stanley Park, exploring the Seawall and coastal areas. The 400-hectare natural West Coast rainforest, one of the most beautiful downtown regions of the urban city, contains famous landmarks and monuments, First Nations totem poles, trails, gigantic redwoods, flora gardens, beaches, local wildlife, and numerous lookouts throughout. Returning to the Y around dinner, we walked in on brouhaha between Gillian and several girls on the fifth floor. Double-teamed by her two roommates, Gill was accused of stealing their dope. The argument had accelerated into fisticuffs. Dons were called from their rooms to break things up between the adversaries. In the end, girls on *our* floor were reamed out for disrespecting the premises and were all sent to our rooms. Otherwise, the day had been near perfect.

Emotional upheaval followed by calm was the rhythm of life at the YWCA. Arriving in short reprieves, peace came at the expense of fighting, drama, or head trips. If it wasn't one or another one whining about somebody stealing food or friends, some other excuse was fabricated, keeping the place on perpetual edge.

The most menacing of all the girls on our floor, perhaps the whole of the building, was Denna, our resident witch — the same Denna that had put herself on public display at The Blarney Stone in Gastown. If Denna didn't like you, she'd cast a spell on you, and kept a wide range of incongruous looking ingredients in her cupboard intended for concocting potions. Because Denna had more enemies than friends, it was important to remain on her good side, however minuscule that side might be.

During our time at the Y, Denna's roommate Carrie once fell seriously ill. When asked if she had a hand in Carrie's sickly condition, twisting her mouth into a wicked grin, Denna began drumming her nicotine stained fingers against her coffee mug as if tapping a secret rhythm to some imaginary co-conspirator. Clearly, she revelled in the compliment. It didn't matter if Denna hadn't actually *stuck* needles into a voodoo doll resembling Carrie. Her watery-grey evil eyes were enough to make you piss your pants. Because she enjoyed assuming credit for the misfortunes of others, no one dared challenge Denna, or put her so-called black magic to the test. On rare occasions, a kinder face was revealed and Denna would offer candy treats. Deb was one of the brave few who shared a reasonable rapport with Denna.

Toward the end of March, shifts at the hotel began getting easier. Rather than doing morning checkouts, Jan and I were on duty to work afternoons. Coasting between three and eleven pm was far lighter, less demanding. Preparing rooms for guests returning to the hotel after a long day required turning down covers, switching on bedside lamps, fluffing bath towels, and placing dark chocolate mints on pillow covers. It was pure elegance. One evening we were invited to peruse the luxurious "Renaissance" suite on the 14th floor reserved for royalty, political leaders, celebrities, the wealthy, and the elite. VIPs included Queen Elizabeth and Prince Philip, various rock bands, and Canada's own Prime Minister, Pierre Elliott Trudeau. Without a doubt, all parties had run their fingers across the marble vanity top, luxuriated in the opulent cast-iron claw-footed bathtub, fondled the gold handled faucets, and cloaked themselves in the plush wedding-white bathrobe draped over the cherry wood armoire in the master bedroom. During our tour of the Renaissance

Room, I placed an empty china tea cup on top of the Steinway piano and learned my lesson from that day forward.

Clocking off after the afternoon shift, there was usually someone back at the Y waiting to put an exclamation mark on the evening, get into a little harmless trouble. Lorraine, a friend from the third floor had recently started work at the hotel. Occasionally, we were assigned the same shift. Whenever our schedules aligned, it was fun to blow off steam.

It seemed that almost daily, new pals came and went and began cultivating life in other directions. Whenever one of our brood was about to depart, our floor would schedule an epic supper. Everybody was expected to contribute a dish.

Most of the girls were not adept in the kitchen. That meant our farewell meals were reasonably flavourful, but basic. In order to stretch our funds, Jan and I had fallen into a naughty habit (now and then) of shoplifting grocery items from Woodward's, a department store located in the east downtown section of Vancouver. In those days, the risk was low — security cameras were not the norm. To get busted, somebody had to personally eyeball you cramming food *into* or underneath your clothing.

The guest of honour at one such farewell dinner was another Debbie, Lorraine's older sister by one year. The two girls shared a room together. Nineteen and still a virgin, Debbie was soon to be married. One week of freedom remained before shuffling off to her family home in Ontario, where Debbie and her husband-to-be would put finishing touches on their wedding arrangements.

In preparation for Debbie's final supper, that afternoon I'd lifted cherries, a hunk of cheddar cheese, and a cucumber from Woodward's store. Jan smuggled out a French loaf and two apples. Stuffing the food beneath our jackets, I shelled out a few coins to the cashier for a couple of diversion items and some candy.

We filed out of the store.

I'm not proud about stealing. As aforementioned, filching wasn't part of my diet. However, as with anything else in life, once you practice a few times, you get better at it. You get bolder. You convince yourself that it's not a big deal. There is that heart-stopping surge in your belly when you skate away scot-free. Though we were never caught red-handed, the threat was always there. Nonetheless, our days of thievery were short-lived. After a close encounter in which we *thought* we'd be captured, it became apparent I had a conscience. Ditto for Jan. I told myself, *from here on in, only when necessary.*

That evening, Yvette, a newer arrival from the fourth floor we'd encountered recently in the lounge, joined our group, contributing a home-baked nut loaf to our soiree.

Yvette and her bread were a hit. The same could not be said about the dinner party.

In mostly good fun, the bride-to-be was teased by so-called experts about what to expect on her wedding night. Shaken, Debbie didn't readily accept good-natured counsel about "lubricating the love channel with K-Y jelly in advance of the big kahuna." Although these infractions were offered mostly in humour, the party ended early with Debbie rushing out in tears. Typically, the evening's undoing was a toxic recipe of overblown emotions, too much alcohol (brought in by Deb), and a couple of shit disturbers.

Sometimes, the right ingredients fell into place. There was musical entertainment, and occasionally, a sibling or friend of one of the residents would come by to visit. One night after putting away an obscene feed of spaghetti and beer, our friend Wendy invited her older brother Derek to serenade us on his guitar. Everybody had a great time. If someone had her own set of wheels and was in the mood for tag-alongs, day trips outside of the greater Vancouver area seldom arose. In exchange for the break, Jan and I usually contributed a food offering.

One radiant Sunday afternoon, Janet, a tomboy of 23, in mourning after having been dumped by her much older, married boyfriend Bob, drove a group of us 40 miles north along the Sea to Sky Highway to Squamish in her sporty white Honda. Having originated during construction of the Great Eastern Railway, surrounded by the Coastal Mountain Range, the rugged, heavily populated Indigenous community of Squamish has long been a favourite locale for rock climbers and mountaineers. Tromping through thickets, indulging in exploration of some of the steep hiking routes, we were eager to sit down to a picnic lunch. As an post-meal aperitif, somebody had the notion to share a couple of joints by the lighthouse. Following a ferocious outbreak of the munchies, our group scrambled to Janet's Honda and raced to the Dairy Queen for hot fudge sundaes, giggling all the way.

During sprees to Kitsilano, Jan and I often returned to Lifestream, the most economical eating establishment in the city. The reward of eating a light meal there made a great excuse for the long trek. In short order, Lifestream food emporium became *the* place.

One mild spring morning, we invited Yvette and Lorraine to come along to Kitsilano and have lunch. Chatting along the way, the distance from the Burrard Street Bridge to Kitsilano was eaten up in record time.

For $2, our group was served homemade cream of barley soup, a glass of milk, chapattis topped with veggie butter, and carrot cake.

Nosing in and out of bookstores along the flower potted street, inhaling a coterie of flavoured incense, we headed into The Equinox, an intriguing little shop, and picked up a couple of postcards. Vetted by Yvette, the quaint hideaway was indeed chocked full of artistic and surprising delights. I selected a card containing a reproduction of a 1975 painting titled "The Arrival" by California visionary painter, Cliff McReynolds. The surrealistic artwork that features a potpourri of deep blue mountainscapes, fairies, moons, acrobats, and a man on stilts, is offset by a fat slice of floating cherry pie. Captivated by the shop's mood, Yvette recounted an incident told to her by her older sister Lily who'd visited there one year earlier. Thumbing through a copy of *Helter Skelter,* Lily was approached by a stranger skimming a similarly themed book. Forcing the paperback toward Lily, in a forbidding whisper, he warned, "If you want to know the *truth* about the Manson family, read this."

Obviously traumatized, the man divulged he'd been a 'Family' member for over two years.

Lily was properly spooked.

Seven years after the homicides, the murders were still fresh.

Everybody was freaked out about Manson.

A few months older than me, Yvette and I shared common interests. Adoring of the Beatles, Gordon Lightfoot, classic Hollywood movies, and classical music, Yvette dreamed of living in a lighthouse in Scotland one day, complete with greenhouse and herbaceous garden beds. Intending to travel across Canada the following year, Yvette worked part-time in an office downtown, stowing away money until the right time to cash in. Tight with her 27-year-old brother Luke, the previous June, Yvette had brought him as her escort to her high school prom. Having grown up close to my eldest brother, Chris, seven years my senior, I felt a strong kinship.

While attending elementary and middle schools, I loved spending evenings sequestered in the back of our basement that had become Chris's realm. Having converted the laundry/furnace room to a makeshift studio, my brother painted, wrote short stories, read, and assessed new LPs debuted on Toronto's Chum FM radio station. In those days, records were played in their entirety on FM radio — an extravagance that fell by the wayside once the video revolution dominated contemporary music and consumerism became an impediment of modern society. Those precious years were a pivotal time for music when artists and fans merged as one.

Introducing me to music, art, and literature, Chris enthusiastically shared his many interests. Reading aloud from a collection of Edgar Allan Poe stories, something my grade four teacher had also done, my brother speculated on morose subjects such as death and reincarnation, being buried alive and other horrors. These tales sometimes scared the hell out of me, but I kept going back for more. My brother Steve and I were close as well; though being less than a year apart, there was typical sibling rivalry. To his credit, Chris was assiduous about dividing his time equally between Steve and me. In turn, we vied for big brother's attention.

Like me, Yvette adored and looked up to her brother, a veteran hippie who'd made an indelible impression on his kid sister.

Returning home that afternoon, someone had pulled a funny prank putting dish soap in the fountain in front of the Bental Centre, a few blocks from the Y. Enormous bubbles escaped into the air, ascending at least twenty feet high before bursting. By the time we reached the fountain, the water had been shut off, but we were able to free trapped suds and help remaining bubbles continue their journey upward.

Inside the Y, passing the lobby bulletin board, a posting caught Jan's attention. Scribbled on scrap paper, a "Walter" sought kids needing rides between Vancouver and San Francisco. The owner of a van, Walter charged $25 per person each way. With an approximate 900 miles between the two cities, it seemed like a reasonable offer.

Throughout the metropolis, hyacinths, crocuses, lily-of-the-valley, and bleeding hearts were now in full regalia rousing a longing to head south. Besides the desire to move on, life at the Y had become increasingly claustrophobic. Dons were constantly on everybody's asses about one thing or another. It felt too much like living at home. Based in Seattle, according to his posting, Walter's next scheduled trip south was April 10 — a week and a half away.

Apart from notifying the Y, and work that we'd be quitting, and needing to pick up a two-man pup tent for camping as backup, there wasn't much to do to prepare to leave. Tearing Walter's phone number from the board, Jan slipped it inside of her purse. One of us would call him that evening.

If indeed we were to leave Vancouver on the 10th, I planned to phone my parents to keep them in the loop. Making up one of the rooms at the hotel recently, I'd experienced an attack of loneliness — one of the strongest waves of yearning since leaving home. Set off by a tangential memory, my gut became a knot that crept up into my throat, blindsiding me like a bandit. A frequent guest of the hotel had placed a framed family photo on the nightstand beside the McMonster bed. In the picture, a man stood next to a woman while two children played on a dock. A blue rowboat floated next to the little group on a calm lake. Fixated on the photograph, the aching that welled in my throat wouldn't let go. Tears were not far behind.

On summer weekends in the early to mid-1960s, my parents, brothers, and I piled into our Country Squire station wagon, driving five hours north to Georgian Bay. By the time our car was securely parked at the landing in Parry Sound, it was long past dusk. From there, we loaded everything into our boat for the ten-minute ride across the lake to a pre-fab cottage on an island.

Throughout July and August, we ate BBQs of charred corn on the cob and gobbled fresh perch that my father caught in the early mornings. Cutting away brush with his machete, Dad constructed a fort in one of the poplar trees where Steve and I lifted our toys from a cedar-strewn bed using a rope lever. Behind the cottage in the forest bordering native land, using dry branches and bark from a birch, Chris had built a tee-pee. Using old blackened pots and pans my mom had given us, the three of us often ventured back in the woods to play house. On warm days, while Mom read on the dock, my brothers and I took turns boating with my dad while he taught us to fish. Much to our father's annoyance, on two occasions, Steve and I dropped our junior-sized poles (Dad had them cut down to size) into the water, and watched woefully as they sunk to the bottom of the lake.

Learning to hook worms as bait, I liked to help my dad clean fish. Once, while scurrying down the wood steps that led from the cottage to the dock, carrying a round container of fish bait, I tripped, spilling the container on to the stairs. Watching the knotted worms squirm between the cracks of the wood planks, I was terrified what my father would say when he found out. To my relief, I never even got a spanking.

Faithfully, every August my family visited my grandparents, who resided in Quebec's Eastern Townships. Our station wagon crammed with luggage and a cooler full of food, while my brothers and I slept in the folded down back seat, to stay alert overnight during the seventeen-hour drive after having worked all day, Dad popped Benzedrine tablets like lifesavers. For two weeks, we swam in the lake, invented games in the playhouse with our cousins, spent quality time making snow pudding with our Nannie, and went for car rides and ice cream at LeBaron's General Store with our Nampie.

Responsible for providing me with firepower, my parents always made travel a priority.

Now that Jan and I had a tentative ride to San Francisco, we drew straws to determine which one of us would telephone Mrs. Ferguson at Hotel Vancouver and give notice. I got the short end. On March 30, following five weeks of work, I called the hotel's housekeeping department and explained the deal. As expected, my news went over like a lead balloon. Contrarily, Jan and I were floating on air.

April 1, after purchasing a two-man tent for $26 at 3-Vets, a camping supply store downtown, we caught the bus to Betsy's house and told her of our plans. Within the company of her two boys, Betsy brought us on a tour of the British Properties, a beachside enclave in West Vancouver. With its narrow winding roads, the pebbly terrain was reminiscent of Christ Church, Barbados, where Jan and I had visited in July 1975. Witnessing the skillful maneuvers of a group of boys skateboarding along the stony surface, I'd never seen anyone do acrobatic skateboarding before — the craze hadn't yet caught on in Ontario. Free styling, flying high with exactitude, the kids were terrific.

That evening, Carrie, Drew, and their three daughters joined us at Betsy's for a buffet style meal. Setting out platters of cold meats, veggies, rye bread, and home baked chocolate cake, Jan and I attractively arranged the goodies in the middle of Betsy and Tim's sprawling kitchen nook. Dinner banter was lively as ever as we conferred about the paranormal; flying saucer revelations, extra sensory perception, and cogitated the existence of true magic. No topic of conversation was prohibited. Unbiased and open-minded, Drew and Carrie were the real deal, and went to great lengths interpreting the complexities of life as they saw it.

Beginning to appreciate how a delicious meal and good company made agreeable bedfellows, our conversation left me wanting more. Returning us to the Y, Betsy reminded me she was only a phone call away. To show our gratitude, Jan and I presented my cousin with a clay vase we'd purchased a few days before.

That night, Jan proposed a bit of extravagance. Before leaving the city, why not spend a couple of days on Vancouver Island and explore Victoria? Leaving from the Tsawwassen Terminal on the mainland, a ninety-minute ferry boat travels several times a day to Vancouver Island at Swartz Bay. This trip would be a short sidebar within our extended vacation. Now that we'd quit work and had some spare coin, I couldn't think of a reason not to go.

Beacon Hill Park, Victoria, B.C.

CHAPTER 5

Victoria, British Columbia

"Express your gratitude
Overcome an old fear
Take two minutes to appreciate the beauty of nature
Tell someone you love him."

ADAPTED FROM AN ORIGINAL QUOTE BY HOWARD W. HUNTER
written on the bathroom wall of The Normandy Restaurant, Granville and
11th Street, Vancouver

Unemployment guaranteed a second cheque in the amount of $175. Monday morning, Jan and I returned to the land of freaks at 535 Homer Street to see about picking up the money.

Not so fast. Before releasing the funds, the adjudicator wanted to conduct another, brief interview. Evidently, there was some concern we might be pulling a fast one.

She would come by the Y that afternoon.

Around 2 pm, Jan left to run errands. The young woman and I had a short chat during which I explained that we planned to return home to Ontario in a few weeks.

"A few weeks" *was* stretching the truth. It was a white lie; the kind of harmless fib my mother said was okay to tell when sparing somebody's feelings. Because I *had* been gainfully employed at the hotel the previous five weeks, pogey docked $95. That left $80 remaining.

Jan returned with good news. Walter had left a message at the front desk, confirming departure on Saturday, April 10. Generally, Walter preferred to wait until he had a full van. In order to accommodate the two of us, he'd make an exception. (Walter redefining his regime should have been our first clue.)

Along with Yvette and Lorraine, that evening in the fourth floor recreation room we watched *Five Easy Pieces* starring Jack Nicholson. Having read *One Flew over the Cuckoo's Nest* the previous autumn, when the film opened I rushed to see Nicholson nail the bad-boy persona in his brilliant portrayal of the womanizing, hard-drinking psychiatric patient, R.P McMurphy. As a result, like millions of females worldwide, I developed a mad groupie crush on the man. *Five Easy Pieces*, a darker, more ominous character study than *Cuckoo's Nest*, shows Nicholson in the role of a husband coming to terms with inner strife as he disconnects from the safety net of his white-collar life in pursuit of seedy motels and bars.

The next night, a group of us headed to the Blue Horizon, a hotel lounge and coffee bar on Robson Street, for a night of carousing. Enhanced by a couple of reefers shared in the ladies' room with a bar regular — the party was our final hurrah before setting sail on the mother ship. At the completion of six weeks residency, as girls continued to move on to pursue other dreams, it seemed nearly everybody had the itch. In less than one week, Jan and I would head south with Walter.

Last minute incidentals had already been taken care of. The day before, Jan gave the Y notice. We paid up our final week's rent. Upon finishing our last shift at Hotel Vancouver, from the Y lobby, collect calls were placed home to notify our parents of our next move. Heartened to hear my mom's voice, she promptly accepted reverse charges and we proceeded to have a short chat. Mostly, my mother cautioned me to be careful in the weeks ahead.

Jan had a tougher time. Coming close to tears upon hearing her father's voice, she later admitted missing her parents every now and then — mostly because she knew she wouldn't likely live at home again. Donning a downcast expression when she returned to our room, one look at my friend's face, I wanted to cry too.

The morning of our leaving, we collected our paychecks from the hotel and were asked to sign papers stating we "wouldn't come to work when required." That sucked, but it was the only way to get our money. Closing out our bank accounts, remaining funds were transferred into traveller's cheques.

Now that our finances were settled, we set off to Woodward's for a few groceries. On the way out of the store, we lifted a couple of bags of hard candy for our travels (old habits). In case there wasn't another opportunity to say a proper goodbye, Yvette and Lorraine met us at Honey's for lunch, where big hugs were exchanged. Choosing to remain at the Y a few months longer, Yvette offered to walk us to the Tsawwassen Ferry Terminal, sliding Jan and me a baggie full of homemade granola for our trip.

At this point, I really wished we hadn't swiped the candy.

It was Thursday afternoon. For a $3.25 fare, Jan and I boarded a 3 pm ferryboat from the Tsawwassen terminal that would drop us at the Swartz Bay on Vancouver Island.

Framed by lazy green mountains and white-capped steel blue water, the 90-minute ferry ride across Tsawwassen to Swartz Bay was under cloudy skies. Despite the lack of sunshine, it was a beautiful trip, an opportunity to get lost inside of your head. Reaching the other side infused by new surroundings, I felt a sense of calm. Noticeably absent was the hustle-bustle of the city we'd left behind. A dramatic change from downtown Vancouver, the short bus ride south from the ferry docks to our hostel in Victoria was through woodlands and green belt where we welcomed the languid pace and expansive terrain.

Located at the corner of Fernwood and Gladstone, for a pittance — a buck and a half a night — our hostel included breakfast and dinner, one of the benefits of staying outside of a major city. Feeling as if we'd pulled off "highway robbery," an expression my dad was fond of saying, we were tickled.

The house itself wasn't anything special. The main floor bathroom looked as if it had been painted by someone on a three-day acid tip, but the residence was roomy, containing twelve sets of bunk beds in two guest bedrooms. In all, there were 23 of us — twenty males to three females — ideal odds.

Two of the boys, Stretch and Guy, invited Jan and I go for a walk and have a smoke behind the hostel. Older hippie types, the folks that owned and operated the Victoria hostel had clear rules: *No Drugs.* With less than a week to go before crossing the border, participating in any conduct that might afford us detention on someone's shit list would not be smart. We made certain to walk several paces away from the residence before striking a match.

In the morning, the male proprietor, Ted, awakened everyone at half past seven for breakfast. Porridge and raw sugar was served with a mandarin and Pekoe tea.

My friend and I were off to see Victoria in the rain.

In the 1970s, and possibly today, it was mandatory for hostellers to spend the day away from the premises and return late in the afternoon.

Except when the forecast called for a heavy downpour, throughout most of our travels, this routine suited us well. Over the months, on a fixed budget, Jan and I usually found ways to effectively spend wet days, dry.

Starting out in gentle rain, we hiked around Beacon Hill Park located along the Juan de Fuca Straight. Exemplifying exquisite serenity, the beautiful oasis consisted of Douglas Firs, red cedars, tulips, trillium, native flora, and lilies. The milder climate, about a month ahead of Vancouver, saw rose gardens and budding trees blanketing sloping hills. When the rain finally stopped, peeling off our rainwear we found a dry spot to sit. Over the ocean crests, snow-capped mountains endowed the shoreline with a protective umbrella; softly flapping their wings, ducks and swans tippy-toed into a waiting pond. Beneath a stellar sky decorated in patches of pink and green, everything pulsated. Chomping on Yvette's granola, I recalled an amusing story she had told me at Honey's and shared it with Jan.

A week before, leaving work, Yvette walked home as she did every day, passing by the Candy Store, a burlesque club on Hastings. Close to the age of Yvette's father, a lone man approached, inviting her to join him for a drink. Deciding to accompany the stranger inside, Yvette sat alongside the man next to a three-piece band. Calculating the dimly lit room while sipping on a Singapore Sling, Yvette gaped at half-dressed tabletop dancers performing strip teases for inebriated clientele, and pondered the private lives of the entertainers and customers. When it suddenly dawned on her the man wouldn't likely buy her drink without wanting something in trade, Yvette waited for him to vacate the table to use the john, finished up her glass, and slinked outside of the club.

Imagining our elfin, wild-haired Yvette, who practically lived in denim coveralls, sitting inside of the Candy Store next to a lecherous old man with naked people all around, cracked both of us up.

The girl had guts. By far, Yvette was one of the best things about Vancouver.

Annihilating my snack, I yanked my journal out of my satchel and began sketching a sea gull standing on one leg next to a discarded wax paper wrapper. Jan began a letter to her grandmother. Enshrouded within the scents and visages of spring, we were content to engage in silent activities.

Mid-day, we wound our way over to the Empress Hotel (also owned by Fairmont) perched on Inner Harbour. An ivy clad replica of Hotel

Vancouver, the Empress had played host to Queen Elizabeth, Prince Philip, and other royals and dignitaries. In the elegantly decorated tea lobby, putting on phoney airs, Jan and I nibbled raisin crumpets and sampled the world's finest tea blends from bone china cups. We headed uptown to tour the Parliament buildings and the Provincial Museum, a three-tiered edifice housing many exhibits (none of which we were willing to pay money to see) and numerous artifacts in the main corridor, including rare stuffed birds — a particularly bothersome sight. Cutting out to do some shopping, we returned to Gladstone for goat soup and veggie salad dinner. A pair of French Canadian boys sat on either side of us. In an embarrassing attempt at communication, half-heartedly, I rolled out my crappy high school Parisian. As is often the case, the boys spoke better English than we did French. Good enough as a matter of fact, that the four of us double-dated at Capitol Theatre, the local movie house where *Cuckoo's Nest* topped the bill.

The ferry ride back to Vancouver next morning was sunny and balmy — the opposite of our trip two days before. Leaving Tsawwassen Ferry Terminal, Jan and I tracked back to the Y. In what had become typical, ceremonial fashion for our generation, parting with our friends was consecrated by the exchange of token gifts: cards, trinkets and food, and books filled with inspiring quotes.

Along with Walter and his youth squad, bright and early next day, Jan and I were on tap to vamoose — all the way down to San Francisco.

Rockies, Vancouver, B.C.

CHAPTER 6

Riding on the Walter Express: Round One

"The mind is furnished with ideas by experience alone."
JOHN LOCKE

Toting backpacks, sleeping bags, and other incidentals, mid-morning we climbed aboard the Burrard Street bus. Clicking along the highway toward Walter's friend's place in the east end of the city allowed time to reconsider what we might be getting ourselves into. The truth was, once Jan eyeballed Walter's offer on the Y bulletin board there was never any doubt. Riding several hundred miles south to San Francisco accompanied by other young faces seemed our destiny. The idea was exciting as hell. Not to mention affordable.

Arriving at a small apartment complex after a short hike from the bus stop, from the building entrance, a middle-aged man limped over to greet us. Introducing himself as Walter, the man explained how he used his "pal's pad to crash" while anticipating another load of customers. Counting three boys and two girls, our group waited until the rest of the passengers arrived before loading the truck. Including Walter, by the time we headed out, there were eleven of us in all. Seven males. Four females.

Besides his limp, the most distinguishable quality about Walter, a scrubby, mid-forties bachelor with a beer belly and three days' growth of stubble, was his offensive body odor. (Later, we would discover that Walter's devastating BO was one his *best* attributes.) At least he was laid back and moderately personable. We didn't expect to become bosom buddies.

Walter's Chevy van was your standard mid-seventies shaggin' wagon, a big, square, steel box on wheels, painted an ugly shade of green — nothing out of the ordinary. Excluding the driver's seat and corresponding front captain's chair, if the passenger seats hadn't been torn out, the vehicle would have seated six comfortably.

Sliding open the side door, Walter instructed nine of us to find our places along the floor, a hard metal surface that would serve as our seating for the eighteen-hour road trip. (No seat belts.) To make the journey more tolerable, a few old army blankets were tossed around. Next to Walter, who had taken his place behind the wheel, sat a backup driver.

As Walter eased out of the driveway, two males which Jan and I'd nicknamed "Curly" and "Poindexter," shifted over to where she and I'd found a couple of spots to sit, and we started rapping. Everybody was in great spirits. Spring had officially arrived in Vancouver. Daffodils, crocuses, and tulips were in full bloom. Garden grass dormant just one month ago, sprang back to life. Next to a fire hydrant, children played hopscotch in the street. Lighting a cigarette, Walter passed around three packages of Bazooka bubblegum to be distributed amongst riders. Wide-eyed, green, and California bound, conversation that morning consisted of "Where are you from and why are you going to San Francisco?" On a natural high, we would remain that way until reaching the Washington State border crossing.

Before leaving Walter's buddy's place, it had been predetermined the only person worthy of claiming the captain's chair next to Walter was Kate, on tap to relieve Walter of his chauffeur duties whenever he needed a break. On the road barely twenty minutes, it became apparent Walter liked to pop pills during road trips. This wasn't foreign to me since my father had done the same, only there was a twist — Walter washed amphetamines down with shots of whiskey kept in his glove compartment. Watching him sneak swigs, it became glaringly apparent why a second commander had been assigned.

The burning desire to go south overpowered any indicators of foreshadowing.

Our trip to the border was approximately 60 miles. Considering that we were eleven people squished into a battered van commandeered by a mildly drunken driver with one official passenger seat, Walter made great speed. Before we knew it, we were in queue at the Peace Arch border crossing in Surrey. The tail end of morning rush hour traffic, vehicle and truck lanes were lengthy, leading to some tense and terse moments inside the truck. People needing relief after downing cups of early morning coffee grew anxious. Waiting our turn near the end of one of the lines, some of our gang got out to stretch their legs until officials corralled them back inside the vehicle.

Jan and I finished the lunches we'd packed helping to pass time. As our van edged closer to the gate, figuring I'd be able to pee somewhere in Washington now just a stone's throw across the border, I held my bladder.

In those days, passports weren't required when travelling between the contiguous countries — a birth certificate would suffice. Walter collected them one by one from our oddball bunch, Canadians and Americans alike, as we joked about being pressurized together for the next seventeen hours in a stinky van.

When it was our turn to pull up to the gate and speak with the border official, Walter eased the vehicle over ever so cautiously. Rolling down his window, anticipating the official's queries about the large number of guests in tow, patiently, he waited. Having been through the same routine before, Walter said he always gave a pat answer, the truth. Before taking off that morning, he'd made it perfectly clear to those who might have thought it smart to carry drugs, "Get rid of your stash. Pronto."

I guessed amphetamines and whiskey didn't count.

Requested by border patrol to step out of the van in single file, we obeyed, keeping our mouths shut as Walter had instructed us to do. Despite what some might consider a motley crew with unkempt hair and non-traditional clothes, homogeneously, we were a polite bunch — quick to appease the death stares of the officials so we could get back to business.

One of the uniformed men suddenly waved Walter over for private consultation. From our vantage point, it seemed there was a problem with the information on one of our birth certificates. When the man and Walter finished talking, Walter turned toward the group of us, beckoning Jan to the booth.

Unsure if Walter was actually talking to her, Jan hesitated.

"Come on over here."

With her short, brown bobbed haircut and freckles, red-faced for being centered out, Jan physically shrunk in size as if scolded by a sour teacher. Covering one hand over her mouth in an effort to rebuke fear, tentatively, she approached the booth.

Staring her down, the official fired a question like a bullet.

"Do you have a note from your parents?"

The border patrol's questioning reminded me of a George Carlin routine, I started to laugh. Not realizing that a permission slip from parents was required to enter another country at age seventeen, bewildered, Jan shook her head.

"Are you able to obtain one?"

Obtaining one certainly wouldn't be a problem. However, it would require time.

Solemnly, my friend responded, "Yes…but why?"

"You're under eighteen. Unless you have written parental consent to travel into the United States, I cannot permit you to cross the border. In case you're thinking about it, verbal permission won't do."

Surprised, Walter attempted to intervene, as did I and some of the other kids, particularly Curly who assured the official he would watch out for Jan on the other side.

No go. It was a matter of guardianship. If only we'd done our homework, Jan and I would have discovered that at eighteen, *I* could have legally vouched for her as personal guardian. Foolishly, we were unaware. Border Patrol weren't about to let us in on that key piece of information.

Walter and our group waited while Jan placed a collect call to her father's Toronto office from the payphone inside Customs. Simultaneously, I called my own father at work. Maybe he could make an alternative suggestion. Dad's advice was to try another border crossing. It certainly wasn't the worst counsel, only once bitten, twice shy.

Jan hung up the receiver and came outside. Her father had avowed to wire a note of consent ASAP to Cousin Betsy's house in West Vancouver. Sympathetic to her impasse, with an assurance he'd be back within the week to bring another group providing there were enough people for a full truckload, Walter returned our money.

The sting of having to bid farewell to our new mates and return to Vancouver to wait an *entire week* until Walter made his way back from San Francisco was one of the first real disappointments of our expedition. Trapped on this side of the imaginary line separating the two countries, Jan and I watched the official give Walter the green light. Then the ugly green rectangle crossed leisurely over into Washington State.

Just like that, there was plenty of time to pee or do anything else that came to mind. After several minutes formulating and extinguishing inventive ways to get ourselves south of the border, funds already allocated, inevitably, it came down to heading back to Vancouver to wait on Walter's return. Officials warned about vagrancy issues, it was necessary to move out of range quickly. Deciding to hitchhike our way back to the city — a common practice amongst youths, in haste, we walked down the highway a couple hundred yards until reaching a moderate distance from the border.

Neither one of us had thumbed a ride before.

This would be another first.

Standing on the Canadian side of the boundary hopeful for a vehicle to come along heading northwest that would deliver us safely to Vancouver, raising our right thumbs, Jan and I waited.

A family would do nicely. Here, that wasn't likely to happen.

Driving south along the California coastal road Route 101 in the summer of 1971 with my family, my dad surprised all of us at a lookout near Monterey when he stopped our rental car to pick up a young hitch-hiker. Our guest, a sixteen-year-old strawberry-blonde surfer girl — a dime a dozen in those days — was heading down to Big Sur. Along with all of our gear; there were already four of us in the car. Turning around, my mom asked Steve and me to make room for our extra passenger, who ended up squishing between the two of us in the back seat. A little in awe of the girl, my brother and I acted out more than usual, attempting to impress the worldly teenager.

Dropping her off to join a gaggle of longhairs already congregated at the famous coastal landmark, remnants of the young woman's zest and enthusiasm endured.

Those first days, I don't believe that Jan or I (openly) panicked about the ramifications of hitchhiking, or we wouldn't have done it. That being said, whenever we stepped into an unfamiliar automobile, trepidation loomed below the surface. Within a few weeks, we would come to adopt a mental exercise that enabled us to override pessimistic thoughts by accepting that whoever gave us a lift would drive us to our destination without any sidebars, threats, or danger.

From that day forward, for the duration of our time away, on both sides of the border, like eating, sleeping, and peeing, hitchhiking would become a staple.

Shell Island, B.C. COURTESY OF ANDREA NELSON

CHAPTER 7

Back in Vancouver

*"Friendship is like a tapestry of intricate design
woven into threads of purest gold — upon the loom of time."*
CELIA K. PARKER

Jan and I didn't wait long for a ride. Feebly holding out our thumbs to the point where it might have caused some drivers to question if we were indeed hitchhiking at all, in less than twenty minutes, Larry scooped us up. On his way to Gastown, Larry was in a hurry. Thirty years of age, the drummer claimed to have played with the Motown Band, partied with folk legend Arlo Guthrie, and shaken hands with the irreverent music meister Stevie Wonder. Not bad for our first pick up. To his credit, even if his stories were complete bullshit, Larry was loquacious and funny. Save for the fact, that even by our middling standards, the drummer appeared on the wooly side, our drive was unceremonious. Larry promptly deposited us at Granville Street in the Gastown district.

Easy peasy.

Now, the Y frowned upon anything less than one month's commitment, and we didn't want to go back to the Y anyway. Unfortunately, there weren't any sufficient alternatives other than to ride the bus out to West Van.

Betsy wouldn't expect to hear from us again so soon. It felt slightly underhanded showing up unannounced, but we'd opted out of calling first to give her a head's up. A surprise visit was the best way to explain Jan's contrary situation.

I knew my cousin wouldn't turn us down.

The city bus dropped us off at the end of Mather's Avenue. Walking along on a sparkling spring day, the sun burnishing onto the sidewalk, the first one to reach the curvature in the road, Jan espied a white and red moving van parked on Betsy and Tim's driveway. Maneuvering a hefty brown leather couch, two men paused along the broad porch steps, reconfiguring their procedure before carrying the furniture to the driveway and loading it into the open van. Suddenly, Tim appeared from around the side of the house. Perplexed by this activity, waiting for sign of Betsy, Jan and I continued to observe the goings on. After a time, we figured Betsy must be out.

Betsy is my father's brother's daughter, making Tim my cousin-in-law by default. On the off chance I should have to face Tim in Betsy's absence, I wasn't comfortable going up to the house and confessing our sob story. It wasn't that I didn't like Tim, but he could be unpredictable and grumpy. On one occasion that Jan and I were at his and Betsy's house, Tim arrived home in an ugly mood, making both of us jumpy.

It dawned on me. Tim was moving out.

Shit. This predicament was embarrassing, not only for us, especially for my cousin if we were to hook up in the middle of Tim's exit from their fifteen-year marriage — if indeed that's what we were witnessing.

Deciding to return to the city, Jan and I walked a quick clip up the street toward the bus stop. Within minutes, I heard our names called out. Turning around, there was Betsy, jogging up the street, imploring us to wait. She caught up quickly. At first, I tried avoiding eye contact, when calmly, she announced, "It's alright, girls. Tim is moving into his own place but I want you to stay. Have dinner with me and the boys tonight."

Not bothering to ask why Jan and I weren't hundreds of miles south of the border, my cousin was astute enough to recognize we had good reason to be back in West Van.

Feeling like an intruder in the private life of my cousin whom I hadn't seen in years prior to travelling to Vancouver, I stood on the pavement like an idiot chewing on my lower lip, searching for the right words. Teenagers have a habit of sticking their feet into their mouths. I didn't want to blurt something out that could be interpreted as overdramatic or insensitive. Finally, I explained to Betsy why we were in the city. "They wouldn't let Jan cross the border because she isn't eighteen. She needs written permission from her parents. We can return to the Y. It's not a problem. I'm really sorry to bother you, Betsy."

Smiling gently, Betsy placed her arm firmly around my shoulder. "Come on. Stay and have dinner with us. It'll help take my mind off things."

Heading down the street toward Betsy and presumably, her soon-to-be-ex's matrimonial home, I tried to ignore the men and the moving van — a brusque reminder that life isn't necessarily unspoiled in paradise. Following my cousin through the front door, Jan and I drifted into the den where Betsy and Tim's two boys were holed up in front of the television set, dividing their time between Looney Tunes and toy cars. Seemingly unfazed, the kids popped their heads up quickly to acknowledge us, and returned to their game.

Sunday, it rained all day. Pulling out family albums, my cousin shared stories of having worked at the hospital in Vancouver where she first met Tim during happier times. Feeling guilty about leaning on Betsy, and not wishing to pry into her private affairs beyond what she wanted to reveal, Jan and I were observant listeners. As it turned out, Betsy's narrative was straightforward. She and Tim hadn't been getting along for about six years. Their separation inevitable, he'd threatened to move out and finally followed through. The previous day was the dress rehearsal.

Somehow, the conversation lapsed to liquor, hard drugs, and painting. The last 24-hours had been stressful and confusing. Betsy was great about allowing us to use her house as a home base while waiting for Jan's dad to wire his note of consent. The only fiddly part — Tim hadn't fully moved out, meaning we would occasionally be crossing paths. Preparing to sleep in Betsy's basement that night, Jan confided how Tim made her nervous. She would be polite, but otherwise keep her distance. Tim kept me on pins and needles too. Maybe I was used to the irregularity of a person's behaviour. Somewhere between his late forties and early fifties, my father had become a serious drinker, vodka being his preference.

Jan's dad drank responsibly.

Next morning, Betsy dropped us downtown at our old haunt, the Y. Finding no one around, we took off for the Granville Street Bridge to douse ourselves in sunshine. Later, we skipped over to Lost Lagoon in Stanley Park. Having brought our journals along, the next hour was spent cozying up to a massive redwood where I sketched a pigeon standing on one leg, and Jan from behind as she sat on a bench wearing her favourite sweater, a yellow, hand-knitted wool cardigan. Returning to the Y, we entered the fourth-floor lounge, and plopped casually onto the couch. Arriving unannounced was worth the identical expressions of disbelief on Lorraine and Yvette's faces. Over lunch at Honey's, Jan and I explained about Walter's tricks and our inability to cross the border without a con-sent slip. Recounting the specifics to our friends made for a humorous saga. By the time our meal was finished, everybody was in stitches.

A cool spring breeze sprung up, keeping the temperature moder-ate. Returning to Stanley Park, we talked about our predictions and imaginings. On the way back, I approached a vagrant woman who appeared to be in some kind of distress. Darting back and forth on the sidewalk, spewing indiscernible language and gobbing onto the asphalt, she was obviously deeply frustrated about something. Probing her several times in an attempt to offer help, the woman finally spun around. Pressing her hands tightly at her hips, in a voice five times louder than mine, she bawled, "FUCK OFF!"

Winter and spring in Vancouver had offered our first unfiltered exposure to street people; the downtown core in particular, a steady reminder how singular the world we'd come from was by comparison. You were never sure how to gauge vocal implosions or self-abuses. In this instance, assuming the woman was a dope head or had some kind of psychological disorder, there wasn't anything to do but walk away.

Tuesday morning brought good news. The official note of permission from Jan's father to travel inside of the United States was delivered to Mather's Avenue. Now we were sanctioned. Yippee! Jan placed a call to Walter to make arrangements with another consignment of kids bound for the United States.

We were set to go Monday, April 19.

The coming weekend was Easter. Anxious for us to meet her brother Luke and the rest of the clan before leaving Vancouver for good, Yvette invited us to spend Saturday and Sunday at her hometown in Aldergrove, 90 minutes southwest of Vancouver. In the meantime, another farewell dinner was organized at the Y for Janet and Hiroko, also heading to California.

Jan and I were asked to bring a salad.

Backtracking a little, shortly before our maiden journey with Walter, dissention broke out within our group. Janet had suggested the three of us (Janet, Jan, and me) travel to California in her Honda. Though tempting at first, I knew it wouldn't work. Janet had wanted to take a different route, see different sights. I also had a hunch that Janet was attracted to me — a sticky situation that could present problems. Too chicken to back out, until I could figure out a way to say no, I made the mistake of letting Janet believe we were "thinking" about going. Not smart. Spending a few sleepless nights worrying how to turn Janet down without suffering consequences (rejection wasn't handled well by anyone at the Y); finally I sucked it up and declined. For a solid week, Janet gave me the old stink eye. It wasn't until she secured an arrangement with Hiroko that Janet's demeanor finally softened. Charitably, Hiroko revamped her own travel plans to align with Janet's.

Now that Janet had lassoed a travel companion, she was in great spirits. I was relieved. Through general mail, the four of us vowed to hook up at a hostel somewhere in Southern California. Without the advent of technology or ability to communicate whenever convenient, itinerant youths relied on standard methods such as the postal services across Canada and the United States to receive and send mail. Frequently, when Jan and I arrived at a pre-destined location, mail from family and friends would be waiting.

There were fourteen of us together for the final meal, a buffet dinner that turned out to mine and Jan's denouement. Even our former roommate, Deb, had quit her job at the bank to head down to Monterey for a couple of weeks, accompanied by Cathy Henry, Denna, and Lois. Difficult to imagine tripping carefree down the highway with Denna in tow, I had to hand it to Deb. If anyone did, Debbie had the stones to stand up to Denna.

One commandment was foolproof. While some might flit to and from the nest, seeking asylum, or needing a good night's rest, a girl's stay at the YWCA was never meant to be permanent.

Honey's with Lorraine and Yvette.

CHAPTER 8
Aldergrove

"Who brings sunshine into the life of another, has sunshine in his own."
DAVID STAN JORDAN

Thursday morning, Yvette and Lorraine arrived in West Van to hang out for the day. Amusing ourselves listening to Jan's cassette player, eating boxes of Ritz crackers, after a few hours, Tim, who seemed to come and go, cooked up brunch, inviting the four of us to join him, Betsy, and the boys. Unsure how to behave, we went with the flow. For a couple who would soon be parting for good, Betsy and Tim never appeared happier. Maybe it was because our friends were there. I didn't pretend to understand it. This was grown up business.

Things grew progressively weirder as the hours wore on. After Tim's big feast, Jan and I brought Yvette and Lorraine down to the pier to watch the sailboats set off on a 143-mile race called the Southern Strait. Returning to Betsy's late in the afternoon, there was Tim, moving the rest of his belongings out of the house. Sitting on the street curb at a safe distance, we waited for the U-Haul to drive away before returning. After Tim had gone, Betsy invited Lorraine and Yvette to stay for tea and squares. There was no mention about her husband's recent activities. The girls caught the bus back to Vancouver minutes before Tim returned to the house — in time for dinner.

On Saturday morning, Betsy dropped Jan and me off at the downtown terminal where we were to meet Yvette. Together, the three of us rode the bus over an hour east to Aldergrove. Before heading to her homestead, Yvette brought us to the local butcher shop, owned by her sister Leila and Leila's husband, for a brief introduction.

A part of the township of Langley, with a population of less than 7000, Aldergrove, an agricultural community cultivates corn, pumpkins, raspberries, and mushroom crops grown by surrounding farms. Just two hours north of Seattle, Aldergrove reveals an astonishing view of Mount Baker, the most glaciated volcano of the state of Washington's Cascade Range.

Situated in a time-honoured part of Aldergrove amidst a handsome apparel of trees and flowerbeds, Yvette's family home is the beneficiary of a sweet fusion of wood and floral fragrances. Inside the dwelling, living and dining room floors are worn maple. A tawny-gold, hand woven braided rug covers a large section of flooring separating the couch, coffee table, and two recliners. Arranged in an amber-tinged Depression glass vase, red tulips curtsy from the top of a rosewood china cabinet standing in the corner of the dining room. Through an archway to the eating area, three yellow walls of the family kitchen are contrasted by a single cornflower-blue papered wall fronted by a pair of vintage end tables. A large rectangular table rests prominently in the middle of the room. A few steps away from the kitchen is a rec room with a plaid upholstered couch and various accents.

The Aldergrove family home is built for growing children.

Yvette's parents, fresh from a holiday in Hawaii, are interested to know how two teenage girls from Southern Ontario managed to find their way West. Questioning out of curiosity rather than judgement, following light chit-chat, Oliver and Jane welcomed us to the fold. Eager to show us her record collection, gently intercepting conversation, Yvette whisked us from the living room, down a short flight of stairs to a plenteous assortment of LPs including Alice Cooper's *Killer*, Paul McCartney's *McCartney* and *Ram*, John Lennon's *Imagine*; *Abbey Road*, *Gordon Lightfoot's Greatest Hits*; Tim Hardin, Leo Sayer, and Aerosmith's *Toys in the Attic*.

In keeping with the rest of the house, Yvette's bedroom is a mélange of new and old worlds, consisting of two antique clocks, an old-time radio and Tiffany lamps draped in dyed violet lace. Floral printed skirts and brightly coloured blouses dust a green velour chair and wardrobe. A pair of overalls lay in a heap on the floor next to powder-blue suspenders. Strewn on the wall over-top of the canopied bed, a velvet tapestry of a polar bear, a gift given to Yvette by her grandmother when she was thirteen, generously covers most of the space.

Every inch of the room bears unmistakable characteristics of the friend we'd grown so fond of in a short time.

Spending the better part of the afternoon listening to records, Jan and I had a hand in making Nanaimo bars (dark chocolate top; walnut, coconut, and cocoa base combined with a custard center). We accompanied Yvette to the trailer camp where she'd spent many summers with her family, swimming, fishing, enjoying cookouts. Returning to the house, dinner was fast and easy — leafy salad, and a tray of cheese and crackers. Half the pan of Nanaimo bars we consumed in one sitting.

Following dinner, Yvette's best chum, Barbie, arrived. The four of us loafed in the rec room watching *Mr. Deeds Goes to Town* (1936), a Gary Cooper film. Unfamiliar with the devastatingly handsome Cooper (one of Yvette's favourites), the actor's trademark reserve and authoritative presence completely won me over.

Laughing about school, boys, camping, travel, we were as tight as any group of friends might have been had we known one another since childhood. It was a beautiful, timely collusion.

After Barbie left for home, Jan crashed on a cot in the spare bedroom where Luke was supposed to sleep next evening, while I crawled into my sleeping bag on the floor of Yvette's bedroom. Within the protection of the dark, in hushed voice, Yvette confided how she'd been worried about our stay in Aldergrove — that I might not consider her as good a friend as I had in Vancouver. Her concern, that once I witnessed Yvette's "real life" and met her parents, somehow I'd be put off, was completely unfounded.

Careful not to cast aside her feelings, it made me sad to think Yvette agonized about the legitimacy of our friendship. Wanting to reassure my friend, that spending time with Yvette in her home and amongst her family was uniquely special for me, I whispered back, "Once we go our separate ways, I promise you, we will *not* lose touch."

With the exception of one more meeting, 38-years would pass before Yvette and I finally reconnected in person. Like a delicate flower, throughout nearly four decades, our friend's ethereal eminence never withered.

Interpretation of polar bear tapestry.

CHAPTER 9

Luke

"Nothing is so strong as gentleness, nothing so gentle as real strength."
SAINT FRANCIS DE SALES

Peering through the bedroom blinds, the sky was a dull grey. Despite the dismal weather, claiming that her mom had a surprise, Yvette had gotten up, dressed, and encouraged us to do the same. Hidden inside of cupboards, next to books, between boxes of Crispy Crunch cereal, dozens of chocolate Easter eggs wrapped in coloured foil were stashed. Jane rightly assumed we might be feeling homesick. It was a caring touch. Gathering up the eggs, we sat down to a hearty blueberry pancake breakfast. Around 4 pm, Yvette's sisters, Lily and Leila, along with Leila's husband and their three children congregated en masse in the living room. Somewhere within the commotion, Yvette's much-lauded older brother Luke called to apologize. He would be arriving late.

Perfect.

The past several weeks, Jan and I'd heard many stories about Luke — all of which contained varying degrees of cool. Whenever that happens, rarely, expectations are fulfilled. In my mind's scenario, I'd manufactured a gorgeous Adonis-like being with supernatural powers sporting a six-foot wing span.

Big brother did not disappoint. Arriving minutes before dinner, standing at a little over six feet tall, peering down from a pair of heart-stopping baby blues and wavy, chestnut brown hair floating past his shoulders, Yvette's sexy older brother easily lived up to the hype.

Once pleasantries were over, we took our seats at the table set for twelve. Supplemented by all the appropriate trimmings, Jane had prepared a marvelous turkey feast.

Somewhere amid a large platter that contained turkey with almond stuffing, and serving dishes overflowing with scalloped potatoes, broccoli, squash, cranberries, and rolls being distributed around the table in conveyor-like fashion, Luke absorbed some well-intentioned flak from his parents for his unconventional lifestyle. Staying with friends in the area, dividing his time between Victoria, Saskatoon, and Mexico, the Jack-of-all-tradesman took on whatever work he could. As many youths aspired to do, for a fraction of what it would cost to settle in a major city, Luke's dream was to live off the land.

The way he explained it seemed completely natural, as if only fools would not want the same.

Despite his fine-looking features, soulful blue eyes, and liberal philosophies, what struck me most about Yvette's older brother was his peaceful deportment. Quietly requesting that his parents keep their words gentle, Luke knew when to hold back.

The back and forth took me back to squabbles between Chris and my parents around the Sunday night dinner table not many years before. Disagreements about my brother's hair length, his "unsuitable" clothing, and what my mom and dad believed was rebellion in general, created friction. The proverbial generation gap, more the size of the Grand Canyon, division between parents and offspring was emblematic of the rapidly changing times. According to Luke, Jan and I exhibited similar attitudes: bucking conformity, resisting societal traditions and parental expectations, trying to find a sustainable way to keep our heads afloat.

I hadn't thought of mine and Jan's experience quite that way before. Yet, when Luke said it, it sounded sensible and sane. Then again, every utterance from Yvette's big brother's princely mouth seemed sound.

Continuing on, Luke drew correlations between himself and his kid sister, another example of non-compliance. His comments couldn't be denied. Yvette surely had both feet planted firmly in her big brother's shadow.

After a time, somebody cracked a joke. Everybody laughed. Levity deflected beautifully, disagreement segued to lighter dialogue. This felt like the norm. Though not unanimous in every regard, Yvette's family was civil, respectful of one another. It was the mark of an integrated and loving group.

Magically, the first course cleared away. Jane served homemade coconut cream pie and Nanaimo bars for dessert. Announcing he'd be returning to his friend Mandy's place in Langley, Luke asked Lily if she'd give him a lift. Prior to our weekend in Aldergrove, it had been decided that Lily, who resided with her husband in Vancouver, would drop Jan and me at the Y on her way home. From there, we'd take the bus back out to Betsy's for one last night before leaving with Walter and company next morning.

Teary-eyed during our goodbyes, the three of us made an oath to meet up in Banff that summer. Unfailingly thoughtful, Yvette wrapped up the remaining Nanaimo bars for the two of us to take on the road.

Mandy's country home was a small, pretty, older house. Outmoded fixtures and a wood burning stove absorbed much of the main living area. Joined by her husband and young son, Mandy was moving to Hawaii and selling off several pieces of furniture. Looking over some of the end tables, Lily purchased two items for her apartment. About ready to leave, Luke made a startling proposal. Though careful not to commit, in a few months after our return from California, he might consider driving Jan and me to Alberta.

It didn't matter if Luke's offer was made in haste and would never materialize.

Enunciating distinctly, I concurred. "That could definitely work."

All decked out with Deb.

Cleveland Dam, B.C.

Jan at Queen Elizabeth Park, Vancouver.

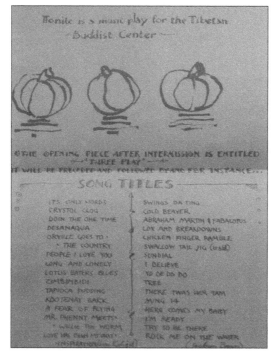

Pied Pumpkin inside program.

Stanley Park, Vancouver.

With Wendy from the YWCA, Vancouver.

YWCA Farewell Supper.

Oregon countryside, near Portland.

CHAPTER 10

On the Road to Find Out

"You are the music while the music lasts."
T.S. ELIOT

Forking over $25 apiece, joining Walter and his roving caravan on Monday April 19, Jan and I hit the highway. Starting out there were nine travellers. A couple more were expected to climb aboard in Seattle. Besides Jan, Walter, and me, our group consisted of "Mouth" (Richard); San Francisco native, Carole; mid-thirties stripper, Gale; "Snowmaker" (Jill), and a young Vancouver couple, Chantal and Guy. You couldn't have thrown together people more different if you tried. Jan, Richard, and I were the only three winging it. Everybody else heading to San Francisco either lived in the city or had a specific purpose. Recently, municipal bus, streetcar, and cable car drivers in San Francisco had gone on strike in protest of unfair wages and unsafe working conditions. Instances of homemade bombs being set in and around the city had been reported. With luck, resolution would soon come.

Breezing to the border, Jan waved her father's note of consent like a flag as we crossed the threshold into our adjoining country. Walter's weathered box on wheels scurried effortlessly beyond the outposts of Northwestern landmark cities: Bellingham, Seattle (where we picked up Bob and Darcy), and Portland, Oregon. In fact, the drive was so smooth, at the next road stop Walter asked Snowmaker if she'd like to trade places with him.

"You'll have the choice spot in the truck." He winked mischievously. "Think about it."

For the first leg of the trip, along with the rest of us who didn't have driving privileges, Jill had been relegated to the back of the van. Guy rode up front next to Walter. Suddenly, Walter wanted to trade places with Jill. Naturally, she was suspicious. Why in hell would anybody *choose* to ride in the back?

The group of us loitered near the vehicle. Snowmaker, a brunette ski fanatic from B.C.'s Okanagan Valley, quietly assessed Walter as he limped toward the van before coming to a clean stop. Having made her decision, approaching the truck, she climbed up onto the dog-eared front seat. "Who wants to ride shotgun?"

All hands shot up. In the end, one lucky adventurer earned the front passenger seat — somebody who not only lived in San Francisco, but could also interpret a road map. That fortunate rider turned out to be Carole, returning home after spending the winter in Vancouver. Guy, who'd been forced to forfeit his place in the front, joined Chantal in the back.

A couple of hours after jumping back on the freeway, Walter's methodology for changing places with Snowmaker was exposed. Joining his passengers in the back, managing to sprawl his sweaty, smelly torso and legs along the floor of the van, conveniently taking up much of the limited space, Walter was quite drunk. Flask handy in pants pocket, inside the van's claustrophobic quarters, Walter's pungent, boozy breath made its presence known. On top of that, Jan counted no less than nine farts since hitting the road. Not having the decency to conceal the sound, the stench was sickening. Everybody was disgusted.

Telltale signs of trouble were evident during our first trip with Walter — we'd decided to give him another chance. Until giving up the captain's chair, Walter presented as a friendly, older brother. With a belly full of whiskey enhanced by the barbiturates consumed while impelling his van that vacillated between 85 and 90 mph, Walter's good nature fell away. He'd become an annoying back seat driver that attempted to contradict our competent pilot who didn't need assistance from a stinky, doped-up drunk. Dismissing Walter's derisory suggestions about "faster roads" or "quicker detours," Jill and Carole formed an impenetrable team. With Snowmaker operating the gears and pedals, aided by the rumpled coffee-stained map retrieved from the glove compartment, Carole helped guide the vehicle in an undeviating route.

Just past midnight, in the faint van light, I noticed Walter's bloodshot-rimmed eyes fixated on Jan's unsuspecting face. Giving her a soft kick in the foot to warn her, my friend already guessed what might be coming. Saddling up to Richard, an intellectual type sporting a head of unruly auburn curls framing a milky white face, Jan put him on red alert should she need him to provide cover. Casting one circumspect eye at Walter, Mouth agreed to help.

Things went from bad to worse.

Strategically repositioning himself, Walter made his play. Complimenting Jan's brunette hair and freckles, placing a clumsy paw on her knee, he told her she was beautiful. Timid and frightened, Jan cowered into the corner of the van.

Back home, if a greasy older man had put unwanted moves on any of us, we'd think nothing of calling him a "perv" and command him to get the hell away. These were not normal circumstances. Hating to admit it, I felt ill-equipped to come to my friend's rescue.

In the interim, Mouth had fallen into a light sleep. When a screech suddenly escaped Jan's mouth, his eyes snapped wide open. Discerning Jan's lips as she mouthed, "He's *bugging* me!" Richard artfully shifted his body weight, creating a buffer between Jan and Walter.

It worked. Walter retreated to the back of the van and everything calmed for a while, the quiet of the ride anesthetizing most of the vehicle's occupants. Then, moving with the speed of a fox, Walter placed two hands around Jan's waist. Startled from partial sleep, she yelped, "I think I'm going to be *sick!*"

Dead serious, my poor friend was certain she was about to spill her guts. Given the close quarters, the image of projectile spewing out over the truck's inhabitants was not a welcome thought. Finally, Mouth called ahead to Snowmaker about the goings on, cleverly choosing his words so not to escalate matters beyond what was already going down. In a heartbeat, Snowmaker made an arbitrary decision. Raising her voice full tilt, Jill announced, "Time to stretch our legs!" Along the reach of sinister highway, it was a welcome break in the wee hours of the morning.

Bursting from the sliding side metal door of the van, glued to Richard's side, Jan and I walked directly toward the bright lights of the convenient store. Now in complete distress, Jan was on the verge of not returning to the vehicle. Turning my head over my shoulder, I noticed the last one to leave the van was Walter.

Ensconced within the safety of the store and company of our group, encouraging her to shake it off, Mouth kept things light. "He's just an old juicer. I won't let him near you when we get back inside. OK?"

While appreciative of Richard's effort to allay her fears, Jan still had doubts. Excusing herself to splash cold water on her face, to my surprise, Jan soon resurfaced from the restroom with a change of heart. She'd try not to let Walter ruin her trip.

Snowmaker refuelled. Everybody climbed back into the van.

Much to Walter's disenchantment, Richard, Jan, and I sat at the other end of the interior — at least six feet away, allowing other bodies to fill the void.

In a fortuitous turn, not long after hopping back on the freeway, like some hideous mutant creature from a sci-fi movie sprawled grotesquely across the floor, our monster snored away the hours as we flew peacefully across the state line from Oregon into California shortly before dawn.

Golden Gate Bridge, San Francisco.

CHAPTER 11

Hotel California

"There is science, logic, reason; there is thought verified by experience. And then there is California."
EDWARD ABBEY

Walter's beat up van pulled discreetly into a parking lot adjacent to a low-rise apartment building on Lander's Street, in Southwest San Francisco. One block north of the San Francisco Mission, perpendicular to Market, Lander's runs between 14th and 16th.

It was almost 6 am. According to our guidebook, Jan (who'd earned the right to take full charge of mapping our hostel stays) figured we were close to one mile from the hostel. Abiding by hostel procedures firmly outlined in the book, we'd have to wait until 5 pm before check in.

Carole kindly offered her apartment to anyone needing a place to crash for a few hours or wash up. Everybody, including Walter, took Carole up on her offer. Alongside capable Snowmaker at the wheel, our first mate had been instrumental in aiding our group to safety, and didn't once complain about fatigue, hunger, or requiring a pee break. Despite Walter's traps, we were grateful for our quick-thinking cohorts.

Small and sparse, otherwise, Carole's apartment was clean and cozy. Following a short introduction to Carole's roommate and lover, Willow, a tall Hispanic woman in her late thirties, rolling out our sleeping bags on the living room floor, Jan and I attempted to grab some shuteye. Others snatched vacant couches and chairs scattered about the room. Stretching out after crunching into cramped quarters dreaming up ways to avoid Walter's hulking, threatening form was a luxury. Neither one of us wanted to go through that again. Especially Jan.

Slumber was short-lived. Shortly after putting down our heads, sunlight crept through the blinds, casting its scope along the surface of the floor. Illuminating tiny dust particles floating in front of a picture window, its span soon engulfed the entire room. Yielding to the morning radiance, despite having spent more than eighteen hours with a bunch of people in a rusty van, surprisingly, I felt rested.

Members of our grungy group took turns using the bathroom for a quick whiz, crap, and scrub up. Thanking Carole and Willow for their hospitality, Jan and I bade our fellow road warriors goodbye. In a short while, we would all disperse in different directions, vanishing from sight as if the entire journey was an apparition. With more gall than brains, Walter asked Jan to stay in touch, telling her she'd be welcome to crash at his buddy's place whenever she returned to Vancouver. Practically pushing me out the door of the apartment, my friend couldn't get away fast enough. Stepping out onto the brilliant concrete sidewalk, we considered how to play the day.

First priority, we needed to find something to eat. Since dining on a turkey feast and all the trimmings in Aldergrove 48-hours before, Jan and I hadn't consumed anything other than Nanaimo bars, pop, and candy. Jane's meal felt like a lifetime away.

Needing to get our bearings, taking a look around, I stared down at the beat up pavement, a platform for damaged, overstuffed garbage containers. Graffiti-laden brick walls barely disguised grubby buildings. I began to panic. Maybe having a wild hair about travelling to the Golden State had been in haste.

Jan and I had been away from home eight weeks. A couple of close calls were the extent of anything remotely insurmountable. However, morning light has a way of throwing a beacon on cracks often overlooked after dusk. Had our trip to San Francisco been less complicated, we'd have felt more optimistic. There was no point dwelling on the past. My friend and I were BIG girls — new to a city upheld by its reputation for liberal attitudes. From what we could tell in a very small window of time, San Francisco surely had verve. Hoping to attach ourselves to that free-spirited fiber, excitement awaited around every corner.

Though sunny and warm, a hard wind blew in off the bay, motivating us to dig sweaters out of our packs — just in case. Finding a grocery-gas station, we cashed in two $20 traveller's cheques and picked out a couple of bagels at the adjoining breakfast bar. Packs secured on our backs, Jan and I walked over to Mission Delores Park to collect our thoughts. According to Jan's guidebook, the green space was one of several parks scattered throughout San Francisco, Golden Gate being the largest. At one point or another we'd try to visit them all.

Sitting on the grass mid-morning, eyes darting everywhere, we were struck by the sedate atmosphere. Overhead, jet stream streaks smeared across a sapphire blue sky, creating an impression of flecks on glass. Other than enjoy the pulsating sunshine and spring foliage, people didn't appear to have anything pressing. Several feet away on the flattened grass, catching winks, slouched a pair of drunks. To our immediate left, an African American couple played peek-a-boo with a toddler.

This was Tuesday morning. Late April. Not an official holiday. *Why weren't people at work?* Around us, men, women, and children engaged in varying groups, eating, snoozing, reading, as if time had stopped. Having been raised in an environment wherein the pace of the status quo often eclipses the simpler elements of life, I wasn't used to this.

Jan opened a book. A brief time out on my sleeping bag turned into a half hour. Regaining consciousness, I glanced over to notice the couple to our left reclined on a blanket, their child next to them playing happily with a Barbie doll. Beginning to kiss, grazing one another's mouths and cheeks, our neighbours soon became more libidinous in their gestures. Sliding his hands around to her backside, the man began to caress the woman's bottom. In turn, through his pants, the woman stroked her partner's genitals. Not paying other park users any mind, opening the zipper, she charitably freed the man's penis. While the man lay flat on his back blissfully aroused, positioning her head at her partner's crotch, the woman began an up and down motion with her mouth.

This sexual action, unfolding not more than ten feet away from where we sat, wasn't lost on Jan. She didn't dare look over at me in case one of us started into laughing and disturbed the couple. Frozen in my tracks, I worried that if we drew attention to ourselves, moved a muscle, got up, or coughed, something bad might happen. In the heat of passion, the man and woman might come at us like wild dogs. Maybe this was commonplace activity in San Francisco parks. Looking around, other folks appeared blasé about the live sex show.

Mounting the man, the woman began rising and lowering her buttocks against his waist. This continued for a couple of minutes until finally, the act culminated in a series of crude emanations. When it was over, I didn't know whether to clap or throw up. Apart from catching a couple of blue movies on the late show, I'd never witnessed anything *this* explicit before. By default, Jan and I'd scored front row seats at a fireworks extravaganza of a lascivious kind.

Dismounting the man, the woman snuggled with her partner in post coital embrace. Doll propped in her lap, the child continued to play. Not even noon, we'd had more than enough excitement for one day.

Leaving Mission Delores Park, lugging our packs like storm troopers for the better part of the afternoon, cautiously, Jan and I roved the neighbourhood, people-watching, window shopping, making mental observations about the rougher brand of hippies, freaks, and greasers loitering outside of storefronts, greasy spoons, and head shops. Marching up and down the hilly San Francisco streets admiring the striking Victorian architecture, doggedness in our steps, we sampled treats at Just Desserts, assessed the frontage at Modern Times Book Shop on 24th Street, and purchased food items from Safeway. Despite being whipped by raw, relentless wind gusts off the bay, my jeans and plaid flannel shirt kept me comfortable. By mid-afternoon, winds calmed. Filling our nostrils with an intermingling sample of salt and ocean fish blowing in from Fisherman's Wharf, the balmy sea breeze reaffirmed why we'd travelled to California.

Jan and I returned to Delores Park. In one hour, we would head over to 101 Steiner Street. Check in at The Holy Order of MANS hostel. Having read rave reviews about the place in our guidebook, according to Jan, a maven in her field, the lodging came highly touted. Disregarding the questionable neighbourhood and unfamiliar name for the place, the residence we'd assumed, was some kind of holy monastery doubling as a shelter for travelling youths. After six weeks living at the Y, anything would be an improvement.

Besides, reviews don't lie.

Charting our map of San Francisco, close to 5:30 pm, Jan and I found ourselves at the foot of a narrow, Victorian style, multi-story structure painted grey. A couple of fan palms and a single maple tree stood on opposite sides of the residence. 101 Steiner Street was the correct address, yet the building didn't appear to represent a youth hostel — more like somebody's private home. Adjacent to Duboce Park in the lower Haight district, The Holy Order of MANS San Francisco Youth Hostel was stationed in a locale my parents would consider a less than desirable part of the city. On the outside at least, the joint looked A-Okay.

Climbing the front steps toward the porch, putting nebulous first impressions aside, Jan rang the buzzer. We waited. Appearing from inside the vestibule, a mild-faced young woman wearing long brunette hair parted in the middle and fastened at the back of her head pulled open the screen door. She introduced herself as Reverend Mary. Appearing at her side in bushy beard and dark, horn-rimmed glasses stood a late-twenties dead ringer for a priest. His name was Brother Bruce. Both were outfitted in traditional Catholic style clergy garb. I studied the couple's attire more closely. Fastened with a woven jute belt, Mary's powder blue tunic covered everything from her neck to her ankles. Her counterpart, a white clerical collar creasing his chin, was neatly dressed in jet-black shirt and black pants. Hand-carved wooden crosses attached to leather cords fell at their midsections. Possessing enormously translucent eyes, Mary and Bruce beamed like a pair of godly Caucasians.

Believing for a moment we'd trespassed into some sort of hard-line Holy Roller church rather than the folksy peace and love communal envisaged from the name of the hostel, I hoped there wouldn't be reason to leave. It had been an exhausting last couple of days.

"We're looking for a youth hostel," Jan piped up. "Are we at the right address?" Reaching out to squeeze our hands, an assurance that we had not made an error, Mary beckoned the two of us inside. Apparent by their bemused faces, our hosts were used to confounded guests.

Jan and I *had* landed in on a class of religious order all right, just not one known to either of us.

No need to sweat it. The uniforms worn by Reverend Mary and Brother Bruce were comfortably familiar, their Zen-like demeanors, oddly soothing. Had they known, our parents would have been relieved to learn that at first chance in our partnering country, Jan and I'd found ourselves tucked within the bosom of presumably principled citizens.

Paying Reverend Mary $2 each for one night's stay, we were shown to the women's dorm (the floor was even carpeted!). Containing six beds, we would share the space with four other girls. Once we were settled, returning to our dorm, the reverend suggested we might like to join fellow hostellers in the common room. Hyped from having covered almost 1000 miles of highway and reconnaissance around the city that day, we anticipated kicking back.

Endowed with a carefree vibe, the central living space contained various animated folks lounging on the floor and on sofas. A couple mingled at a book shelf set against the wall in the middle of the room. Two women worked on a jigsaw puzzle next to the window overlooking Duboce Park. People drank coffee, munched donuts, talked, and joked. There was nothing calculating. No Walter scavenging about. Chantelle and Guy, co-passengers from our drive from Vancouver to San Francisco, huddled next to the stereo. Jethro Tull's *Thick as a Brick* played on the turntable.

Jan and I traded favourable glances.

New faces consisted of Maggie, Daniel, Michael, "Big Mouth" Ray, "British Mike," Allister, Judy from New York accompanied by her yellow canary Tinkle-bell, and other nameless youths full of energy and enthusiasm. As friendships merged organically throughout the evening, one or another took his or her turn in the spotlight, sharing stories of where they had been, where they were headed. Everything seemed to flow in nutritive ambiance. Quietly presenting ourselves to the group, Jan and I were encouraged to share our expeditions. By way of an unspoken act of induction, day-old-crullers were offered. Accepting the unequivocal endorsement, we partook of eight-hour standing black coffee. Prior to arriving at HOOM, I'd never tasted coffee before. Believing that it would stunt our growth, people of my parents' generation did not generally permit kids to drink coffee. Providing you masked the harsh gut-rot taste with a shovel full of Coffee-mate (when it was available, which wasn't often), HOOM's generic brand wasn't half-bad.

At one point, holding up what appeared to be a pair of barber shears, one of the boys, Daniel, approached me. Would I trim his beard?

Dumbfounded, I thought he couldn't possibly be serious. I hadn't trimmed anyone's beard before, nor had I even cut hair, except my own. A onetime experiment. Never to be repeated.

Overruling my hesitation, Daniel convinced me a simpleton could trim a beard, and led me down the short hallway separating the common room from the kitchen. Approaching a round wood table a few feet from the counter, Daniel positioned the "barber's chair" across from where I postured nervously. Holding the shears awkwardly in my right hand, I looked to my left where Brother Bruce stood over the stainless-steel sink washing broccoli hearts in preparation of dinner with Brothers and Sisters at the manse, a short walk down the street. Looking up from his task, noting the duty I was about to perform, he smiled encouragingly in my direction.

Skimming my eyes over Daniel's smooth, suntanned face and thick black eyelashes, gripping the scissors tightly, I let the sharp, pointed edges dangle inches from his dark facial hair. Hunching over my subject carefully, I began to clip the coarse prickles neatly as I could, taking pains not to leave any visible bald spots on his chin or cheeks. Confident in my newfound skill, I cut and snipped until paring the hair down to about a half inch from Daniel's face. When the task was finished, nervously holding up a small hand mirror, I allowed him to inspect my handiwork. Taking the looking glass from my hand, Daniel carefully studied his face and chin. Then his chestnut eyes lit up like rockets. "Thanks!"

When eventually, we rejoined the others in the common room, excitedly, Jan caught me by the arm.

"I'll be sure to recommend this place."

Statue at San Francisco's Golden Gate Park.

CHAPTER 12

A Small Circle of Friends

"Eyes reveal truths."
JILL C. NELSON, APRIL 1976

People gathered in the main living area of the house for the morning ritual of day old donuts and black coffee. About to spend the day hiking up and down the perpendicular streets of San Francisco, edibles of any kind were welcomed. Our second day in northern California, Jan and I anticipated covering a fair bit of ground. Setting off with a city map in pocket, we made our way down Market Street, the main thoroughfare in the downtown core. Along the southeast side, the non-stop activity of streetcars and electric trolleybuses volleyed people of colour and ethnicities to and fro. We ventured over to Saks 5th Avenue, walked over to St. Mary's Cathedral, ordered chocolate sundaes at Gaylord's Ice-Cream Shop. Finding ourselves in neighbouring Twin Peaks, as our map outlined, starting at Castro Street, Jan and I navigated our way to the city stairway and managed to climb Eureka Peak-North Peak at Twin Peaks Mountain, one of two sister hills standing roughly 650 feet apart with an elevation of nearly 925 feet. The ecological and medicinal reserve is home to several classes of insects, wild berries, blue butterflies, and small game. Closer to the top, from Christmas Tree Point, we snapped a couple photos overlooking San Francisco and the bay.

Before returning to the hostel late afternoon, for dinner Jan suggested Communion, an "all-you-can-eat for $1" she'd read about, located on Folsom Avenue. Hoofing it all the way down there (about two miles), we were greeted by a tiny red sign on the door that read, "Closed." Back at Steiner Street early evening, we shared a bag of dried coleslaw with mayonnaise dressing.

While chatting with a soft-spoken boy, Michael, an attractive man strode conspicuously into the room whistling an unfamiliar tune. Brown hair tied back in a ponytail, half-smoked cigarette sticking to his bottom lip, in his hands were freshly picked daisies. Dressed in a light brown corduroy jacket, the two-toned pair of green and black leather shoes on the man's feet looked brand new. Apparently familiar with the place, stopping at the window, the ponytailed stranger placed the flowers in a mason jar on the sill before pivoting toward the record player.

Flipping quickly through a collection of albums in an effort to find something to his liking, Ponytail discarded one LP after another — a virtual who's who list of talented artists — all of whose music I'd have been more than moderately happy to hear. Pausing, he held out a shabby album jacket donning the face of a serious-looking man beneath a Scottish tweed cap. Dressed in a suede overcoat and scarf tied around his neck, the expression of unrest on the artist's face was unusually disquieting. Sliding a large black disc from the sleeve, the man positioned the record on the turntable. Needle secured on the edge of the black surface, the first cut of the album began to rise up and down like a sheet flapping in the breeze. Eyes closed, Ponytail started to hum along.

Turned off by the stranger's musical choice, several of the hostellers demanded another record and were promptly ignored. Irritated, people dispersed to other areas of the house. Clutching onto the sleeve, the young man continued to become engrossed within the song's haunting melody. Emerging from the kitchen carrying a cup of coffee and chocolate dipped donut, Jan grabbed a chair next to mine. Captivated by the vocal stylings of the mystery artist, along with Michael, she and I remained.

Introducing himself as Teddy, the man informed us we were listening to *Pleasures of the Harbor* by the late folk singer Phil Ochs. Ochs had taken his life two weeks earlier.

Political activist, song writer, and performer, Phil Ochs enjoyed an inimitable, prolific, albeit uneven tenure throughout a fourteen-year musical career. Alongside American singer-songwriter and contemporary Bob Dylan, Phil Ochs came up through the ranks of the 1960's New York folk scene in Greenwich Village. Throughout their scrappy early years, the two musicians became close, competitive friends. Coinciding with Ochs's escalating psychological issues, once Dylan's star power took hold, camaraderie began to unravel.

Ochs committed suicide by hanging in his sister's home in Far Rockaway, New York. The final act became the bookend to a self-destructive last couple of years wherein the singer was diagnosed with manic-depressive disorder.

The ironically titled third track of the album and best known offering, "Outside of a Small Circle of Friends," according to Teddy, was penned by Ochs to make known the point that bystanders are reluctant to intervene even when witnessing a violent assault.

The song is particularly jarring.

Set to a cheerful, catchy melody, "Outside of a Small Circle of Friends" recounts the story of Kitty Genovese, originally reported by *The New York Times* to have been stabbed to death in broad daylight outside of her apartment building in Queens. It was the summer of 1964. Purportedly, neighbours who witnessed the attack ignored Genovese's cries for help.[1]

"'Outside of a Small Circle of Friends,'" Teddy contended, "is Ochs's musical trademark." He went on to opine the singer's principal talent was his ability to offset complex, sardonic lyrics with jaunty, stirring melodies. Choosing to play the LP was his way of paying homage to the "poet and anti-war counter culture hero" who'd penned the controversial tune almost ten years earlier. In Teddy's mind, Ochs would forever be relevant and profound.

You couldn't help but pay attention — to the music — and to Teddy's compelling dissertation. Jan and I were about to have our ears and eyes further broadened in the company of our arresting new occupant.

Born in 1948, Teddy was raised in Boston's Irish Ghetto by an Irish Catholic mother. Hearing impaired in one ear, Teddy claimed to have once sung with the Boston Symphony. During his younger years, he dabbled in all constituents of the arts. Supporting himself as a typist and later journalist, in the late 1960s, Teddy was drafted to serve in the Vietnam War where he met a Vietnamese woman whom he married and later divorced. Together, they'd had a baby girl. Having gone "crazy" from the war, Teddy was temporarily institutionalized. Experiencing a psychotic episode that caused her to pull out all her hair, Teddy's young bride became strung out on heroin and was committed to a facility for the mentally insane. The couple's baby daughter was taken into child custody.

When death and loss became too much to bear, like many of his compatriots, Teddy (whom we would soon give the nickname, "Good Samaritan") took to numbing himself, doing street drugs, having indiscriminate sex with prostitutes. Eventually, he wound up in jail where he was strangled, beaten, and left for dead by a fellow inmate. The same prisoner to cause him bodily harm later apologized to Teddy.

1. In 2016, *The New York Times* amended their original Kitty Genovese story, stating there were fewer witnesses to the Genovese murder than originally reported, and that witnesses observing only portions of the crime believed it to be a domestic dispute.

With every word articulated, this interesting, ponytailed man became increasingly impassioned, as if his string of bad luck had happened recently. In fact, it had only been a few years. Despite the pain of his past, Teddy knew how to work a room. Like a pinball machine, his energy and mania ricocheted up, down, all around.

There was more.

Preceding his arrival at 101 Steiner Street, this charismatic young man claimed to have lived in the desert for seven weeks working on a novel. It was never clear how Teddy found himself in San Francisco, though he was actively seeking another place to live. More importantly, until he got his "shit together," Teddy had an extended guest pass at HOOM.

At the conclusion of Teddy's disclosure, there was prolonged silence. Then, as if on cue, Brother James, a pipe-smoking, premature grey member of The Order casually entered the room and sat down. Through semi-transparent green eyes, Brother James began to elucidate the reasons why Teddy had survived not only the war, but also drug addiction and his assailant.

"Instinctually," James said, "Teddy possesses the intrinsic will to live. Every one of us creates our own reality. All that happens throughout our lives is a result of our own self-visualization. What we fundamentally *believe* will manifest in our existence."

Pausing briefly, Brother James turned his eyes toward Teddy. Difficult to discern what Teddy was thinking, I know what I was thinking: *Is Brother James suggesting that Teddy willed himself to endure all that pain, and then willed himself out of it?*

Later, I looked up "self-visualization" technique at the library. Originating in Russia during the training of Olympic athletes, the practice was incorporated with relative success. The first occasion that either Jan or I'd heard of the New Age philosophy, it made sense as much as anything did.

To reflect upon later, to the best of my recollection, I recorded the Teddy/Phil Ochs/Brother James information/conversation in my journal.

Alone in our bunk beds later that night, Jan and I chatted about Teddy and our day, and then turned out the light.

It was difficult to fall asleep.

Intentional or not, the Good Samaritan had left an imprint.

Next morning, we slept late. Approaching nine o'clock — it was time for hostellers to seize the day. Michael, one of the Steiner Street gang whom we'd met the night before, invited Jan and me to tour the city. Any opportunity to socialize with newfound friends — we jumped.

Setting out in the cool foggy morning with intermittent sunny breaks, we made our way toward Golden Gate Park, not far from HOOM. Along Market Street, we espied Teddy and Brother James handing out leftover day-old donuts to street people. Acknowledging the two with a wave, Jan, Michael, and I continued along the street until we encountered a mammoth marble structure decorating the walkway in front St. Mary's Cathedral. Sitting on the tall sandstone steps regarding the carving, while Jan and Michael studied our city map, I took my journal from my bag. Preparing to sketch a rough incarnation of the stone sculpture, I studied the sword held in one hand and sheath draped across the statue's body. The imperial expression on the face of the long-bearded man resembled a king; his potent, dignified presence a metaphoric reminder how diminutive we are in all respects. Beyond admiring the statue and intricate composition of the pipe organ inside of the Cathedral's sanctuary, we continued along our way.

Arriving on the convivial grounds of Golden Gate Park, charmed by the Japanese Tea Garden, the three of us were drawn to break at The Tea House. Seated at the small outside patio, Michael ordered a pot of jasmine tea. Sipping from dainty ceramic cups, nibbling on fortune cookies, I retrieved my fortune typed across pink paper, and shared it with Jan and Michael. It said, "You will step on the soil of many countries."

Originally from British Columbia, 21-year-old Michael had recently travelled throughout South America. Slowly making his way back home, the next morning he would fly to Vancouver. The past two years, Michael had become a self-taught student of the book of *I-Ching* (also known as the *Book of Changes*), one of the oldest of classic Chinese texts centering on traditional Chinese writings. Deeply respectful of the disciplines associated with I-Ching and its principles, Michael carried in his pocket special coins.

Turning the coins in his fingers, he divulged one of I Ching's fundamental tenets: "When trouble finds its way onto your doorstep, don't stamp your feet on the ground in anger or despair. Make yourself like water. Water flows through everything. Once you transpose your being, you can positively affect an outcome depending upon your hopes and dreams." Corresponding with the self-visualization practice Brother James had spoken about the previous evening; Michael had purposely chosen to share the water analogy.

Reasonably open to considering the values of Eastern religion (two favourite novelists and spiritualists to that point, Herman Hesse and J.D. Salinger, were greatly influenced by Buddhism and other alternative Eastern philosophies), mysticism and New Age hypotheses associated with the secular world — I was also hesitant. Not a religious girl in the customary sense, truthfully, I didn't really know what I was.

In mid-seventies North America, faith in God was routinely accepted as a highly lauded human merit. Believers were considered "good" people. Ascribed with the responsibility of forming the solar system and leading to the eventual creation of the world, growing up, God's hand was presumed the reason for all living entities, specifically the existence of human life. The practice of Christianity, and subsequently a happy ever-after life was accepted by those who "believed." Bearing in mind this supposition was in place centuries before the growing acceptance of scientific evidence pointing to the contrary, like many people, I didn't feel convicted. Yet, in general, I *believed* in God more than I disbelieved in Him. On any given day, it was a crapshoot.

Important that my brothers and I had a foundation in the fundamentals of Christianity, church was introduced to us by my mother, who attended semi-regularly. As a kid, I prayed *"now I lay me down to sleep"* every single night, attended church on a part-time basis, and was confirmed in the Anglican Church before I was thirteen. After the ceremony, as many kids do once other forces and influences take hold, I stopped attending. Required to attend Presbyterian Church three times on Sunday throughout his childhood and teen years, as an adult my father let himself off the hook.

I recall Dad attending church on one occasion. It was Christmas Eve, 1974. My friend Liz's dad had passed away suddenly from a heart attack a few days earlier. Only sixteen, Liz took her father's loss hard. Inextricably, her father's death was a wake-up call for my own dad whom (I believe) felt guilty about his personal lifestyle choice — squandering evenings and weekends in a vodka fog. Not that I wanted my father to die, I just didn't understand how the deck was stacked. Liz's dad was a God-fearing, church going man. When my dad attended church with our family that Christmas service, I remember feeling sublimely happy. The best part of all, Liz had come with us.

Despite mounting scientific support and the fact that globally, human beings are rapidly acquiescing to the evolution theory over God, one never knows when faith in something or someone saintly might come in handy. My motto: Keep God in your back pocket, just in case.

Delighted to learn there was no entrance fee, after our tea break, Michael, Jan, and I headed to the de Young museum to visit the art gallery. Housed within the exhibit halls, exquisite papier-mâché works jumped out while some truly magnificent paintings depicting decorative American art from various periods — costumes, textiles, landscapes, and images, aligned the walls.

In the afternoon, we roved through Golden Gate Park's passages.

Renowned as one of the largest urban parks in the world, in part for the sheer elegance of its delicate flower gardens, scores of alcoves, groves, lakes, and museum; over the past five decades the park has played center stage to some of the world's most legendary musical assemblages. During the height of the sixties, the likes of Jefferson Airplane, Hot Tuna, Buffalo Springfield, and The Mamas and Papas honed their crafts at Golden Gate Park. To this day, free concerts are still held at the concourse almost every Sunday afternoon.

Wandering amongst the park's free-flowing meadows and statues scattered endlessly among eucalyptus, cypress, and pine trees, Jan made a startling statement. She might *not* attend university in the fall. Before coming away, school had been her elected autumn plan. Now, she might consider travelling until December and start the winter semester instead.

I asked my friend what caused her to reassess the situation.

"I like travelling too much right now." Jan grinned. "I want to keep going until the end of the year."

Seeming to be on the same track, within the last forty-eight hours, something irrefutable, the presence of newfound energy had altered our former state of reality, lifting us to a plane of enlightenment. Whether valid or imagined, since coming West, Jan and I would remain on auto-alert for new opportunities.

Late afternoon, the temperature rose substantially. The fusion of sunshine and balmy breezes filtering off the bay turned the day into a dazzling one. Wandering down Polk Street, we encountered the Good Samaritan outside of The Art Show, a gallery owned by local dealer, Fred Mattes. Employed by Mattes part-time, Teddy offered us a quick tour inside the shop. Leaving us to tend to a browsing customer, we headed back outside. Along the steps of a nearby community church, people milled about while a smiling, heavyset woman wearing a red cotton dress with long kinky hair to her waist passed out pamphlets to passersby. We were invited inside.

The sanctuary space, a far cry from the gathering place from my days at St. Christopher's Anglican Church, resembled a vacated store rather than a place for worship. Copying the informal attitudes of the folks that had congregated inside, we removed our shoes. Kneeling before the makeshift altar, where worshippers offered flowers, coins, incense, and candles, we were informed that on this morning, the spirit-guided message would be delivered by Father Donald, affiliated with San Francisco's HOOM chapter.

Holding onto cups of water, snacks in hands, raising their beaks, the flock perched ready to receive the spoken word of the lean, clean-shaven preacher. Taking his place at the altar, Father Donald blessed the sanctity of the shelter. Then he began to speak reverently of God and how "He has made us Perfect." Designed to spiritually purify the disparate collection of parishioners, various proclamations followed until finally, in closing, the pastor cautioned, "Until you grasp the truth, that every one of us is perfect, you will fail to identify perfection in other human beings."

Once session let out, descending onto Polk Street, Jan, Michael, and I became caught up within the annual Chinese parade and pageantry in full force, an astounding succession of vibrant sequined costumes and carnival of floats embellishing the main thoroughfare. It seemed a fitting end to the day.

That evening, the excitement within HOOM's epicenter was raw. In the background, *Sergeant Pepper* played at high intensity. Assembled in the main room, our comrades planned to hit the bars. Approaching Jan and me, Teddy invited us to come out drinking with him and Michael. Uncertain if I'd heard correctly, I asked if he could please repeat the question.

One month into spring in the city by the bay. Everything was possible.

Holy Order of MANS holy book: The Golden Force.

CHAPTER 13

The Golden Force

"I looked for my soul but my soul I could not see. I looked for my God,
but my God eluded me. I looked for a friend and then I found all three."
THOMAS BLAKE

Jan and I would have given our eyeteeth to go bar hopping with Teddy and Michael. Unfortunately, while most of the group left for drinks and dancing down on Market Street; we sucked it up at HOOM.

Both of us carried fake I.D. It had worked as effective camouflage in Vancouver. Now that we were no longer in Canada, things were different. The legal drinking age in California was 21-years-old. Passing ourselves off as young twenties presented a challenge. If only our roommate Deb was around to apply a little polish as she'd done the night we went out to Charlie Brown's nightclub in Vancouver. Resembling the two typical teenagers we were, there was little Jan or I could do to help our cause. Upon discovering our ages, Teddy looked ready to load his pants.

We were sufficiently bummed.

Disappointed to stay home while everybody else was out partying, we occupied ourselves in other ways. Assuaged by Donovan's *Sunshine Superman*, a few rounds of checkers and games of Crazy Eights were had. In the cabinet below the turntable I discovered another Phil Ochs album, *Tape from California,*[2] and put it on.

Noticeably pared down instrumentation-wise compared to its predecessor, *Pleasures of the Harbor*, in the liner notes, the LP's theme is described by Ochs as a commentary on the spiritual decay of America. The title song's chorus, in which Ochs contends being in a hurry but

---

2. *Tape from California*, released in July, 1968, is described by music critic William Ruhlmann, as "a portrait of a desperate, debased society and [Ochs's] own sense of personal decline." Ruhlman goes on to describe the record as a "frighteningly accurate portrait of its times of the most tumultuous year of the tumultuous '60s."

will send along a "tape from California," would become emblematic of our time spent in the Golden State.

Mid-way through the evening, eager to drop his hulking pack, a new drifter filed into the room. He was 19-year-old Gary from New Zealand — an extroverted Mick Jagger clone (only taller), and he knew it. A total peacock, hilarious from the start, not surprising, Gary was a *huge* Stones fan.

Enormously verbose, fortified with machismo and swagger, Gary proposed to visit every American state and as much of Canada as possible before his sixth month visa expired and he had to return home.

The tone of the evening had suddenly changed. Happily whiling away the hours listening to records, joking around and playing cards, Jan, Gary, and I made plans to visit Fisherman's Wharf in the morning.

Nearly time to retire to the girls' dorm, some of the barhopping crew returned, the Good Samaritan among them. Dressed in blue jeans and brown corduroy jacket, beneath his arm, Teddy carried a couple of oil paintings from The Art Show.

Aided by the effects of drink, everybody was in great spirits. Firsthand accounts were shared about what had gone down at one of the clubs, the room erupting in laughter. Several eyewitnesses claimed that one of the *Orderly* women of HOOM had peeled off her blue gown and panties to a stinging cover of Zeppelin's "Stairway to Heaven." Bored by the silent porno film that played on a monitor during the striptease, others left the bar to appraise other clubs before returning to the hostel.

That evening, Teddy was attentive toward me in a manner that could only be interpreted as fatherly. Having brought along a couple of bags of food he'd picked up at the nearby Safeway store, gently, he approached. Handing over one of the sacks, Teddy asked that I open it. Inside the bag were loose carrots, an orange, a bottle of grape juice, and container of peach yogurt.

"Here's your lunch for tomorrow," he stated, candidly.

The slightest nuance of attention from an attractive male easily stole my affection. Eyes and heart swelling, I made a motion to hand the items back. Refusing to accept the food, Teddy advised, "It takes courage to accept a gift, no matter how small. Right now, I work and have a bit of money. Maybe one day you'll do the same for me."

Wondering where his concern for my daily nutrition had come from, not to mention the innocent conjecture about my future, gratefully, I received the gift. Turning on his heel, reaching his hand inside of the other bag to retrieve three lemons, Teddy asked, "Who wants to try their hand at juggling?" Finding there were no takers, the Good Samaritan stepped into the center of the common room, spacing his feet apart. Nimbly, he tossed three lemons into the air, and then began circulating the pieces of fruit in a fluid arc. Commanding the room before a sweep of yellow amidst clapping and shouts of approval, folding the lemons into his hands, he finally sat down. Brother Bruce asked could he give it a try. Placing the lemons into Bruce's hands, Teddy good-naturedly offered to monitor the Brother's attempts to get the food in motion. Chucking the citrus in opposite directions, much to Bruce's surprise, all three lemons whacked down onto the floor.

Everybody booed.

Bruce sat down.

Teddy invited me to try.

Nervous at first, after a couple of rough attempts, I could get two lemons in sync. Adding the third was a bust. Soaring through the air, the errant lemon smacked the Good Samaritan firmly in the cheek.

I was horrified.

Teddy didn't flinch. "You'll get it next time." He grinned.

Most of the others started to head to bed. A few remained, including Jan and Gary. Now well past midnight, not wanting the evening to end, the friendly mood within the remaining group felt encouraging.

Somebody scurried away to make tea. Minutes later, mugs in hands, spiritual matters dominating the tone, Gary, Brother James, Brother Bruce, Marianne, Michael, and Teddy engaged in chatter. Mostly, Jan and I listened, taking it all in while people interjected opinions, theologies, and personal views. Cracking jokes, Gary questioned the reliability of some of the stories espoused by the brothers.

Somebody asked about The Holy Order of MANS. What did it represent exactly? From his shirt pocket, Brother James withdrew a worn copy of HOOM's bible, *The Golden Force*, written by founder Earl Blighton.[3] The

---

3. Manifested from Christian roots, Holy Order of MANS (HOOM) was first established in San Francisco in 1968 by founder Reverend Earl Blighton, retired electrical engineer turned mail-order minister. A New Age religious denomination with complete autonomy, The Holy Order of MANS was developed from esoteric teachings. According to Wikipedia, the condensed definition of the origins of HOOM is as follows: "The Mission and Purpose of The Holy Order of MANS is to guide humankind to union with the Divine Self of God within. Full experiential knowledge of God beyond merely intuitive spiritual insight is true redemption. The principal means of affecting this insight is by the practice of theurgy, the practice of rituals."

Considered magical in nature, sacrament is essential to achieving oneness with God and the perfection of self. The acronym 'MANS,' stands for Mysterian, Agape, Nous, and Sophia in Greek. In English, MANS is representative of mystery, love, mind, and wisdom.

forest green cover depicts a logo of a small gold cross, enflamed. Lodged inside of a gold triangle, the symbol is housed within a circle within a golden square.

From the inside flap, Brother James read aloud the organization's mission statement:

> "The Holy Order of MANS is officially a non-sectarian, non-denominational service and teaching order of minister-priests, Brothers and Sisters, who have dedicated their lives to the service of all men by teaching and living the universal law of creation in accordance with the teachings of Jesus Christ and other great avatars. The Order maintains Brother-houses throughout the United States, where members and missionaries train. This is a universal Catholic Order. Its doctrines are adopted from the teachings of Paul and the ancient Christian mysteries."

Intriguing were the "mysteries" and "other great avatars" portions of the introductory text. What did they mean? During conversation, Brother James eluded that Order members of a higher spiritual echelon could pass through solid barriers such as walls and doors. Shedding human form, evidently, this act of transference made it possible to mediate more directly with God.

The concept of human bodies transporting through portals seemed cool. According to James, there were eyewitness accounts. Myth or fact, I wasn't about to judge out loud. Anyway, the Holy Bible professes some fantastical claims. Supposedly, Jesus Christ turned water into wine and returned to life after death. Throughout the ages, surreal, metaphysical episodes purported to have occurred involving native tribes, Yogis, and spiritual mentors, have been documented. Some of these incidents allegedly came to pass after the ingestion of peyote buttons and other edible plants with transformative powers. Writer and anthropologist Carlos Castaneda composed several books inspired by the mystical influences of various herbs and hallucinogenic plants.

James went on to elucidate his point. "Just as we have ability to create physical bodies, we also possess the faculty to disintegrate physical form by defying laws of nature if we become part of the Universal Law. Scientific in its origins, the Universal Law operates and exists within linear function and principles."

Though fun to participate in the discussion, some of what Brother James had read *did* seem far-fetched, and it was confusing. Out of the reach of the others, I couldn't wait to get Jan's take on the evening.

That wouldn't happen right away.

On my way to the girls' dorm, Teddy approached me in the hallway, taking me aside. Believing I seemed to be upset, he asked what I was feeling. Thinking about it for a moment I replied, "Given everything, I find the subject of God, the afterlife, and people floating aimlessly around difficult to understand." Scarcely able to imagine *myself* around in twenty years, understanding the planet and its relationship with my life at eighteen years of age was unfathomable.

I told Teddy so.

Taken aback by my indifference, the Good Samaritan didn't hesitate to bring me up to speed. "The world is a *good* place. It's getting better all of the time, you know. Don't ever forget that." To reinforce the importance of projecting positive thoughts, Teddy explained how he walks in dangerous parts of the city and isn't harmed because he whistles, presenting a self-assured front to outsiders. His newfound perspective on life had taught him to trust that nothing evil or vile would ever fall upon him again.

"From here on in," Teddy swore, "things are looking up."

I wasn't so sure.

Climbing into the top bunk of our dorm, stomach tingling with excitement, my brain raced through a web of possibilities.

I was young. I wasn't stupid. Part of the reason for my exhilaration and disorientation that night resulted from my escalating crush on Teddy. Captivated as I was — by him, by everything else that was happening, I cautioned myself not to get caught swimming upstream.

Next morning, mind clearer, I gobbled a couple of day olds, and rinsed them down with bitter black coffee. Next to the record player, Jan and Gary huddled together scripting the day's itinerary. In the kitchen, wearing the same denims and shirt from the night before, a green kangaroo jacket over top, Teddy stood beneath the window preparing to wash a sink full of dishes. Lifting a dry tea towel from the stove handle, hovering next to the sink, I offered to pitch in. This would be my "good deed" to counterpoise the one Teddy granted the night before. As I expressed my intentions, laughing uncomfortably, the Good Samaritan proceeded to light a cigarette. Inhaling deeply, he set the smoke on the window ledge and plunged his hands deep into the water.

Watching the swirl of grey dance back and forth before the window pane until accelerating upward, I sensed there was something on Teddy's mind. The next several minutes, standing quietly side by side, he sponged the plates, mugs and cutlery while I dried. No one said a word.

Finally, looking up from the sink, Teddy snuck another quick drag. "I'm going to join The Order."

Turning slightly to the right, I looked closely at Teddy. For a young man of 28, the Good Samaritan's face reflected every personal victory and defeat. Tiny lines beneath his tender blue eyes exposed a burden of anguish beneath the foundation of his features, reminding me of someone who wished his life had turned out differently.

Grasping to extend an appropriate comeback, I chirped, "That's great news!"

Muttering something indiscernible about having to cut his hair before entering the novice stage, Teddy changed the subject. He'd heard a rumour Bob Dylan was in town and might play an impromptu gig that night. "Keep your eyes and ears open," he warned.

Overhearing the tail end of our conversation, Jan and Gary joined us in the kitchen. While working as a freelance journalist during the late 1960s, Teddy told us he'd contributed articles to *Marijuana Review* and other alternative publications. He was still connected to the "grapevine." The expansive world map on the wall between the kitchen and the living room suddenly drawing his attention, Teddy traced a lone finger around the British Isles, explaining how his grandparents had migrated from Ireland in the early part of the century. Raising his head, teeth gleaming, fondly, he looked over at Jan and then at me. "See you happies later."

Preparing to collect his belongings from 101 Steiner Street, the Good Samaritan would be moving across the road to the manse where HOOM's novices-in-training slept.

Gary: San Francisco, April 1976.

CHAPTER 14

Fisherman's Friends

"There may not be a Heaven, but there is a San Francisco."
ASHLEIGH BRILLIANT

The previous day, touring the grounds of Golden Gate Park and the de Young Art Gallery with Michael acting as our unofficial tour guide had been an honour. Hanging with Gary was akin to being in the company of someone amped on speed, or at the very least, twenty cups of coffee. Given that breakfast at HOOM was a limited regime with coffee as the primary sustenance, the latter was likely the case.

Outside, on the street, Gary poked fun at Teddy and the Brothers and Sisters of The Order, referring to the Good Samaritan as "Brother" Teddy. Drawing our attention to same-sex couples strolling along Market Street holding hands, Gary sniped "queer" and "fag" nearly loud enough for people to hear. Looking for laughs rather than trying to be callous, Gary's remarks were not altogether kind either. Upon our first encounters with gays and lesbians along Polk and Market Streets, Jan and I had snickered a couple of times. In the presence of somebody else doling out insults, it wasn't so funny. Ashamed, I told Gary to quit it.

Home to the largest gay and lesbian community in the world, in 1976 San Francisco celebrated its sixth annual LGBT Pride Parade and Festival. Over the decades, the parade has expanded to include up to 200 contingents. Where we'd come from, sexual preferences other than heterosexuality were considered a less than desirable alternative lifestyle choice. Overt displays of affection by same sex couples made many people uncomfortable, even threatened. Observing Gary's actions and the demeaning labels he lobbed, I doubted things were different in Christchurch where he was born and raised. I couldn't help stare, not in judgment, but from a position of curiosity and awe. Trim men with trimmer beards embraced. Women of various shapes and ages walked arm in arm with female partners. Observing couples through juvenile eyes, I read genuine affection. It wasn't that big a deal.

Cashing in $10 worth of travellers cheques apiece, Jan and I were rich again. Navigating BART (Bay Area Rapid Transit) would enable us to visit The University of California, Berkeley's historic campus located in northern Alameda County along the east shore of the San Francisco Bay. Boarding the bus to Fremont which stopped at Berkeley, for more than an hour we hiked the area, though didn't end up spending much time on campus. Mostly, it was to say we'd been to Berkeley.

From there we caught a ride with two red-haired Englishmen driving a white Austin Mini that vibrated, backfired, and made a loud racket all the way to Market. After we were let out, Gary took off like a shot, running wildly down the narrow streets darting between cars, screaming at passersby for no apparent reason until coming across the first record store in sight. In search of *Black and Blue*, the Rolling Stones' (pronounced "Stines" in Gary speak) recent release, Gary was on a mission.

Thunderstruck by the astounding collection of vinyl; 33s, 45s, 78s, and an endless motif of music magazines that included *Circus*, *Creem*, and *Rolling Stone*, from one end of the store to the other, racks overflowed with LPs and posters showcasing Pink Floyd, Zeppelin, The Beatles, The Who, The Doors, The Yardbirds, Canned Heat, Country Joe and the Fish, Velvet Underground, The Beach Boys, The Mothers of Invention, Bowie, The Strawbs — some of the most celebrated bands to have garnered acclaim during the sixties and seventies' decades. For pop, rock or underground aficionados, the photo collages alone were a banquet for the eyes.

Seizing his prize, a freshly pressed copy of *Black & Blue*, Gary paid the clerk and rushed out the door in hunt of a photo booth. With its cover depiction of three of the band's notorious members, Mick Jagger, Keith Richards and Bill Wyman, our New Zealand friend was as infatuated with their surly mugs as he was with the records' contents.

Locating a booth on Polk, dropping four quarters into the metal slot, Jan and I were invited to join Gary behind the black curtain as he summoned his most impudent Jagger sneer. Shooing us from the booth with both hands after one quick shot, Gary wanted to pose alone with the boys for the remaining three pictures. To shush us up from distracting him from the task at hand, he bellowed, "Shut up! You bloody idiots!" causing Jan and I to double over with laughter. Gary planned to send the black and whites back to friends in Christchurch.

Taking the trolley down to Fisherman's Wharf, conductors don't mess around. Riding any tramcar in the city, you hold on tight. Sitting hands free, I got the surprise of my life when the driver yanked hard on the clutch causing the car to lurch forward, the momentum of the trolley's velocity hurling me to the ground. Struggling to my feet, I observed Jan pinned between two hefty women while Gary roared with laughter. Quick to haul me up by my arm, unmoved, the driver hurried me out the door behind descending passengers.

Heading down the steep slanting sidewalk toward the Wharf, gazing out over hundreds of tourists, a party of colourful sailboats slept in the harbour. In the distance, the radiant shimmer of spring light settled comfortably along the indigo bay. Warmed by the morning sun, predictably, the fog had lifted its veil over the waterfront by noon.

Fisherman's Wharf is home to a variety of shopping areas, seafood restaurants and museums, an aquarium and park, and includes Pier 39, Ripley's Museum, and Ghirardelli Square. A healthy sea lion colony sits adjacent to the pier. Throughout the last few decades, the area has evolved into a universally admired attraction. Falling in with the celebratory atmosphere that featured a network of face-painted acrobats, unicyclists, magicians, musicians, performers, and vacationers of all races and creeds, like a maestro, Gary wove his way through the mobs and vibrant caravans dotting the sea and land. Deciding on a serving of battered shrimp for lunch, he suggested we splurge on a few beers. (With Gary in tow, the odds passing for 21 were better than fair. Servers would have to assume we were the same.) Locating a place serving pub food, the three of us hustled inside.

Saddling ourselves on barstools, tossing out hilarious comments about other customers, Gary's one-liners made it impossible to keep a straight face. When the barmaid arrived to take our drink orders, dialing it down on the wisecracks, Gary turned on the charm. Coolly, he ordered, "Bud, please. And one for each of my girlfriends."

Without balking, the young woman scampered away from the table to fetch our drinks. No doubt sucker punched by the allure of Gary's accent, she probably couldn't be bothered to check ID. Either way, we were *in*. It meant that Jan and I probably could have gone barhopping with Teddy and Michael without suffering the humiliation of being booted out.

If only.

The barmaid returned, setting three ice-cold bottles on the table. Feeling my face light up like a winning slot machine, I pretended not to care. Raising our bottles triumphantly, Gary made a quick toast about new friendships. Drawing from the narrow brown neck, I didn't think there was anything more divine than the cold golden brew coating my throat. It sure beat the hell out of tasteless, day-old black coffee, the oily tar that had become a fundamental element of our diet as of late.

Sharing a plate of battered shrimp and fries, we scarfed down the food as fast as it was set down. Gary put in a bid for one more round of Bud. By the time the bottles were drained, it was time to leave.

Outside, sunshine sparkled and danced along the bay, clearing a straight path to the island of Alcatraz, little more than one mile from the Wharf. The subject of various Hollywood productions, the one-time maximum-security prison is known to have housed some of the country's most notorious cold-blooded criminals. Over the years, several daring escape attempts were made. Due to cold water conditions and rough currents surrounding the penitentiary, none were successful. After 29 years in operation, in 1963, the prison was finally closed down. Between the years 1969 and 1971, Alcatraz was reclaimed as native land before it was taken over by Federal Marshals. Reopened years later as a tourist attraction, with the availability of self-guided tours, the former penitentiary continues to function as a popular destination site for visitors to San Francisco.

The remainder of the afternoon we wandered throughout various stalls at Ghirardelli Square, where artists, musicians, fortunetellers, and metalworkers, eager to dispense their wares before sunset, would expend daily earnings on food and drink. Displayed across plush velvet fabrics, exquisitely designed silver pieces portraying faces of leopards, lions, snakes, dragons, even garish medieval gargoyles were fascinating if not a little frightening. Excited to visit a tarot card reader, upon learning the $5 fee — I quickly changed my mind. Denna, our resident witch back at the Vancouver Y would have happily read my cards free. I could only imagine what despicable disasters she'd have giddily foretold.

Keeping an eye on the time, we caught the trolley partway to the top of the city, took in a fine view of Telegraph Hill, and checked out Lombard Street. Known as the "crooked" street, it was exciting to be back on the arterial road made famous by actor and professional driver, Steve McQueen in the 1968 film *Bullitt*. As Lieutenant Frank Bullitt, McQueen scorches down Lombard in a green mustang at a prohibitive speed in pursuit of a couple of mobsters, and cleanly maneuvers the road's eight sharp turns and switchbacks before skating away in heat.

Flopping into one of the lumpy couches back at the hostel, I looked forward to drinking more cruddy coffee and munching on another crusty donut. Two straight nights we'd eaten cupcakes, apples, and dry coleslaw for dinner (the stove and oven were off limits). The lunch that Teddy had brought me the previous evening was stored in the fridge, soon to be shared with Jan.

Two guys from Montana, Hal and Bill, planned to leave San Francisco for Los Angeles the next morning, and were looking for riders to help share gas. Knowing that we were soon headed down to Santa Cruz, Brother James mentioned to Hal he might know a couple interested customers. Jan and I were growing more comfortable at 101 Steiner Street than either one of us cared to admit. Intuitively, the Brothers and Sisters of HOOM sensed when it was time for hostellers to move on.

Strategic or not, their ill-fated timing coincided with dangling just enough rope to mess with my head.

San Francisco accident site. Hal and Bill (in behind) wearing hats.

CHAPTER 15

Cruising to Santa Cruz

"One's destination is never a place, but a new way of seeing things."
HENRY MILLER

Hal and Bill were anxious to hit the road early. Knowing that everybody had to clear out of the hostel by nine, Jan and I were up and showered. A couple of the others, Judy and Ross, would be along for the ride.

We forced down donuts and coffee, our last for a while. Offering to clear the table dishes, I noticed the Good Samaritan stooped over a sink full of bubbles. Inasmuch as I looked forward to Santa Cruz, leaving HOOM and San Francisco felt premature. Mostly, I felt deprived not getting to know Teddy better.

Watching him roll up his sleeves about to plunge both hands into the hot soapy water, I wondered would I ever see the Good Samaritan again? The notion seemed audacious, even to me. Ten years my senior, Teddy had already racked up lifetime's worth of hardships. In principle, he wasn't the sort of person to bank on for any serious purpose. Still, Teddy was someone with whom I'd liked to have invested more time. Possibly a lot more time. I was positive about that.

Approaching the sink I said, "I'm sorry to leave the hostel and San Francisco already. It seems we just got here."

Surely able to discern between the lines, Teddy didn't let on. In an attempt to mollify my regret, he countered, "It's always hard to move on. In the same way that you never really leave any place, you're never ever home." Smiling broadly, the Good Samaritan lowered his head to peer out the kitchen window where the tawny morning sky held promise of a splendid outing down the coast.

"Besides," he added, "it's a beautiful day for a drive to Santa Cruz."

Not about to disagree, I replied, "Well, it's my last morning here. I'll help you with the dishes, OK?"

Communing in light conversation about places we'd like to visit some day, and other matters, Teddy mentioned he'd donated blood the night before, an incident that had apparently laid him "flat out." Recently, he'd picked up a book at City Lights bookstore in North Beach containing the poem, "Journalism" by New York newspaper columnist Franklin Pierce Adams. Missing his days as a writer, Teddy told me the poem, apparently an analogy for tempestuous relationships such as marriage, had galvanized him.

Recognizing I had zero knowledge about Adams, he proceeded to recite a few lines.

"Journalism's a shrew and scold, I like her. She makes you sick, she makes you old; I like her. She's daily trouble, storm and strife. She's love and hate, and death and life. She ain't no lady. She is my wife. I like her."[4]

Revelling in the enchantment of the moment, I smiled favourably.

Bulging red knapsack protruding behind her back with sleeping bag attached, Jan entered the kitchen followed by Gary (I had a feeling she was sweet on him, but we hadn't yet talked about that). Drying his hands on a dishtowel, Teddy announced he was late for work. Arms outstretched, the Good Samaritan blessed Jan and me on our journey. In turn, we wished Teddy all the best in The Holy Order.

In a wink, he was gone.

Hal and Bill packed their light blue Dodge before a small group that had gathered in front of the porch at 101 Steiner Street. For the 75-mile drive to Santa Cruz, Hal charged $2 for each rider. Along with some of the others remaining in San Francisco a few more days, Gary had come to see us off. Taking our places inside the vehicle — Jan in the front between Hal and Bill, I in the back next to Judy and Ross — each of us received a kiss on the cheek from Gary, who pledged we'd get together somewhere down the line before he returned to New Zealand.

Coasting up the street toward the traffic light, barely retrieving my arm from the open window, I felt a sudden hard *thud*. Smashing glass followed a loud *crash*. Though I hadn't eye-witnessed it, as Hal eased through the intersection, another vehicle crossed over and T-boned the front end.

From her place in the front seat, Jan complained about a sore jaw.

Managing to scramble out of the car, I watched our friends run toward us. Gary had to clutch onto his stomach he was laughing so hard. Arriving at the accident site and realizing that Jan was hurt, he dropped the dumb act — then,

4. According to colleague Nat Benchley, Franklin Pierce Adams (1881-1960) included the poem "Journalism" in his column in the final issue of *The World*, a New York newspaper which folded in 1931.

sweetly, wrapped both arms protectively around my friend. Waiting for police to arrive on the scene, placing her fingers to her lips, Jan discovered the inside of her mouth had been cut. Her jaw bruising from the force of the steering wheel that had smacked her face during impact; she was positive that every one of her teeth had been broken. Thankfully, they were all intact.

That's what you get for privileged seating.

Taking down the pertinent information for his report (there were several eyewitnesses), the motorcycle cop charged the driver of the other vehicle (a woman) with negligence, delaying our trip almost two hours. Reestablished inside Hal's crumpled car that miraculously still functioned, Jan (mostly recovered from shock) rode next to me in the back seat. Anxious to put fresh emotions behind us, after our setback, I was happy to get on the road and encounter new territory.

Arriving just south of Santa Cruz at Brighton National Park mid-afternoon, planning to spend at least one night, Jan and I prepared to assemble our two-man pup tent. In an effort to save a couple of bucks, we'd snuck into the campground past the ranger. Situated at a large site between two giant Monterey pines, our tent was rigged with little effort.

Stuffing our backpacks into our tiny triangular structure, setting out to explore the park, we headed down toward the beach area. Modest imageries of sand, sea and sky, reminiscent of the dazzling beaches Jan and I'd hiked along on the south coast of Barbados the summer before brought about an intoxicating sense of elation. Wading out into the cold Pacific Ocean, the two of us ruminated about some of the people we'd met during that two-week vacation. Surprised to learn that we were sixteen and seventeen, other hotel guests couldn't fathom why, at such tender ages, our parents consented to a Caribbean vacation. Not realizing we'd done anything out of the ordinary, Jan and I prided ourselves on securing a group rate — once again, our part-time jobs enabled us to afford the trip. As long as we were able to pay our own way, we had permission to travel.

Watching the ocean ripple and crash reckless onto the beach, we commiserated about Teddy and Gary. My instincts that Jan had more than a passing crush on Gary were correct. On the slim chance that either guy might still be kicking around, on our way back to Canada, we decided to return to HOOM.

The sun's far-reaching rays kept us warm that late afternoon and into early evening. Once the yellow lantern in the sky began to fizzle, it was startling how quickly our campsite grew dim and chilly. This was typical northern California in spring. Prone to travelling light, apart from our tent and sleeping bags — not down-filled ones at that, we didn't have supplementary camping gear. Nor did we think about the necessity of a kerosene lamp or fuel. Late afternoon, I attempted to light a fire, with little success. To stay warm, it was decided we would turn in early. Splitting a can of cold Beefaroni, (flip lids come in handy), my friend and I sipped on water and used the nearby pump to wash up before bed.

Tucked deep inside of my sleeping bag that night, desolation crept over me. Fear escalated quickly. Reflecting upon where we were and what we were doing, the only thing that meant anything was that we were two girls in the middle of nowhere. Apart from a handful of campers, several sites down the dirt pathway, Jan and I were alone. In spring, pre-season, unless you were diehard, it wasn't uncommon to find few tents occupying a lonely state park. Making ourselves scarce so not to attract attention of park rangers, other inhabitants probably hadn't noticed us.

I thought about the folks in Barbados the summer before, that had asked about our parents. Putting on a front, we were so sure of ourselves. Feigning bravery is an easy thing while the sun is shining high in the sky. Trying to get comfortable on damp, hard ground in a remote dark-wooded area is a different story. You cling to your defenses.

Cloistered within the bosom of northern California pines, talking quietly, Jan and I tried to avoid entertaining thoughts about the cold, the uncomfortable surface, or negative forces. Hoping that it might provide comfort and heat, for the very first time, we practiced Brother James's positive visualization technique. The stunt seemed to work for a while until shadows loomed large against our nylon shelter. The human brain can mislead you under the best conditions. This night was ripe for an onslaught of hallucinations. Imaginings of wild animals scavenging for scraps and bodies to eat ransacked my head.

For the last couple of years, I had been unable to cry. Since leaving home in the winter, I'd wept only once when caught unaware by a guest's family photo during an afternoon shift at Hotel Vancouver.

Crying soundlessly that night fraught with doubt, maybe it wasn't a smart move after all casting familiarity aside in an attempt to sidestep the norm.

Beautiful Big Sur, California.

CHAPTER 16

Big Sur to L.A.

"It takes a minute to learn something and a lifetime to find that minute."
LEON SAULTER

Shortly after dawn, light peeked out from between the trees, nuzzling us from a restless doze. I heard a truck not far away. Not paying it much attention, poking my head outside the tent, I thought about going for a morning pee and noticed a park ranger approaching. Stopping about ten paces away, he began writing something down on a pad. On task to retrieve payment for one night's stay in the woods, the ranger wasn't happy.

Shit.

Approaching our tent, the camp cop deadpanned, "You owe $4 for last night."

Wiping sleep from one eye, I attempted to make a valid case for why he might want to consider giving us a break. We were on our way to Los Angeles after all and needed to conserve our cash.

Even I thought my explanation sounded lame, and wondered how often he'd been insulted by the same unimaginative excuse. Still, I pressed on, hoping to impress upon him just how tight our funds were.

"We're *hitchhiking* to L.A.," I pleaded, as if it would make a difference. The ranger could care less. Again, he demanded payment for one night's stay.

Overhearing our conversation, Jan unzipped the tent door. Inside her right hand were four American $1 bills. Receiving the money from her, like holding onto a hot potato, I hurriedly passed the money over to the ranger. Clearly unmoved by our stunt, lowering the brim of his hat, the ranger's mouth formed a straight line. "I'm warning you not to try skipping out again."

We'd been defeated, but watching the park monitor's truck roll away from our campsite in the opposite direction, Jan and I couldn't resist snickering a little.

After making use of the modest park restrooms, we returned to the pump to wash and brush our teeth. It was still early back east. Remembering my fright, the night before, from the park payphone I made a collect call to May in Ontario. Promising to be brief, I vowed to pay her back once I was able.

Delighted to hear one another's voices, we quickly caught up. Considering travelling to Alberta in the summer, May would meet up with Jan and me if she could get time off from her job.

This was the best news in a while. Especially heartening after the rough night we'd had.

Disassembling our tent, Jan and I shoved our belongings into our backpacks leaving no trace, and lugged our gear out to the road. Figuring we'd continue moving south into foreseeable warmer weather, Big Sur State Park campground would be our next destination.

A blonde man driving a shiny-green luxury Cadillac convertible slowed down his prized set of wheels. On his way to Monterey located centrally, about 30 miles down California's jagged coast, the driver opened the passenger side, beckoning us inside.

Tossing my pack into the back seat, I hopped in front. Because of our accident the previous morning, Jan wasn't taking any chances. Making a B-line for the rear, she placed her backpack against the white leather interior and climbed in next to it, clinging to the red bulge like a long lost friend.

Reminiscent of many of the slim gay men we'd seen along Polk Street in San Francisco, I presumed our driver wouldn't try anything funny. A few miles up the road, my suspicions were confirmed. The blonde-haired individual affirmed he was of the homosexual persuasion. Not knowing why, he felt compelled to share, this was perfectly fine by me. Apart from the sight of his extremely long, manicured fingernails, our driver was a decent enough fellow. About halfway to Monterey, the man pulled over at a truck stop and offered money so that we could purchase refreshments.

After our break, the man shifted his vehicle into cruise. Sailing down the coastal highway, California State Route 1 (also known as Cabrillo Highway), we drove beyond miles of purple tinted ocean, pockets of green space, and ginger-coloured apricot fields. Entering a small seaside town, the caddie crossed beneath an extended varicoloured arc stretching from one side of the road to the other. Etched across the banner in tall bold lettering, "MONTEREY" leapt out.

Letting Jan and me out of his car on a red light, the man sped away.

Before coming away, my brother Chris had talked about Monterey. Known for its striking waterfront and marine life, throughout the fifties and sixties, the beautiful coastal town became home and muse to a community of artists — jazz, pop, folk musicians, and writers — many of whom were unfamiliar to me at the time. As an early teen, I'd watched a film about the June 1967 Monterey Pop Festival; the internationally recognized three-day concert held at the Monterey County Fairgrounds. The show was memorable, in part because of the outrageous behaviour exhibited by some of the headliners. The Who's Pete Townsend smashed his electric guitar to smithereens at the end of the band's appearance. In a riveting, sexually charged implementation, virtuoso guitar legend Jimi Hendrix set *his* axe on fire. Along with her band Big Brother and the Holding Company, raunchy blues songstress Janis Joplin wowed audiences in one of her earliest public performances. Unofficially elected as the kick-off to the 'Summer of Love,' the 1967 Monterey Pop Festival became the predecessor to Woodstock in 1969 and later, Live Aid in 1985.

Unfortunately, the hostel guidebook didn't show any listings for Monterey.

Our Christmas-coloured backpacks resting on the sidewalk in anticipation of our next ride, one that might take us straight to Big Sur, Jan and I stuck out our thumbs. Straight away, we got lucky. A large black man propped behind the wheel of a silver-grey pick-up eased his truck to a lazy stop. I snagged the middle seat next to the driver. Jan chose the seat by the door. A jokester from Alabama, the man could drive us only twenty minutes down the road to Carmel. The upshot, he had us in stitches during the short time we were together, buying us beverages before parking his truck downtown.

Scanning our eyes around at Carmel's scenic bluffs and Cypress trees, the quaint yet chic beach community (part of Monterey County on the Monterey Peninsula), an appealing locality for seasoned writers and artists, made us wish we had the wherewithal to burn a couple of days. Excluding those with pocket books able to afford high-priced hotels or upscale rental properties, in 1976, Carmel did not provide friendly accommodation for young travellers. The possibility of remaining was a pipe dream.

A rusty blue sports car carrying a driver and one passenger (two males) drove past then put the vehicle in reverse. Jan and I didn't hesitate to jump in. (We would learn to be more cautious about accepting rides with a driver that had second thoughts about slowing down.)

Journeying south along the coastal highway was even more beautiful than I'd remembered. Gliding through the outskirts of Carmel, the sports car brushed past ornamental touches of reds and oranges bordering the landscape, and pink bougainvillea embracing earth-toned adobe houses and garages. Threading between dirt cliffs hugged by palm and Cypress trees hovering above swirling blue waves, overlooking the Pacific Ocean from several hundred feet up, it seemed eons ago we were freezing our asses in a dinky tent.

A couple of hours later, the sports car wheeled into Big Sur State Park campground. In a hurry to make it to Los Angeles by nightfall, our driver and his buddy cut our farewell short.

Standing together for a few minutes in the parking lot, Jan and I took stock of the brilliant visual splendor that surrounded us. Shouldered between robust mountains, cerulean sea, sun, and sky, from the mouth of the Big Sur basin, up and down the coastline, the landscape was simply extravagant. Northward and southward, daunting cliffs accentuated by a profusion of coloured cacti perched on jagged rock, stretched around roads winding far beyond where the eye could see.

This was the ultimate respite for body and mind.

Employing the same deceitful tactic as the night before, while a park official attended to a young man driving a small station wagon, Jan and I sleuthed past the visitor's booth and into the campground. Safe beyond the front entrance, popping into the general store, we picked up a couple dinner items and then searched out the most idyllic setting to drop our tent.

Below a wooden bridge, not far from a pebbled pathway adjacent to a brook, we found the perfect location. Large fir trees, gentle ocean spray, and the rugged Santa Lucia mountain range would keep us in good company. Setting up our tent, we unfurled our bags. Still ill equipped for light and fire, I prayed the temperature would remain relatively stable overnight. Not wanting to give rise to adverse thinking, there was no point in expressing my concerns.

Jan suggested we get our bearings.

Suspended on a fallen tree trunk bathed in blonde sunshine, I began to compose a letter to my family and others. Depicting present conditions and our recent San Francisco introduction, I briefly mentioned our fender bender and then went on to describe Teddy, Michael, Gary, and The Holy Order. Almost two days since leaving Steiner Street, I was surprised how much I missed the place and the people there.

In the morning, Jan told me she'd dreamed about Gary and Teddy coming to take us away. When she opened her mouth to cry tears of joy, no sound would come out. Sharing Jan's dream in a letter to Liz, I found myself elaborating about Teddy, far more than what I had in my letter home. Re-reading the note, I thought it made Teddy and his life sound depressing. Much of his life *was* depressing; it was true. However, I didn't want Liz to think he was a loser, which he wasn't. Adding a little frill to my note, as an addendum I wrote that when Teddy entered a room he often whistled or carried wild flowers. I told her that he was helpful, a good listener, and fatherly in many ways. I conveyed Teddy's reaction when Jan and I had told him about Jan's refusal at the border, how he'd sided with the officials.

That impressed me.

There were strong feelings.

Liz and other friends knew that once something or someone got a hold of me, I could be over the top. Careful not to divulge information that might give cause for concern, no doubt my family would be wary about some of the things I'd expressed.

When nightfall came, our good cheer fizzled. The night before had been unforgiving. This one would suck too, only worse. Here we were, nearing the end of April in California. It felt like January in Southern Ontario. Preposterous as it might seem, the thought that occurred the night before, freezing to death in our tent, flashed through my brain. It didn't help that we were hungry — a bag of Fritos corn chips split between two people and an apple apiece doesn't cut it. I felt responsible for dragging Jan along on this unpredictable excursion. She had wanted to travel; there was no question in her mind or in mine. Still, Jan was sixteen months younger than I was — a relatively big age gap. No doubt she was petrified. I know I was — of all sorts of things — wild animals and rapists running through the forest, seeking unsuspecting victims to overtake and kill. I should have been the prudent, protective older sister. I was, however, able to take comfort in the knowledge that Jan was above holding someone hostage for her own choices.

Turning toward the tent side in my sleeping bag, wide-eyed, shivering, I felt increasingly guilty. As of late, our trip seemed to be hitting the skids.

Overnight, the temperature dipped to almost zero.

At daybreak, the world seemed brighter again. Talking most of the night to distract ourselves from our numb hands and feet, future camping would be put on hold until temperate weather was here to stay — or until we were southern enough in the state for mild temperatures to carry overnight. Peeking outside of our tent, Jan noticed we weren't the only early risers.

The day before, two brown-haired teenagers set up camp a few sites down from ours. To say they were amorous would be an understatement. Having spent the late afternoon and evening pawing one another, at dusk, the couple finally turned in to their tent. Early morning, the boy dragged a single sleeping bag outside of the tent, strategically placing it adjacent to smoldering embers — remnants of their fire from the previous evening. Tossing a few pieces of dry wood on top of the pit, the kid gave it a couple of stokes and the logs sparked. Voila.

Emptying the last of the granola, Jan and I bitched lightheartedly about the frigid night we'd spent and saw that our neighbours had gotten friendly again. Facing one another on their sides next to the fire, the couple began kissing, mouths wide open. This activity carried on for a few minutes before the boy, bare-chested, wearing shorts, lifted his girlfriend on top of his torso. Covered by an oversized, plaid flannel shirt, the girl's garment likely belonged to her boyfriend.

Lifting the back of her shirt, the boy smacked his partner's bare bottom, hard. As if it was the funniest thing in the world, the girl erupted into a fit of giggles. Was the entire state of California comprised of one big horny population? Obvious where this scenario was headed, Jan and I weren't about to pass. This was going to be good.

Pretending to be interested in my book, over my shoulder I heard Jan stifle laughter. Something juicy was happening, no doubt. Overcome by temptation, I craned my neck around. The girl had removed her shirt. Two olive-coloured breasts with dark, pert nipples were exposed. Recognizing there was a good chance we might see her boyfriend's penis, I was curious how considerable it might be.

No such luck.

Both completely naked now, the couple switched positions. Simultaneously on top of and inside of the girl as if keeping ¾ time in a four-piece rock band, the boy thrust away, his mystery member neatly ensconced. Every so often, a pleasurable feminine sigh was audible.

Neither the boy or girl appeared to be concerned about park rangers lurking, but *we* were. Remembering that Jan and I'd snuck into the park, we needed to beat it out of there before we were caught again. Providing use of the campground was paid for upfront, it seemed that people and park rangers in California were oblivious to campers' activities, which included sexual exploits and acts of exhibitionism. This was important to keep in mind should I ever be caught with my pants down, so to speak.

My cousins Vic and Mark lived in L.A. Before leaving Vancouver, I'd written Vic asking if we could stay with him and his family for a few days while in the vicinity. Gathering our packs, Jan and I disassembled the tent and skirted it out to the coastal Highway. From there, we hitched a ride with a mid-fifties man (whom we dubbed "L.A. Man"), travelling 300 miles from Big Sur to Los Angeles.

The owner of a white Volkswagen van, L.A. Man turned out to be an overzealous conversationalist. Ploughing his way through a torrent of topics — life in Los Angeles, our 'Canadian' accents, dope, movies, sports, snow skiing, and surfing — an avid participant of the latter of the two activities — our driver revealed his atypical work hours allowed for surfing multiple times a week. Mastering the board was L.A.Man's passion.

Before reaching Los Angeles, Jan and I were driven on a short detour. Wanting to surprise his son stationed at Vandenberg Air Force Base — about 10 miles northwest of Lompoc, after a quick trip inside the base, we made the discovery that recently, L.A. Man's son had been transferred to the east coast. This news was a major disappointment. He'd really wanted to see his boy.

The astounding thing about L.A. Man was that he put in extra miles to ensure we would arrive safely at our destination, the YWCA, and did this by crisscrossing canyons and stretches of heavy rush hour traffic to deliver us in Los Angeles before dark. I thought some more about Brother James's visualization technique. If it had the potential to be *this* effective, it wouldn't hurt to trial it on a regular basis.

That morning, after scurrying out of the park, Jan and I'd made a pact. Before resuming hitchhiking, we would recite a silent prayer prior to setting out. It wasn't anything elaborate. A few simple words sufficed. Entrusting that this implementation would aid in developing a tracking system that could isolate the depraved from the innocent, we envisioned good kismet in our forecast. As individuals are prone to do when feeling vulnerable, in exchange for our safety we pledged to give back.

Jan and I took our vows very seriously. If our textbook ride to L.A. was any indication, our prayers were answered.

So far so good.

So much for confidence.

L.A. Man drove us to the Westchester YWCA as planned. Adjoining the building was a hostel that didn't open until summer. Cousin Vic and his family (living in Canoga Park) were eager to have Jan and I come stay, but I didn't want to burden them just yet. They weren't expecting us for at least another week.

While pondering our next move, L.A. Man waited patiently in his van. Eventually, we headed outside to explain the situation. Offering to take us to his son's downtown apartment, L.A. Man suggested making a few phone calls to find out which route we'd need out to Canoga Park.

It was late afternoon. There were no other hostel listings for L.A., a sprawling, somewhat formidable metropolis unfamiliar to both of us. As much as I'd wanted to avoid bothering my relatives before necessary, it was looking more and more that it would be necessary.

L.A. Man's son's one bedroom apartment was about a mile away, within L.A.'s nucleus. It was soon determined our best bet was to ride a bus to Canoga Park from the airport. With one transfer at Van Nuys Boulevard, the bus would offer us the most direct course.

This felt like retracing steps, but who were we to question the logic of somebody's father?

Following a pit stop at a McDonald's drive-thru for a couple of vanilla milkshakes, L.A. Man sped to L.A.X., a walloping aerodrome. Stepping out of the van for the final time, I found myself holding back tears. L.A. Man's concern for our welfare was greatly appreciated.

From the airport payphone, I bit the bullet and placed a call to my cousin's house. Vic's wife Patti answered the phone and offered to pick us up from the Canoga Park station. No questions asked.

My second trip to Los Angeles within the last ten years, riding through the city in a sweaty bus looking out through dirty rectangular windows at traffic, pasty low-rise buildings and passersby felt disillusioning, in a hollow-in-your-gut kind of way. Becoming acquainted with the sprawling, dispassionate environment would take time I reminded myself. Putting things into perspective, we hadn't exactly landed in Beverly Hills, Malibu, or Santa Monica. Jan and I were on Van Nuys Boulevard, travelling west on the orange line. Tucked between Chatsworth and Woodland Hills in the region of San Fernando Valley, we anticipated a friendlier community in Canoga Park.

Along the way, a man introducing himself as Keith badgered us to take his calling card "in case you get into any trouble." No matter how many times we tried to ignore him, he wouldn't let up. In two days, Jan and I had hitchhiked 400 miles without incident. One hour inside Los Angeles, we were hit on by a creep on a foul smelling city bus. Perhaps, I thought, the City of Angels is impervious to Brother James's "create your own reality."

My California cousins and their children. Canoga Park, April 1976.

CHAPTER 17

Encounter
with "Hot Lips"

"The final story, the final chapter of Western man, I believe, lies in Los Angeles."
PHIL OCHS, *Liner Notes from "The Broadside Tapes, 1"*

Pulling up to the Canoga Park bus stop at half past eight, I recognized Patti dressed in blue jeans and a yellow sleeveless cotton shirt standing next to a green station wagon.

Back at their house on Owensmouth, sheltered within the natural light of a typical (according to Cousin Vic) California style stucco abode with open concept interior, Patti made cheddar cheese sandwiches and poured us each a tall glass of milk. Recollecting my cousin's wife from years before, Patti was fun, lively, and always ready for a joke. Nothing about her had changed. In all honesty, it was a relief to have somewhere bright and shiny to stay for a few days that didn't necessitate being sneaky or bearing up under faux winter temperatures.

When my family visited relatives on my mother's side in Los Angeles in 1971, there was a huge drunken reunion. My parents hadn't seen my Uncle Bud (my mother's brother) and his wife, Aunt Laura, since the late 1940s (a period in which Mom and Dad lived in Southern California). Understandably, the weekend was party central.

Many years before, Laura had been a glamorous business girl. On the living room wall in my grandparents' upstairs apartment where Laura and Bud's wedding photo was proudly displayed, the two resembled old Hollywood.

Fast forward twenty-five years. The mild-mannered woman that greeted my family at the door in Reseda in 1971 wearing a faded printed housedress, hair cropped down to a brush cut, missing nearly all of her teeth, was a far cry from the woman smartly dressed in a suit jacket and matching skirt on my grandparents' living room wall. To be fair, eager to get reacquainted, my family had arrived earlier than expected. Returning to Reseda a couple hours later for the first of two reunion bashes, Aunt Laura's appearance had improved substantially. Her dentures were in; she had on a stylish, bronze-coloured wig and wore a turquoise pantsuit. Laura and Uncle Bud showed us a grand time.

Amidst the calamity, celebrations, and Mom's dramatic ride on the back of Cousin Mark's motorcycle, the best part about that weekend was catching my parents unaware as they cozied up side by side on the sofa in my aunt and uncle's living room. Snuggled against the chest of my father's pale blue golf shirt, Mom appeared happier than I'd ever witnessed when Dad casually slipped one arm around her slight tanned shoulders.

The sweet overture of affection stood out for me as the landmark of our vacation.

Vic arrived home from work that night later than usual. For several years, my cousin was employed by Technicolor in Burbank. An excellent mother and partner, Patti was a proud homemaker. Along with their two children, a secure salary and terrier named Taffy, Vic and Patti lived comfortably in their modern ranch home nestled within the quiet Canoga Park neighbourhood. A compelling storyteller and history buff, proud of his considerable knowledge of L.A.'s history and cultural heritage, Vic was also politically well informed. A lifelong Democrat, my cousin loved debating politics, classic Hollywood movies, and the L.A. Dodgers. (Eventually he would switch his allegiance to the Angels.) Reflecting on the madcap family reunion years before, Vic showed us photos of relatives known and not known to me. We shared a few laughs. Reconfiguring several episodes from the previous two and a half months, Jan and I exaggerated more than necessary.

Intrigued by our hitchhiking adventures, out of Cousin Vic's listening range, Patti said she thought she would like to try hitchhiking herself, halfway joking that if she found a guy irresistible she might not be able to restrain herself.

Saturday May 1, Jan and I chattered more with Vic while Patti drove the kids to their Saturday activities. On Sunday, Patti planned to throw a bridal shower for Cousin Mark's fiancée, Sarah, and had composed several to-do lists.

Cousin Mark's impending marriage was an interesting prospect, and based upon my memory of him, difficult to fathom. I hadn't attended a shower before, nor had I met Sarah. According to Patti, Sarah had two children from a previous marriage. The kids were going to be living with Mark and Sarah at Mark's house on Calvin Avenue in Reseda. Mark becoming a stepdad was beyond imagination. My memory of Mark was that of a lovable teddy bear. I had a clear image in my head of him and his best buddy, Bobby, riding off into the sunset on their Harley's, bound for British Columbia — two badass bachelors taking on the big, badass world.

Penning a couple more letters that afternoon, I reiterated to May how I felt about the Good Samaritan. Indubitably, I guessed by now he'd become versed in the ways of The Holy Order and would soon cultivate a hierarchy within the group, accruing a surplus of data, possibly to be dispatched when we returned to Steiner Street.

If Teddy had stuck it out at HOOM.

Addressing the envelope to the General Post Office box in San Francisco, Jan mailed her first note to Gary. Because of uncertainty where he was headed after leaving Steiner Street, it was a long shot.

Late afternoon, Patti suggested I call home. I knew my parents were both at work, but Steve might be around. Smiling at the thought of talking to my brother, the image of our appalling collection of more than 60 rabbit's feet came to mind. Creating our private world, as children we collected various colours, shapes, and sizes, naming each one "Bea" (short for Beatles) according to their dyed colours and physical characteristics. The Beas played concerts, had families and distinctive personalities, and drove toy cars. In order for the Beas to communicate with one another, simulating ventriloquists, Steve and I spoke in high-pitched voices that sounded something like Alvin and the Chipmunks. My favourite, Daddeo, a blue-green paw, liked to belt out in falsetto, *"Steeeveeeee!"*

To my surprise, after a few rings Chris answered the phone. He'd stopped at the house to borrow an item — never to be returned, no doubt, as was his habit. When prompted by the operator, my brother accepted reverse charges. Good to go, I gushed about all of the places Jan and I'd visited in recent months. His turn to talk, Chris dropped a bombshell of his own. Since he and Mark kept in touch on a semi-regular basis, Mark had invited Chris to attend his and Sarah's wedding.

My big brother would be in Los Angeles in three weeks!

Once I finally calmed down, Chris informed me that during his visit to Los Angeles, he expected to visit a friend, Hollywood actor Sally Kellerman. Two years earlier (four years after her starring role as nurse "Hot Lips Houlihan" in the 1970 smash hit, *M*A*S*H*), Chris had met Kellerman when she was invited to address the student body at Sheridan

College. Employed by the college as its liaison officer, my brother was assigned to pick Kellerman up from the airport. Ever since, they'd kept in touch.

Chris suggested I call Sally and say hello — from him. "You never know," he tantalized. "She's very nice and might even invite you and Jan over for dinner and a swim in the pool."

If I was daring enough to call Kellerman's residence, there was the possibility that Sally's (adopted) daughter Claire might answer the phone, and not to be put off. (Claire and Tatum O'Neal, child star of the 1974 film *Paper Moon*, were roommates at private school.)

On a piece of scrap paper next to the phone, I copied down Kellerman's phone number.

Once Patti and Jan got wind of this information, they were both ready to bust a gasket. There was no backing down. The mere notion the actress might be *home* induced a panic attack. Maybe Ms. Kellerman would even *speak* to me. Gathering myself at the kitchen counter, lifting the receiver, I dialed the Kellerman house in the Hollywood Hills, and hoped I wouldn't crap my underpants.

Listening to six long rings, my heart pounding in my ears, just when I figured nobody was home, somebody picked up on the other end. It was a woman. Channelling a proper telephone voice using an intonation my mother instructed us to do when talking to older and unfamiliar people, when asked, I introduced myself as the sister of a friend of Sally Kellerman. Kellerman's assistant or housekeeper told me to hold on. Soon, a man came to the phone wanting to know, "Who *are* you, precisely?"

The aid was polite, though not about to waste Kellerman's time. Explaining how "my older brother Chris, from Canada," was an acquaintance of Sally's, I informed the man that Chris had asked me to call on his behalf to let Ms. Kellerman know he'd be making a trip to Los Angeles within the month.

Taking a deep breath, it was all I could do to hold my composure. Just like when we were kids, my brother had cunningly copped me into doing his dirty work for him.

The bugger.

To my great surprise and relief, the man told me to hold on a moment. Spinning around, I looked over at Jan and Patti, both jumping up and down like a couple of clowns, and waved furiously at them to quiet down. In less than one minute, Kellerman took the call. Enunciating a simple "Hello" by way of her signature husky inflection, Sally's reception was pleasant, not overly. Sticking to my script, I replied, "Hi. I'm Chris

Morton's sister. I'm staying in Los Angeles with relatives. He asked me to call and say hello."

Before I could mention anything about my brother's imminent visit to L.A., her tone softening, Kellerman gently cut in. "Oh, Chris. Well you thank him very much. He's a lovely person." Then she paused, enabling me an opening to blurt out that my brother had given me her telephone number. (Even in those days, I didn't want anybody to think I was a stalker.)

"Did he receive the letters my daughter and I had written him?"

Chris hadn't mentioned anything about letters.

"Yes," I fibbed. "I guess that's how he got your number."

Skating over my flippant reply, in a friendly manner, Sally said, "Well, he showed us a very good time when we were in Toronto. You send him my love."

Not wanting the conversation to end so soon, I told Ms. Kellerman my friend and I were staying at my cousin's house in Canoga Park. Curious how long I'd been travelling, she queried, "Are you and your friend also from Canada?" Verifying that, we, too, were from Canada, I informed Sally I hadn't seen my brother since winter. Again, she sent Chris her love, thanked me for calling, and hung up.

Our short chat hadn't garnered us an invite to the house, not even close, but it was the first time I had spoken to an A-list movie star. The funniest part of all, despite my desperate hand waving, signalling her to shut-up, witnessing Patti bent sideways in a fit of laughter was well worth the effort. Suddenly panicked that I might not have returned the receiver to its cradle properly, thereby opening the potential for Sally to listen in on the mayhem, once I realized everything was cool, I joined in with Jan and Patti in the pandemonium. Confused about what the hell was going on, full of questions, the kids soon spilled into the room.

Reinforced by our brush with fame, that evening Vic and Patti treated everyone to dinner at the legendary Bob's Restaurant in the San Fernando Valley, topped off by ice-cream cones at Farrell's. Turning out the light in the living room that night, Jan on the cot, I on the couch, I swore I'd never call a movie star again. It was far too much pressure.

Sunday morning, waking early, we helped Patti hang decorations and prepare snacks for the bridal shower. Patti was good enough to loan Jan her long, pink and white gingham dress. I picked out my best clothes: light brown cotton wrap-around skirt and cream-coloured t-shirt. It was neat to have a reason to dress up, even if only a subtle change.

The shower turned out to be a lot of fun, mainly because nobody seemed to take the upcoming nuptials too seriously. Mark's fiancé was nothing short of a fireball, a shit-kicking cowgirl type who didn't seem the kind to put up with a lot of nonsense. I liked her.

Accompanied by his buddy and best man, Bobby, at one point, all silly and charming, Mark barrelled into the room crashing the shower. It was apparent my cousin hadn't much changed. Possessing his father's good looks and sociable personality, Mark enjoyed a good time. For all his carousing in those days, Mark (a mechanic and War vet), was a big-hearted person. While residing at his parents' house, my cousin had helped tend to his aging folks' daily needs, pay the bills, and care for their three dogs. After my aunt and uncle passed away, choosing to remain in the Calvin Avenue house, Mark's digs were your typical bachelor pad, with several animals running about. According to Patti however, since Sarah entered the scene, feminine touches were everywhere.

His wingman Bobby along for kicks, that evening Mark invited us all over for a BBQ, showing Jan, me, Vic, Patti, the kids, and a couple of neighbours a grand ole time. A supreme host, we were treated to good old-fashioned burgers (Jan loaded up with cheese and veggies), spud salad, and all the cold beer we could handle. This was our first real chill out since arriving in California.

Sitting in Mark's fenced-in yard sipping beer, eating Southern California BBQ, my friend and I easily fit in. Though we continued to miss Teddy and Gary, the friendly diversion of the group helped to mitigate our youthful pangs of the heart.

Once the party wrapped, Bobby offered to drive us back to Canoga Park in his raven T-bird convertible. Whipping down the freeway, top down, wind slapping our faces, looking beyond the periphery of the Santa Monica Mountains, I entertained the notion what it might feel like to be a full-time California girl.

Grauman's Chinese Theatre, Hollywood, California.

CHAPTER 18

Universal Studios and Hollywood

"Tip the world over on its side and everything loose will land in Los Angeles."
FRANK LLOYD WRIGHT

Hopping into Vic and Patti's Ford Galaxy, we drove over an hour to the Pacific Ocean to spend the day at Zuma Beach. Acting as our personal tour guide, Vic swept us past mountains, canyons, palms, and desert flowers in varying phases of evolution and colour.

Overloaded with sun worshippers on the sunny Sunday afternoon, beneath a cool blue sky, we barely managed to find a sand patch to place our comforter, towels, and picnic basket. Adjacent to Malibu, Zuma Beach was inhabited by swarms of people and families that had come to swim, surf, and hang out. The ocean temperature a little chilly, we didn't care. You got used to it. Jan and I built sandcastles with the kids, threw the Frisbee, swam and jumped waves. Patti had thrown together an enviable picnic lunch. As many people who prefer to eat in the fresh outdoors can attest, there is nothing better than a baloney sandwich enhanced by the flavour of sea salt.

Treating us like daughters, Vic and Patti made us feel that we could relate to them on any level, something I wasn't able to do with my own parents. Self-assured, considerate, and equipped with a wry sense of humour, in both physical and personal characteristics, Cousin Vic reminded me of my favourite uncle, Ralph, another of my mother's brothers. Trusting Vic implicitly, I valued his opinion. When Jan and I discussed the possibility of going south to Tijuana after San Diego, cautioning us strongly against it, Vic emphasized the danger of being locked up in a Mexican jail for no justifiable reason. Firm in his resolve that we'd be placing ourselves at unnecessary risk, reluctantly, we deferred to his experience.

My cousin wasn't bossy. He had good reason to be wary. In the news and from talking to fellow travellers, reports of people being framed south of the American border, mostly for drugs, apparently wasting away in decrepit Mexican lock ups with marginal chance of convincing crooked authorities of their innocence, were common. Years later, when I visited Mexico City, Amatlan, and Cuernavaca, we were briefed by two female guides about the importance of partnering up with others, especially when travelling the rural terrain and interior, as there were numerous reported incidents of rapes and murders of women by drug cartels. I adore Mexico and its people, but the unscrupulous criminal undercurrent could not be ignored. Locals and long-time residents inhabiting some of the more dangerous parts of the country did not refute these claims.

Back at Canoga Park, following a light meal, we watched the 1967 thriller, *Wait until Dark*, featuring Alan Arkin and Audrey Hepburn, both terrific in leading roles. Near the end of the film, Vic received a call from Sarah. Mark was "in the hoosegow." Yukking it up at the Renaissance Fair that afternoon in Pasadena, he'd flattened his bike in front of a patrol car and was promptly arrested. Sarah was chauffeured to the jailhouse on the back of Bobby's Harley.

Scheduled to be released that evening, the deputy decided to delay the process, probably to give my cousin a chance to sober up.

Monday morning, psyched about touring Universal City in Burbank, Vic's position at Technicolor (adjacent to Universal) enabled him to snag a pair of discounted tickets. Not wanting to miss out on the "full Hollywood experience," at $5.50 a pop, Jan and I didn't hesitate to splurge.

A stellar 86 degrees that morning and clear under sunny skies — typical Southern California daytime temps in May, Toronto news told a different story, predicting snow in the forecast (not common in spring), causing us to be doubly thankful to be kicking back in sun-drenched So Cal.

Vic dropped us off at the Sheraton Hotel — an ideal spot for celebrity sightings according to my cousin. Sipping black coffee, we sighted actor-comedian Charlie Callas checking in at the front desk. Ironically, we'd mistakenly identified Callas as another comedic actor, Sid Caesar. Point being, Jan and I recognized Callas as *somebody* important but weren't positive of the Hollywood bloodline.

Touring Universal, we visited film lots, television and movie sets used in various mainstream Hollywood pictures. The house where Boo Radley (played by actor Robert Duvall in one of his earliest roles) had lived in the award-winning film, *To Kill a Mockingbird*, was the first famous location we visited. Having watched the movie and read the novel in English class a few years before, it was a rush. Our tour guide pointed out grass huts, props used by Cary Grant and Leslie Caron in the 1964 film *Father Goose*, another beloved flick from my childhood.

Hopping a tramcar and travelling over a bridge to a fabricated river, we were subjected to a series of surprise special effects consisting of avalanches, flash floods, submarines, and the mechanical shark used in the 1975 summer release *JAWS* — a recent addition to the theme park. Coming face-to-face with the giant automated mammal, its bloody, razor-sharp teeth and slimy body lunging itself onto our tram scared everybody shitless.

In the costumes pavilion, the navy pinstriped suit worn by Robert Redford in *The Sting* and sleek charcoal tux donned by Paul Newman were on display. As visitors to the studios, we skimmed through portions of original scripts for *The Miracle Worker* and *Gone with the Wind*. Our pass also included three live shows. By far, the animal exhibits were my favourite, particularly the cockatoo, Fred, that had starred as Robert Blake's number two on the television series *Baretta*. The bird kissed, hugged, rolled over, and aced a hilarious drunk routine. Actors demonstrated how to fall off three story buildings during a cowboy stunt show without fracturing bones. Nearing the end of our tour, we participated in a screen test for the debut TV program, *Emergency*.

That night, Jan and I had an opportunity to try artichoke for the first time, one of Patti's specialties. Dipped in melted garlic butter with a dash of salt and pepper, it tasted divine.

Next morning, Patti drove us to the bus stop at the corner of Ventura Boulevard and Topanga Canyon. Getting off at Highland and Hollywood, we meandered through many of Hollywood's hotspots. Along the Walk of Fame on Hollywood Boulevard, hub of the Hollywood district, we read aloud the names of highly lauded celebrities, famous enough to have their very own gold star along the sidewalk. Stopping at Grauman's Chinese Theatre, we took photos of signatures, hand and feet prints of popular Hollywood stars. Happy to spot Jack Nicholson's prints at the front of the theater, I searched for Charlie Chaplin and came up empty. A longtime fan of Chaplin's work, I felt cheated and sensed the reason why. Having spent three decades of exile in Switzerland because of accusations of Communist ties, the actor was yet to be forgiven by the Hollywood power structure for his rumoured involvement. A genius and trailblazer, along with contemporaries Douglas Fairbanks and Mary Pickford, in

1919 Chaplin had co-founded United Artists. In doing so, the filmmaker opened the floodgates to the prolonged achievements of his successors. At the very least, Chaplin should have been included amongst his peers at the famed theater.

Remaining at Grauman's for more than an hour, Jan and I continued to marvel at other cement blocks belonging to luminaries in the entertainment world — entertainers such as Red Skelton, Steve McQueen, Greta Garbo, The Marx Brothers, Jimmy Durante, and Al Jolson (who had also placed his knees in cement). Inside the theatre, *Bad News Bears* starring Walter Matthau and Tatum O'Neal played on the big screen. A mediocre film at best, nevertheless, it was a treat to sit within the interior of the theatre elaborately decorated with ornate fixtures and facings of intricate design and detail. Back on Hollywood Boulevard, an eclectic assemblage of characters dominated the sidewalk. Performance artists, Elvis impersonators, panhandlers, and hookers, flamboyant and effectively working it in every conceivable way left no doubt who the keepers of Hollywood's lunacy and anarchy were. Following up with a stint at Pickwick Book Shop — reputed to be one of the exceptional literary sites in the world, Jan and I rode the bus back to Canoga Park empty handed and were greeted by Mark, Sarah, and Sarah's two children. My cousin's face was beat up, particularly around the eyes and mouth. Overall, between the bike crash and clash with the cops, I thought he'd fared well.

Alone in Vic and Patti's living room that night, Jan confided how disappointed she was not being able to afford a book at Pickwick's. A book lover from early childhood, more than any celebrity sighting or dispensable trinket, a new work of fiction was something my friend craved.

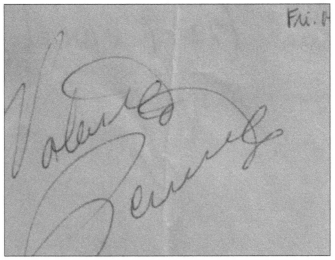

Valerie Perrine's autograph.

CHAPTER 19

Valerie Perrine and Company

"I'm not anti-Christ or anti-religion, I just think it's encouraging that people are leaving the Church and going back to God."
LENNY BRUCE

Reading recently received letters from our friends back home (we'd given out Vic and Patti's address), Jan and I responded with dissertations. May and Liz questioned why *they* were still in Southern Ontario while we were "wild and free in La-La Land." Hah! We weren't exactly "wild and free," but the scenery was great and there were no worries as of late.

One afternoon, after dropping the kids off at a farm, Patti brought us on a drive across L.A. County past blackberry bramble and desert brush, through valleys separating the Santa Monica and San Gabriel Mountain ranges. Marvelling at Southern California's unparalleled topography and climate, Patti told us how many individuals prided themselves on surfing and snow skiing the same day. Soaking up the irresistible majesty of palm and eucalyptus trees flanked by cactus flowers within an abyss of dusty canyon chasms, in my gut, I knew Southern California had become second home. Happening upon a cemetery along the way, Patti turned the car into the lot, looked over at me and said, "This is where we placed Bud and Laura's remains."

There were no headstones, only flat plaques embedded within the perfectly manicured lawn. Patti explained how this was the "proper way to respect and represent the dead." Apparently, that included my uncle and aunt who'd both chosen to be cremated rather than opting for the burial route. As far as permanent resting places go, this one was exquisitely serene. Reading the inscriptions on my relative's plaques, I reflected again on the weekend spent with Bud and Laura not many years before, when they were both in reasonable health.

One of the beautiful aspects of youth: teenagers don't generally think about mortality and have no concrete measure of time. Life beats on ad infinitum until eventually you begin to count the decades and mentally fight to slow down years. Even if I forfeited school, evaded finding a job to procrastinate against the inevitable duties of life, time was on my side. I *could* sustain travel, and was pig-headed enough to resist, as money would allow. Standing before my deceased relative's remains reinforced these inclinations, prompting thought about our imminent journey to San Diego in the next couple of days.

Another fresh start.

Winding our way back to Owensmouth, Patti retrieved the kids from school and had an idea to try to track down Sally Kellerman's residence (no stalking here). As if on autopilot, my cousin's wife nitpicked her way toward Mulholland Drive, a two-lane road that follows the rim along the eastern Santa Monica Mountains. Stopped at a traffic light on Mulholland driving a silky black 450 SL Mercedes sports car — a relevant piece of information Jan later recorded in her diary — comedian Redd Foxx looked in our direction from the other side of the intersection. Opening the driver's side door, Foxx suddenly stuck his head out to check a noise or something that had piqued his attention. Waiting for the light to change provided ample time to assess Foxx's familiar face, cap, and beard.

Celebrity interludes were becoming more of a common occurrence, and it was exciting as hell. I couldn't wait to tell Vic, whom, it turned out wasn't impressed in the least. After having spent more than two thirds of his life in L.A., movie star glitz and gossip didn't interest my cousin one iota.

Unsuccessful in tracking Kellerman's digs, we finally turned the car around. Our final stop that day provided a bird's eye view of a knoll in Box Canyon, Topanga area, former hideout used by Charles Manson and his followers seven years earlier. Standing within a stone's throw of the breeding ground for Manson and Family members and their terrifying rampage of murder felt completely surreal.

I wouldn't have missed seeing it for the world.

An unsolicited box addressed to me arrived at Canoga Park. It was from my mother. On top of a few articles of clothing, was a sheet of paper on which my mom had written she felt I needed "proper clothes" for Mark and Sarah's wedding. Mom had taken it upon herself to send a care package, recommending (not suggesting) I pick something from the items inside.

Despite my mother's practicality, the conservative skirt, blouse, and summer dress didn't resemble anything I'd worn the last couple of years living at home. Learning about the wedding only a few days before, I hadn't asked my mom to send anything, making me wonder if she and Patti were in cahoots. Other, kinder daughters might have believed this a considerate gesture. Because of our prickly history concerning my clothing choices, I didn't.

The last couple of years, my mother and I'd wrangled daily about my preferences in school clothes — a steady regimen of patched jeans and plaid flannel shirts. Though I refused to comply, I understood the reasons why she felt strongly. Having grown up during the depression and, later, working in a women's shop, my mother believed a person's apparel suggested a certain socio-economic status. Not giving a fig about those things, I perceived this action as means to control. It angered me.

Determined not to become sucked in by my mother's need to micromanage, I left the house to take a short walk. Around the corner, a cute blonde boy about six feet tall crossed over from the other side of the street. Passing one another, looking me over, he said "Howdy" and gave me a sure smile. It wasn't much but it was enough. As if reading my mind, the boy let me know that everything was okay. My spirits regenerated, I returned to the house.

Our last day in Los Angeles was Friday. Jan and I didn't have anything set in stone. When my cousin surprised us with four free passes to attend a live studio taping of the popular *Dinah Shore Show* that afternoon, we were ecstatic. He'd even scored front row seats.

Comedians Rick Granat and Jim Carrogo were Dinah's first two guests. Next, distinguished film actor Hal Holbrook took the stage to discuss two of his more notable roles, Abe Lincoln, and Mark Twain in a one-man stage show. Holbrook's praiseworthy appearances in *All the President's Men* and *Deep Throat* (the mainstream version) were also discussed. At the show's halfway point, The Four Man Band performed. They were okay, but the audience was clearly jacked for Dinah's special upcoming guest, Valerie Perrine. Known for her highly lauded performance opposite Dustin Hoffman in Bob Fosse's *Lenny* (1974), Perrine had competently characterized "Honey," a stripper who becomes Bruce's accomplice following a ban from nightclubs for obscenity and throughout his downward spiral of drugs and alcohol.

Entering the stage to cat calls and resounding applause (before the show we'd been instructed to make lots of noise whenever one of the guests took the stage, especially Perrine), Ms. Perrine greeted the audience warmly, looking every inch a sexy glamorous movie star. Crossing her shiny long legs on a cushy pink chair next to Dinah, beaming, Perrine answered Dinah's queries about her latest role as Carlotta Monti (an actress and W.C. Fields companion) in the recent biopic, *W.C. Fields and Me.*

This was mine and Jan's first live taping of a Hollywood talk show. When it was over, she and I waited around the back entrance of the studio to obtain autographs. Hal Holbrook and the two comedians were the first two out of the exit doors, filing past flashing cameras and autograph hounds while spectators, five rows deep, waited patiently for Perrine. Minutes later, all sparkly and twinkly-eyed, Perrine stepped outside to a landmine of flashbulbs. To her right, a young man in a wheel chair with atrophied legs waited by an emergency exit door. Kneeling to eye level, Perrine and the man engaged in private conversation. Midway through, the fellow dropped his pen on to the pavement. Stuttering nervously, he made a few failed attempts trying to retrieve it. Swooping down to scoop up the ballpoint, sweetly, Perrine handed the writing instrument back to the fan. In turn, the man returned the pen to Perrine and they both started to laugh. Perrine happily signed an 8 x 10 glossy photo he'd carried with him.

Once the crowd began to thin out, Jan and I, the two lone holdouts, were about to approach Ms. Perrine when a black jeep sped into the parking lot and swung around to stop in front of the exit doors. Graciously, Perrine hurriedly scrawled her signature on the papers in our hands and then thanked us for coming. Apologizing for signing and dashing, the actress explained her mother had arrived and begged off to join her in the waiting jeep.

Following dinner at the Spaghetti Castle, Jan and I packed our duffle bags for next day's departure. Mark had arranged it so that he and Bobby, a licensed pilot and owner of a small four-seat aircraft, would fly us directly to San Diego — a quick flight that would cost what Bobby paid to fuel the plane, $8 each.

The bus to San Diego was costlier.

That afternoon, letters had arrived from Yvette and Lorraine. Stuffing the notes into our packs, we would read them once we got settled in downtown San Diego. Jan called her parents from Vic and Patti's informing them we'd be heading south to San Diego the next day. Unlike the previous time, hanging up, Jan told me how proud she was she hadn't cried.

Desiring to recreate the recipe prepared by Valerie Perrine on *The Dinah Shore Show*, Saturday morning, Patti surprised us with a delicious feed of omelets and brown toast. After helping with clean up, Jan and I showered and dressed so we'd be ready when Bobby and Mark arrived to pick us up for our flight. Whimpering at the front door, Taffy longed to be taken for a walk. Joining Vic and his pup on a jaunt around the block afforded the two of us an opportunity to chat in private. Expressing gratitude for opening his home to Jan and me, I assured Vic I'd make it up to him somewhere down the line. In a couple of weeks, we would return for Mark's wedding.

"Just don't do anything brainless without checking in first."

My cousin was referring specifically to Mexico, among other things.

A reasonable request, I pinky swore to honour Vic's warning.

San Diego, California. COURTESY OF ANDREA NELSON.

CHAPTER 20

San Diego: Fear of Flying

"Travel is fatal to prejudice, bigotry, and narrow-mindedness."
MARK TWAIN

Swerving his truck from lane to lane, Mark cut a tiny path through L.A.'s uninterrupted labyrinth of traffic. Pinned in the middle seat between my cousin and Bobby (Jan on Bobby's lap), we were on our way to the Van Nuys' Airport in San Fernando Valley — a mere 15 miles down the freeway. Bobby had it in his head to leave the airport at noon, land the aircraft in San Diego an hour later.

Arriving at the small airstrip, the grey tarp had already been removed; the small plane's tank filled with fuel. Bobby's four-seater was ready to go. Detracted from meeting Bobby's noon departure time due to traffic, at half past, it was close enough. Providing everything went according to Hoyle, we'd arrive at the San Diego airport at 1:30 pm. Intending to stay at the YMCA (no hostels in San Diego), Jan and I expected to sign in long before dusk.

Assigned with the task of fulfilling co-pilot duties (Mark also flew but didn't have his full license), Mark hoisted our packs into the plane's under-carriage while Jan and I stepped up, taking our seats behind the small cockpit.

I'd been in a small aircraft only one other occasion. I was eight years old. It was spring on a Sunday evening under a pale-yellow sky. My father had arranged for a friend to fly Steve and me above the Burlington escarpment near Rattlesnake Point. I remember coming close to clipping the tops of fir trees as we sailed across the night sky, dipping and diving, our little vessel creating an arc below a small arrangement of stars.

A thrill.

At Van Nuys' airport, the sky was clear, ideal conditions for a short flight. Eager to get a panoramic bird's-eye view of Southern California County from the firmament, we couldn't wait for take-off.

Before setting out, Mark turned around to inform us that once we were out on the tarmac, the plane could *not* get airborne unless Jan and I lifted our feet high in the air, tall as we could. Staring at my cousin blankly for not knowing this essential tidbit of information, Jan and I did as we were told. As Bobby revved the engines and eased the plane along the airstrip, Mark gave us the queue, waving his arms madly for us to raise our legs high, high, high up in the air. Once there was liftoff and it was okay, he'd signal us to put our feet down on the floor.

Like two neophytes, Jan and I raised our sandaled toes, high as we possibly could, dangling our legs in the air until my thighs hurt like hell. Finally, thank god, Mark motioned at us to lower our legs and we stretched them out to rest.

The flight was exceptional. Gliding below clouds at a speed of 163 MPH through infinite blue sky, we looked down on tanned desert brush and green tinted foothills — breathtaking and surreal topography that can only be fully appreciated from the air. Swooping over land, a blue-green sea floating along the periphery, the scenery analogous to the dreamy, fantastical paintings created by illustrator Roger Dean, whose brilliant artistry glorified Yes album covers for several years, we marinated in the beauty of it all.

Approaching San Diego airport, Mark and Bobby requested we do the opposite of what we'd done earlier to get the plane airborne. The trick, Mark insisted, was to press our feet down, hard as we could on the floor base until instructed otherwise. If not, the aircraft might run the risk of an unsafe landing.

Clutching onto the sides of our seats giving the aircraft greater leverage (we believed), faces reddening from the strain, with all our might, Jan and I pushed our feet down on the floor of airplane.

I don't know how Mark and Bobby managed to hold it together during take-off and landing but they didn't let on, instead giving us high praise for our efforts. (Incidentally, over the years, the story of two gullible Canadian girls flying from Los Angeles to San Diego has grown legs. In fact, the next time I saw Vic, who did a lousy job hiding the smirk on his face, he didn't hesitate to inquire about our San Diego flight. "Did you remember to lift your feet during take-off?")

Around half past one, the aircraft touched gently down on the landing strip at San Diego airport.

Giving us each a squeeze, Mark reminded us to be safe, and then climbed back into the plane next to his pal for their return flight. Seeing them off, Jan and I dashed to catch the airport bus that would take us to the downtown San Diego YMCA on Eighth Avenue.

That's when things went from the sublime to the ridiculous.

The Y turned out to be co-ed. Co-ed was not a problem. But the sleazy clientele had potential to create a predicament. There was no point bothering to look for an alternative. At a day rate of $6, we decided to hang in for one night.

Room 507 was similar to a tiny studio apartment, not much bigger than a jail cell. Painted a dull blue-grey, I noted spider-sized cracks along the entire surface of the walls. Mould visibly lined the baseboards. The room had a sink and there was a community bathroom down the hall. Judging by the filth quotient in our room, god only knew what infestations lived and grew there. Rolling out my sleeping bag along the chipped floor tiles, scanning our room in one long glance, I watched Jan place her pack and sleeping bag on top of the single bed. No way in hell anybody was getting under the covers. We'd swop the next night — if indeed there was a next night.

Outside, creeps and dope heads conspicuously lurked. A cafeteria within a block of the Y offered something reasonable to eat. Obviously taking pity on us, the server insisted on doling out double portions of coleslaw. On the way back to our accommodations, the sky started to darken. Quickening our steps, upon entering the building, a kindly Latino man dressed in a tired navy-blue suit greeted us in the lobby. No doubt he was security, or at the very least, an authoritative presence. Signing in earlier, a surly youth had been working the desk.

Upstairs on the fifth floor, Jan made motion to turn the key in the door to our room. Entering stage right, a skinny, abject looking woman approached us in the hallway, claiming she hadn't eaten solid food in six months. Matter of fact, our new next-door-neighbour announced she'd been in no less than five psychiatric hospitals over the past three years. *Was she was bragging or complaining?* According to the woman, upon release from her last stint in the loony bin she'd come to live at the Y, a facility she alleged that functioned largely as a halfway house for drug addicts and parolees.

Maybe I'd read too many crime novels but there was the eerie sense a person could go missing in a hovel like this one without anyone bothering to look until it was too late. More than a week since we'd put Brother James's positive visualization technique into play, if good fortunate was expected in our futures, the procedure couldn't be executed soon enough. In the middle of the night, turning on the light to go pee, Jan spotted a small unit of roaches climbing the walls. Thankfully, she waited until morning to tell me about it.

Next day was Mother's Day. Still peeved about the box of clothes shipped to Canoga Park tucked away in a spare room at my cousin's house, I wasn't in a rush to have a conversation with my mother. Sure, it was juvenile to hold on to anger. I could be one ornery bitch when I wanted to be. Anyway, the event was dutifully taken care of. I'd mailed my mom a card from Vic and Patti's.

We woke up to a mild 74 degrees. Heading over to Denny's for breakfast, for $1 we filled our bellies.

Pondering why there were so many men walking around wearing crew cuts, eventually Jan and I clued in. There was a huge naval base in the area. Many of the young men were either in training or already fully-fledged Marines.

The 32nd Street Naval Station based in San Diego is the largest Marine base in the United States. Now, I didn't have anything personal against Marines or the Navy, but a "shorthair" was usually the criterion indicating a person was straighter than a line of track. Therefore, he could not be trusted. Granted, this kind of preconception is not only superficial but a load of bullshit. Right or wrong, our attitude was another one of those incomprehensible decrees youth of our day lived by.

Venturing beyond Balboa Park to Washington Street, we headed out to the residential area. Similar to San Francisco, many of San Diego's downtown streets have steep inclines fringed by attractive bows of pink and purple flowers embroidering the concrete. At Jan's suggestion (using our tourist guidebook she usually sought out the best art galleries and shops — freebies that were entertaining if not educational), we stopped in to grab a bit of culture at the Thackeray, characterized by Western-themed exhibits that included oil and water colour paintings and several Indian artifacts. Leaving the Thackeray, we crossed over Cabrillo Bridge, entered Balboa Park, and settled beneath the gigantic red oaks.

The largest urban park in the nation encompassing more than 1000 acres, infringing upon some of San Diego's older neighbourhoods, Balboa Park accommodates Spanish Colonial Revival buildings, fifteen major museums and lush gardens, a theatre, musical venues, and the San Diego Zoo. In 1976, the park was as prepossessing and tranquil as it is today. With its generous lawns, ornamental horticulture, nooks and niches, Balboa Park represents the kind of expansive recreational acreage wherein a girl can lose herself for a few hours. The public toilets however — unofficial headquarters for a mire of iniquitous activity should have a sign posted, "Enter at your own risk."

Cloistered beneath the big tree's sinewy boughs, for the better part of the afternoon, we relaxed. After a while, a guy, Peter, rode his bicycle up to the bench asking if we wanted to get stoned. Reeling off his surname and service number, both of which Jan later recorded in her diary, Peter boasted that he was in the Navy — as if that was supposed to impress us.

Several weeks had passed since we'd gotten a good buzz on. What was the harm in having a couple of puffs amongst acquaintances? Peter smoked us up, and the three of us shot the shit until it became apparent he wasn't about to leave until we made the first move. Eventually, Jan fabricated some benign excuse that we needed to be elsewhere.

Before riding away, Peter gave us another joint to stow away for later. Instincts told me there was something untrustworthy about our neighbourly friend. We weren't sorry to see Peter go.

A good hour after riding away on his ten-speed bike, Peter returned driving an orange VW van, slowing near the oak where he'd approached us earlier. Putting the vehicle in park, he rolled down the window. "Come on. Get in. We'll go to my place to get high." When I told Peter we had other commitments, he sensed I was fibbing and became belligerent, grilling us about what and where, as if it was any of his business.

Holding our ground, I thanked Peter for the joint, but was firm. Jan and I were not going to his apartment. Defeated and incensed for looking a fool, the blue jacket drove off and out of the park.

Paranoia set in — impractical thinking that results from smoking too much weed. I began formulating outrageous scenarios, such as how *did Peter suddenly acquire a van after riding a bicycle into the park?* Relying upon simple rationale, Jan and I should have put it together that in all likelihood, he'd stored his bike inside the vehicle, or had ridden it home. Too baked to string that hypothesis together, we talked ourselves into believing he'd been plotting and planning on kidnapping us from the onset. To avoid risk of bumping into Peter again, we footed it back from Balboa Park to our luxury palace.

Cashing in a couple of traveller's cheques at the front desk to pay for another night's stay, we met a single man signing up for a room. Visiting from Vancouver, Bob worked for the West Coast Seaport doing outdoor maintenance. Feeling the lasting effects from Peter's joint, Jan and I made easy small talk with Bob from Vancouver who obviously had money. Of all places, why had he elected to stay at the Y, even temporarily? Before deliberating on this pressing question, Vancouver Bob invited us to tour the downtown.

Two invites in less than two hours.

Here, Jan and I'd turned down Peter's invitation to go to his house, yet were perfectly amendable to joy ride with Vancouver Bob at night. Bob felt like a surer bet. Besides, Bob was from *Vancouver* — a good Canadian boy. Anyhow, in the morning, he was leaving for Mexico.

Rambling around for a couple of hours, we three Canucks explored San Diego's downtown neighbourhoods: the Core district, Little Italy, Cortez Hill, and along the harbour through the Marina by way of the drive by. Returning to the corner of Eighth Avenue, Vancouver Bob made his pitch, asking us to join him for drinks at an amusement park.

Jan and I turned Bob down for two reasons. First, the amusement park was a financial extravagance we couldn't justify. Second, a *legit* I.D. was an ongoing issue. Possibly, Bob would have covered our entrance fee and taken care of the drinks.

He hadn't offered.

Maybe the bar wouldn't bother to look at I.D.

There was greater chance they would.

Feeling lonely, horny, or both, poor Vancouver Bob looked pitiful when we extended our regrets. Despite not accompanying Bob on his quest to get blasted, we did get lucky a second time that day. Prior to making his exit to investigate the club scene, Bob handed Jan a tightly wound joint. As he drove away blurring into the city lights, I had a minor epiphany. Much of the day was spent in the company of two men seeking female company. Jan and I'd done our best to oblige. All said and done, there had to be something bigger and better out there ripe for the picking.

Guilty about holding onto the anger toward my mother, tucked into my sleeping bag that night I decided to forgive her.

Underneath my breath I whispered, "Happy Mother's Day, Mom. Love you."

Balboa Park, San Diego, California.

CHAPTER 21

Rehearsal for Meadowlark

"Walk with caution. Move with care. Camouflage is everywhere.."
ELLA WHEELER WILCOX

Breakfast was pancakes at IHOP, where Jan and I had a sober discussion about our money dilemma. It wasn't that we were broke, but with at least three months of travel ahead, we needed to find lodging that included breakfast. What's more, the Men's Y wasn't cutting it. We'd hit town a few weeks shy of the summer season for backpackers — an important, skimmed over tip when strategizing our trip south of the border.

Leaving a small gratuity to our waitress, rechecking our guidebook, we hurried back to Balboa Park for a little inspiration. Tucked deep inside my jean's pocket, I fingered Bob's joint, knowing full well that if we lit up the next few hours would unquestionably prove to be counterproductive. In the same respect, it might just be the ticket.

Tapping my fingers lightly against my pants' leg, I smiled sheepishly at Jan. Running with the tease; my friend deduced that sharing one measly joint would do no harm.

I didn't need convincing.

Two fuzzy hours later, we were no closer to figuring out our next action. Worse, we had sunburns, felt cruddy and hungry after coming down.

Smoking marijuana, an extracurricular activity that Jan and I (and some of the other girls) began indulging in during grade ten, became a mutual pursuit that probably drew us closer in friendship. As most smokers can attest, pot has redeeming and converse qualities. In the way that you remember your first time riding a bicycle hands free, everybody remembers their preliminary high.

I bought my first nickel bag ($5 for readers born after 1980) from a friend's older sister. The same older sister used to buy us six-packs at the beer store when we were underage. Back then, practically every kid had connections in one way or another. They probably still do.

Smoking grass helped flatten out the bumps. When things were rolling, we'd light up a doobie and celebrate. If a situation went south, we'd fire up the pipe. Smoking on a semi-regular basis became a function of teenage routine. Because of our part-time jobs, we could afford to buy pot. Bearing in mind, this was several years before Nancy Reagan embarked upon her "Just Say No" campaign, like most kids of our generation; we were a couple of girls who wanted to have fun. Getting high was a sure-fire way of eliciting laughs.

Even in those days however, mostly everybody (who is honest) knew that dope smoking is one of the greatest procrastinating activities on the planet. A pot habit doesn't become problematic until you're faced with responsibilities and require lucidity to execute. We weren't exactly carrying the weight of the world on our shoulders, but I'm certain Jan and I would have been out of that fleabag sooner had we not hoodwinked ourselves into accepting the notion that we could allay our impasse with a couple of toots.

The most conspicuous obstacle impinging our financial circumstances was the lack of an American work visa. Foreigners could earn wages legally in the U.S. for up to a period of six months before applying, but employers hired their own first before scavenging for seconds. Pickings were slim. We weren't versed in anything other than clerks and maids. On the other hand, Jan *did* have work history as a librarian — possibly our ace in the hole. To keep costs at a minimum, our objective was to spend no more than $5 a day, including food and lodging. This was doable we believed, so long as we could find accommodations that didn't exceed the going rate per night.

Perhaps the marijuana had helped us wade through the thicket after all.

By evening, we were back to feeling dejected and sorry about our present state of affairs. In the room adjacent to ours, a portable radio played Gary's new favourite *Stines* single, "Daddy, You're a Fool to Cry." A poignant melody will do a number on you every time. It hurts worse when you're lonesome and pitiful. Teddy's face flooded into my head; a blatant reminder how dense and fickle I was. Admitting that she, too, had been thinking about HOOM and Gary every single day, perhaps Jan was being considerate, but this knowledge brought about a level of reassurance.

Talking about San Francisco and the people daily, returning to Steiner Street seemed artificial somehow.

That night, Jan slept on the floor while I took the single bed.

There wasn't much difference between the two.

The next day was Tuesday May 11. Eating a couple of bites of breakfast in our room, we decided to stick out the dump another week. Entering the corridor, I came close to smacking head on into Gregory, a mid-thirties black man. Arriving from Florida the day before, Gregory lived to the left of us in room 509. Our new next-door-neighbour was friendly enough. Apart from formalities, as a precaution we were careful not to engage. Excluding Vancouver Bob, Jan and I kept our distance from everybody at the San Diego Y. Men *and* women. It was too risky otherwise.

A promising morning weather-wise, we set out early to visit the Natural Museum of Mans and the Fine Art Gallery at Balboa Park, where collections of sculptures and paintings from various countries, mostly modern art, were housed. Not overly enamoured with conceptual art, much of the work looked like something I could have painted. What did I know about art anyway?

In the afternoon, Jan and I ventured over to the Spanish Village and finished breakfast leftovers, a couple of ripe bananas, at Balboa Park. At one point, a man ambled up and sat next to Jan on the bench. Dressed in dark rumpled pants and an oily baseball cap, the guy absolutely reeked — even worse than Walter had. Our stinky, piss-stained buddy thought we might appreciate his company.

Without much difficulty, Jan shooed him away.

Random men haphazardly approaching us had become an epidemic as of late, creating a compromising situation. How did we know if we could trust these individuals? Prior to our arrival in the city, being waylaid by men had not been a serious concern. At the Y, most of the males were not only weird and antagonistic, but behaved if they hadn't seen a female in years. Figuring it might be in our interest to move on rather than waiting another week, Jan and I elected to leave San Diego within the next couple of days. Maybe elsewhere the men would be less assertive, less creepy. Fingering through the guidebook the night before, Jan had read about a *Meadowlark* hostel in Hemet, located in the California desert. The name had a ring to it. Better yet, Meadowlark was only 90 miles northeast of San Diego.

Any place had to be a step up from the San Diego Y. Unsure if the Meadowlark hostel was open — there was no way of finding out in advance — but even if we had to sleep under the stars, we would take our chances and hitchhike to Hemet in two days.

Our escape to the desert was not without drama. Late that afternoon, standing outside of his room shit-faced drunk, Gregory tried to maneuver his key in his door. Not wanting to ruffle feathers, when he glanced our way bleary-eyed, Jan and I maintained a polite distance. Finally able to finagle his key to fit inside the hole, magically, the door to Gregory's room flung wide open. Surprised by his good fortune, our neighbour began to crack up. We started to laugh too — nervously, when suddenly, Gregory stopped moving. He was no longer laughing. Staring in our direction, jaw clenched, and dead eyed, quietly, he asked our names. Not making a move to approach, Jan offered the information. Weaving back and forth, a satisfied smile pasted on his face, Gregory stumbled into his room. Seconds later, the door slammed behind him.

That evening, we ate blueberry muffins for dinner and took a short walk. Feeling stoked about leaving the city in two days, Jan and I looked forward to putting San Diego behind us. Not that anything bad had happened, but the town wasn't all that it was cracked up to be either — at least not where we'd ended up.

Unsure how to spend our final day was a nonissue. Maybe we'd revisit Balboa in the morning. Laze the day away. Whatever would happen would happen. Anxious to start into *The Stepford Wives*, a book she'd borrowed from Patti, Jan hoped to finish it before our return to L.A.

Stepping off the elevator, we headed around the corner to our room. Leaning against the wall smoking a cigarette, slouched Gregory.

A little freaked out, managing frivolous conversation, we watched carefully while Gregory swayed in a circular motion, his equilibrium still out of whack. Pleasantries out of the way, once a respectable amount of time had lapsed, I informed Gregory we were wiped out and going into our room. As Jan placed the key in the door, in a hushed, accusatory voice that caused the hairs to stand up on my neck, Gregory piped up, "What's the matter? Are you two prejudiced?"

Goddammit.

Feeling my body swivel as if on auto-polite, I took a deep breath and locked eyes with the hefty man to our left. Ignoring the sound of my heart beating in my ears, calmly, I answered, "No. We're just tired. It's been a long day. Nice talking to you."

I hadn't exactly been truthful about it being a long day — an excuse your grandmother might make — but it was all I could muster on short notice. To be honest, in our WASP-y hometown, Jan and I hadn't had much exposure to people of colour. Most definitely, though, we were *not* racists.

Not even close.

Gregory burst out into a scary, *just kidding — I'm only serious* sounding cackle, making me leery about whether it was safe to head into our room or would there be a confrontation. This was prime time to employ Brother James's positive visualization theory. Possibly needing an adrenalin reserve for later, I was too weak in the knees to rally energy for courage, much less meditation or prayer. Looking over at Jan, I noticed her face had gone redder than the exit sign on the wall where greenish-brown paint the colour of vomit gave way to decay.

I knew exactly what that cherry face meant, Jan was scared shitless.

She wasn't the only one.

Three doors to our right, wearing a loose blue net covering long grey hair, a man exited his room. Entering the hallway, the skeletal figure tip-toed his way to the community toilet. White paper slippers were encased over top of his shoes — footwear that somebody with OCD might choose to put on to stave off contamination. I didn't blame him. Filth, grime, and dust cakes were everywhere, from the sinks to the radiators to the windowsills. With Gregory's attention distracted by our new pal on the scene, Jan and I slipped into our room. Closing the door, I locked the deadbolt and slid across the chain.

Not daring to speak or make a move, my friend and I communicated using eye contact and hand gestures. It was a good fifteen minutes before one of us checked to see if the coast was clear. Observing the empty corridor, determined that Gregory must have gone back to his room, we were confident we'd seen the last of him. Every night since our arrival, at all hours through tissue-thin walls, you heard people coming and going, screaming, laughing. There was a constant flushing of toilets. Surely, if Gregory was lingering in the hall we'd know it. It seemed he had enough alcohol or dope in his system to pass out dead to the world until morning at the very least.

For the next hour, all was quiet. Taking extra precautions not to raise our voices above a whisper, we engaged in reading, a silent, non-disruptive activity. About to retire, there was a deafening crash against our door followed by Gregory's booming and demanding voice. *"Jan! Jill!"* In a feverish pitch preceded by thrashing and laughter, he roared, *"Open the door! I want to taaalk to you!"*

Fuck. This can't be happening.

We didn't respond. The banging and yelling continued, growing louder, more desperate with every new assault on the wood. In a King Kong voice, Gregory bellowed, begging us to let him into our room. The pounding incessant, we were terrified he'd succeed in breaking down the door, kill us both.

Like a cat, I sprung onto the end of the single bed. Barely distinguishing one another's faces in the pitch black, unable to move, from our stations at opposite sides of the mattress, Jan and I trembled in silence. Meanwhile, Gregory's voice broke into a wail. "JAAAAN! OPEN THE DOOR! I KNOW YOU'RE IN THERE! COME ON! I'LL FUCKING BREAK IT *DOWN!*"

The decibel levels of my voice rising to an extreme pitch in a matter of seconds, I screamed, "GO AWAY! LEAVE US ALONE!"

My pleas only exacerbated the situation. Gregory's commands became more hysterical. Ear-splitting. A litany of intoxicated-fueled profanities chased a quiet reprieve. Suddenly, his voice broke, as if he'd started to cry. Depending on the psychological state of an individual, weeping and maniacal laughter are first cousins. Reloading, Gregory's whining slyly reverted to yelling.

There was little left to do except call down to the front desk, inform whomever might be on duty that we were in danger. Paralyzed by shock and fear, I could scarcely believe Gregory's shouting hadn't awakened the entire building. The man's persistent threats had apparently fallen on rotting, needle-ridden bodies with pulp for brains.

Waiting for the door to crash down, our emotions alternated between tears, and nervous, stifled giggles. Shrieking at Gregory, I'd taken a stab at dispelling the situation. It was Jan's move. Even in dire straits, we were about balance. Sharing responsibility. Taking turns. Pointless maybe, but it'd worked so far. This wasn't time to change things up.

Rising from the bed, trance-like, Jan threw off the covers. Creeping in the dark toward the 1950s phone on the wall, lifting the scummy receiver from its resting place, she dialed down to the front desk. In a frightened murmur, my friend informed a phantom on the receiving end that we had a "real problem" on our hands. Either completely deaf or a dope head himself, the night clerk *had* to have heard Gregory screeching in the background. Unbelievably, while Jan and I lay sobbing beneath our covers, management (if you could call them that) took their sweet ass time sending someone up to haul our perpetrator away.

Gregory was physically removed from the premises, screaming and cussing his way in restraints. Tired of shivering in the dark fraught with fear, the braver of us mustered the nerve to switch on the light. Reaching for the bus route and roadmap from the outside pocket of her knapsack, assuming a confidence I'd never heard in her voice, Jan avowed, "That's it. I can't hack this place. We're leaving this shit-hole before dawn."

Meadowlark Centre, Valle Vista, CA, May 1976.

CHAPTER 22

Finding our Place in Space

"A man is more than his symptoms."
DR. EVARTS LOOMIS

Following the Gregory incident, sleep was fitful. Negligible. Reluctant to hitchhike and take a chance on another stranger, Gregory's steel-toed boots against our door had desecrated our emotional well-being, kicking our confidence all to hell. Not wanting to put ourselves at more risk, there was one regret. Jan and I had failed to explore Old Town, the site of the first Spanish settlement in San Diego.

So much for foiled plans. Old Town would have to wait.

To arrive in Hemet the same day, Jan and I would walk the few miles from the Y to the terminal and catch the 12:15 pm bus. This excursion was not going to be cheap — $10 total. I hoped our decision to skedaddle would be worth the investment. Knowing absolutely nothing about the hostel, we were placing our bottom dollar on a hunch.

The San Diego bus would take us to Riverside, and then we'd need to transfer onto another bus out to Hemet. Arriving at the depot well ahead of schedule, stuffing our packs into a locker to conserve our backs while waiting around, Jan and I passed an hour or so reading and people watching. Before long, it was time to board.

The eastbound bus pulled out of the terminal on schedule. Thankful to leave the city and our worries behind at the Men's Y along with the dopers, head trippers, and ex-cons, the 100-mile ride would take about two and a half hours. Physically drained from the terrifying night we'd endured and long walk to the terminal in blazing heat, after a time I could barely hold up my head.

Pulling into the Riverside station, we had an hour to spare before catching the last bus departing from the depot for the desert at half past three. At the mercy of the mid-afternoon sun, I was completely over-dressed in a pair of green cords, work boots, and long-sleeved, light blue peasant blouse. Already, we were running out of clean clothes and would have to find a laundromat once we got settled at the hostel.

The distance between Riverside and Hemet wasn't far, around 36 miles. Travelling on a rickety old school bus over dusty, two lane roads, under better conditions, our journey would have been much shorter. Crawling up and down canyon rifts at an achingly slow pace scattered amongst five other passengers, I halfway expected Rod Serling's grave face to pop up on the other side of the glass and announce we'd crossed into a void called *The Twilight Zone*.

It wasn't that bad, but it occurred to me what might happen if the bus were to break down in the singeing heat. Trying not to dwell, I sat back to enjoy the ride. This was a piece of cake after the Gregory fiasco.

Clocking into the Riverside terminal close to 5 pm, the temperature rising to 104 degrees and climbing; our journey wasn't over yet. We still hadn't reached the Meadowlark hostel, a couple of miles away in Valle Vista within the San Jacinto Valley. According to AAA, there was no transportation going Valle Vista way.

It figured.

A brief detour at nearby Robert's Health Food Store provided a couple of glasses of icy cold water offered by a pleasant Hispanic girl. Walking up the road a short distance, Jan and I stuck out our thumbs. There was no other way. For an agonizing hour, vehicles, few and far between, trickled by without giving us a look. If we hadn't been up at the crack of dawn hustling our asses to the bus depot, we might have considered footing it to the hostel. In the torrid desert heat, covered in too many clothes and the possibility of sunstroke on both our minds, walking was out of the question.

Ahead at the corner, an old gas station sat in plain view. From the looks of things, it was open. Surely, somebody inside might be able to suggest a way for us to get out to Meadowlark, or drive us there for a small fee. Poor Jan had been relegated to call down to the front desk to dispose of Gregory the night before. I was on tap asking for favours.

Entering the gas depot, his head buried inside a newspaper, I approached an elderly man seated on a stool. Posturing lazily in faded denims and white undershirt marked by yellow sweat stains beneath his pits, I presumed our man's itinerary was open.

Moving closer, he looked up, surprised.

"Can I help you?"

A brief introduction followed, in which the man said he was the pro-prietor of the station. In turn, I explained how we'd journeyed from San Diego earlier in the day, arriving in Hemet from the Riverside station one hour before. We were looking for a lift out to the Meadowlark hostel in Valle Vista. Pausing, I asked the man if he had access to a car. If so, would he consider doing the honours? Drive us up there?

Eyebrows raised, the man appeared alarmed when I mentioned the part about the Meadowlark *hostel* in Valle Vista. Familiar with Meadowlark at Valle Vista, he didn't know of a hostel "anywhere in the Hemet region." I pointed to the photo of Meadowlark represented in the guidebook. Frowning, the man suddenly looked up at me through questioning eyes. "Hmm…That's definitely the doctor's ranch."

Following him outside to a muddy brown station wagon, I introduced Jan to the gas station proprietor. Tickled that our scheme had worked, I thought it best not to mention I might have talked us into a ride out to a phantom shelter in the middle of the desert.

Double-checking Meadowlark's address, 26126 Fairview Avenue in Valle Vista (Hemet), driving down the road a way, we pulled up to the front gate of a ranch house situated on a beefy chunk of land. Flanked by several smaller buildings, sure enough, the sign at the stone-gated entrance beneath a peaked overhang read, "Meadowlark." Supposedly, the hostel was somewhere within the well preserved grounds.

What if it wasn't?

My heart sunk.

First glance, it appeared that no one was on the premises. Moving his eyes suspiciously over the property, from inside his wagon, the man from the station watched after us as we walked beyond a white, circular adobe structure resembling a chapel, and up to the front door of the main house. Across my left shoulder, an interesting weathervane shaped like a cat spun wildly on the green roof of the chapel-like building.

Jan rapped on the main entrance door. No answer. Venturing around to the side of one of the secondary buildings, we discovered an office. Seated inside at a broad desk was a slender young man. On the wall hung a sign that read "$2.00/Nite." Elated, we were about to fork over our money when the boy informed us the hostel wasn't "officially" open for business. "Not until summer," he said.

Groans of exasperation escaping our mouths, one of us dispatched a pithy version of our last 24 hours.

The man had an idea. Since we'd travelled a fair distance, there wasn't any reason we couldn't stay as long as we didn't mind sleeping in the horse stable and shower at the manmade stall outside the barn.

We sure didn't.

Returning to the car, Jan and I thanked our gas station friend for the lift, returned to the office to pay for one night, and proceeded to follow the man around to the stables where the temperature was several degrees cooler. Next to burnt-orange barnyard hay, stood a horse tied to a stall. He was accompanied by two colts, a rooster, and several hens. Good to get out of the sun and within the compliant company of furry and feathered creatures, finally, we could lay down our packs, shower, and rid our bodies of damp, sticky clothes. Not far from the premises, a small grocery store stocked fruits, vegetables, and other inexpensive food items for supper.

Things were turning around.

In a very short time, Jan and I would find out that Meadowlark provided far more than a layover for youths with little to show but a rambling heart on their sleeves.

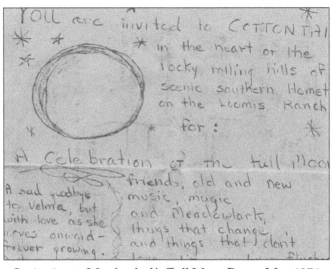

YOU are invited to COTTONTA[
★ in the heart of the
rocky, rolling hills of
scenic southern Hemet
on the Loomis Ranch
★ for : ★

A Celebration of the full Moo[
friends, old and new
A sad goodbye music, magic
to Velma, but and Meadowlark,
with love as she things that change
[cu]rves onward— and things that don't
[fo]rever growing.

Invitation to Meadowlark's Full Moon Party, May 1976.

CHAPTER 23

Meadowlark:
Full Moon Rising

"Look and listen. Move slow. Tread softly.
Stay open and be a part of what the place is being."
MEADOWLARK, *Valle Vista, CA, May 1976*

Situated on twenty glorious acres of desert ranch land in the foothills of the San Jacinto Mountains, Meadowlark was not only equipped with horses and fowl, the property contained a massive organic vegetable garden, several species of birds; coyotes, snakes — scores of wild life. Rows of lemon trees and orange groves enveloped the property. Cloaked within the natural beauty of the mountains, poignant and imposing lay a mysterious, mystical aura. Compared to where we'd come from hours before, Jan and I were suddenly accessories at an out-of-the-way gem that could be described only as heavenly. Perhaps Rod Serling had arbitrated on our behalf. Either that or we were clicking on all cylinders practicing positive visual imagery.

Padding our bunks with straw from the stable to create comfortable makeshift mattresses, wandering outside, we found our way to the kitchen area of the main house. The epicenter of the ranch resembling a farmhouse, the Centre's generous kitchen stood self-assuredly atop a red terra cotta floor. Throughout the room, mature wood beams and overhead strapping secured the ceiling and foundation. Raw strips of barn wood extended vertically from the baseboards to the rafters. On top of a hearth pad next to at least fifty feet of counter space running the length of four walls, a black cast-iron stove provided the foundation for a large aromatic pot of simmering spinach and lentil soup. Suspended over top of a considerable island were cooking tools, iron-laden pots, pans, and utensils. Serving trays, fresh herbs, vegetables, and fruits smothered the surfaces of the countertops.

Perplexed by the well equipped the kitchen, despite it being early in the season, I wondered why then, only two hostellers on the premises?

Bruce, Corey, and Jack, a few of the folks who lived and/or worked at the ranch full time, explained that Meadowlark functioned as a holistic health resort year round. The hostel was an afterthought. Retreating to the Centre from all over the world, guests sought treatments for various types of cancers, respiratory problems, high blood pressure, allergies, weight control, and other maladies. More than thirty patients occupied the private casas propagated throughout the property.

Formerly owned by movie mogul, Louis B. Mayer, in 1958, the Meadowlark estate was purchased by physician and surgeon, Dr. Evarts Loomis.[5]

Favouring the complete utilization of homeopathic practices and natural remedies, rather than conventional medical treatments and over-the-counter narcotics, Evarts reopened the property as a fully functional spa/holistic health and personal growth retreat. In its early years, inviting international visionaries in their respective fields to confer about program development and expansion, Loomis hosted regular conferences at Meadowlark. Among esteemed guests were physicians, psychiatrists, sociologists and psychologists, scientists, ministers, business leaders, spiritual healers, musicians, and artists. Hollywood A-listers Dolly Parton, Kenny Rogers, and John Wayne are all rumoured to have been treated at Meadowlark. According to Bruce, Corey, and Jack, Dr. Loomis (who preferred to be called "Evarts") believed in treating the "whole" person. He achieved this by introducing wholesome vegetarian eating habits and integrating physical, spiritual, and mental components through therapeutic health management. Some of the healing techniques employed at the ranch were simple as dispensing love and prayer, or innovative as administering polarity[6] treatment, the practice of balancing natural electromagnetic energy for restorative purposes. Dr. Loomis tailored specific regimens based on need. Patients of the Centre committed to a two-week stay.

5. Regarded by many as the "father of holistic medicine," Evarts Greene Loomis (1910-2003) was an internationally known physician, lecturer, author, and visionary in the field of alternative health.

6. A procedure that had been discovered by Austrian-American chiropractor, osteopath, and naturopath, Randolph Stone (1888-1981), who integrated Eastern and Western models of healing prior to the implementation of polarity treatment's subsequent relevance in the Southwestern United States.

It wasn't cheap.

This unexpected flood of information aroused our interest. Warmed by the friendliness of the employees and intrigue of the health spa, we talked some more. Jan and I had apparently arrived in time to take part in a special event. To celebrate the approaching lunar phase of the full moon, a shindig was scheduled the next night up at Jack's farm. The party would feature music, dancing, and sumptuous vegetarian cooking — organic dishes prepared from Meadowlark's own garden.

Reaching his arm over to the counter for a pair of invitations, Bruce placed one in each of our hands. Scribbled across the sheets of yellow paper in black marker next to a crude sketch of a full-bodied moon bore a message that read: *"You are invited to* COTTONTAIL *in the heart of the rocky, rolling hills of scenic southern Hemet, on the Loomis ranch for: A Celebration of the Full Moon, friends old and new, music, magic, and Meadowlark. Things that change and things that don't — love, life, and liver flushes."*

On the back of the invitation, a map outlined the route between Meadowlark and Cottontail, a smaller ranch in south Hemet, also owned by Loomis. It was the location of Jack's place.

A tender smile drew Bruce's lips together. "You two must come."

Following a restful sleep, Jan and I awakened to the sound of wind chimes nudging eucalyptus trees hovering outside the stable door. Dappled sunlight filtered through the slats in the barn. Though cool throughout the night, snuggled deep inside of our sleeping bags, we stayed cozy and warm. Not yet oppressive as it had been late afternoon the day before, the morning brought a dry heat. In our enigmatic new setting, Jan and I were eager to greet the day.

Scattering dried fruit, cheese, and crackers along the counter of the main kitchen, within the Meadowlark Centre's kind light and gentle ambiance, the food we'd carried with us from San Diego tasted better than expected. On the pantry wall, a plaque was tacked up. Unable to make out the words of what appeared to be a poem, getting up from my chair, I edged over closer to have a better look.

FINDING OUR PLACE IN SPACE

"Clear your head. Clean up your dreams.
Get easy and believe in the new possibilities.
Move about. Look around. Pick a place.
Come down gently and tune yourself to the natural vibrations.

Live lightly on the land. Share. Recycle.
Do less with less.
Dream small. Feel big."

Returning to the stables to retrieve my journal, I copied the poem verbatim.

Navigating the grounds of the ranch, we were swallowed up by fields of orange groves and lemon trees, iridescent and enchanting in the morning light. The sky, an arid, hazy blue, cast a glow over the aloes and succulents. Fringing the border of the land, delineating a tableau of mauve, burnt sienna, yellows, and greens, the Jacinto Mountain Range created an explosive spectacle. Encouraged to pick from the fruit trees on the premises, Jan and I were delighted to accept this gesture. Not only would it cut down on food costs, the juicy oranges tasted delectable.

Paying $2 apiece at the office to secure one more night, we headed into Hemet on foot to scope out summer clothing. Anything either one of us carried in our backpacks was far too warm. Sadly, the cotton Mexican tops we admired were out of our price range. Instead, we delighted in picking out a few groceries.

On our return, his black lab Raisin by his side, Jack offered us a lift back to the ranch by way of his place where the Full Moon Celebration party would be held that evening. Glad to get out of the sun, we hopped inside the truck.

Sitting atop 600 acres of rock-strewn land like a trophy, the communal living residence, "Cottontail," had an elevation high enough to allow for a cyclopean view of the Jacinto Mountains. A fixer upper with temperamental fridge and toilet, the farmhouse managed to hold great appeal. Residing at the Cottontail farmhouse for more than two months, Jack, a part-time artist and painter and one of Meadowlark's full time chefs, was waiting for a room at Meadowlark to become vacant. Though brief, the detour to Jack's ranch was long enough to offer a glimpse of what we might expect come evening.

Despite the temperature climbing to a searing 106 degrees early afternoon, Jan and I assisted Meadowlark's sun-gnarled elder gardener, Hal, weeding and watering plants at the main garden. Afterwards, we cooled down in the stable to read, sketch, and nap. While afternoon siestas were encouraged at Meadowlark, because of the ruthless heat, gardening duties were generally carried out in the mornings.

Earlier, I'd purchased a postcard from the office depicting the Meadowlark ranch, and bookmark bearing an image of the flowers of Judea and cross of the Garden of Gethsemane in Jerusalem. A short poem was printed on the opposite side. On the off chance that he was still there, when we returned to San Francisco, I would give the bookmark to Teddy.

Inside the office, I met Carl from Ontario, Canada. Emaciated and pale, Carl was on seven-day fast, juices only. When I asked how he was feeling, Carl replied, "Polarity treatment has been prescribed by Dr. Loomis to help strengthen muscle tone and encourage vitality."

The term "polarity" had been bounced around since our arrival. Jan and I would soon learn more about the process and its applications. Uncertain what kind of illness had befallen Carl, examining his sallow face, I hoped that whatever remedy Evarts recommended would surely improve his health, and told him so.

Nodding gravely, Carl made his way toward the door.

Late in the afternoon, Velma, another of the Centre's chefs, circled her Volkswagen into the ranch carting a load of prepared foods, veggies, and fruit from the Meadowlark gardens. Through her friend Bruce, the young Meadowlark groundskeeper who'd invited us to the party, Jan and I'd managed to secure a ride to the Full Moon Party. Velma was moving out of state. In gratitude for her hard work and fellowship, in part, the Full Moon Party was held in her honour. It was rumoured that Evarts planned to attend. His aura ubiquitous, it was exciting to imagine meeting the guru doctor in the flesh.

Next to Velma in the front passenger seat, between his knees, Corey balanced Tupperware containers containing condiments and perishables. Amidst the labyrinth of food, spices, and sweets infusing the atmosphere with aromatic delight, cheerfully, Velma commanded, "Squeeze in!" Squeeze we did, me crunched on top of Jan's lap, my head pressed against the windshield of the Volkswagen as we rolled away from the house, down the laneway and out toward the road. One of a small caravan of vehicles creeping its way along Florida Avenue toward Balboa, eventually, we climbed several hundred yards along stubble and rock before traversing Cottontail's long laneway.

A gathering of bodies had already collected at Jack's farmstead, an even blend of seniors, youths, and middle-aged. There were women, men, children, and babies as young as one month. Disembarking from the Volkswagen, The Kinks' "Sunday Afternoon" discharged loudly from a pair of oversized speakers positioned outside one of the barns. People rushed the car, helping unload food, packages, trays, transferring the items from the vehicle to the pantry where a profusion of cakes, fresh fruit pies, cookies, home baked breads, cheeses, and crackers piled high. Eyes widening, Jan and I gaped at the smorgasbord of mouthwatering goodies.

As if they'd practised weeks ahead for the occasion, people congregated in the back yard, on blankets, in chairs, at the few tables in preparation for the party. Fastened within an impressive reach of mountains and bleached desert hues, as the food was meticulously arranged in the kitchen, guests were offered water, juice, and cold beer. Poking his head around until finally locating us outside, Bruce handed us a couple of bottles of Corona.

No one bothered about age of discretion at the Full Moon bash.

Before long, the pleasing scent of marijuana filtered through the air. Acquiescing to the sweet smell permeating the atmosphere, I tracked a goat and four dogs chasing one another in and amongst guests. A group of new folks arrived: Doug, Zoran, Karen, and their eight-year-old son Jake. Mandy, Denny and Judy introduced themselves. Two attractive blonde boys, Steve and Keith, invited us to smoke some hashish from a small bamboo pipe. Between the beer and the hash, perfectly mollified, I was about to help myself to another Corona when a distinguished, older man wearing a generous crop of white hair, headed in our direction. Walking with purposefulness, the man was accompanied by our friend Bruce.

Recognizing the strong facial features from photos, I knew it was Dr. Loomis.

In this world, Evarts was a rock star. I didn't want to do or say anything that might sound brainless. Jan and I were unofficial hostel guests — would Loomis mind that we were crashing on the Meadowlark property — as trespassers — sort of?

Spotting Evarts from a few yards away, breaking free from another group, Jan hurried over.

"Jill, Jan," Bruce smiled wide, "I'd like you to meet Evarts."

Considering the man's stature and reputation, Loomis's name sounded informal. Wearing a blue denim shirt and khakis, at first impression, Evarts appeared casual. Down-to-earth. Our short meaningful exchange would prove it so.

Echoing one after another, Jan and I blurted out hellos. To our surprise, Evarts knew who we were. With luck, whatever he'd heard was good.

"You're the two girls from Canada," Loomis grinned.

Referring to our staying out in the horses' stable, he asked how we happened to find our way to Meadowlark. Jan told the doctor about the hostel guidebook, listing Meadowlark's location as accommodation for travellers, and explained how we'd taken the bus from San Diego to reach Hemet the day before.

Looking thoughtful for a moment, Evarts allayed, "Ah, yes. The listing is still up. You know, the hostel *has* been a big part of Meadowlark in past years. Actually, we won't be opening it this summer."

Stunned, I asked why.

"We've decided to close the hostel permanently. The entire ranch functions primarily as a health facility now. Because of the great need to expand for more guests seeking homeopathic treatments, we're in the stages of renovating the Centre to accommodate more patients."

Evarts' reasoning made sense. Still, there was something serendipitous about the two of us sliding in through the cracks before the actual shutdown — even if we were in the stable.

Dr. Loomis was called away to socialize with some of the other revellers. Before departing, he extended an invitation to attend Sunday morning worship at the home of his 95-year-old mother, Amy. Eyes crinkling persuasively, Evarts guaranteed. "You won't want to miss it."

When dinner was announced, Loomis encouraged everyone to gather around as he prepared to read a few words before the meal. Encouraging each one of us to embrace the prayer for "improved digestion," Evarts proceeded to recite a short poem written by Austrian philosopher, author, and esotericist, Rudolph Steiner.

"As plants germinate in the Earth's night…As herbs send forth shoots through the atmosphere's power. As fruits ripen through the strength of the sun…So blossoms the soul in the shrine of the heart…So sprouts the spirits' strength in the light of the world…So matures the strength of man in the light of God."

Met with billowing clouds at the start of the party, now, the air charged static-electric. Picking up paper plates and plastic utensils, our group of thirty lined up outside of the kitchen pantry, ready to partake from a mouthwatering mixture of appetizers, breads and rolls, nut loafs, salads, and a multiplicity of cheeses combined with a menu of meatless main dishes such as zucchini lasagna, sauerkraut casserole, enchiladas coloradas, and turnip soufflé. For dessert, carob nut brownies and pumpkin pie sat next to a vat of homemade lemonade. Peppermint, ginseng, alfalfa and licorice teas were on hand to wash (and cleanse) everything down.

When the feast was over, everybody pitched in clearing and cleaning up. Several in the group that had brought along instruments started to set up outside. Accompanying a couple of acoustic guitar players, Bruce played bongos. Denny provided vocals.

For the next couple of hours, there was singing, dancing, and celebration. Then, as if within arm's reach, dressed in engorged splendor, the plump, pallid moon rose elegantly from behind the curtain of the desert terrain. Escorted by its ally, a star-speckled sky, the glowing sphere shone with a patina I'd never witnessed.

Gathering in a large semicircle, stirred by a sense of tranquility gripping the group consciousness, lifting our eyes, we gazed spellbound at the heavenly pumpkin, brilliantly satiated as it levitated in the galactic playground. Ecstatic to be part of this exclusive event, Jan and I paused to regard one another's incredulous faces.

It felt unbelievably good.

The spectacularly beautiful evening had opened a torrent of privilege and humility. After a time, stepping quietly aside, I started toward the back of the house. Taking few strategic paces down the mountain, my right foot parked behind a rock for safety, reflecting upon the moon's compassionate face, I started to cry.

Later, driving along the dirt road down to Meadowlark just after midnight, seated on the open flatbed of Steve's pickup truck, stars above, bare feet dangling over the edge touching tips of desert scrub — Jan, Bruce, Denny, and Judy nestled around me, I was barely able to contain joy.

Meadowlark ranch, the dusty San Jacinto Mountain Range in behind.

CHAPTER 24

Polarity for Dummies

"Spirit is where the energy flows, and all the modalities we used at Meadowlark encouraged this healing flow of energy."
DR. EVARTS LOOMIS

Following breakfast, Jan and I helped Hal weed the main garden. Mostly, Hal didn't say much. Whenever he felt like talking, Hal chose his words carefully. Whatever he had to say you hoped to remember.

Originally from the area, Hal had once been a Navy man, and later, a ranch hand. Several years earlier, before finding a permanent home at Meadowlark, Hal drifted from farm to farm, earning enough money to eat, buy smokes and the odd bottle of whiskey — habits that were no longer a part of his repertoire. Apart from his question-mark posture and grey thinning hair, what stood out most about Hal was his leathery, coffee-tanned skin — a badge for having spent too many years baking in the desert sun.

In summers, Steve, May, Jan, and I had worked on local farms. June weekends, we'd get up early, ride our bicycles a few miles away to a nearby rural road to pick strawberries. Doing our utmost not to eat all the plump ones, it was our job to ensure the boxes didn't contain any rotten fruit. If our collection of quart-sized boxes met with the farmer's approval, we were paid $4 apiece for eight hours labour. Once strawberry-picking season ended, riding out to another farm in the same vicinity, Jan and I secured tomato plants to stakes for twin middle-aged bachelors. Because of their contrasting sizes, "Three Pounds Underweight" and "Three Pounds Overweight" addressed one another appropriately. As a reward for enduring the incorrigible mid-day sun, "Three Pounds Overweight" usually offered ice-cold beer after our workday was finished.

"Three Pounds Underweight" wasn't quite so liberal.

Jan and I settled in quickly to our new routine at Meadowlark, watering, weeding dehydrated soil between vegetable beds in the cooler morning air. Bit by bit, we got to know Hal, a wise and introspective human being. Hal was kind. He was helpful. Working on the ranch alongside Hal made us feel that we were contributing to Meadowlark's values and sustainability.

Near the front gate one morning, I'd set out to sketch the mountains and landscape behind the ranch. Stopping over on the way to the house, Bruce told me he knew of an idyllic setting in which to sketch, and guaranteed I'd agree. Packing a picnic lunch — whatever was on hand — Jan and I accompanied Bruce to his magic spot.

Within the core of desert wilderness less than a mile from the ranch, we found ourselves encircled by a jamboree of taupe, gingers, and soft blues. Steeped within the Jacinto Mountains, accentuated by supplementary jades and the aroma of citrus fruit arising from acres of thriving orange groves and lemon trees, I couldn't help feeling spoiled by our superlative surroundings. For the past six months, under Dr. Loomis' employ, Bruce helped in the kitchen and assisted in the daily caretaking of the grounds — work that Hal was unable to manage. Often teaming forces with Hal, Bruce attested that Hal was one of the most disarming and intelligent individuals he'd ever known. Having exposure not only to the senior employees but also guest lecturers at the Centre, Bruce was privy to some of the healing techniques applied by Evarts and his team of specialists. That spring, he was studying the benefits of polarity treatment. As a workable means for curing physical and psychological diseases and disorders, Bruce described polarity as a "massage therapy technique" designed to relieve tension and infuse life energy as means of purging disease. By applying pressure at different points on the body, Bruce explained the administrator is able to reinstate positive energy flow.

Combined with polarity therapy, Meadowlark patients were required to eat "good, healthy food" as a primary restorative healing ingredient. They were encouraged to strive toward a pleasing demeanor. Guests participated in regular liver flushes (4 tbsp. lemon juice, 2 tbsp. olive oil, 2 cloves garlic and juice of 1 orange or grapefruit) and consumed herbal teas at every meal. By introducing and reinforcing routines that promoted wellbeing, Evarts taught people how *not* to become sick.

According to Bruce, Evarts believed human beings were responsible for developing symptoms. During a patient's pre-assessment at Meadowlark, Evarts would probe, inviting individuals to explain why they believed to have fallen ill at a specific stage in their lives. Loomis helped them to discover that good health is a matter of will. Once patients decided to become better, physical symptoms would dissipate.

May 1976, Meadowlark Holistic Health Spa celebrated more than twenty years' success. In my mind, finding ourselves at Meadowlark was not a fluke. Since leaving Vancouver, life back home was beginning to seem antiquated.

Supper that night was a repeat of cheese and crackers — food I could easily live on. During a walk out to the canyon, Bruce caught up. Would we be interested in joining some of the patients for the evening's program, a recording of psychologist Dr. Murray Banks? Apart from the atrophied man I'd encountered one day ago, this was an opportunity to fraternize with other guests.

As we'd imagined, the main living area of Loomis's residence, where evening sessions took place, was ample and comfortable. Unpretentious, yet rich in tone and texture, there were plenty of sofas, generous sized chairs, and a couple of hand-woven Indian rugs covering honey wood floors. Duplicate crystal chandeliers hung from the ceiling on either side of the room. Fifteen to twenty people or more, mostly in their forties, fifties, and sixties scattered about the room. Everybody appeared to be comfortable with the drill. Bruce, Jan, and I sat on the floor, leaving remaining seats for those who might join mid-session. Evening program attendance was optional.

Introducing the lecture, Loomis praised the comprehensive work of former clinical psychologist, motivational speaker-turned comedian, Dr. Murray Banks. Without delay, Evarts placed a record on the turntable.

Banks opened the dialogue with a catchy one-liner that would become his trademark, "Anyone who goes to a psychiatrist should have his head examined." Most of the LP played out similarly, bending truths and realism with jokes thrown in throughout the routine to underpin Banks's opinion that when it comes to preservation of mental health, human beings are self-sabotaging. Stressing laughter as the road to personal wellness, Banks closed with the parting message, "The blue bird of happiness is you."

Acknowledging the psychiatrist's clever use of satire, from what I could gather, Meadowlark patients enjoyed the show.

Once applause died down, stepping up to the front of the room, Evarts encouraged everybody to mingle. Jan and I were introduced to Casey, (who asked if we'd walked to Hemet from Canada!), a woman who trained animals for Disney and other major Hollywood studios. We met Bert, who claimed to have invented his own language, and demonstrated it for us — a sort of customized Pig Latin. A linguistics specialist might have decreed Bert's unsystematic construction of vowels and consonants illogical, maybe even a bit nutty, it was a good laugh all the same.

Amalda, a stout woman who travelled from Germany with her physicist husband, had convalesced at Meadowlark for more than two months. On a strict liquid diet, so far, Amalda claimed to have lost over 60 pounds. Excitedly, she pressed for details about our travel adventures to date, giving me the sense she missed her children back home. Handing each of us an American $1 bill, in a heavy German accent, Amalda encouraged, "Have a svim in the pool, I know Dr. Evarts vouldn't mind."

Generally, the pool was restricted to patients only.

Returning to our straw beds, Jan and I chose a couple of prime oranges from the grove, and then bade Mandy, Meadowlark's token horse, goodnight.

At dawn, we helped Hal with the weeding and watering until it got too warm. Taking shelter in the stables, Jan and I planned to follow through with Amalda's suggestion, use the money for a swim at the Centre's large, kidney-shaped pool located behind the main house. Last place we'd gone swimming was Zuma Beach. Here, we were in Southern California, with access to sun, fun, and sea. As of late, we'd been consumed (though happily) by a gamut of nature, community, and philosophical theories leaving little time for simple pleasures.

A swim might balance things out.

Changing into our suits, we walked around to the back of the ranch toward the gateway, leading to the concrete pool deck. At the opposite end of the pool, seated beneath red and white striped umbrellas, were six other guests. Two of them appeared to be napping. Nobody seemed to care that we intended to have ourselves a bit of recreation.

Swimming conditions were ideal. At an optimum temperature of 84 degrees — almost 20 degrees cooler than the air, the saltwater was pristine. Completing a few laps, hare-brained flips, and fun with pool toys, reclining on chaise lounge chairs; tall glasses of lemonade in hand, slices of lime within reach, for the next couple of hours Jan and I conceived what it might be like to be two of Meadowlark's well-heeled guests.

In the evening, we set off on foot to discover Bautista Canyon, another site just off the ranch property Bruce had mentioned earlier. Appraising miles of orange groves, grapefruit, lemon, and avocado trees, I noticed a warning. It was an offense to pick from the trees. If caught, trespassers would be fined $50.

For now, Jan and I were law-abiding citizens.

Looking outward, the San Jacinto Mountain rock cast a grey shadow over the dusky brush. I imagined that during early spring, before draught set in, vegetation was much more robust. Nevertheless, even in late May, when many of the overhangs were dry in the lower regions, it was tough to avert your eyes from the iridescent sight. At dusk however, without the benefit of streetlights to guide our way, it was necessary to head back before desert coyotes and other wild game started making rounds.

On our way home, magically, the night air cooled everything down. Looking across the canyons as we headed cautiously down the path, set off by the lowering sun, the orange groves transformed the sky into a phantasmagoric exposé of red and gold — a most handsome colour-shifting sight.

Back inside the stable, Bruce reappeared, knocking at our door. Would we like company?

So far, Bruce hadn't tried to put a move on either one of us. Rather than a lack of interest in sex, I believed his laissez-faire attitude had something to do with the laser sharp focus Bruce had on everything going on around him. Besieged by the full-on Meadowlark experience, the virus had clearly taken hold. Dropping casual hints about the possibility of Jan and me finding work in the Hemet area was Bruce's way of saying he approved, and would like us to stick around.

Working and living in Hemet for a few months *was* an intriguing proposition.

Sharing red grapes and corn bread he'd brought from the kitchen, Bruce began to emphasize the importance of living in the "now," and talked about "reality" in relation to "concepts."

Reminded of the John Lennon song, "God," in which Lennon describes God as a creation and concept devised by man to measure pain, I mentioned it out loud.

"God is within every person," Bruce cautiously countered. "He shouldn't be perceived as a concept or belief." Ratcheting up a couple of notches, conversation fragmented into telepathy and astral travel. We wondered: *Is astral travel the same as time travel?* I recalled that on a couple of occasions as a kid, sitting next to my mom in church, there was the sensation of becoming invisible — as if I could watch myself from outside of myself. In my head I'd repeat, "I am here..." believing that saying the words aloud would prevent me from disappearing altogether. Questioning the others to ascertain if these occurrences were exclusive or possibly even brief episodes of astral travel, Jan shared how she distinctly remembered flying around the apple tree in her yard when she was five years old. Claiming to be wide awake at the time, these mini flights had taken place during daylight hours.

Throughout the duration of our stories, Bruce became increasingly quiet. Finally, he acknowledged something he'd been keeping to himself. "I think I might be from another planet."

Early Sunday, a piccolo played melodiously outside, rousing Meadowlark guests to consciousness. Excited to attend the meditation session up at Amy's house, Jan and I worked early in the vegetable garden before the mid-morning temperature became intolerable.

This was the first time I looked forward to a spiritual service of any kind.

Late morning, Jan, Bruce and I arrived at Loomis's mother's house, an attractive residence embedded neatly within the folds of the canyon. Evarts was already there, shepherding invitees out to the backyard, where eye-popping beds of violets and roses, periwinkle and hibiscus bowed as we settled upon the soft green grass. A fusion of melodic music and rustling trees stirred the air while active insects dallied near various garden sculptures modelled in shapes of angels and fairies. The San Jacinto Mountain crests, lightly dusted in snow, tantalized in the late morning sunshine.

In the middle of the lawn in a folding chair, ankles crossed, daintily dressed in a cotton-printed dress dotted in mauve, pink and yellow, sat Meadowlark's unofficial matriarch, Amy Loomis. Anchored by a few loose wisps of white floating freely before keen green eyes, the 95-year-old woman shone like a beacon of light. Greeting the group with a kindly smile, from an open leather-bound book upon her lap, Amy began to read a poem titled, "How to Run to God."

When she finished, Loomis closed the book, looked to the sky and then turned her palms to direct us to the solace of our surroundings. Encouraging everybody to take slow deep breaths, Amy asked that we concentrate our thoughts on God's presence. Fingers massaging the soft grass, I attuned my mind to bird songs, busy insects, and other organisms, faithfully and diligently executing daily garden tasks.

Quietly, Evarts stood. Addressing the group, the doctor reiterated his mother's message of gratitude, respect, and love. Then Loomis turned things over to one of his eminent therapists, Doug Barton, expert practitioner in the administration of polarity.

Handsomely dressed in flowing white robe and sandals, long dark hair and beard, Doug Barton looked every bit the part of a new age healer. According to Bruce and others that had been in his care, Barton could walk the walk.

Through aquamarine eyes, Doug proceeded to outline the effectiveness of the polarity procedure and other applications. While he spoke, I heard a woman seated next to me whisper to her neighbour that Doug's soul was so "intensely innocent," when he conducted polarity treatments, the energy emanating between therapist and patient was in its purest form.

Barton demonstrated "yogic flying," a technique designed to help humans achieve levitation for extended periods. To "tune in" to the natural inner life energy of the universe or "Chi," adopting the lotus position, Doug began bouncing vigorously back and forth and up and down along a thick rubber mat. At one point, carried by the momentum of his movement, Barton elevated approximately three feet in air. Applause followed. Completing this short overture and flying feat, Doug began making the rounds to a select few.

Barely home from our morning up at Amy's house, Jan and I were encouraged to join Meadowlark guests for Sunday brunch. On the verge of feeling as if we were taking advantage of the good nature of just about everybody since our arrival, this charitable act was well beyond expectation.

In a couple of days, Meadowlark would be a blissful memory. In my heart, I already missed it.

Broccoli-rice bake and spinach patties were paired with bean sprout salad. New cabbage slaw and greens, mixed with cottage cheese, dates, raisins, celery, nuts and chives, were crowned with avocado and tomato garlic dressings. Marjoram and Yerba Santa herbal teas, orange cake, carrot pudding with whipped cream complemented the first course.

Our stomachs satisfied, returning to the big garden, we worked furiously until late afternoon.

Accompanied by Bruce, before dusk, Jan and I returned to Bautista Canyon. Walking clear past the end of the road and into an open field, again, we were engulfed by a multiplicity of colour schemes.

Bruce asked if we'd like him to read our auras. Carrying out this act, to detect peripheral light, he fixed his eyes on the center of our foreheads. Raising both hands during the process, it was a foregone conclusion, our aura signatures were positive. This was good news. Explaining how auras are partly composed from body temperature, Bruce demonstrated how to trap natural energy. Rubbing his palms together rapidly for several seconds creating friction, he then placed each of his hands between our hands to feel heat sensation from the energy generated.

"This is it," he beamed with pride. "This is how polarity works."

Bruce had read three books about polarity. Using this energy heat treatment, by coincidence, he claimed to have healed someone not many months before. A friend had fallen off a bicycle fracturing his right arm. With little time to react, rubbing his hands together for several seconds, Bruce applied pressure to the man's arm. When the injured bone appeared to mend and the man was no longer in pain, Bruce became convinced of polarity's credibility.

Years later, recollecting the conversation with Jan, we agreed our Meadowlark friend was not a liar nor was he fraudulent. Bruce told his own truth. Possibly, the friend's arm wasn't completely broken. Maybe it was sprained. The fact remains, Bruce recognized he was party to the budding stages of something powerful.

Settling into our stable beds that night, there was a lot to chew on. Asserting the importance of determining which one each of us is predestined to be, weeks earlier, Brother James volunteered there are two people in the world: teachers and students. Gauging everything to which we'd been exposed since first meeting him at Meadowlark, more than a friend, Bruce was a veritable guide.

That made us students.

In front of the chapel at the Meadowlark Centre,
Valle Vista, CA. May 1976.

CHAPTER 25

Savouring Meadowlark

"Think healthy. Teach Children. Maintain yourself. Steward the earth. Love and we will all have a place in space."
MEADOWLARK PHILOSOPHY — *Valle Vista, CA.*

Buzz saws awakened us from sleep. Jack and his buddy Kent were busy converting two of the horse's stalls into a bedroom so that Jack could move to Meadowlark in July as scheduled.

Over breakfast, Jan and I chatted with a late arrival roomie, Richard, and then helped Hal in the garden until noon. Used to our new groove at Valle Vista, I intended to drain every drop from remaining time.

After a grocery stop, Jan and I walked 2 miles down Bautista Road, taking photographs of one another and of the landscape. With any luck, our pictures would elucidate the panorama in a way that my marginal artistic skills had failed to do.

Passing Jack and Kent as they continued building, returning to our bunks, we changed into bathing suits for a final swim. The sun's penetrating lens filtering through the leaves of a regal oak, our suits wet, Jan and I surrendered to the heat. Spring, summer, and autumn, the only occasion in which anybody would deliberately sit outside in Valle Vista in the daytime was when soaked to the skin.

That evening, Doug Barton was the delegated speaker at the Centre. Jan had inquired earlier about sitting in on the seminar. One hour before show time, we learned we were *in*. Sitting before Barton was to connect with a divine creature. Not only was he mystical and saintly, Doug was sexy in a Cat Stevens kind of way. It didn't matter what he was peddling, he'd have our undivided attention.

At the main residence that night, the program commenced on time. Barefoot, legs covered in stark white pants, donning a light blue Indian shirt with Nehru collar, in suspended calmness, Doug Barton entered the room. Seated near the front, Jan and I noticed how beautiful his hands appeared (another prerequisite for a sage), slender and strong. Opening the session sharing stories about a recent backpacking expedition, how he'd survived on wild berries and nuts, smoothly, Barton modulated his anecdote to the detriment of frozen foods and the health benefits of sprouts and fresh fruits and vegetables. Commenting on the linkage between harvest and human health, Doug stressed the significance of diet as the heart and soul of the polarity program.

Patients of the treatment began giving testimonies. Not only had Barton helped assuage aches and pains, but he'd renewed the physical and psychological health of customers. A half hour polarity session with Doug Barton cost $12 — a bag of shekels in exchange for fawning over a fine specimen, I thought.

When the tutorial ended, people milled about. Glad-handing his way toward the rear of the room, Doug suddenly stopped next to where Jan and I were seated. Kneeling before me smiling, Barton clasped both my hands between his.

My god, did Bruce put him up to this?

Holding a hypnotic gaze, Doug's pastel aquamarine pools were merely inches from mine. Trying to match his stare, I attempted to will sexual thoughts from my mind. This was not a simple thing to do. The man was idiosyncratically handsome in a most devastating way.

I'm not sure what transpired during our moment, if anything. I'd *like* to believe that Doug Barton imbued me with some superior sagacity I could latch onto, perhaps indefinitely. Slowly releasing my hands, turning his attention to Jan, Barton repeated the exercise with unadulterated ease.

Unquestionably, this was the closest either one of us would ever come to experiencing a telekinetic orgasm, perhaps the best possible kind. At the very least, our experiences were on par with encountering the Dali Lama in person. In the looks department however, Barton had the edge.

Next day we had "energy" oranges and milk for breakfast. On tap to leave Meadowlark imminently, final hours were commemorated taking more snapshots of the area surrounding the ranch, and Hal's garden. I captured an image of Bruce tending to the grounds outside of one of the smaller stucco buildings. In turn, Bruce took a photograph of Jan and me posing in front of the round adobe chapel, the little house that had caught our attention that first day, the cat weathervane whirling around on the roof. It would be tough leaving the Centre and the friends we'd made, especially Bruce, whom we promised to write.

That morning, Bruce made another plea for us to locate work in the Hemet area. Apart from financial limitations, Jan and I were invited to Cousin Mark's wedding on Saturday and wanted to be there. Additionally, my brother was expected to attend. Privately, I worried that if we stayed on at Meadowlark, it would lose its luster somehow.

I didn't ever want that to happen.

Labouring one last time in the big garden, watering, prepping soil, extracting as many weeds as possible, when the time came to check out at the office, the money paid during our stay was returned to us. The good folks determined since we'd assisted Hal every day but one, we deserved a break.

This was a huge bonanza and would help cover bus fare from Riverside to L.A. The entire week at Meadowlark, Jan and I'd spent a combined $10.

Making final rounds, wishing us safe on our journey, we were embraced by everybody on site. Thanking us for our participation, Evarts came out from his study to see us off. Even Jack's black lab, Raisin, appeared sad to see us go.

When it came time to say goodbye to Hal, bending over carefully, the man held each of us softly against his chest, the way a father holds his own flesh and blood. An integral part of the Meadowlark experience, Hal had been our surrogate grandpa, a man whom Jan and I would never forget. Looking one last time at his brittle, ripened body, I wondered how many years Hal had left exploiting skin and muscle to maintain his vegetable family, the last of his true loves.

Walking us down the laneway toward the road, Bruce put in one last pitch about staying. Then, stepping gingerly toward the white chapel, he waved farewell. As if willing us to change our minds, holding four fingers in the air, not once did his eyes waver from our faces.

Jan started to cry. I prayed I wouldn't.

A middle-aged man behind the wheel of a red Datsun truck slowed at the side of the road. We climbed inside. Pulling away from the curb, I turned toward Bruce. Standing next to the chapel, the cat weathervane spinning whimsically in the wind, he continued to watch.

Perhaps one individual's hopes and dreams can infiltrate another's.

Gary posing with "Black and Blue."

Universal Studios #1.

Universal Studios #2.

Patti clowning around at Van Nuys airport.

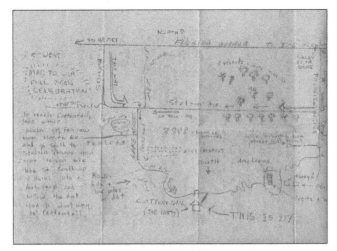

Directions to Full Moon Party.

Raw sketch of Gilbert O'Sullivan.

Jan in Meadowlark's main garden.

Bruce Flagg.

Magnificent Southern California coastline.

CHAPTER 26

Big Brother

"A brother shares childhood memories and grown-up dreams."
UNKNOWN

Our driver was going as far as Hemet. Jan and I paid for two bus tickets from Hemet to Riverside and from Riverside to L.A.

Still gun shy about taking risks, the bus was the most direct and safest way to reach Canoga Park. Waiting at the Riverside terminal for the 4 pm RTD bus to L.A., chatting with our bus driver Stanley, cafeteria food seemed a total come down from the organic cuisine we'd grown accustomed to at Valle Vista. Nobody was complaining. Food was food. Feasting on Wonderbread cheese sandwiches, I marvelled in the amazing kismet of having stayed at Meadowlark for a full week. Not only did we save money, no price could be levied on our exposure. Thanks to Jan for that one.

The ride from Riverside to L.A. was a beautiful one, helping to alleviate the sting of leaving the desert and remarkable locale behind. A change of scenery however proved to be an advantageous tool, teaching us not to get comfortable in any one place. Moving on enabled us to continue to build new relationships. Find our place in space as it were.

Back at Canoga Park around 9 pm., we were greeted by Vic, Patti, and Bobby. Confirmed to attend Mark's wedding, my brother would arrive Thursday — two days away.

In our absence, more mail arrived. Two letters were from Lorraine. She'd found work at the Banff Springs Hotel in Alberta. Jan was ecstatic to learn Gary had sent a note. Incorporating his signature "bloody idiots" on almost every page, amongst a lot of rambling, Gary's letter was hilarious, not different from the way he communicated in person. Currently employed at a hostel in Vancouver, he hoped to save enough money to visit Ontario in the late summer. A visit from Gary would definitely give us something to look forward to, when and if we found our way back home.

With specific instructions, Gary scribbled seven kisses on the last page of the letter. We were to divide three kisses apiece and would have to "fight over the seventh." Even on paper, Gary's ego and screwball personality came across loud and clear.

Secretly, I was delighted to receive a letter from my mom. Abandoning my grudge for sending the box of clothes I would never wear, in the spirit of Meadowlark, I realized it was futile clinging to negative energy attached to a silly incident weightless upon the scales of life.

My life.

Jan received correspondence from her mother and grandmother and there was a ten-page letter from Liz. Diligent about communicating back and forth as much as our nomadic lifestyle would allow, Liz informed me she had started taking the birth control pill. This was surprising news. She'd been having difficulties with menstrual cramps — the standard justification in those days to get the green light from a physician for a prescription. It didn't mean Liz wasn't telling the truth. As far as I knew, she wasn't sexually active, yet. Of course, *that* could have changed in our absence. Anything and everything could have changed. I supposed she wanted to be prepared for when somebody came along. That made sense. In the event that I was to meet someone and eventually become intimate, I'd want to be prepared, too.

So far, all was quiet on that front. I remained a virgin — not exactly an albatross around my neck, though I seriously expected I'd still be chaste upon our return to Canada. Jan and I'd met some great people. Excluding Gary who was more Jan's type, the only person I continued daydreaming about was Teddy — my infatuation fuelled, in part, because he was untouchable.

And older.

And broken.

Teddy's speedy metabolism was incredibly sexy too.

Returning to San Francisco in a few weeks, would I feel the same way?

The following day, Patti drove us to Northridge Plaza for appropriate wedding apparel that wasn't exorbitant. Though I'd forgiven her, I still rejected the clothes my mother sent, but didn't exactly have an extensive wardrobe either. At the mall, I managed to find a white peasant blouse I could wear overtop my wrap-around skirt to cover the bleach I'd managed to spill on it. Jan purchased a scarf, and cream-coloured, Indian style cotton blouse.

We were set.

That evening, Patti and Vic planned to fly with Bobby to Las Vegas and asked Jan and I to babysit. The day before, Mark had driven his car to Vegas so that he and Sarah would have a vehicle handy on Saturday after Bobby flew them there for their honeymoon — his wedding gift to the couple. Once Mark was picked up from wherever he'd parked his car, Vic, Patti, Mark and Bobby would fly back together later that might.

Anticipating his Thursday arrival, Chris called next day to say he'd be late. His plane delayed, my brother would meet us over on Calvin Avenue on Friday, one day before the wedding.

It was determined the three of us would stay at Mark's house and look after the three dogs and cat while Mark and Sarah honeymooned. At the end of the week, Jan and I would leave the city for Fresno, then move on to Yosemite National Park. My brother would return home.

Relieved to have an opportunity to relocate out of Canoga Park, we'd be giving Vic, Patti and their children space. Recalling a wise crack Bobby made the day before while downing half a pack of Coors, about the two of us "taking advantage" of Vic and Patti's kindness, he'd intimated we'd been there a month, which wasn't true at all. Not only that, Jan and I'd offered Vic money to cover us food-wise.

Ever the diplomat and standup person, Vic had come to our rescue. "You are not intrusive in the least. You've helped with the kids and pitched in making meals." Since neither Vic nor Mark had visited Canada in several years, Vic appreciated the opportunity to spend time with his Canadian family.

I believed him.

In the early 1970s, my cousin made a onetime voyage to Canada. Part of the vacation, Vic and Patti had stayed with my family. Extending them the same generosity the couple would (later) show us in Los Angeles; my parents brought them sightseeing, prepared home cooked meals, and treated them out to dinner. In addition to our seven-day visit a couple of weeks earlier, our return to the house in Canoga Park would last three days. If it weren't for the impending wedding, Jan and I wouldn't have returned to Canoga Park. The fact my brother would be in the city was another reason to track back to L.A.

Chris arrived at Calvin Avenue on Friday, mid-morning. Mark, Patti, Jan, and I were there to greet him. When my brother stepped out of a blue Ford Pinto rental vehicle, I rushed from the porch down the driveway and threw myself into his arms. Almost four months since leaving my family back home, clutching my big brother, I realized how much I missed them all.

Everybody piled into the house. Not for long. The day before the wedding, there were many pieces to put into place. Leaving Patti and Mark to take care of final details, speeding off in the Pinto, Chris, Jan, and I shot out to the coast. Driving the Pacific Coast Highway, arms straight out the window to caress the ocean breeze, proved a welcome change from the desert heat. Not only that, alone with my brother, I felt freed from stress and sensitivities.

The three of us huddled near a sand dune, we watched dedicated surfers give way to the adrenalin rush of the sea, as their boldly painted boards bounced robustly north and south, until the milky foam eventually delivered riders to shore. Then it started over again.

Single and looking for kicks during his California vacation, thrills for Chris included an invitation to a party at his friend Sally Kellerman's Hollywood Hills estate.

Jan and I were not invited.

Scouring the Malibu Beach area, locating a trinket shop, we selected a wedding card with an appropriate generic sentiment. Deciding to bestow our cousins with a financial gift, Chris's contribution would be substantially more.

Mark's final night of bachelorhood, everybody met up at a Cantonese restaurant near Calvin Avenue. Not having tried Cantonese, the cuisine tasted like Chinese take-out, only ten times better. Patti ordered a drink that combined Kahlúa, vanilla ice-cream, and ice. Insisting we sample it, she explained, "Learning to enjoy liqueur is a cultured thing to do."

Vic and Mark insisted on splitting the bill.

Worried earlier about the expense of eating out in a decent restaurant, Jan and I felt we had no choice. This was a family affair, meaning Bobby was absent. That was okay by me. I liked Bobby well enough but didn't want to get slammed again. Having had first-hand exchanges with individuals under the influence of alcohol who behave in ways they might not otherwise, I also knew about the pecking order of friendship.

Bobby was Mark's closest friend and best man.

We would try our damnedest to get on his good side.

Bride and Groom.

CHAPTER 27

The Wedding

"It's tough to stay married. My wife kisses the dog on the lips but won't drink from my glass."
RODNEY DANGERFIELD

Mark and Sarah's wedding was scheduled to take place at half past noon on Saturday, May 22. An outstanding start to the day, lustrous sunshine and a fairytale thermometer reading of 75 degrees had to be a solid indicator. The couple was off to a good start.

I showered, washed my hair and shaved my legs (they'd grown furry beneath my blue jeans). Arranging my new peasant top over my light brown wrap-around skirt, the bleach stain was appropriately concealed. Slipping into the pair of Roots Earth shoes I'd purchased on sale at Hotel Vancouver in the winter, I divided my long hair into two wet pieces, braided it and blew it dry. Unbraiding it, I brushed it out to give it a crimped appearance and fastened back two front strands with a gold barrette.

Accompanied by Jan in her red skirt, cream-coloured top, and sandals, two hippie girls who normally didn't attend formal functions, we looked presentable. Wearing matching green outfits, Vic and Patti left the house early to join the wedding party. Shortly ahead of schedule, Chris arrived in his Pinto to escort us to the chapel.

Outfitted in a white lace bodice and lengthy gown, Sarah's lace train extended to the bottom step of the altar. Her long blonde hair scrupulously styled in an up-do, eyes heightened by turquoise eye shadow and coral lipstick, Mark's new bride was easily a Catherine Deneuve clone. Dressed in complementary shades of green, peach, yellow and lavender, likewise stunning were Sarah's four bridesmaids. Matching his fiancée in the Hollywood glam department, donning a coiffed moustache, slicked black hair, blinding white tux and tails, black bow tie, and white shoes, Cousin Mark was pure class.

Before the ceremony began, Sarah presented Jan and me with twin bouquets of lavender flowers tied by yellow ribbons. It was a sweet inclusive gesture. Proudly decked out in their dress-up clothes, Sarah's two kids were happy as clams. They were getting a new dad after all.

Mark and Sarah vowed to respect honour and conform until death, and then Mark placed a big fat smooch on Sarah's lips for the adoring crowd. Smiling happily, the bride and groom posed outside for photographs.

Lanni's Inn, a bar/lounge combo in Reseda, had been reserved for the post-wedding bash. Adopting the role of chauffeur, in grand style, Bobby escorted Mark and Sarah to the Inn in a spanking new red Lincoln Continental rented for the occasion. Pulling up in front, Bobby hopped out first, gallantly holding the door for Sarah and Mark, who subsequently ushered Sarah and her protracted lace train into the restaurant. Lanni's was open daily to the public for dinner; the reception was scheduled for four hours.

Ensconced within an army of charcoal portraits of famous cowboy heroes from 1950s film and television shows, within the black and red interior, Jan, Chris, and I found our name plates on a table in the company of relatives we'd not met. Darren, our great Uncle Joe's son on my mother's father's side, and his wife Jeannette were practicing psychologists in the L.A. area. Chowing down on cheese and crackers, Doritos, and spicy homemade guacamole dip — a new best friend in the dip department — we conversed easily with Darren and Jeannette. In midst of multiple toasts to the bride and groom, filling our faces and drinking Bud as if our lives depended on it, Darren extended a dinner engagement at their home in Sherman Oaks the following Thursday.

Appetizers and half-drunken speeches preceded the presentation of a delicious, three-tiered vanilla wedding cake. During the calamity and celebration, Mark and Sarah were insistent the three of us take the leftover slab back to Calvin Avenue. Otherwise, the cake would have been trashed.

Driving back to Reseda in Chris's Pinto, most of the back seat consumed by half the cake, to prevent the vanilla icing from melting onto the car's vinyl interior, Jan and I rolled the windows all the way down.

Tossing our gear into the back bedroom of Mark's house, we changed out of our wedding attire and then headed out to the Van Nuys Airport where the newlyweds would fly away on their adventure. Concluding a few days in Vegas, during their three-week honeymoon, Mark and Sarah had plans to visit British Columbia and Alberta. It would be Sarah's first trip to Canada.

Following their departure, taking a ride out to Westwood, we checked out the UCLA campus and returned to Calvin Avenue to watch an old flick and eat pizza and leftover wedding cake. Hyperactivity likely brought on by their father's sudden disappearance, for the better part of the evening, Mark's three frenzied dogs, Fred, Mitten, and Sammy chased one another up and down the hallway. Immune to the rambunctious behavior exhibited by his siblings, eying the other three, Mark's calico Joe shot them a stern look that suggested, "Better not do anything stupid while Dad's away or he'll hear about it."

Sunday morning, three tidy piles of dog shit were dispersed in various patches on the living room carpet. From the looks of the hardened vanilla icing spotted in their fur, Sammy and Mitten had helped themselves to the cake that was too big to fit into the fridge. After a midnight snack, Jan and I'd absently left a big chunk on the dining table. Fortunately, the dogs saved us some leftovers.

Now, cake is great any old time, but after several gluttonous helpings the day before, we were nauseated by the sight of it. Not having discussed the grocery list for the week ahead, I didn't want to lean on my brother for handouts. Expert at making do with less, unless Chris suggested otherwise, we would stick to our usual menu that included cake.

While I cleaned up the shit, Jan scouted a hiding place for the cake on the top shelf of the hall closet. Mid-morning, the three of us left for Canoga Park for a day trip to the Santa Barbara Mission in Vic's beloved Ford Galaxy.

A trendy, attractive upscale resort destination ninety miles north of Los Angeles, Santa Barbara rests comfortably between the Pacific Ocean and the Ynez Mountains. With the habour and hiking trails, wine tasting opportunities, lively nightlife, educational institutions, wilderness exploration sites and a terrific view of the sea and mountains from practically every point in the district, Santa Barbara easily embraces its reputation as the "American Riviera." Unable to afford amenities barring free ones, Jan and I stuck to the basics as usual. A dedicated history buff, Vic's aim for bringing us to Santa Barbara, to educate his Canadian cousins, began with a tour of the Mission.

Founded by the Franciscan Order in 1786, The Santa Barbara Spanish Mission (known as the 'Queen' of all California Missions) is a grand, distinguished structure; tenth of its kind. Constructed for the conversion of the indigenous Chumash Tribe to Christianity, many of the exterior clay edifices were built by the hands of the Chumash Indians, including the reservoir and water treatment system. Meticulously crafted, elemental fabrications bearing symbols of early Christianity are etched into stain glass windows in the sanctuary at the front of the chapel, and detailed comprehensively on painted murals along the interior walls on either side of the wood pews.

It was an impressive historical sight, though after an hour or so we grew restless.

We headed to Rocky Nook Park to picnic. Like a magician pulling a rabbit out of a hat, Val had snuck a case of Schlitz beer into the cooler — a great stroke of foresight.

Down at the Santa Barbara marina and beach area, we perused the works of local artisans. On sale were handmade arts and crafts. Hoping to score with affluent tourists that had come out in droves on the sunlit Sunday afternoon, artists displayed works representing the history of local native tribes. Continuing along the boardwalk, Chris purchased an original piece; a delineation of horses and stagecoach illustrated on canvas, and watercolour of a lone palm tree.

Returning to Reseda early evening, we fed the dogs, cat, and fish and surveyed the disorder infesting inside the house growing more menacing by the minute.

Jan and I decided to do something about it.

To be fair, we three hadn't created most of the mess in our short time at Calvin Avenue. Accumulating in the days and weeks leading up to the wedding, crap was strewn everywhere. As unpaying guests, bringing a semblance of order was the least we could do. Cleaning the place would be our official wedding gift to Mark and Sarah. Consequently, to say thank you for their hospitality during our visit, Jan, Chris, and I invited Vic, Patti, and the kids for dinner in a couple of days. Keeping the place orderly not only for our company, but for the duration of our stay would be tough. With four animals, a fish, and three people in a small house our work was cut out for us. Short-term employment at Hotel Vancouver wouldn't be in vain.

Jan and I dusted, vacuumed, scrubbed, scoured, and scraped until we were hot, exhausted, and ready for bed. Since we hadn't eaten any dinner, sustenance was required to calm our grumbling stomachs. Upon helping myself to a big hunk of wedding cake, I brushed my teeth and lay down on top of my sleeping bag in the steamy back bedroom. Listening to Mitten whimper to sleep, little did she know her master had swapped allegiances.

Mark and his new bride wouldn't be returning to Calvin Avenue any day soon.

Los Angeles patio. Home of photographer Joel Sussman.

CHAPTER 28

Revelations

"Los Angeles is 72 suburbs in search of a city."
DOROTHY PARKER

Mitten pined for Mark most of that second night. Poor thing. She'd taken the abandonment a lot harder than Fred, Sammy, or Joe, who pretended not to notice or care.

Monday breakfast, Jan and I hacked off another sizeable piece of wedding cake, only to discover my brother had risen early and gone. Stealthily, he'd snuck away for a feed of bacon and eggs at Duke's in West Hollywood, a notorious Los Angeles food chain.

When he returned, the three of us set out browsing used record stores in Westwood. In addition to picking up a Carlos Santana LP for Dee back home, I treated myself to *Pleasures of the Harbor*, the same Phil Ochs album the Good Samaritan had introduced to us at HOOM. The downside to acquiring these fine purchases was carting *two* records in my duffle bag for the next couple months at least, along with the fear of damaging them. Not about to ask Jan to share responsibility, I was on my own.

Chris treated us to a bite at the Hamburger Hamlet, and then drove down to Santa Monica to the American Youth Hostel Association. A handful of the listings advertised in our current guidebook had turned out to be a bust, so we were keen to pick up an *updated* manual. Destinations such as Meadowlark were few and far between. To our surprise, because Jan and I weren't American citizens, United States hostel books were off limits unless we wanted to register as (paying) members of the Association.

Leaving Santa Monica, feasting our eyes on the homes of the rich and famous, we crept along Coldwater Canyon Road before taking a drive to Old Town Calabasas in the hills, west of the San Fernando Valley, northwest of the Santa Monica Mountains. Once an old Western town, the village had been converted into an upscale shopping destination. Judging

by many of the original adobe-styled structures and austere beauty, despite
its prosperity, Calabasas managed to retain much of its original charm.

Jan and I purchased a couple of postcards. Armed with his new Nikon,
my brother captured area attractions.

Since his arrival, I'd wanted to talk to Chris about the specifics of
our adventures, particularly HOOM and Meadowlark. Eager for his feed-
back and input, most of all, I longed for my brother's stamp of approval.
Somehow, the synthesis of the two communities had elucidated my scrap
of faith reforming it into something relatable. A splintering of my psyche
was at work, causing me to question whether I might be a veritable candi-
date for The Holy Order. Simultaneously, my sensible self reproached my
other self for being susceptible and rash. In some ways, the whole thing
seemed laughable. Why was I toying with the idea of joining a religious
order anyway? Maybe I was seeking an escape route. Joining The Order
could feel like a permanent vacation from the expected.

I had to come up with a better reason.

Dropping half-assed hints to Jan about the logistics of carrying out a
harebrained scheme such as joining The Order, the fact that she hadn't
balked was promising, even a little surprising. One thing was certain; any
debate about joining a cult was not a discussion for Cousin Vic's disbelieving ears. Armed with a healthy cynicism and skeptical view of the world,
undoubtedly, he would eyeball me narrowly through my rose-coloured
glasses and snip facetiously, "You're crazy."

I hadn't done anything crazy yet.

Returning to the house around dinnertime, downing another couple
of pieces of wedding cake, we washed the food down with homogenized
milk. The television running interference, I confiscated the opportunity
to feel my brother out about HOOM, and started out by explaining how
the organization's philosophies supported similar practices utilized by Dr.
Loomis (a reputable physician!) and the Meadowlark Centre.

Voicing my feelings out loud was scary. To spare Chris from finding
out I was a nut, or worse, a loser, I didn't deluge more than necessary, and
neglected to mention anything about possibly *joining* The Order. My
brother was on vacation. Why spoil his trip?

Extolling the virtues of the people and places we'd known and seen, on
my brother's end, there was no visible recoiling of the body or eye rolling.
Absorbing my little speech like a Dharma convert, Chris didn't pass judgment on my passion or sense of logic. In essence, we were kindred spirits.

Influenced by the anti-establishment, and counter-culture phenomenon that swept North America and parts of Europe during the 1960s, as a teenager, my brother embraced overtures initiated by the Yippies, a radical movement that merged hippies and the New Left activism instigated by two New Yorkers, social activists/anarchists, Jerry Rubin and Abbie Hoffman. Through his interest in journalism, in 1970, Chris became a non-paid member of a subversive media group that peddled underground newspapers in Yorkville, a onetime underground faction of Toronto. This voluntary task carried out in an effort to educate people about the evil and destructive tendencies of the conservative and corporate classes, spun off into the study of Scientology. For a few years, Chris even subscribed to monthly Scientology newsletters.

Flashing his eyes at Jan who hadn't spoken a word, I sensed Chris attempting to read her thoughts. Cringing, I held my breath.

"It all sounds on the level," he finally said. "Just don't jump into anything."

"Thanks." I agreed. "I won't."

Nonchalant as I'd ever known him to be, Chris's tidy advice was the best I could have hoped for. Anyway, an agenda more crucial weighed on his mind. Sally Kellerman had arranged a Friday night date at a Hollywood restaurant.

My brother would be having dinner and drinks with "Hot Lips Houlihan."

Patti called in the evening to let us know more mail had arrived. Having made plans to see the new Western feature, *The Missouri Breaks*, starring Jack Nicholson and Marlon Brando at the Encino Theatre, Chris, Jan, and I would swing by Canoga Park on our way to the late show.

Three letters addressed to me lay on the kitchen counter. There was an artsy postcard from Yvette bearing a photograph of an Escher painting I hadn't seen before, a note from Jen, and the first piece of correspondence from my father. *Had my mom persuaded him to write?* My dad was a man of few words. If one of us approached him about a subject or concern, he was open for business, but wouldn't dream of offering advice for the hell of it.

Waiting until we were back in the car, tearing open the envelope, I began reading.

Conveying on paper what he would never be able to say in person, my father wrote how he admired my spirit and courage to set out.

Leaving home at fifteen to join a swing band, much to the disappointment of his parents who held aspirations of him attending Julliard or even med school, Dad never finished high school. Impatient to earn a degree to study music, my father wanted to be free to chart his own course and make his own mistakes.

Accomplished in most everything he set out to do — musician, arranger, and bandleader — Dad also conquered the game of golf and learned to water-ski. My father had travelled overseas, debated politics like nobody's business, and was a better-than-average painter. Realizing his dream of becoming an entrepreneur, he had wholly succeeded. In his heart of hearts however, big band jazz was what invigorated and calmed his soul. Long after leaving the music business in the mid-sixties, consoling what-should-have-been with alcohol, Dad had fallen into a routine of pining for the good old days.

I missed my father's poker face, his nervous gum chewing. Most of all, I missed our quirky talks.

In conclusion, Dad told me he loved and was proud of me. If he'd ever said those words in person, I couldn't remember. Next chance I got, I would write both my parents.

Pocketing the letter, inside the Pinto's alcove, I concealed my emotions. Rereading my father's words three times more back at Calvin Avenue, I tucked the note in the envelope, and placed it beneath the head of my sleeping bag for safekeeping.

Tapia Park, Los Angeles, California.

CHAPTER 29

Life is (Sex on) a Beach

"Count the scattered crystals below your feet;
I will reward you with the ocean."
JILL C. NELSON, *May 1976*

We were on tap to host Vic and the family for dinner on Tuesday. To make some kind of impact on our guests' appetites, we'd keep it simple, and with luck, the food would be edible. Needing a little inspiration, Chris, Jan, and I returned to Malibu to lust the sun and sand.

The tourist quotient at Malibu that morning was a dull roar. Not officially summer yet, on Tuesday, most of the grown-ups were occupied working day jobs. The fact we didn't have to scrounge for beach space made for a pleasurable afternoon. Adjoining an emerald painted ocean and azure sky, portions of the beach were open to the public in those days. The Mediterranean-like "Bu" was the natural world's answer to a psychedelic episode — it was simply brilliant.

Jan and I swam a little and checked out the guys. Intent on presenting a slapdash edition of homegrown California beach boy for his Friday dinner date with Sally, my brother was fastidious about getting a suntan. Four hours later, the three of us scarlet red, we returned to Reseda. There was no way to camouflage our burns, but a few cold Genesee's made it easier to put on game faces.

Half past six, Vic knocked on our front door. Bowing chivalrously upon his entry into the house, Jan and I were presented with duplicate bouquets of pale pink tulips. Guardedly impressed by how tidy the place appeared (on the surface, anyway), Patti exclaimed how Mark's house hadn't looked "this good" since my aunt and uncle lived there.

This had to be an exaggeration. Using limited cleaning supplies, improvising, Jan and I'd gotten creative — meaning there was a lot of sweeping under the carpet — in the truest sense. Good thing Patti hadn't witnessed the dog shit the morning before, I doubt she would have given us high marks for cleanliness.

Our dinner menu was as diverse (and scaled down) as what our combined culinary skills allowed. Essentially, Jan and I'd thawed everything from the freezer that was edible. Serving fried shrimp as the main, sides were Brussels sprouts, peas, cauliflower, and a green leafy concoction — my poor woman's attempt at emulating the fabulous California salads whipped up by Patti.

On the surface, nobody objected to our carte du jour. Nobody exited partway through the meal to throw up.

Compliments to the chefs.

At the head of the table in the small dining room sat my brother. Considering that he too was living on borrowed time, this was an amusing posture. Enjoying play-acting California homeowner and doting host, throughout the meal Chris kept the conversation and beverages flowing.

In those days, folks didn't give much consideration to the dangers of drinking and driving. Out on the highways and freeways, it was every man and woman for themselves. Though indulging like the rest of us that night, Vic and Patti were two conscientious people who wouldn't subject their kids to a scary ride back to Canoga Park. They knew when to pull back. A couple hours before the evening wrapped, Patti switched to soda.

Later, Chris switched on Mark's gargantuan television (my cousin was always ahead of his time), flipping through channels until he settled on the *Dean Martin Show*. One of Dean's guests was comedian Charlie Callas. It suddenly dawned on me: Jan and I had actually seen *Callas* in person the month before at the Sheraton Universal Hotel, not Sid Caesar as we'd believed. Known for screwball comedy skits and riotous sound effects, Callas had old Dino splitting his gut.

Without much arm-twisting, on Wednesday I persuaded Chris to drive Jan and me to Disneyland at Anaheim. Whittling down our wish list to determine how to best allocate our cash, Disneyland was the exception. Only a hard-boiled grouch can resist the draw of insatiable crowds and the amusement park's attractions — we had a ball. Even so, everybody has a limit as to how much theme park one can tolerate.

Picking up a warrior doll, a new relic for his farmhouse in Troy, Chris had something to show for his trouble. Jan bought herself a Mini Mouse silver charm for her bracelet back home, while I purchased a pair of hoop earrings.

Too early to return to Reseda and the animals, my brother suggested we take a drive to Manhattan Beach, (then) a quiet, undeveloped setting along the Pacific Coast Highway. Lolling on the damp white sand at twilight, eavesdropping upon the roar of the ocean's calling, we joked about slipping into an idyllic beach existence, camouflaged in a van or hut. Fixed within that gypsy state of mind, for a time, everything seemed practicable.

That evening was one of the best times spent with my brother.

Thursday morning, we set out for a hike in Tapia Park.

Lodged within the Santa Monica Mountains in Calabasas, Tapia is the threshold to Malibu Creek State Park. While Malibu Creek runs directly through numerous peaks and plateaus, weaving amongst Tapia's 7000-acre integrative recreational region are hiking and riding trails.

It was a dusty hot day, the kind that encrusts your body in a film of grime and sweat, attracting elements like a magnet. The key, stay hydrated and wear sun protective clothing, you'd hardly think to carry a canteen while hiking, much less cart around designer water bottles or consider lighter coloured garments. Sunscreen was not in vogue. Winging it was the order of the day. Rather than be proactive, habitually, we dealt with fallout.

Trying to cope with intense heat in jeans and t-shirts (Jan and I never did purchase additional summer wear in Hemet); the three of us embarked the sandy trails. Chris in the lead, we hiked up and down footpaths along the creek until venturing upon an extraordinary canyon vista. Seeking refuge from the throbbing heat, shaded under the able arms of a colossal oak, Jan and I took a time-out. In a zone shooting the wide-open clefts with his Nikon, my brother meandered along dirt pathways and rock. Keen to photograph the landscape from an alternative perspective, when he returned, Chris suggested we walk the backbone terrain back to the car.

Stepping in single file along the powdery laneway, glancing ahead to the middle of the corridor leading to another opening, I saw two figures in the distance wrestling on the ground. About thirty feet ahead at the forefront, Chris led Jan, who divided a straight line between us. Edging closer to the two shapes before us, I distinguished one male and one female. They weren't wearing any clothes.

Here, in the midst of nowhere, the couple was screwing — in missionary position. Bodies, thighs, and feet entwined one another's torsos. There was no alternate bypass through to the clearing without walking past the lovers, nor was there time to call ahead to my brother and say, "Um, do you think maybe we should *turn* around? Take another *route*?"

Now practically on top of the couple, from my vantage point, it didn't appear that Chris stopped to gawk. Dashing past the pair, he was almost completely out of my line of view. Mimicking my brother's actions, darting quietly along without so much as volunteering a hand wave or greeting, Jan ignored the grunts and groans until well beyond the deed.

Bringing up the caboose, by the time I approached, the duo was so enthralled I panicked the guy would shoot his load — the absolute *last* thing on earth I wanted to witness.

Whatever happened to their clothes? There wasn't a stitch anywhere in sight. One could deduce either they were nudists, living in the rocks or knolls somewhere on the park premises, or they'd stashed their clothes in a nearby tree or behind a boulder. The perimeter of the passageway mostly enclosed, the closest trees were two to three hundred feet away.

Confounded all the way back to the car, I tried to approximate at which point did they discard their clothing, figure out where they'd *do it*, and walk all the way over to the pathway to begin (or continue) foreplay, if there was any. I suspected there wasn't. This act was born from a primal need.

Reaching the parking lot, sitting in the Pinto, Chris busied himself with a roadmap. Though embarrassed to say anything about the copulating couple to my big brother, I could tell Jan was ready to bust a gut. Addressing our sexual encounter of a third kind, she and I entertained the notion, maybe three times really *is* a charm.

Signs were pointing everywhere. Sex could conceivably happen to me.

Sketch of actor Jack Nicholson as R.P. McMurphy in One Flew Over the Cuckoo's Nest, *May 1976.*

CHAPTER 30

Sherman Oaks

"Let your soul stand cool and composed before a million universes."
WALT WHITMAN

Part of the San Fernando Valley, Sherman Oaks is principally an upper middle class, Caucasian-dominated, urban Los Angeles environ. Inside and out, Cousin Darren and Jeannette's tastefully groomed two-story spread suggested long time money.

Formal mahogany interior embellished by heavy drapes, posh furnishings, a fine collection of Native American art, and intriguing bobbles reeked of success and prosperity — the ultimate American Dream. Interestingly, Darren, a gangly man with black balding hair and dark moustache and his pleasantly round, attractive partner, didn't look or act the part of a well-oiled couple. Down-to-earth and accommodating, Darren hurried the group of us through the main foyer, introducing Chris, Jan, and I to their spry, five-year-old son Joseph named after Darren's father. Patti, who'd hired a sitter for her own children, was startled to learn of Joseph's inclusion in the adult evening.

Folding everybody into the den, Darren encouraged everybody to get comfortable.

Excitable, superficial chatter followed.

Though we'd met only a few days before, I immediately liked Darren and Jeannette. Well into their forties, at the prime of their lives and careers, the two full-time working professionals had chosen to take on the challenge of raising a gifted kindergarten aged boy; a virtual mop of blonde hair who was not their biological child. Precocious and intellectually inclined, evidently, Joseph had taken favourably to his privileged environment. As smart as the boy was, by contrast, Vic and Patti's children, a pair of delightfully clever, unsophisticated kids, seemed unsullied by the distractions of the grown-up world.

Like Patti, Jeannette was an excellent chef. Paired with generous help-ings of sparkling California wine from a seemingly endless bottle, guests were served chicken and beansprouts, brown rice, honey-glazed carrots, shredded noodles, and baked green beans. Educating us on the origins of grape varietals, a wine connoisseur, Darren encouraged our group to tease our palates with differential nuances, textures, and faint colour dif-ferences. Green around the edges and everywhere in between, Jan and I were not patronized because of age or inexperience. Doing my best to live up to expectations, I made sure not to become a drunken fool. On the other hand, liberated from their children for a few hours, Patti was well on her way to becoming the life of the party. Effervescent and witty, her free spirit and sense of adventure was enviable. In his quieter way, it appeared that Darren liked to party too. Through his work and other avenues, occasionally, Darren rubbed elbows with Hollywood pedigree. He and Tom Laughlin, creator, writer, and star of the 1971 hit film *Billy Jack*, were good friends and played golf together. Darren had even been to Laughlin's home. Learning this newsworthy information, I pumped my cousin for the scoop.

What was Laughlin's house like? What was *he* like, *in person*?

Darren played it cool. Clearly, he was amused. Promising to pass along my admiration of Laughlin's portrayal of the anti-everybody, Green Beret Vietnam Vet and martial arts expert Billy Jack, according to Darren, Laughlin's onscreen character wasn't much of a diversion from what he'd come to know about Laughlin in real life.

Engaging us with stories about our mutual family, Darren's father Joe had come to California in the 1930s and built rental cabins in Encinitas, an ocean town where my mother and father lived a few years after they were first married and had learned to make ceramics. Like Vic, Darren had once visited his father's Quebec hometown. Unable to detect a resem-blance to anybody on my mother's side of the family, Darren ventured to guess that my blonde hair, lightly freckled fair skin, and brown eyes conveyed a Netherland heritage on my father's side. He was off base (my father is Scottish descent), but I wholeheartedly approved of this assessment.

Moving into the family room following dinner, we were served Sambuca from tiny crystal glasses and frozen cherry yogurt on sticks. Darren put Cat Stevens' *Teaser and the Firecat* on the record player; con-versation segued into a pot-smoking debate. Uniformly, Chris, Jan, Darren, Jeannette and I favoured legalization. Vic and Patti were opposed. On the political front, both families supported the Democratic Party and anticipated that Georgia Governor Jimmy Carter would oust their current Republican President, Gerald Ford, in the autumn election. Despite their similarities, approaches to parenting between the two couples were markedly different. Darren and Jean allowed their son the kind of freedom Vic and Patti wouldn't abide. As cute as he was, Joseph could be a little hellion and proved to be annoyingly hyperactive. Like a monkey with its ass on fire, to win his parent's attention, during dinner, the diminutive Einstein proceeded to jump on every piece of furniture within range — interrupting conversation umpteen times, screaming, even kicking — guaranteeing that everybody was aware of his presence. Considering their academic competence and urbane qualities, I thought Darren and Jeannette were amazingly patient people.

The evening soon wound down. Darren took Jan and me aside, inviting us into the study. Astonished by a staggering library of books, films, and memorabilia, I longed to stay long enough to graze Darren's collection. Reaching inside of a rosewood desk drawer, my cousin retrieved two white, letter-sized envelopes. Waving one of them in the air, a self-conscious grin opened his kindly face. "Here," he said, "I'd like you to have these."

On the drive back to Reseda, Patti rambled on about how permissive Darren and Jeannette were with Joseph and that they'd allowed him to use their home like Disneyland. Vic and Patti were typical parents, the way most kids expected and trusted adults to behave. Conviction, discipline, and dependability will usually trump being your kid's best pal. Despite being stuck on the experimental channel, there was also a lot to be admired about Darren and Jeannette. In the end, the two couples' hearts were in the right place.

Tearing open the envelopes, Jan and I discovered a crisp, $20 American bill folded neatly inside each one.

Nauseated from over consumption of alcohol, Friday morning Jan stuck to a liquid diet. She was the smart one.

I ate the remainder of wedding cake.

On the hunt for a housewarming gift for Sally, in the afternoon, Chris, Jan, and I set off for Northridge Plaza. While I searched through gift cards to find an appropriate 'Thank You' note for Vic and Patti, Chris settled on a philodendron in a decorative rattan basket.

Confounded about which route to take to Sally's, leaving Northridge Plaza, Chris inched the Pinto along Laurel Canyon Road. Winding our way through the Hollywood Hills, snaking along Woodrow Wilson Drive, we eventually stopped directly in front of a four-digit number marked on the curb of the sidewalk.

Appropriately concealed by liberal lime foliage and Loquat trees, Kellerman's property was attractively located. Satisfied having found his way, heading confidently down Sunset, my brother grabbed the PCH exit toward Malibu.

Growing increasingly anxious about his dinner engagement with Sally, trying to manage expectations, Chris reminded himself he'd dined with the actress before, in Canada. Now, he was on Sally's turf, and Kellerman was a legitimate movie star. My brother wanted to make a good impression.

Late afternoon, Chris dropped Jan and me at Vic and Patti's as pre-arranged, and then departed for the Hollywood Hills. As much as we looked forward to hanging out with Vic, Patti, and the kids, Jan and I were antsy to move on. Too polite to say it, I knew my cousins would be happy to have their routine restored. Retrieving family albums that had belonged to his parents, my cousin told a few juicy stories and showed us pictures of my mom during her early twenties. Jan was the only one to point out the resemblance between my mother's appearance and the way I looked that spring. Everybody else agreed I resembled my dad's side of the family.

Up until the point when somebody reintroduced (what had become) the litigious subject about travel, Bobby had been well behaved. Tensing up, I zipped my trap. There was good reason to keep quiet. For the next fifteen minutes, much the same way he'd done prior to Mark and Sarah's wedding, Bobby centered Jan and me out for "cashing in" on Vic and Patti's good nature. Trying his best to intercede, Vic soon gave up.

Bobby was on a roll.

The same age as Mark, Bobby had many good qualities, albeit, listening uncomfortably to his pessimism and negativity about a number of subjects, I wondered if possibly Bobby was envious of Jan and me. Maybe he was envious of Mark. Or lonely. Reflecting later that night on the low blows and judgments cast about youths and the two of us (thankless ingrates) in general, I thought about Chris's evening. Thankfully, he'd bypassed all the nonsense and was hopefully having the time of his life.

Our final full day in Los Angeles, Vic thought Jan and I might enjoy a trip to Chinatown and L.A.'s Grand Central Market. Part of the afternoon was eaten up window shopping, walking around the market area, sampling free French stick and cheese. Pointing out MacArthur Park, the same one mentioned in the song recorded by actor Richard Harris, helped fill time while waiting on news from my brother.

Close to twenty-four hours, there was no word.

On the patio early evening reading (I'd recently started *Helter Skelter*) while everybody else (Bobby included) left for the movies, around half past seven, Chris called the house. Dining in Hollywood with Sally, Claire, and Claire's friend, he would meet us later in Canoga Park.

My brother was excited, that was unmistakable. Devising scenarios about how Chris and Sally had spent their time, Jan and I'd made bets that over the course of two days, something sexual had taken place.

One hour later, a car engine slowed outside. I ran to look out the front window. Pulling into the driveway, the Pinto stopped. I heard the engine cut. My brother, appearing frazzled, stepped outside of the car wearing the same clothes he'd had on the day before. The only difference, they were crumpled. Glad to finally get first dibs on all the news, Jan and I rushed out to the driveway.

Even in fading daylight, Chris looked spacey, worse for wear. He and Sally had dinner Friday night, and then returned to Woodrow Wilson to party. By the looks of him, Hollywood parties are far more heinous than any bash my brother had previously attended or even hosted.

Inviting a few friends to her home, the evening was comprised of a generous picking of the popular Hollywood crowd — mostly producers and sycophants. Sally's guests also included veteran movie director Robert Altman (*M*A*S*H*, *Come Back to the Five and Dime*, *The Player*), and Don Brewer, drummer for Grand Funk Railroad. Scoring an invite to Robert Altman's estate the following Tuesday evening, which consisted of a grouping of prestigious household names including *Jack Nicholson*, because of his already booked return flight home from Los Angeles on Sunday, my brother took a rain check.

I wouldn't say Chris spilled the beans — at the very least, he blew a few stray farts. The Kellerman party was categorically outrageous. While the patio bartender kept hard-to-pronounce drinks rolling all night long, a live band performed by an octagon shaped swimming pool. The eventual blowout, a nudie affair that combined booze, some sexual escapades, and illicit drugs, was the first time my brother had sampled cocaine.

This piece of information blew my mind. As far as I knew, Chris stuck to alcohol and smoked very little weed. Never much interested in chemicals, in those days, my brother was a beer aficionado who later grew to appreciate wine.

In any event, Chris had a major buzz on that was wearing thin. Whether it was the adrenalin kick or something else, I couldn't be certain. Never having witnessed him amped on anything other than alcohol, this observation was fascinating to realize. For a brief interlude, Chris was the most effusive, animated person in the room. Hands down, my brother had experienced a frenetic time, never to be duplicated. After the party fizzled around dawn, he crashed in one of Sally's guest bedrooms. Probably, he'd wilted into bed. Knowing how Chris preferred intimate gatherings and quiet conversation to big whoop-it-ups, the highlight of interacting with the Hollywood crowd was probably dining in the company of Sally, Claire, and Claire's friend.

The gang arrived home from the movies. Once Patti got the kids off to bed, Chris regaled with highlights from the last couple of days in the company of "Hot Lips Houlihan." Understandably cagey, it was apparent he wanted to keep minutiae of the events to himself. That was cool. I'd have prattled on to everyone in the room, and after coming down from the buzz, regretted it. My brother had more class than that. Either as a means to protect himself or my family, sometimes to the detriment of others, Chris was notorious for withholding incidental details.

Before heading back to Calvin Avenue, somewhat of an imbroglio ensued. Opinions about society, travel, the establishment, and other divisive topics I would have preferred to avoid, were expressed. In defense, I made some tempered statements about youths and individualism, opinions that were immediately squashed by Bobby, who really seemed to have it in for me. Beer propped in his hand, friendly and neutral, though not at his best, my brother didn't offer much in the way of an opinion. Jan, who wisely avoided conflict by remaining quiet as I'd done the night before, was suddenly called on the carpet to offer her views. Muttering a couple of vague statements, by wisely keeping her comments generic, the girl could not be contradicted or misconstrued.

I had a lot to learn from my friend.

Striking off on our excursion together, at different points, I'd been proud of and in awe of Jan. Especially, I admired her nerve that final night in L.A. Her handling of the situation, effectively holding the wolf at arm's length, scored big points in our favour. The conversation finally mitigated, we returned to our respective corners of the ring.

No hard feelings.

Documenting in my journal some of the points raised that evening inferring irresponsibility and selfishness of young people, I couldn't help feeling frustrated. Nevertheless, sitting unarmed in the line of fire had facilitated a constructive finish. Maybe it was another test to see if we could hold our own. Either way, it felt good to extract from the well of positive fortification again. Something I'd neglected to do since returning to Los Angeles.

Evangel Home, 1955. Opening as a boarding house, its first resident was an alcoholic woman. PHOTO FROM HTTP://EVANGELHOME.ORG/

CHAPTER 31
Evangel Home

"I'm actually an evangelical atheist, but there is something I recognize about religion — it gives people a chance to surrender."
BRIAN ENO

Jan and I cleaned Mark's house, starting by washing and drying an intimidating week's worth of dirty dishes. By the time we were packed and ready to go, the place had little trace of anyone having set foot inside. Giving special attention to Fred, Mitten, Sammy, and Joe, I would miss caring for Mark's pets and took comfort in the assurance they would be in capable hands. On task to pick up where we left off, Bobby would assume the daily duty of feeding and nurturing.

Over at Vic and Patti's, Jan and I presented our California family with a card of gratitude, along with a clay figurine from The Mission in Santa Barbara. Squeezing each family member tightly before proceeding with all our gear toward the Pinto, there were mixed emotions. Likely years before I would see them all again, the reality brought me down.

Insistent that we stay in touch, kindly crediting our adventurous spirits, my cousin told me not to change a thing.

Reading between the lines, Cousin Vic's words did my heart good. I certainly didn't feel like an opportunist anymore than anybody would that spent time with family living 3000 miles away. Vic's confidence in us was his way of letting me know he and Patti were happy to oblige.

They were on our side.

Though we were intent on hitchhiking to Fresno, my cousin wouldn't hear of anything contrary to a proper lift. On his way to the airport, my brother offered to drop us at the Greyhound depot in North Hollywood. Scheduled to depart late morning, the bus was due to arrive in Fresno at half past four. The trip was expensive, $10 each. Both $20 richer now after our dinner at Darren and Jeannette's, the extra money would be put toward the fare.

Splitting with my brother at the North Hollywood bus station proved more difficult than I'd anticipated. The week in L.A. together was the first occasion wherein our schedules intertwined; I sensed things would never be the same again. Discussing the possibility of my moving in with Chris in the fall at the farm he rented in Troy, it was hard somehow to imagine living there, possibly with Steve as well, as if the three of us were kids again. Even so, the proposal made it easier to go our separate ways. In case I burned through every other option, Troy was another alternative.

Pulling out of the North Hollywood station half past eleven, the Greyhound ferried past sites and attractions halfway familiar to us. The combined two and a half week's stay in Los Angeles provided Jan and me with an armload of memories — mostly good ones. Passing by the willowy network of red narrow track at Magic Mountain, an amusement park Gary had raved about, I was awestruck by the way in which the metal elaborately twisted and turned rising into the clouds. Nudging Jan's shoulder, I announced, *"next* time, we'll have to take a spin." In truth, I was terrified of roller coasters, or any fast ride that turned you upside down.

Riding north through Bakersfield, my mind turned to HOOM, Teddy, Brother James, and others at Steiner Street. Within the week, Jan and I planned to return to San Francisco. I imagined what had changed, if anything. Would Teddy stick out his new assignment with The Holy Order?

I couldn't imagine anybody or any group housebreaking him.

The YWCA in Fresno was a short distance from the Greyhound terminal. Having been confined to our seats for five hours, we didn't mind the hike. Walking the mile or so along sparsely populated streets from the terminal to the Y, looking up and down the road at pale houses in dire need of fresh paint, chain link fences framing every other property, Fresno felt very unlike Canoga Park or even Reseda. Disquieting, as if someone might bust out from behind a half-demolished building, hold us up for lack of something better to do, I reached my hand into my jean's pocket to ensure the few American bills I'd stuffed inside were still there.

Arriving at 1033 H Street in Central Fresno, fee for one night's stay was $6.50 — too rich for our blood, especially after the bus fare we'd coughed up. Lately, we'd lived the high life, working for our keep at Meadowlark, staying free at my relatives' homes.

Not anymore.

Evangel Home, a private residence located at 137 North Yosemite Avenue, was another possibility, but too far to walk. We'd have to hitch a ride. Administration working the Y's front desk hadn't offered much information about Evangel Home other than its availability. Moreover, it wouldn't cost us anything. Calling ahead, she let them know we were on our way.

Retracing a couple of blocks, standing aimless in this unnerving new city, Jan and I watched automobiles and trucks pass one another going opposite directions. Holding my right thumb near my face, before long, we had a proposal. A family of four driving a rusted out shell of a car, were on their way home from a grocery trip. Certain they couldn't afford to use up gas other than what was necessitated, my heart sunk. No matter. The man drove us 5 ½ miles to North Yosemite Avenue before turning left at an intersection, five houses east of our destination. Feeling sorry for their trouble, Jan and I offered the man and his wife a couple dollars. They didn't turn our money down.

Procrastinating on the front porch beneath the overhang at the one-story white stucco house on North Yosemite Avenue, I noticed an oval wood plaque fastened to a lamp post at the foot of a palm. In simple white letters, a name and street address stated *Evangel Home 137*. "Evangel" could only imply one thing. Frowning, I complained to Jan, "This place doesn't look like a hostel to *me*." Glancing down at her watch, lifting her head, Jan started to laugh. "How bad could it be? We can put up with anything for one night. We've done it before."

Before I could argue, the front door opened. There stood a mid-60ish woman, presumably Fanny, the person whom we were supposed to ask for. Presider of the home, Fanny was expecting us. Administration at the Y had indeed called ahead.

It was true. Jan and I were *not* required to pay a fee. Food and lodging would be provided. Uncertain of the terms and conditions that preau-thorized our remaining at Evangel Home without any cost, I thought there had to be a catch.

"I understand you two girls are travelling," Fanny attested. "You'll be our guests at the Home under different conditions than what usually brings teenage girls to Evangel Home. I'll expect you to dust, vacuum, and clean the two bathrooms daily for the duration of your stay."

Is that all?

Jan asked for details about the premises. Happy to fill us in, Fanny explained that Evangel home operated as a "Christian centered charitable facility housing transient women and their children." Founded in Fresno in 1955 by Pauline Baker Myers, Evangel Home functioned as a respite for pregnant and unmarried mothers and girls.

Neither one of us had gotten knocked up. Yet, we were welcomed. There was another caveat. Every morning, we were expected to attend chapel services.

Jan was right. How difficult could this *be*? Feeling as if we'd pulled off the perfect crime — at the very least, petty theft, flipping my hair confidently over my shoulders, I smiled. "No problem."

Fanny showed us to our room on the west side of the house, a pretty twin bedroom decked out in pink motif overlooking a flower garden ensconced by a periwinkle wreath. Soft mattresses were covered by lightweight, down-filled duvets — refined furnishings compared to what youth hostels generally provided. Usually, you were lucky if you had a mattress. Then again, as we were informed up front, at Evangel Home it was mandatory to partake of daily devotionals.

We couldn't fake it.

I found out the hard way.

Clearing away dinner dishes (we had take-out Chinese food, if you can believe it), Fanny approached me, and began to press about the status of my faith. Did I consider myself a Christian? Had I accepted Jesus Christ as my personal savior?

There was no soft peddling at Evangel Home like at HOOM. This was hardline questioning encroaching into aggressive territory. Short of offending her, I answered Fanny's queries to the best of my ability — with one shrug, and one "I never really thought about it seriously," leaving myself open to be railroaded. Wanting to avoid Fanny's shit list and screw up our opportunity to stay free at Evangel Home for a couple of days before continuing to Yosemite, I played along.

Fanny posed thorny questions pertaining to differences between the Old and New Testaments. Questions I couldn't answer with any kind of authority simply because I didn't know what the differences were. My biblical knowledge negligible at best, I hadn't read either Testament. (Attending church irregularly as a kid didn't require Bible study. You only had to show up.) Disturbed by my theological ignorance, Fanny promptly handed me a bible and suggested I bone up on my (lack of) knowledge.

A phone call interrupted her lecture. By the time I slid away, I was nerve wracked.

Jan must have had an inkling Fanny was on the warpath. Conveniently, she'd disappeared into our room.

So much for sticking together.

Following pancake breakfast and devotionals — not a snappy process — we started into our chores. Jan was sent off to buff up the kitchen and dining room. I was assigned the job of cleaning the ten-foot-tall stained-glass window in the Celestial Sanctuary — a task that required a fifteen-foot stepladder. Deciding I was up to the challenge, I found myself almost nose-to-nose with a glossy oil painting of J.C., *The Man* himself, on the south wall of the chapel. Bearing soft, yearning eyes and strong facial constitution, the world-renowned martyr smiled at me like a tragic clown. Or was it Batman's Joker?

Within the beveled window, there was a cross, embodying everything Evangel Home represented. Skillfully crafted, comprised of equal measures of purple and gold cut glass, the cross reached from the top wood frame of the window to the bottom. It was extraordinary, an encapsulating piece of handiwork that yielded you to it — exactly the reason why Fanny had assigned me this task, being the heathen, I was.

Certain that she wanted to save my soul, manic thoughts ran rampant through my brain. Maybe Fanny had read my mind and knew I'd been ruminating about joining The Holy Order. In her eyes, I was certain there wasn't anything more sacrilegious. Was I so transparent that she could telepathically burrow deep into my subconscious? Hold dominion over my future? The woman hardly knew me. Well meaning on the surface, maybe, but Fanny was the pious sort, full of condemnation. I had suspicion she'd never had sexual relations with a member of the opposite sex — or even her own gender if that happened to be her preference. The epitome of a single, older woman who didn't get out much, I didn't want Fanny's apparent sexless life to be my fate.

Cleaning the window and all of its apertures from top to bottom required precision, enabling me ample time to reevaluate my prospects and my fears. Pummeling me the night before with questions, was it possible Fanny had gained access to my insecurities by imposing her spiritual will?

Did she put something in the food?

Hating myself for thinking like a dope, I kept on. Alone in the chapel with the iconic emblem and lifelike oil painting of Christ instilled the desire to take personal inventory. It's exactly what Fanny wanted, I thought. She bullied girls into subservience playing mind games. Fanny was a head tripper. Boy was she good. Joining The Order *was* incompatible with my nature, no argument there. Yet, in their defense, HOOM, and particularly Meadowlark encouraged freedom of expression *and* free will.

Far as I could tell, Evangel Home did not.

A pattern had started to form. HOOM, Meadowlark, and now Evangel Home all shared a strong saintly undercurrent. I needed levity — something that would help balance everything out. What I *really* wanted was to smoke a joint and suppress my thoughts until I was out of range of Fanny. Reminiscent of those old horror flicks where one sister is invested in driving the other one over the brink while pleading innocence, apparently Jan was ignorant of the goings on. No matter. The whack job in our friendship had finally materialized.

It wasn't Jan.

The notion of Jan and Fanny being in cahoots loitered in my brain. In my heart of hearts, I knew this was preposterous. Completely false. Still, Jan needed to understand that Fanny was out to convert. The woman spoon-fed her agenda until the minions caved to her beliefs. If I was correct, that Fanny picked on the weak-minded and the vulnerable, she certainly had my number.

Of course, maybe I was making a big to-do out of nothing.

Over lasagna and bean lunch, Fanny introduced us to some of the other young women and families staying at Evangel Home for brief intervals and longer. All at once, we were privy to the sad and sordid details about their hard luck-lives. Introduced as my new roommate, Michelle, a sweet sixteen, five months pregnant Latino runaway, had lived in a women's correctional facility — juvenile division, prior to coming to Evangel Home. She would reside at the Home until after the birth of her baby. At the encouragement of the facility, Michelle was in the process of completing her GED within the year.

Chalk one up for Fanny.

There was Mary Meddas, her visiting husband, and their four children, Rachel, Danny, Alfie, and Poops. Another Mary, originally from Texas where she'd lived with her mother and four sons, found herself at Evangel Home after a run-in with the law. With three of her boys in tow on a waiting list for welfare, Mary hoped to return to Texas soon and reunite permanently with her youngest child.

While the other women were chatty, eight months pregnant Dixanne and her eleven-year-old daughter Karen sat side by side at the dining table quietly eating. Rounding out the group were other parentless children. It didn't seem to matter that we were at different places in our lives, favourite TV sitcoms and pop and rock bands level the playing field.

Jan would now be rooming with 32-year-old Margurat, another of the mothers who'd resided at Evangel for a few months. Hitting it off right away, Jan and Margurat talked about children and the Fresno area. Since our arrival the day before, we hadn't seen much of the city. Save the odd, jacked up greaser car here and there, the neighbourhood was eerily quiet. As far as I was concerned, nothing about Fresno stood out.

After lunch, I cleared dishes and Jan took care of garbage duty. As we were about to break away, Merabelle, Evangel Home's director, entered the dining room. The antithesis of Fanny, gifted with a loving nature, Merabelle was eager to get to know Jan and me as people, not converts. Having spent nearly six years under Evangel Home's employ, Merabelle and Fanny worked as a team.

A shock.

A group of us set off for the grocery store. During our errand run, Jan wanted to double check bus times for our trip to Yosemite State Park the following day. I invited Michelle to tag along. Out of range of Evangel Home renewed by sunshine and a mild breeze, I laughed at myself for behaving like a nut. Pushing Poops in the stroller, flanked by Sherry, Johnny, and Susan, the older kids in our entourage, we purchased everything on the grocery list, called the terminal from a pay phone for route and departure information, and headed over to Roeding Park so the kids could play on the swings.

Open seasonally, bountiful Roeding Park contains lakes and orchards, flower gardens, oak, eucalyptus, pine, and maple trees. There are two tennis courts, playground areas, a dance pavilion, the Chaffee Zoo, and a Japanese War Memorial. Not all of these amenities were available when we brought the children there years ago, but the park was easily accessible, a short distance from Evangel Home and the heart of Fresno.

The kids took turns on the swings, climbed monkey bars and scampered to the top of the slides. Letting them go wild, the brood finally tired themselves out. Having a go on the swings, Jan, Michelle, and I chatted about Evangel Home and Fanny. Cosseted by the beauty of the blossoms and park, I kept silent about my obsessive thoughts from that morning inside the Celestial Chapel. Jan was aware of my tendency to be irrational at times. I didn't want word to get around.

Judging by her omission of the elephant in the room, I gathered that any discussion of Michelle's pregnancy was off limits. Except for her protruding tummy, like Jan and me, Michelle had ambitions about future work and travel and talked of typical teenaged shenanigans. In many ways, we were mixed up girls just as she was. To her credit, Michelle knew how to stay in Fanny's good graces. If there was a chance of keeping her unborn child, she had to watch her back and not do anything that might be considered a misstep.

Michelle was hoping for a baby girl.

On the way to my room, I was interrupted by Dixanne standing outside my door.

I invited her in.

The reserved young woman we'd met earlier that day suddenly became Chatty Cathy. Out of the hawk-eye range of Fanny and with a private audience at her disposal, Dixanne grew animated, gossiping about the other women at Evangel Home and bad-mouthing the various "assholes" she'd screwed. She bragged about the "stupid" laws she had broken and bitched about what a drag it was to find herself and her daughter living at Evangel Home.

Though I felt sorry for Dixanne, I didn't want any self-destructive karma to rub off. According to her, Evangel was the "absolute last place on earth" she wanted to be. I suspected Evangel Home was probably the most stable and safest environment Dixanne had ever lived.

Her wish for a change of scenery would come soon enough.

Jan set the supper table for carrot soup, rolls, and cookies. Fanny was a big believer in the nutritional benefits of a mid-day meat and potato meal. Light dishes were reserved for dinner.

Come morning, Jan and I would be gone. Fanny would be a microscopic speck on the radar screen. Realizing I was being juvenile not to mention groundless in the way in which I'd perceived Fanny, it was time to give her some rope. Fanny *had* taken us in, few questions asked. She'd even allocated us with the duty of babysitting her charges.

There is a lot to be said for that level of trust.

Next morning's temperature was fair, 66 degrees. Though excited about going to Yosemite, recent memories of our last two camping expeditions in Santa Cruz and Big Sur were lucid. This time around, we anticipated more suitable conditions.

Merabelle cooked eggs and bacon for breakfast. Afterwards, Jan and I swept the paths leading up to the front entrance of the house, along the side walkway and around the back porch. As expected, we joined the others to take devotions in the Celestial Chapel.

Determined to go with the flow of the ritual, kneeling on the red leather padded bench, closing my eyes as Amy Loomis had instructed, I began meditating on the things that created discord in my being. *Will our money last? Will we return in one piece? Shall I join The Order for real?* Crediting the people who'd made a positive impact on our journey, I included Fanny.

Surrounded by an invisible protective shield — perhaps a guardian angel of sorts, Jan and I had been fortunate thus far. If in some way we'd reaped the intervention of a holy defense, I didn't know how. I could think of many reasons why we didn't deserve help from above. Whatever and whoever God was, I prayed our safe shelter would carry forward.

Returning to my room for the last time, I placed the Bible Fanny thrust upon me on top of the table next to my bed. Not ever having opened it, I'd kept it for security.

Mid-day, we thanked Fanny, said goodbye to Michelle, Margurat, Dixanne, the two Marys, and all the children at Evangel Home. To our surprise, Dixanne and Karen were packed and ready to leave Evangel Home too. Whatever the reason for their departure, I hoped Dixanne would be able to settle somewhere and take proper care of her daughter and soon-to-be-born child. Measuring the expression of sadness on Karen's face, I wasn't about to put a wager on Dixanne choosing the right path.

Merabelle offered a ride to the Fresno terminal to catch the late afternoon bus. Stepping up onto the platform, she placed a kiss upon each of our cheeks. After she left, Jan told me that Merabelle had reminded her of Mrs. Calloway, an elderly co-worker she'd grown fond of at the public library.

Merabelle was the very best that Evangel Home had to offer.

Jotting a note in my diary that evening, I wrote, "From here on in, we'll have to be *extremely* careful with money. Paying nearly $8 each for the bus trip hurt. Jan and I will hitchhike back to HOOM, and eventually home. We'll also need to ask people for rides, and divvy up gas costs. Only when *absolutely necessary* will we take a bus, boat, or train."

Drawing out our residual cash, the balance of the trip would involve a leap of faith.

For all concerned.

Camp Curry, Yosemite, California.

CHAPTER 32

Curry Village, Yosemite National Park

"We are disturbed not by what happens to us, but by our thoughts about what happens."
EPICTETUS

Moving beyond acres of wheat fields buoyant against strong gales, throughout the three-and-a-half-hour bus trip from Fresno to Yosemite Valley, this defiant act of nature intensified the mood of passengers. Surrounded by cheerful folks headed to Camp Curry, espying the tall gold strands dancing back and forth before a blue cloudless sky, I was lulled into a state of wellbeing. Beginning in the pit of my stomach, like a flash flood, a tingling sensation swept through my body. With every mile logged, the road seemed to magically widen; my inner self and the world twinned, harmonious.

I'd experienced euphoria before — the phenomenon of being awash with pure ecstasy that saturates your soul without being subpoenaed. When it occurred during our trip, presuming they were stand-ins for the Supreme Being, I was induced to take stock in personal angels. In recent weeks, the presence of a guardian seraph, an assenting sign had been revealed in unexpected places and people. These little motions were starting to mount; a crossroads of absolution had crept upon us. A verdict would need to be settled. It wasn't up for debate.

Jan and I arrived at Camp Curry early evening to a remarkable view of the Sierra Nevada Mountains, and assembly of mammoth sequoias staged outside our back door. Mapping out the park, paying a $7.95 fee for two nights would be justified. Not only would our stay be a unique opportunity, to camp directly inside the Sierra Nevada

Mountain corral, it was the first time in two weeks Jan and I paid for accommodations.

Within the boundaries of Yosemite National Park, Camp Curry is as rich in history as it is in inherent, aesthetic wonder. Established in 1899 by David and Jennie Curry, the couple's mandate was to provide the means for people to enjoy the beauty of Yosemite at an affordable price. During their start up years, the Curry's charged $2 per day, including a bed and modest breakfast.

Located in the Yosemite Valley silhouetted between Glacier Point and Half Dome, the park's elevation is just over 4000 feet. Provided with a tented cabin, we were guaranteed one meal daily in the small cafeteria and hot shower, with access to drinking water. The premises contained a general store and post office. Outfitted with an organic geological landscape, Yosemite offered plenty of hiking trails for day visitors and challenging tracks for the practiced rambler. Over the decades, Camp Curry has continued to grow as a family centric setting equipped with amphitheater, skating rink, and swimming pool.

Like matching hooks on a fishing line, our canvas tent was adjacent to several other tents in a row. We didn't feel confined. In this friendly, populated park, fear of prowling animals or serial rapists was disbanded. On the second day of June, a few weeks from school letting out, the campground was nearly choking with visitors. No small wonder. From our small dwelling and from any other vantage point within the park, the backdrop was awe-inspiring. Bold sandstone overhangs, formidable waterfalls, streams winding in and around mountain vessels, and sequoia groves were daunting as they were stately. Grateful to be among nature without external manipulation, we looked forward to exploring the vicinity on foot.

The park offered free shuttles to transfer people within the self-contained community.

Built on top of a plywood structure, our tent was slightly slanted, similar to a modern day yurt assembly with ample room inside to fit two identical beds, two crudely made wood nightstands, a couple of lamps and writing desk.

Jan and I slept deeply that first night, comfortable and warm beneath wool blankets tucked overtop of clean sheets. Our heads supported by feather pillows, it was like a motel, only better, and far cheaper.

Greeted with a favourable temperature of 80 degrees the next morning, after washing and dressing, we joined fellow campers in the cafeteria for porridge and maple syrup.

Following breakfast, we hurried to catch the shuttle parked next to the cafeteria. The bus made regular trips to Yosemite Village where Camp Curry's store, post office, and laundry facilities were located. Hopping onto the platform, we discussed what food items we'd need. Milk, cheese, crackers, peanut butter, and apples hadn't failed us yet. Buying daily, very little went to waste. Protein would provide the necessary fuel to climb mountains and maneuver trails.

Selecting a few postcards and sundries at the general store, Jan and I started out hiking into the woods along the short path that led to Yosemite Falls. Taking easy steps through the brush, I reached out to touch the leafy foliage moistened by morning dew. Studying the skinny red veins rooted within the lined green pads, looking up, a pair of Western Tanagers crooned harmonious in the forest. Continuing the length of the spongy tree-lined path strewn with wood spindles from fallen branches, eventually, the forest opened up and we found ourselves less than 50 feet from a cascading waterfall. Moving closer until standing at the foot of the faucet, the fresh spray spurted gently against our faces, and wet our clothing.

Climbing on the rocks to gain closer access to the top, we soon reached the halfway mark and discovered a riverbed that ran beyond our line of vision. Jan clambered after me on the granite until we were next to the tributary, close enough to reach down and taste the water. Bending on one knee, I placed my hands into the translucent stream, watching it spill into my palms. Raising the fluid to my lips, it tasted crisp and clean; easily supplanting anything I'd savoured before — even ice-cold beer. Mimicking my actions, Jan kneeled next to me. Drinking from two cupped hands, she looked surprised when the water tickled the tip of her tongue.

It was a golden moment.

Shortly thereafter, positioned across the stomach of a fat boulder, we spread out a red-checkered cotton serviette scooped from breakfast. From our bags, cheese, crackers, apples, and two small milk cartons were unpacked.

Lunchtime in the mountains.

Irregular canyons and shapely symmetry encircling us, we acknowledged how happy we were to have travelled to Yosemite. Having spent nearly every waking and sleeping minute together for several months, apart from sporadic quiet periods, amazingly, there hadn't been any serious disagreements — an astounding achievement. With one other to fall back on, occasionally, the right amount of interference from other parties came into play. Having had the recent discussion regarding money and future transportation, because of corroding funds, Jan and I delineated our approaching route from Yosemite to San Francisco. There was approximately two and a half months remaining of our trip. Leaving Camp Curry, we would hitchhike 200 miles to San Francisco, and then continue moving north. Returning to Canada, we'd fill out job applications, maybe in Alberta or even Saskatchewan.

This was tentatively speaking.

Everything was riding on developments once we returned to HOOM.

According to letters received from our friends back home, there was a misconception that Jan and I seldom met females. Leaving Yvette and the girls back at the Y in Vancouver, we had met our share of guys; it was true — Gary and Teddy being standouts. At the moment, maybe forever, things were platonic. Still, they counted. Save the grebes encountered at Balboa Park, and the Men's Y in San Diego, Jan and I wouldn't mind meeting more men. Though most were spoken for, there was certainly a lot of eye candy at Camp Curry.

In recent correspondence, our friend Jen (who also worked at the library) mentioned my mother had visited the week before. They'd had a chat, mostly about places Jan and I had stayed. Jen went on to say that as of February, my father faithfully visited the library every Wednesday night. According to her, Dad shared details of letters I'd sent home.

In other news, May was going to a Blue Grass Festival late June accompanied by her new boyfriend, Tim. A pair of soul mates in the making, I was extremely happy for her.

Lazing on top of our beds, slathering peanut butter across white bread to take the edge off, Jan and I talked about dinner. A line had formed outside near the cafeteria. If we joined, we'd end up spending money that wasn't in our budget. Jan left to check on the menu while I scratched in my journal. Shortly afterwards, she returned. The supper menu consisted of potato soup and a bun for $2.

The price was reasonable enough. Anyway, we'd sleep better with full bellies.

A couple of farm hands from Georgia, Bill and Mike assisted in Yosemite's park stables. Earlier in the day, we'd observed horses and mules for camp visitors who preferred sightseeing on horseback rather than slogging trails on foot.

Bill and Mike invited us to join them at their table.

The two men were all right. Talkative. Occasionally vulgar. Bill was married and had three kids. Mike was single. Like a comedy duo, Bill played the straight man to the idiotic jokes Mike cracked during dinner. Scraping the remains of our bowls, Jan and I deposited our dishes in the bins provided. Peripherally, I noticed Bill shoot a glance over at Mike. Then they both looked over at me.

Did we want to join them for a couple of beers on the bar patio?

Loving nothing more than to toss a few back, we simply couldn't afford it. There was also the testy point: We were three and four years younger than the legal drinking age in the state. Even if Bill and Mike paid for us, our appearances were too juvenile to pass for early twenties. If the men had been on the ball, figured out a way to stock beer inside their tent, that would have been cool. Alcohol was available for purchase at the makeshift outside bar area only. Visitors that got caught sneaking booze into the park were given the boot.

Standing next to Bill and Mike at the garbage bins, Jan started to giggle, baffling the two poor buggers who had simply invited us for drinks. Suspecting the reason for her outburst, it would have to wait until we returned to our tent to go full tilt.

I told Bill and Mike straight out we couldn't go to the bar with them. Following up, Jan revealed our ages, and then waited as their eyes bulged from their heads. Our roommate, Deb, once told us most men can't distinguish between teens and young twenties — even thirties. She'd done her homework. Noticing Bill appeared more disappointed than Mike, I clued in. Bill's plan, to catch a little nookie up at Camp Curry, 2000 miles away from the wife and kids, was foiled. Guessing which one of us he'd had his eyes on, I decided on Jan. She was the closest thing to jailbait.

Men liked to live dangerously.

Safe inside our tent, zipping it tight to keep the critters out, I fell onto my bed in a fit of laughter. Jan was beside herself. Honestly, the reason for the outburst wasn't that funny. Maybe it was the fact we'd been out in the sun all day, hadn't had enough to eat, or were tired.

Poor Bill and Mike. Unknowingly, they'd invoked memories of Bobby and David, two oversexed men Jan and I met in Barbados the summer before.

Barbados, 1975

July of 1975, the dry run for our trip west, Jan and I travelled to the Caribbean for two weeks to the Welcome Inn (now Barbados Beach Club) located in Christ Church.

Jan was sixteen. I was seventeen. The legal drinking age anyone's guess in Barbados in 1975 was one of the reasons we'd decided to vacation there. Taking advantage of the combination of sunshine and lax laws, routinely, we made trips to a sleazy bootlegger one block from our hotel to purchase cheap boxes of Banks beer.

Late afternoon, Jan and I generally headed downstairs to the buffet in the hotel dining room. One evening, a couple of men ambled over introducing themselves as Bobby and David. A 37-year-old blonde divorcée (so he said) and father of a teenaged girl, Montreal native Bobby Shields worked as a travel agent. Twenty-nine-year-old David was born and raised in Puerto Rico. Handsome, with a ready accent that came at you in a fast clip; it wasn't clear what David did for a living. For all we knew, he could have been a gigolo. Next morning, David was leaving for home.

Bobby and David weren't guests at our hotel, but liked to party in our lounge where vacationers were deluged umpteen times daily by the popular (and irritating) Hot Chocolate song, "Sexy Thing." The two pals hooked up days before we met.

Suffice to say, Jan and I were toasted the night we made Bobby and David's acquaintance — obvious to them and to anyone else in the bar. Two teenage girls a long way from home — like kids gone wild after leaving home for college, it was not abnormal for youths to tie one on when opportunity presented itself. Accepting Bobby and David's invitation to join them at the bar, in flirty moods, we proceeded to indulge ourselves with more Banks beer.

The four of us soon left the bar area and eventually the hotel. Bobby had rented a dune buggy and suggested we take a drive to the beach. At this point, Jan and I'd ventured beyond the hotel to the bootleggers only, a short road veering a sharp left from the Welcome Inn's front entrance. When Bobby made a right turn out of the hotel and started driving down the two-lane dirt road, I became conscious of the fact that we were jeopardizing our safety — only it was too late. Driving a few minutes, Bobby parked the jeep in a vacant lot and we walked out to the Caribbean shoreline. Leaning against the cement break wall separating sand and water, we began talking. Jan and I disclosed our ages. The guys didn't flinch.

This was Barbados. Prime destination spot. Earlier, David had procured a joint from a local — a middle-aged Caucasian who'd traded a high-paying white-collar job, wife, and family for the simpler island life. Since 1971, the man had been living incognito in the Caribbean, smoking, illegally selling marijuana and hashish.

Jan and I got delightfully high with Bobby and David, sharing tokes and laughs before it hit me, we weren't going to ditch them anytime soon. In for the long haul, these guys would wait it out. To ensure I hadn't missed the irony of my prospective situation, taking me aside, Jan teased about Bobby being the father of a teenaged daughter. Not to worry, I reassured my friend. I wasn't about to make out with an old man, especially one with a kid my age. However, before they out-wised us, it was imperative that we engineer a tactic. Holding out his arm, David waited until Jan touched his elbow. Off they strolled, down the beach, away from Bobby and me. As long as Jan believed she had the upper hand, I knew she wouldn't allow herself to go too far, geographically, or otherwise. Now that we were separated however, Bobby made his play.

He told me he longed to kiss me. For a while, I gave in and let him kiss me on and inside the mouth. It was all right, though I wasn't seriously attracted to him, not in the way he said he was attracted to me — something Bobby surely said to all the girls. Course, the booze and pot made him seem appealing for about five minutes longer than he would have been if I hadn't altered my state of mind.

Likewise, I'm sure.

Convincing myself of our safety providing we didn't stray too far from our hotel, I suggested we return to the Welcome Inn. At this point, there was some commotion. Turning to certify that Jan and David were still close by, I saw David on his hands and knees in the sand desperately searching for something.

The man was royally pissed. Meanwhile, Jan was completely giddy.

Bobby and I went over to see what was going on. Apparently, after David had tried to put the moves on Jan, she knocked his hand upward, and one of his contact lens dropped of his right eye falling directly on to the beach. Learning this information, I felt my own laugh reflex emerge and had to swallow it to the back of my throat.

David was positively agitated, I wasn't about to add fuel.

Dividing up, we formed a small search party. Kneeling on the ground, everybody felt around in the sand for the missing lens. It was fruitless. The light from the boardwalk lampposts was too dim to distinguish anybody's face let alone anything else. A minuscule lens buried within bazillion grains of sand was next to impossible to find, even in daylight. We all knew there was no way in hell David would ever find it.

Once he succumbed to this reality, I (again) recommended we return to the hotel. What I really wanted was for Bobby and David to leave us alone. Still feeling the effects of the pot, I'd started to sober up from the drink. My cogent brain eased back into cruise control mode. Bobby and David were fun to hang out with for a while, but their act was wearing thin. Feeling guilty that maybe we'd lead them on, I blamed it on the booze.

Finally giving in, the guys drove us back to the Welcome Inn. Entering the lobby, Bobby and David weren't ready to return to their hotel. Their evacuation, my M.O. for the shift in scenery — the guys weren't having any of it. Wanting to come up to our room and drink some more, the two became persistent. If only we were in better control of our faculties and more experienced with men, Jan and I would never have permitted those two jokers into our room. It was a trade off. To get them out of our hair, we went along. There wasn't time to confer about our predicament anyway. A decision had to be made. The logic being that if we enticed them with more beer, they'd go home happy.

Unfortunately, life is never that straightforward — nor should anybody be so naïve.

Like two lost puppies, Bobby and David followed us into the elevator. The four of us rode up to our double room located on the second floor. I already had it in my mind, once inside, we'll usher them out to the balcony and show off the view of the beach.

Using the key kept inside of her purse, Jan unlocked the door. Immediately, I clucked, "You guys have got to see the moon from our balcony. It's amazing." Bobby and David would have done just about anything to appease, the way most horn dogs do when they think they're about to get a piece of ass. Banks beer in hands, more than half a case of full bottles on standby, Bobby, David, Jan, and I gathered on our balcony watching the half-moon shimmer and shake over the Caribbean Sea. Twenty or so minutes passed, Jan slipped away to pee. I planned to follow shortly. When she didn't return, I figured she'd probably passed out.

Hoping to have our first real chance to talk alone since hooking up with these two dickheads (I'd demoted them to this by now), it was starting to look as if the conversation wasn't going to happen. Racking my brain, I made an excuse to exit the balcony, go check on Jan. As I'd reckoned, fully clothed, Jan appeared to be passed out cold on top of her bed. Stealing quietly to the sliding balcony door, I slid it over, pushed the lock across and bolted it. Incredulous, Bobby and David turned in cohesive motion to gape at me through the glass. Trying to absorb the ludicrous action I'd pulled off, their expressions soon changed from bemusement to confusion.

I didn't give a shit what they thought. Acting as if nothing was out of the ordinary, calmly, I closed the drapes, changed into my pajamas and went into the bathroom to brush my teeth.

For the longest time, it was quiet out there. Stealthily quiet. Both of us in our beds, the lights off, I fantasized they'd jumped over the balcony and on to the beach.

Directly below, the beach was a clear fifteen-foot drop. I figured they could land it in one-piece, the soft sand cushioning their fall. I didn't want them hurt, I just wanted them gone.

Tempted to try to fall asleep and not worry about it, I soon realized it was unreasonable to think they'd jump off the balcony, or do anything other than leave our hotel the conventional way, through the door. Inevitably, retribution was going to come down, probably hard. To my surprise, Jan whispered in the dark from her bed.

"How'd you get rid of them?"

"Shhhh!"

"What's wrong? Why are you whispering?"

When I told her the news, Jan was understandably horrified. Not only were Bobby and David technically, still in our room, they were about eight feet away. The only reasonable way off the balcony was through the sliding glass door and into our room.

Somebody banged on glass. That meant one thing. The men had finished the case of beer that provided distraction for a while. Now they were outraged. Maybe they'd even pissed themselves. I could hardly blame Bobby and David for their sour moods. I wouldn't want to be locked outside on a balcony at 3 am either. In my warped mind, it looked good on them to beg us to let them out, or rather, into the room. I hadn't considered the danger that, in fact, they might try to teach us a lesson for behaving like a couple of bitches.

Starting to yell, Bobby demanded we let them in the room. Soon, in repetitious rhythm, four closed fists beat furiously on the glass. Jan and I both knew we were going to open the door; it was a matter of when.

Bucking up, I switched on my table lamp and got out of bed. Remaining in her bed, panicked, I knew Jan was anxious for the night to be over so that she could pass out for good. I felt like shit, too, but as the pounding continued, pulling on my robe and slippers, I pushed open the curtain. His face beat red, David was about to raise his fist to the glass when I took him by surprise. "I'll unlock the damn door if you both leave! Right now!"

Relieved to be reassigned from their balcony detention, our two enraged male acquaintances surrendered. They would leave us alone and go. If it was a lie, we didn't have a plan B.

Unlocking the latch, I slid open the door and waited to see what would happen next. Hands moulded into fists, David, the angrier of the two, shouted a few choice expletives. Then the drunken men stumbled across the carpet, past our bathroom, through the entrance to our room and out into the hallway. Slamming it behind them, I locked the door in a hurry and turned the deadbolt.

It would be a whole week before either one of us wanted to look at or speak to a man again.

Mist Trail below Vernal Fall, Camp Curry Village, Yosemite, CA.

CHAPTER 33

The Mist Trail

"I always say, keep a diary and some day it'll keep you."
MAE WEST

Thursday June 3, Jan and I had officially been on the road for fifteen weeks — a milestone. In a good way it was starting to feel like a lifetime. To celebrate our landmark, we put down money to reserve one more night at site 660 and then headed into the cafeteria for porridge and banana breakfast. At 77 degrees, the morning mountain sky was clear and sunny, a patented image of the day before. Deciding to visit three park locations, we planned to ride the shuttle to Mirror Lake, Happy Isles, and then take in Nevada Falls. There would be a lot of hiking, 8 miles up and down the crag between shuttle trips. Fanning through the brochure the night before and speaking with fellow campers, we could not forgo exploration of the park's high points.

The shuttle at Loop B brought us up to where we could access the pathway to Mirror Lake situated in Tenaya Canyon, the west portion of the park. In danger of disappearing into the abyss because of sediment residue near the end of the last ice age, Mirror Lake is one of the last of the glacier lakes to devour most of Yosemite Valley. A frequently photographed locale, glimpsing into the center, the diminutive body of water resembles a virtual reflective image. Perched above, creating a shadow effect is Half Dome. By summer's end we were told, the lake usually dries up into a dribble. Late spring 1976, Mirror Lake was deluged.

From various angles, Jan snapped pictures of the still clear lake and contiguous boulders. Before hiking back through the meadow, I managed a quick sketch. Resting in the field, we watched various hikers wander into the area, one of whom, a mid-twenties man of medium height with long dirty blonde hair and a pensive brow, was particularly good-looking.

Dressed in a red and green plaid shirt, he wore a pair of baggy khaki pants probably picked up at an army surplus store. Hiking alone, the young man didn't pay us any mind.

Jan and I often encountered people who preferred to trek alone without having another body to consider. For those comfortable in their own skin, according to people who have done it, travelling solo is an unbeatable way to explore. I respected their courage, but didn't get it. Safety in numbers is what we were always taught.

Unaware that he was being undressed and violated in the minds of a couple of teenaged girls, the handsome heartthrob took his time exploring the path in his brown leather ankle high hiking boots until finally, Nature Boy dispersed to the other side of the field and into the recesses of my brain. Deciding to continue, trailing behind a few of the others, we discovered the American Indian caves scattered about the vicinity. Concealed inside boulders were caverns that contained spider-like fractures. Others, located beneath the overhang of large rock cliffs, indicated where Indigenous peoples sheltered themselves from treacherous weather and rival tribes.

From there, we hiked nearly 6 miles, beyond Vernal Fall, straight up almost to the top of Nevada Falls to reach a signpost designated "The Mist Trail." Mounting rocky steps, we reached the pinnacle. Nearing the apex of Nevada Falls, a towering triple rainbow formed a rich, multihued vision.

Beneath the sweep of the rainbow arc, joining a small group, Jan and I gawped out over a helm of devastating strength. Like two giant valves pouring 600 feet down from the top of the mountain, twin falls calmed to a hush, while stream bands, nestling comfortably in the riverbed, swirled in circular pools. Beholding the exquisite liquid shapes enfolding in graceful motion like allied flickering flames, any grievances of late were gently disarmed.

Hiking down The Mist Trail on stone steps proved easier than trudging to the top. Considering all the climbing we had done that day, every step of the way felt rejuvenating. Jan and I were in excellent physical condition. During our months away, I'd carried two pairs of shoes, hiking boots, and the used pair of sling-back Earth shoes in reserve for hot days. Designed to withstand mud, wet, and slush, Jan owned a pair of leather-bound footwear and carted a pair of tan leather sandals for lighter days. Walking varying distances, between 5-10 miles per day including portions of our L.A. visit, if anything, we had endurance.

Shuttling back to camp, we stopped at the Yosemite Village Mall to pick up milk, more crackers, cheese, and a "health" sandwich for 60 cents.

Hurrying to site 660 to engage in a miniature feast, the decisive payoff after a satisfying day, we decided to turn in early that evening.

Reinstating Brother James's dormant visualization technique, standing at the top of Nevada Falls that afternoon, Jan told me she'd had a premonition. We would have a good (as in harm free) drive to San Francisco.

One of the things I liked about Jan, she was always anticipating. Truthfully, the security of our 200-mile journey to San Francisco weighed on my mind as well. It was time to polish off rust, regain confidence, and ward off unforeseen threats or danger. Apart from invoking our trusty system: concentration, meditation, and prayer for a risk-free journey, there wasn't anything else.

Turning out her table lamp, Jan went to sleep right away. Uncustomary for her to leave her diary open anywhere, especially on a desk in plain view, I deliberated for a moment about peeking. Unable to curb my curiosity, getting up from the bed, padding quietly to the desk, I glanced down at the crayon red bound book. There, upon crisp, lined pages, blue ballpoint displayed Jan's neat, distinctive penmanship. My own journal, a mess of black ink in hurried scratchy handwriting, exposed a carcass of scribbles, sketches, poems, and lyrics smothering every spare space of page. A sloppy writer, I confess. I was a bonafide slob in other ways, too.

Casting sheen on two open pages of the book, the night lamp enabled me to read the few lines Jan had entered earlier that evening: "I think we will get a good safe ride to Frisco. Jill has been chatting about Toothpick (Jan's nickname for Teddy/aka the Good Samaritan because of his rakish physique) for almost six weeks now. I will be glad for her to see him again.

I hope to get lots of mail at the hostel when we return. Even crazy Gary had better have written.

It was a nice, exercising day today. You sure know something else is going on when you see those waterfalls." — J.M.

The first week of June, the concept of time was intangible. With the days tallying up, there was the desire to emboss every memorable moment, every friend and encounter upon my brain. A journal is one way of safekeeping time and activities, the relevance of every facsimile of the excursion. Of equal importance within the systematic pattern of things, adverse incidents were also duly recorded.

"It's the I Ching way," Michael had said at the Japanese Tea Garden in Golden Gate Park, when referencing the yin and yang that describes the interconnection between opposite forces. Though reticent about moving on from Yosemite National Park so soon, with every day growing warmer, the campground was becoming ever crowded. The desire to return to San Francisco and HOOM, both pivotal at this point of our expedition, was driven by auspicious intentions.

Apprehensive yet excited to see Teddy, I was enthused by the real possibility of joining The Holy Order. Maybe there'd be an epiphany and I'd know exactly what my choice would be. Talking often about revisiting HOOM, Jan and I'd danced around the real issue. She and I were coming to a metaphorical fork in the road. There was exactly one day left to circumvent the topic. If everything worked out, by nightfall, we'd be asleep in the small girls' dorm on Steiner Street.

Dropping my overstuffed knapsack on the floor of our tent, I regarded Jan sitting cross-legged on her cot, scrutinizing our guide book. Looking up for a moment, she offered a casual smile, as if to say everything is cool.

Freeze framing her lax expression inside my head, I had suspicion there'd be reason to revisit that smile. Possibly when in bed wide awake in the middle of the night trying to exorcise self-doubt.

Artwork featured on stone, Northern California.

CHAPTER 34

San Francisco, Act II

"Nothing matters very much and very few things matter at all."
LORD BALFOUR

Standing at the shoulder of CA-120 W, Jan and I held out matching right thumbs. An old brown truck that had known better days pulled up to the Village Mall at Yosemite Park. Obviously delighted with his fate to discover two teenage girls looking for a lift, upon learning we weren't headed in the same direction, the eager driver was more disappointed than we were.

One down.

Next, a gentle-natured, older man stopped to give us a short ride, taking care of a few miles.

One hundred and eighty-five left to go.

After he dropped us off, we spotted a couple of guys ahead of us waiting at the side of the road. They'd fabricated a small sign, a green marker drawing of a mountain range with an arrow and the word "Vancouver" written next to it. A reasonable distance to travel, the boys were in greater need than we were.

The last thing you want when hitchhiking is competition. Luckily, Jan and I were young and female. Those two factors will usually override a male in his twenties waiting on a ride any day of the week.

Unless the driver happens to be a woman.

A mile down the highway, a black Pontiac Parisienne emerged from an artificial horizon. Weaving around three vehicles, it stopped on the shoulder. The heavy passenger door pushed ajar enabled us to easily make our way inside the vehicle where a dark-haired, heavyset man sprung out from the driver's side to help us with our backpacks.

The Parisienne was en route to Lake Tahoe.

Discouraged, Jan courteously declined for both of us. Observing our interface with the driver from a respectable distance, our competition almost tripped over one another sprinting toward the vehicle. Regretfully, as the big boat squealed from the curb with a vengeance, dust and stones kicking and spitting at the wheels, slapping us in the face as the driver tore up the asphalt, we watched in silence. Wondering if the fireworks display was for our benefit, hanging my head, I looked over at Jan. "That could have been *our* ride if only we were going to Tahoe."

Peculiarly cheerful about our misfortune, my friend was convinced a vehicle would soon appear with our names on it. Doubtful of her wishful thinking, sitting down on a rock, I freed my foot from my boot and wiggled my toes in the air. A relatively cool morning so far, it would become progressively warmer as the day wore on.

Because of walking up and down The Mist Trail, my right foot had become sore and swollen. Friction from my boot against the back of my heel irritated the callous that had surfaced in Vancouver months before. In recent weeks, it had gotten worse. Considering making the switch to sandals, the downside was I'd have to strap my boots to my backpack. I didn't want to create any extra weight. The desert sun out in full force, carrying a pound or two is one too many.

Ten minutes passed before another anonymous automobile creased the junction between earth and sky. Advancing unhurriedly into focus, a banana-yellow Toyota station wagon appeared. Drawing closer, the car slowed and eventually stopped. Inside, a handsome blonde in his late-twenties introduced himself as Grace. Grace's equally attractive fair-haired girlfriend Jude greeted us from the front passenger seat. On their way to San Francisco, the Australian couple would eventually drive northeast to Montreal to attend the summer Olympic Games. In a few months, they were headed to Europe to continue travel by way of a Euro-rail pass.

Her intuition spot on, Jan didn't hesitate to shoot me an all-knowing glance. Returning the stare, I presented her with a mock bow.

Touché.

Not about to tempt fate staring us flagrantly in the face, before Grace and Jude had a change of heart, we climbed into the rear seat and unloaded our weight into the back of the wagon. Following an exchange of pleasantries, Grace and Jude told us about their adventures since touching down on American soil a few months prior to our chance meeting. On an extended two-year break from work, the pair had opted to see as much of the world as financially feasible. Once funds ran low, they would seek employment before returning to Australia.

Looking forward to spending a few days familiarizing themselves with the sites of San Francisco, Grace asked if we could recommend accommodation. Jan and I reassured the couple there would be "room for all four of us" at 101 Steiner Street once we arrived.

Concerned about the state of their '69 vehicle, (it had been stalling since purchasing the car second hand in Washington), before driving much further, Grace suspected the wagon required a battery transplant. That morning, they'd gotten a boost. Stockton was only a couple of hours away. Once we reached the city's periphery, Grace had it in his mind to track down a repair shop. Chugging along for a good stretch at a 60-mile clip, Jude suddenly pointed to an exit this side of the Stockton border. If a mechanic's shop could be located, we'd get the work done and arrive in San Francisco early evening.

While the car was in the process of being overhauled at a Stockton garage 1½ miles off the freeway, the four of us walked across the road to a truck stop to grab lunch and wait. Grace had been correct about the battery's status. Additionally, the alternator needed replacing. With several hundred miles to conquer, the young apprentice was given the green light to make the repairs to ensure the car was road ready.

In midst of dipping donuts into coffee mugs between fragments of conversation, I noticed the Aussie couple seemed to be congruent in every which way. Even their attractive faces and fit physiques mirrored one another. Standing nearly six feet tall and sporting a trim yet strong build, Nestlé's chocolate brown eyes and Robert Plant-like blonde ringlets falling to his shoulders, Grace was conspicuously handsome. Offset by a luxurious long blonde mane and slender form, with mellow blue eyes, Jude was stunningly beautiful. The 1970s avatars of flower children, Grace and Jude treated Jan and me fondly, like long lost kid sisters.

Once the car was repaired, Jude next to him in the front seat, Grace took his place behind the wheel. Handing Grace a few dollars to go towards gas, an effort they both appreciated, Jan and I retired to the back. The four of us sped down the freeway on a straight stretch of smooth pavement, the kind of level plane that wills you to catnap even if you haven't had a late night the day before. Assuming it'd be a couple hours before reaching our destination, noggin against the headrest; I closed my eyes and fell into a light sleep.

Hitchhiking is about being at the mercy of the driver. You must remain on alert. Under normal circumstances, unless we knew our drivers, Jan and I never dared close our eyes, no matter how tired or hung-over.

Grace and Jude were the exception.

People pick up hitchhikers for a myriad of reasons, the most apparent, to drive somebody to a designated location. On long or short hauls, folks enjoy the company of riders unfamiliar to them. Having a guest on board provides opportunity to make breezy conversation, share personal stories, and purge guilt. Convening on common ground, between driver and rider, there is an equal distribution of power. Moving down the line, reasons for picking up hikers becomes more dubious and suspect. The same can be said for solicitation.

Along the highways and freeways during those days, it wasn't uncustomary to encounter exceptional people like Grace and Jude, especially during the seventies decade when youths were relatively ripe and unsullied. The flower-power experiential that governed the sixties one decade before our journey was little more than a smoldering ash in 1976, yet many of the tenets and free form philosophies held tough. Teens and youths were encouraged to seek sovereignty and independence. Travellers risking the open road trusted that most people encountered were intrinsically decent and of sound mind. Anything to the contrary was extreme, an aberration rather than commonplace.

Driving up to San Francisco in the company of Grace and Jude as they traded stratagems and told stories was an endorsement for hitchhiking, relinquishing any dread I'd had before leaving Yosemite Village.

The little wagon pulled in front of 101 Steiner Street around half past five. A couple of weeks shy of official summer, once high school, colleges, and universities let out, kids and young adults migrated to San Francisco like hornets to a nest. The hostel almost at capacity, Jan and I were given the green light to roll out our sleeping bags along the floor in the girls' dorm. Our charge was $1 each. The men's dorm was also full, leaving Grace and Jude no choice but to find lodging somewhere else for the night.

Jan and I both felt lousy about Grace and Jude being turned away. Our Aussie friends had driven us all the way from Yosemite and were two of the nicest people we'd met so far. Promising to check in again the following day, Jude anticipated that some of the backpackers would disperse.

Settled in, Jan and I walked over to Safeway to gather up our usual — crackers, cheese, peanut butter, and fruit before returning to the hostel to hang out with some of the new gang.

Brother James and Brother Bruce were on the premises. A good sign, I thought.

The Brothers seemed genuinely delighted to see us, going so far as to say that we'd changed in the six weeks since we'd been away, the transformation for the better. Finding our features to be "more acute," according to Bruce, Jan and I had come into "focus."

Providing Bruce with a Reader's Digest of time spent at Meadowlark, he wasn't surprised by anything we disclosed.

Hesitantly, I asked about Teddy. How was he adapting to life in The Order?

As a novice, Bruce said, Teddy was adjusting well. In the beginning, Teddy hadn't liked the transition but was getting used to it. He had cut his hair — a big deal. I told Brother Bruce I'd brought along a small gift from Meadowlark for Teddy, and anticipated giving it to him soon.

Steiner Street had a delightful new permanent fixture, a soft ball of black fur, a kitten named "Happy Sweet." Happy Sweet fit right in with the commotion stemming from a high volume of visitors to the hostel.

Crammed within the finite space of the main room, the pulse of affection between people from all over the world was tangible. The liveliest of the bunch, Marco, a 19-year-old student from Zurich, among other things, fancied himself an aspiring actor. Beneath a helmet of dark brown hair reminiscent of Moe from the The Three Stooges, Marco was a mustached beanpole. Bright, jovial, single minded, and providing he was in control, it was evident that Marco liked to kid around. As it had happened with Gary, Jan, Marco, and I clicked from the start.

We played a few rounds of cards, drank too many cups of coffee, and listened to Zeppelin and Grateful Dead. There was a lot of ground Jan and I had yet to cover. In the morning, we would meet up to do some sightseeing.

Before turning in, Brother James presented Jan and me with letters from home. May reiterated the possibility of meeting up with us in Alberta in July. My brother Steve had written that he missed having me around the house, which touched my heart. Missing Steve, too, I was glad to hear from him. As close as we were growing up, wreaking havoc with our crazy antics, I was doing my thing and Steve was involved in his own life, which consisted mostly of playing music. Gifted with an exceptional ear, my brother is a talented keyboard player, trumpeter, and composer.

Mom wrote that I'd been accepted into St. Lawrence College in Kingston. She'd even sent in the $35 registration fee to hold a spot for me. Prior to coming away, at her encouragement, I'd submitted an application to their applied arts program. It was something to hang my hat on, in case.

When communicating through the written word, people are inclined to be thoughtful, plainer spoken. Pen and paper have a way of eliciting sincerity like truth serum. Since winter, my mother conveyed, she believed I had matured.

If Mom only knew.

Wide awake in my sleeping bag from the combination of caffeine and hustle bustle of the day, I tried counting sheep to see if the exercise might help me become drowsy. During a bout of insomnia at the age of eight, I'd started sheep counting. As a kid, it was torturous, tossing and turning in bed on auto-alert until early morning, knowing I had to get up for school in a few hours. Eventually, once my mother began crushing half a valium into a teaspoon of raspberry jam, giving it to me before bed, sleeplessness was cured. Our family doctor had suggested the remedy.

Tallying imaginary animals jumping over fences hadn't worked then. It didn't work now.

The girls' dorm room was as black as a pocket, not the tiniest glimmer of light emanated from the hallway or from outside of the window. Secure inside of my sleeping bag while Jan and three other girls basked in slumber heaven, I shut my eyes tight, making the black velvet shade inside of my head even darker. My body soon began to relax. Breathing slowly, concentrating on every single breath, I could zone in on the sound of my breathing, easing in and out like an accordion playing busker on a lazy Sunday afternoon. I imagined the whooshing sound of an evening ocean tide cooling down the Pacific shoreline as it blankets over sand crystals.

Eventually, I'd have to fall asleep. My body would be overcome by fatigue.

Eyes still closed, I noticed a white glow the size of a golf ball gradually increase in size with every breath I drew. Remaining focused on my breathing, I watched the ball balloon larger until it disassembled to a million little sparks, the way fireworks disseminates into fragments. Feeling as if I was being pulled out of myself, I opened my eyes to make it stop. Closing them again, like pushing the play button on a cassette recorder, the tugging resumed.

Cognizant of people claiming to have had out-of-body experiences — a discussion that Jan, Bruce, and I'd had at Meadowlark, I questioned if I'd ever undergone anything of this nature and thought again about being a kid in church with my mom. An unknown energy source mimicking a game of cat and mouse was toying with me. To find out if I could muster the self-control to resist going whatever direction I was being lured like a vertical pull, I kept my eyes open.

The visual could have been my imagination playing tricks on me, as my mother used to say after a long, cranky childhood day. It also seemed plausible a part of me was reacting to something different going on — an opening up, first sensed during our preliminary visit to San Francisco. Michael said he'd first tapped into his "chi" life energy travelling abroad. Didn't Brother Bruce say he noticed a change in both of us? Maybe that change unlocked something inside.

Giving my soul permission to depart from my physical shell while conscious might transport me to a place that isn't good.

When exhaustion finally crept throughout my body, I gave in to a long, bottomless slumber.

Marco at Golden Gate Park, San Francisco.

CHAPTER 35
Flower Ladies

"The Cool, Grey City of Love." (San Francisco)
GEORGE STERLING

Next morning, I discovered everybody had gotten up and vacated the room. Yanking on a pair of jeans and t-shirt, scurrying off to the main room, I hoped to find leftovers. In the pantry, a couple of decrepit looking day olds gathered dust. Thankfully, a full coffee carafe sat warming on the burner. I didn't require much; a couple of bites and few sips would tide me over until dinner.

Seated at the table, mugs in hands, Jan and Marco looked ever the cute pair. Joining them, I bit down on a hard chocolate donut and diluted my coffee with milk. Brother James promised we'd be charged $2 a night (in a bed) if we helped tidy breakfast dishes and keep the kitchen clean. Jan and I were on duty.

Completing our tasks, we headed outside where Marco waited on the porch, a freshly rolled Drum cigarette dangled from his lips. A windy morning, skies were overcast. There was a bite in the air, yet it was mild enough. Live bands frequently played at the Oakland Coliseum. With any luck, we'd slink in and catch a live show. Heading down Steiner Street, our trio would need to grab a lift. This was the first time Jan and I had company thumbing a ride.

Our threesome didn't seem to deter prospective drivers. In two rides, we made it to the Oakland Coliseum, about a half hour away. Climbing out of the second vehicle, the driver had tried to pawn general admission tickets off on us for $10 apiece — "A real bargoon."

The man had no clue about which bands played on the bill.

Good thing we had little spare cash, the tickets turned out to be phony. A police officer witnessing the solicitation didn't hesitate to bust the man on the spot. Turns out, the guy had a reputation for attempting to lay bogus tickets on unsuspecting rock fans. According to the cop, fake scalped tickets were a common occurrence.

Circling the perimeter of the stadium, listed on the marquee were Blue Oyster Cult, Bad Company, and Santana. Sunday, Jeff Beck was scheduled to appear. There was no point sneaking in, security was tight. We'd have had a better chance with counterfeit tickets.

Hitching a ride to Emeryville, Marco suggested we stop for lunch at Denny's, one of the largest growing food chains in the U.S. New to America, in his estimation, Denny's was a hot commodity. Not expecting to chow down again until suppertime, I couldn't wait to unload on salty fries laden with ketchup and vinegar — next to potato chips, probably the greatest comfort food of all time.

Stuffing the greasy sticks into our mouths, Marco dropped a bombshell. Slated to go into the Swiss army on July 1, less than one month away, Marco asked Jan to marry him. "If you will become my wife," he pressed persuasively, "I wouldn't have to leave the country."

Knowing full well she didn't have American citizenship, Marco's end goal was to make his base in the United States. Marrying a Canadian girl was the first piece, allowing easy access to American soil.

It sounded like a sleazy con, particularly because I suspected Jan was falling for Marco.

We'd see how this prank would play out.

Jan's initial reaction, to bust out in laughter, induced Marco to lobby harder. Expressing his libidinous desires to my friend, straight and to the point, he was emphatic, "I vant a voman."

So, Marco wanted a wife, now he "vants a voman." The sound of desperation in his voice when he rolled out the "I vant a voman" really got to Jan and she laughed even harder. Stunned to have his proposal snubbed so straightforwardly, in a scolding tone, Marco implored he was dead serious.

Genuinely flattered to have been asked, my friend buckled down. Barely knowing the boy, Jan informed Marco that getting married would be a "dumb idea," adding she was only a kid.

Not about to give up, Marco asked Jan to at least think about it. Assuring him she would, the subject was abruptly dropped. In the time it had taken to squeeze a few blobs of ketchup and vinegar on top of a plateful of plump fries was the extent of the marriage conversation. Figuring out what to do next, we decided to eat up and hitch back to San Francisco to spend the balance of the afternoon in Golden Gate Park.

Hiking a mile or so out to the freeway, reaching the bridge, Marco produced a reefer.

With a snappy flick of his lighter, Swiss Romeo inhaled deeply before passing the joint to Jan, who in turn took a lengthy toke before extending the stick to me. The marijuana's capacities impelling the three of us straight away, we fell about in fits of hysterics until a blue Caddie convertible interrupted our clowning around. Pulling over to the curb, Herb Harvey from Pacific Heights offered a ride.

A classy fellow who expressed concern for our welfare, Harvey didn't hesitate to warn about the dangers of petitioning rides, and then dropped us safely at a downtown intersection. Handing over $5, Herb urged us to use it for bus fare and food. Thanking him for the free piece of advice and kind offer of money, deferring to Harvey's counsel, we decided to spend the cash on bus fare out to Golden Gate Park.

On Saturdays, hordes of people actively use Golden Gate Park, particularly families with small children. Wandering around, eventually we parked our butts on the mossy grass in the botanical area, a lush reservoir off the beaten path called Stow Lake. Appointed with a stone bridge, Stow Lake is quietly delightful. Comfortably sequestered from the rest of the world, Marco hauled out a pouch of Drum tobacco and Zig Zag cigarette papers. I hadn't smoked rolled cigarettes before, and wasn't much of a fan of smoking cigarettes at all. Adamant that rolled cigarettes were in a class alone and tasted better than manufactured smokes, Marco swore that given half a chance, we'd both love Drum.

He offered the tobacco and cigarette papers to Jan, who politely passed. Marco turned to me. "Would you like to try?"

Lifting a pinch of tobacco from the pouch, clumsily, I rolled myself a bulging cigarette, far fatter than what it should have been. Lighting the end of the pudgy cylinder, I inhaled. Raunchy tasting, the harsh shag made me choke.

Standing on his head a few feet away, hands planted firmly on the grass, Marco giggled at my inexperience. Holding his pose straight as a dart, tan leather boots extended high in the air, ankles squeezed tightly together, Moe walked me through the process of inhaling a hand-rolled cigarette.

Taking another drag, I started hacking my head off.

Still, I was not impressed.

Righting himself, Marco snatched the tobacco and papers from my hands and rolled a perfect cigarette in less than thirty seconds.

Now I was impressed.

Jan suggested bringing Marco to the Japanese Tea Garden where we'd gone with Michael during our first trip to the city. Trotting through the sunshine-doused grounds, we found ourselves before the watchful eyes of the large bronze Buddha, prominently positioned at the garden gateway. Outside of The Tea House bordered by cherry trees, the moon bridge, coloured lanterns, and a pagoda engulfed in a multitude of radiant flora, were sculpted shrubberies and trees decorated by festooning branches.

Romanticized by the alluring serenity, Marco popped the question a second time to Jan.

Answered by charged silence, he made one more attempt. Again, Marco was shut down.

Our persistent Swiss Romeo had one apparent weakness. He'd failed to calculate the willful sovereignty of my friend.

Returning to Steiner Street, we stepped down from the bus to make a pit stop at Safeway. Undoubtedly feeling like a weasel for pestering Jan, Marco insisted on making things right. He would prepare us dinner that evening.

Knowing exactly what he was after, our trip to the grocery store was brief. On the menu, an all-natural yogurt would be served with a basic assortment of fresh fruit. Fingering a tub of plain yogurt, Marco knew where he would purchase his ingredients. It was not the Safeway store. Two blocks from the hostel, a middle-aged female proprietor waited at a fruit stand. Wandering contemplatively down the street, Marco suddenly paused in front of the woman's stall.

Strands of long greying hair hung loose from the vendor's bun, the wind had twisted the fibers askew across her face, making it difficult to look directly into her eyes. Once the wind calmed, I distinguished two soft dark globes with delicate long black lashes. Moving about the stand, the woman carried herself like one who might have once worked in the theatre.

Oranges, apples, bananas, strawberries, kiwi, and melons sat upright on the wood shelf. Next to the fruit, long-stemmed red and pink roses, 25 cents apiece, lay across the table. Selecting several items, inspecting each one closely, Marco turned the individual shapes in his fingers as if they might break if he used too much force. Paying for the goods with a pocketful of coin, he received his purchases in a brown paper bag. Timidly, the woman smiled and, with a flourish, waved a few slender fingers across the end of the stand like a magician brandishing a wand.

Eyes full of trust, she asked, "How would you like pink roses for the two ladies?"

Marco's funds were scant, as were Jan's and mine. Fresh flowers were surplus. Excess. Besides, we could pick wild ones free. Embarrassed to confess he couldn't afford the roses, not wanting to hurt the woman's feelings, Marco vowed to return before the end of the week. Knowing his refrain by heart, bending her head gracefully, the woman waved goodbye.

Starting away from the fruit stand, I looked over my shoulder at the merchant's wistful eyes as she watched after us.

Nobody buys flowers from the flower lady.

View of San Francisco en route to Sausalito.

CHAPTER 36

The Holy Order and Sausalito

"Man is condemned to be free."
JEAN-PAUL SARTRE

Returning to HOOM, Jan and I were pleasantly surprised to find Grace and Jude. The Aussie couple was planning on staying two nights.

With much of the same crowd sprawled throughout the main room, hostellers drank stale java, talked travel, music, politics, and prepared cold impromptu meals in the hostel kitchen. Someone approached me about our pup tent. Would we consider selling it? I hadn't thought about ditching our tent just yet. When the guy offered $14, I checked with Jan.

Ecstatic to rid ourselves of the tent, not only would we each be $7 richer, purging ourselves of the nylon accessory would immediately lighten our load.

Liz had sent a letter to say she'd secured a summer clerical job working for the steel company in Hamilton. Her dream had finally come true. Liz would be an official "city" girl, "learning early how to open doors with just a smile" — a favourite lyric of hers from the Eagles song "Lyin' Eyes." Looking forward to meeting someone tall, dark, and complicated, I was confident Liz would settle for a steady guy with a car and a few bucks in his pocket.

She would keep us posted.

Carrying his groceries into the kitchen, Marco amassed the fruit along the counter top. The large plain yogurt tub lay open between a sharp utility knife and bananas, oranges, apples, and grapes. Efficiently slicing the goods, Marco told us he'd once worked at a café in Zurich where he'd learned to prepare inexpensive dishes consisting mainly of fruits and vegetables.

Allowing Jan and Marco to get to know one another better (Jan didn't want to marry Marco but she was intrigued), I slipped into the main room where Grace and Jude had befriended a fellow Aussie. Before long, Marco announced dinner was served. Out from the kitchen he strode; above his head, long fingers balanced a large ceramic bowl containing yogurt, with sliced fruit fragments arranged attractively on top.

I had to admit; Marco's dish looked fine and tasted even better.

Following dinner, Bruce introduced us to Sister Rose, one of the new women of The Holy Order's San Francisco chapter. Small in stature, Rose had straight, jet-black hair drawn into a bun at the back of her head. Her brown inquiring eyes shone like lighting sparks, emphasizing a youthful, freckle-spattered face. Dressed in a pale blue gown fastened with the HOOM women's obligatory rope belt, Rose could easily have passed for a child playing dress-up.

Since leaving home, my own hair had grown quite long. Providing I could track down a pair of sharp scissors, rallying Jan, I asked if she wouldn't mind giving me a cut. Pre-occupied sewing a patch on Marco's pants, Jan looked up from her task with a cheeky grin. "I'll be free later."

Swiss Romeo hadn't wasted a moment in his attempts to woo Jan, who appeared deliriously happy fulfilling personal requests. Positive that Marco could thread a needle and sew a patch, this was an obvious test to see if he could bring Jan around to accepting his proposal of marriage.

If she could mend, she was good to go.

Though not consciously part of the burgeoning women's liberation movement of the 1970s, setting out on our undetermined journey, a symbolic chord with the female liberation crusade had been struck. In 1976, women and men still had a long road ahead. Performing subservient favours for a male could be interpreted many ways. My friend didn't over think this assignment. At the very least, she was being helpful. If Jan was happy, I was pleased.

Having heard from one of the others that I was looking for a trim, claiming she usually shortened her own hair including her bangs, Rose kindly offered to oblige.

As far as I was concerned, this was more than sufficient résumé in the hair styling department. Promptly, I took my seat in the kitchen chair allocated for haircuts, dye jobs, and beard trims, the same chair that Daniel had perched in as a guinea pig back in April.

Using a plastic water bottle to spray the ends of my hair making it wet and flat, Rose lifted the heavy shears and proceeded to snip. As she clipped, Rose and I interacted the way a loyal customer and hairstylist might during a cut, perm, or colour. Inviting her opinion, I told Rose how Brothers James and Bruce alleged that Jan and I had come into focus since we'd first left HOOM. Thinking over my comments, after a moment, Rose asserted, "I believe the two Brothers meant that with each new experience, you and your friend are growing into your true selves. Each encounter along the path is a key, unlocking the door to realization, awareness and perception. Not only who we are as people, but our spiritual faculties, nurtured as we walk through life. It is part of the continued process of seeing."

Rose's interpretation of the Brothers' observation of our return was strangely reaffirming. The first female member of HOOM I'd spoken with, Sister Rose revealed a reassuring, simpatico way about her. In a short window of time, I could tell Rose was well liked. A devotee to The Holy Order, Sister Rose didn't project a manner of strict authority or obedience displayed by some of her Brothers and Sisters. What made HOOM different from other religious denominations (as far as I could tell) categorized under the label "cult," members never imposed their will or belief system upon outsiders. Non-members were not solicited to join. It had to be an individual's own decision.

The privilege of becoming part of a little known elite spiritual society wasn't enough to push me over the edge just yet. I wanted to be convinced.

I looked forward to talking with the Good Samaritan.

Next morning, my throat hurt. Assuming I'd contracted the beginnings of a cold or flu virus, living in and out of a backpack for several months amongst strangers, sleeping on floors, suspect beds, and tenting, it was only a matter of time before one or both of us became vulnerable to bugs.

I'd drawn the first unlucky card.

After breakfast, somebody took pity and gave me a throat lozenge. Then, along with a few HOOM members, a group of us piled into a red van to attend Sunday morning services at Cole Street Community Center where HOOM's tribe practiced their faith. Presided by Father Allen, the sermon's message was strong and reflective in tone, proffering motive to take personal inventory. I didn't exactly feel guilt or that I was trespassing into heathen territory. What came into question was whether I was sucking up space living a hedonistic, throw-caution-to-the-wind existence. Certainly, my life could resemble something more dignified.

Feeling wedged between remaining a teenager and transitioning into adulthood, which would surely come soon enough, there was also the matter of sex, a foreign entity. Something told me I'd need my head audited to forfeit carnal familiarity in exchange for a life of celibacy. Not that I knew if HOOM members practiced abstinence. From everything I'd gleaned, religious commitment and sexual gratification were not synonymous. If I was wrong, nobody volunteered to clarify.

Of one thing, I was certain. HOOM members could only marry affiliates of the organization. They were very strict about that.

Descending the hill from the Centre to Steiner Street, despite my raw throat, mid-morning sunshine helped to disregard symptoms. Brisk as ever earlier, the wind had finally died down and the temperature hovered in the low-seventies. Next to the front window of the manse, a non-descript, white brick building located across the road, a scrawny young man swept the porch steps. Despite his scalped head, short-sleeved black shirt, white collar, and wood cross, Teddy's quick, jerky movements gave him away.

My stomach started to churn. Wiping sweaty palms on my jeans, I told myself, *Appear neutral, you moron. Act nonchalant.*

Gradually approaching the bottom step, Jan and I patiently waited. Suspecting a foreign force in his trajectory, looking up from the broom, a grin flooded Teddy's hollow cheekbones. He shouted, "Wowee! Hiya, happies!"

In one fluid motion, putting aside his brush, the Good Samaritan asked what we'd been up to in the weeks since leaving HOOM.

Talking over one another at first, and then remembering how I'd been waiting for this opportunity for weeks, Jan sweetly begged off. Dispensing a jumbled version of some of the peaks and valleys of our travels to Big Sur, L.A., San Diego, Hemet, Fresno, and Yosemite, I felt Jan's eyes bore into the side of my face. Privately, I knew she was rating my performance.

Having worked in Fresno for a year as a farm hand, Teddy said he had fond memories of the sedate, tranquil life. Difficult to envision the Good Samaritan toiling away in sun-saturated fields harvesting iceberg lettuce until dusk, I realized how little I knew about the man, except that I liked him — a lot. Thinking it might be wise to preserve the short time we had, I asked a pointed question.

"So how do you like being a novice so far?"

"It's not a bad gig," Teddy started, "but I've got a few things to teach the Brothers and Sisters about rock music among other screwy ideas. They say it upsets the pattern of The Order. They're under the assumption that anything other than classical music is interference, which is a crock of shit. I stood up and let my feelings be known. I don't think they appreciated that."

Not surprised to learn that Teddy struggled under a regime of con-formity and capitulation, for better or worse, I'd opened a can of worms.

Hands and arms oscillating wildly in the air, in the span of several minutes, Teddy paraded through a repertoire of traits that had initially attracted me to him. The more invested he became in his repartee, the more exaggerated his actions. Without naming names, Teddy relayed disdain for "People in positions of authority who attempt to chastise those merely questioning certain policies in the face of life, supported by validity and legitimacy."

Damning the torpedoes and regulations enforced, in the end, Teddy confessed he was "learning to adapt."

Wondering about those in authority who Teddy might be inferring, I recalled several folks at the manse we'd never formally met.

The Good Samaritan glanced warily over his shoulder. "Sorry, I have to cut our conversation short." With work still to finish, Teddy didn't want to "piss off" his superiors more than, presumably, he already had. Smiling wanly, he said goodbye.

Documenting our conversation with Teddy would have to wait until later. That morning at Cole Street, Jan and I'd encountered Manny Libowitz, a tourist and family therapist staying at HOOM. Libowitz had invited the two of us to tag along with him to Sausalito. No strings. Beautiful weather conditions inspired Libowitz to decide to take the ferry to tour the scenic island, a hub for artists.

Predicated on our short conversation at Cole Street, I had a sense that spending time in Manny's company might be worthwhile.

Possibly edifying.

Meeting in the common area of HOOM, Manny, Jan, and I proceeded to catch a ride with a schoolteacher driving a fire engine red Volkswagen. Zigzagging along Market Street until reaching the ferry docks, the driver let us out. For 75 cents each, we picked up three tickets at the wicket. The next ferryboat would depart for Sausalito in fifteen minutes.

During the sun-bathed voyage, the three of us sprawled out along the yellow painted benches lining the deck floor. Nestled amongst deep blue breakers and a show of colourful sailboats, gliding gently past Alcatraz Island, Manny, a native Southern Californian, imparted the particulars of his clinical practice located on Kelton Avenue near the UCLA campus. The stresses of his workload bearing down on him, two days previous, Manny broke from the program and flew to San Francisco, a city he'd loved since childhood. Later that afternoon, he planned to return home.

Sporting three houseboat communities along its waterfront, Sausalito upholds a contentious boundary between wealthy developers, impoverished artists, and borderline income people. For the past four decades, the squads continue to clash in conflict as the "rich people on the hill" fight to have the low-income houseboat residents extinguished to make room for growth.

Today, the communities, approximately 400 boats in all, continue to subsist, two of which are located within the Sausalito city limit. They remain a large part of the city's allure.

Docking approximately 30 minutes after setting out, we recognized a young German man, Casper, from the hostel. One of the kiosks was selling fish and chips, a tempting combo I hadn't eaten since home. Standing before a booth manned by an awkward-looking teenaged boy, we watched and waited as the fish and fries crackled and hissed in six inches of grease. When our two orders were ready, Manny insisted on picking up the tab.

Dividing the food between the four of us, following our feed, we took a walk.

The sloping Sausalito streets contain sharp, ascending gradients that swath in and around cedars and Redwoods, augmented by hardy vegetation and floral bands of flourishing growth.

Following behind Manny and Casper, Jan and I mounted the incline to the top of the hill to scope out an attractive neighbourhood of houses, shops, and wine tasting rooms. Looking on at a bevy of enchanting cottages and boats poised soporific on the sea; I imagined a daily regime of sunshine spanked ocean right outside my doorstep. Breaking the spell, Casper began to scoff at the wine tasting merchants. Claiming that European grapes were far superior than fruit produced on California vines, the German insisted homeland characteristics surpassed most of the varietals he'd sampled in California, grapes that were grown in the Northern California interior, considered a prime growing region. Begging to differ, Manny assured Casper that California's flourishing wine industry was much more than a thriving innovation. Recognizing potential for worldwide market share, Libowitz explained how several Californians were entrepreneurs, planting and cultivating their own vineyards, even in the San Francisco Bay area.

Ignorant about wine as we had been at Cousin Darren's when the conversation was introduced at dinner, neither Jan nor I advanced an opinion.

Each one unwilling to bend, Manny and Casper continued arguing about grape superiority in 'my dad's better than your dad' fashion. Soon enough, Casper begged off, making his way down to the docks to catch the ferry back to San Francisco.

We took another walk.

The climate close to perfection for the feathered friends, Manny gestured to birds of varying species that had migrated to Sausalito. Observing a flock of seagulls pouncing mightily down on crushing waves while honing on an afternoon snack, Manny pointed toward what appeared to be an estate. Summoning us to follow him on to the deck, upon closer look, The Alta Mira Hotel was indeed a stately property.

Close to 90-years-old, The Alta Mira ("altar mire" meaning "high view" in Spanish), once a private residence with tennis courts and swimming pool, had been converted to a hotel in the 1920s. After the changeover, The Alta Mira became a coveted destination for weddings, parties, and meetings. The original cocktail lounge was eventually expanded to a vast octagon shape, catering to its many patrons and socialites. A strict dress code in effect, during the mid-1950s, a generous outdoor terrace was constructed, enabling guests to take advantage of the health benefits of salt suffused air. Dining on delicacies from the ocean, patrons and invitees drank in a majestic view of the San Francisco Bay.

More than thirty years after our visit, much to the discontent of long-time vicinity residents, to accommodate the ever-growing need for a treatment facility in the city, the Alta Mira was again renovated to a 48-unit drug and alcohol rehab facility.

Seated at one of the hotel's aluminum tables beneath a canvas umbrella on the expansive outside patio, the server came over to greet us. Insistent on indulging his two guests, Manny asked our preferences.

Contented to nurse grapefruit juice on the rocks, the sour juice soothing to my increasingly raw throat, imbibing in the sights and sounds of our surroundings, we watched flirtatious couples rendezvous over colourful drinks. Amusing us with anecdotes from his L.A. practice, most days, Manny confessed, counselling clients was a herculean task, far from the romanticized ideals he'd conceived when first entering the field of social work in his early twenties.

Manny asked if we enjoyed hitchhiking and wanted to know if we'd ever been fearful. Jan explained how we focused, meditated, prayed on receiving a ride with a "quality" person that would drive us where we wanted to go. Surprised but not dismissive of our (flimsy) method of protecting our own safety, as Jan and I took turns citing examples how successful this ploy had been for us to date, Manny dipped his head up and down. To show how resilient we thought we were, I added, "Sometimes, we'll even try to imagine the model and colour of the vehicle."

It was time to head back to the city. Rising from the table, eyes twinkling, Libowitz half-smiled, "Let's give your self-visualization theory a try."

The route out to the main artery was a distance. Hiking along a few hundred yards, the three of us conspired on the imminent arrival of a car, truck, van — any mode of transportation that would advance a lift.

A white panel truck halted along the shoulder of the road, sparing us time and energy on foot. Next, a couple of teenagers scooted us across the Golden Gate Bridge, stopping in front of the Fillmore. Climbing out from the front seat, a grin pleated Manny's face.

Our strategy had worked.

Beneath the Fillmore's façade, next to a couple buckets crammed with white carnations, three Hare Krishna's chanted in sync. Unbeknownst to us, Manny had purchased a couple of bus tickets so that Jan and I could take BART back to Steiner Street. Approaching the Krishna troupe, thoughtfully amused, Libowitz extracted two snowy-white carnations from the pail. Placing spare coins in the palm of a maniacally smiling disciple, turning in semi-circle, Manny postured for a moment and then handed each of us a blossom.

"Thank you for a lovely afternoon."

Hugging us one at a time, reaching into his wallet, two business cards were retrieved. "If you ever decide to return to Los Angeles and need anything, don't hesitate to call."

Waiting for the next bus to arrive, I thought about the woman's disappointed face the day before at the fruit stand. Somehow, Manny's modest act of kindness had reinstated balance in the universe. Returning to HOOM, Jan and I placed our carnations in a drinking glass, proudly setting it in the front window of our room.

That evening, Grace and Jude planned to go for a drive around the city. Despite the condition of my tender throat, it was a thrill crossing the Golden Gate Bridge, bonding the bay and the Pacific Ocean, brilliant and candescent at night.

Returning to HOOM around 11 pm, Marco appeared outside on the sidewalk. Evasive when asked where he'd spent the day and evening, I suspected that possibly, Marco had been scouring the downtown Tenderloin district, a well-known haven for drug activity. It was also plausible that somewhere in the nefarious underbelly of San Francisco's shadowy streets, Marco had found a voman. If Marco scored drugs and got laid, maybe he'd be sated.

Jan headed to bed. Though my body longed to retire, still psyched from the drive, I was determined to hold out.

Before leaving the common area, Jan mentioned something surprising. That morning, Marco had presented her with a seashell-strung necklace. She figured the dowry was a down payment, authentication of his marriage proposal.

Marco could never be accused of stupidity or waving the white flag.

"Lotus Flowers" watercolour by Barbara Mills. COURTESY OF CARLY MILLS

CHAPTER 37

Swiss Romeo Departs and Rose is Still a Rose

"The path is steep with no rail to guide. But the powers of the Universe are always at your side."
"CALL TO DUTY," *The Golden Force*

Sister Rose was the single female transplant from a nearby HOOM chapter. Thirty-two-year-old Brother John, a lanky, handsome man, was the male.

After most of the others had gone to bed, in the company of Brother John, discussion of spirituality was opened.

The word "spiritual" wasn't actually voiced that night. Instead, it danced along the margins of our talk, peering into my essence as the vendor had done when Marco failed to purchase the flowers. There were many unanswered questions about The Holy Order and related subjects.

Carefully, I probed.

If nothing happens by chance, then perhaps Jan and I had been divinely guided to choose The Holy Order of MANS hostel in April. Add Meadowlark and Evangel Home into the fusion, and you have holy germination. If in some way we were sent to HOOM et al, then why?

Brother John spoke about the differences between reality and the perception of reality. A slightly different spin on Sister Rose's talk the night before about seeing, basing his beliefs upon personal life accounts and expectations, according to John, our sensitivity to reality differs. An auteur on reality versus unreality, prior to life reformation, from the age of fifteen, John had undergone several scrappy years on the streets of San Francisco. The last seven years, he'd worked hard to effectually create distance between old and new routines.

One of the HOOM's vital teachings Brother John pointed out, was learning to disregard preexisting information that hints at a fundamental root of truth. Unless an individual visits Paris firsthand, how could anyone possibly know that Paris exists?

"Seeing is believing. Seeing is truth. Seeing is personal knowledge."

This is akin to creating one's own reality, I thought. Brother John's rationalization seemed to align with the concept of existentialism (which, according to some definitions denies the universe of intrinsic power), a popular term then that was not part of my vernacular in those days, though my brother Chris had once tried to explain it to me. Creating our own reality was consistent with what I'd come to understand about HOOM. Yet, the assertion seemed to deny acknowledgement of God.

Didn't HOOM members believe in God?

Feeling my brain might implode, thanking Brother John for his company, I headed to bed.

Something that had been told us when we were kids: Sleep on it. In the morning, it will make sense.

I doubted it.

Dawn was overcast and 55 degrees — about the same as my body felt: listless, chilled, and punk. Gratefully, Brother James allowed me to remain in bed longer than usual.

Youth hostels don't take kindly to illness. It's not that those in charge don't care, but it's very unlike being a kid sick at home where Mom appears carrying a tray of chicken noodle soup, dry toast, and glass of flat ginger ale. In the vagabond world, you must buck up.

It was my own fault I felt shitty. I should have gone to bed the night before when my body demanded it. Essentially, I got what I deserved. I guess that meant I'd created my own reality.

Sarcasm didn't help me to feel better. A cup of stale black coffee might. At least I'd get enough of a caffeine kick to souse me with energy for a few hours. It had worked before.

Following thirty minutes in comatose heaven, I hauled my ass out of bed and prepared for the day ahead. There were no set plans. Usually, Jan and I talked with friends and fellow hostellers at breakfast and took it from there. Settling down at the big pine table, mug in hand, I was met with some bad news. Grace and Jude had their tires slashed overnight. Preparing to leave Steiner Street for Montreal that morning, the Aussie couple hadn't expected to incur more car expense.

Shit.

The tire incident was a definite bummer. For one, it felt like a bad omen. Wishing I had excess funds in my bag of tricks to help them out, all that was left were precious dollars (little more than $100) I'd managed to squirrel away to last the rest of our journey — at least until we found jobs. Precariously closer to reaching a point where we would need to work before returning home, neither Jan or I were afraid of work or working hard. Unless you found something under the table, without a permit, employment in the U.S. was unlikely. That same old bugaboo. Short-term employment — cleaning or gardening bartered in exchange for food, lodging, or both, we'd wrangled since crossing the border. Trading labour for food and bed was an excellent bargaining tool for anyone wanting to explore North America, only demand was the essential requirement for it to fly. Sometimes folks got creative finding jobs for you. Often, there just wasn't the necessity or priority.

In lieu of a money loan for replacement tires, I offered Grace and Jude my home address and telephone number, assuring them they were welcome to "stay anytime" during their visit to Canada. Determined to be on their way, since they didn't carry a spare set of tires, Grace called a tow truck to pick up the Volkswagen and drive it to a garage. Exchanging earnest hugs with Grace and Jude, it was yet one more leave-taking.

Curious to see the oldest and one of the most storied California academia institutes, Marco, Jan, another one of the short-term HOOM hostellers, Charlie, and I, hitched a ride out to Berkeley. Technically, Jan and I hadn't stepped on campus when visiting Berkeley with Gary a couple of months earlier. We'd merely meandered along the periphery.

Having accrued a worldwide reputation for drugs, open love, demonstrations, free speech, and friction, Berkeley University was held liable for permanently branding the mid-late 1960s youth movement, melding together and mobilizing groups deemed by straights as hippies, activists, Yippees and apolitical wasters united with the radical left. Telegraph Avenue, a 4 ½ mile street beginning in Oakland and ending at the southern edge of the University of California campus in Berkeley, had become a daily trough for hippies and rebels until the end of the Vietnam War in 1974. Walking the campus site, you felt a current in the air still rife with vestiges of the previous decade.

Following lunch at the school's cafeteria, trailing the fringes of the campus grounds, we explored Telegraph Avenue where we'd been told there were clothing and bookstores galore. Snooping inside a couple of record stores, Marco sniffed out and examined every single Eric Burden and The Animals LP. Looking over at Marco, then down at the various albums in his hands, I was struck by his resemblance to Burden, the British band's lead singer. In April, Jan and I'd consorted with Jagger's twin, now we were hobnobbing with Eric Burden's clone. Mostly because of his hairstyle, Marco continued to remind me of Moe from "The Three Stooges."

I let him know.

Marco was annoyed.

We split up. Jan, Charlie and I got a lift in a pick-up truck while Marco hung back. Instructing the driver to drop us off at the wharf, I hoped the scent of saline water would be almost as restorative as a day's bed rest. Unless you were at death's door, the hostel was off limits during the day.

Returning to HOOM with a case of the sweats compounded by throbbing headache, burning throat, fever, and aching muscles, stepping into the vestibule that afternoon greeted by a small network of co-travellers; Brothers James, John, and Sister Rose, I felt cloaked in solace. It wasn't only the effects of flu — a transmutation continued to take place. If I'd learned anything since coming away, it was to revel in the nebulous blush.

From the kitchen marched Marco, all dressed up with somewhere to go. Leaving him behind on Telegraph Avenue, evidently, he'd met a woman. Details about her physical description or whereabouts were not disclosed. Marco made a point of letting us know he'd met someone and bragged about hooking up with her later that evening.

Not that it was my business, nor did I entirely care, save wanting Jan's feelings spared. I was curious if Marco's voman in question was a streetwalker. His girlfriend might very well have even been a ghost, a figment of Marco's imagination, or wishful thinking. Infuriated that she'd turned down his premature marriage proposal, it was entirely plausible Marco was trying to make Jan jealous.

In the interim, Marco and one of the girls had a contest to see who could sketch more skillfully. Determined to make the greater impact showing off his artistic dexterity, setting about to draw a pencil portrait of Jan, Marco accurately depicted her freckles and russet brown hair. This was another staged effort no doubt to win Jan over. Though flattered beyond compare, Jan hung tough on the "no marriage" deal.

Marco did a disappearing act upstairs to the men's dorm to sulk.

Two new arrivals entertained our group playing acoustic guitars, perfecting beautiful harmonies. Busking their way across America, adeptly, the pair covered an arm's length list of popular folk songs. Suddenly surfacing from the Men's dorm, cheerfully, Marco announced he was leaving for the night. His date was waiting out front.

It was a quarter past eleven. Glancing lazily over her shoulder, in a sing-song voice, Jan cried out, "Have a good time!"

Sitting in our PJ's, sipping red zinger tea with lemon; we continued to enjoy the live tunes. Around midnight, obviously upset about something, Marco returned from wherever he'd gone and again headed directly toward the men's dorm. Torn about whether to console him or let it go, Jan decided against walking into his trap.

The man had needs. He wasn't going quietly.

Next morning, backpack strapped against his young, strong body, a keen certainty flashing in intense dark eyes, Marco entered the kitchen leaving no doubt, Swiss Romeo was about to move on to the next plateau. Not surprising perhaps for Marco, a master at maintaining an austere expression, there had been no mention about leaving Steiner Street to anybody the night before.

Following Marco down the front steps and out onto the sidewalk, Jan received kisses upon both cheeks. Exchanging addresses to their respective hometowns, the pair made small talk. Marco accepted Jan's offer of fruit and chocolate chip cookies for the road, and then disappeared into a funnel cloud of exhaust smoke.

Indeed, Jan had liked Marco. How would she accept his leaving?

As I watched my friend silently watch Marco vanish from view, turning around, she finally said, "And so much for Marco the actor."

Stunned by her nonchalance, I asked Jan if she was okay.

"Sure. I'm fine."

Case closed.

Cool and overcast, Jan, Charlie, and I made plans to venture to Ocean Beach in the west part of Golden Gate Park. With a free day on her hands, Sister Rose asked if she could tag along. Apart from her old-fashioned clothing and knowledge of ethereal things, Rose was one of the gang. And there was familiarity between Charlie and Rose. Charlie's older sister, Dina, also a member of HOOM, was a friend.

There was no sense bellyaching about feeling crappy. It had been pointed out by Rose and some of the others that perhaps my body was overdue for a cleansing. Apparently, physical illness is something to rejoice not abhor. Presumably, constructive thinking on my part could ease some of the nastier symptoms of cold and fever. If I remembered to carry throat lozenges in my canvas bag and adhered to red zinger tea and lemon before bed, I should feel better soon.

Rose's orders.

Chilly and blustery, Ocean Beach was spacious like an outdoor gymnasium, untouched by human debris and crass commercialism — a contrast to several of the beaches along the Los Angeles coastline. Walking against the east wind, we knelt on the sand to scrutinize miniscule sea creatures still housed within their shells. A historic pavilion-type edifice, The Cliff House hovered over the Pacific Ocean. Below the overhang, a colony of seals spread their slippery, tawny bodies along the rocks in the sun. The unremitting steady smell of migrant salt water felt regenerative.

Rose soon left to meet Reverend Mary for a lunch engagement. Coinciding with the wind's shift, the Sister's sudden parting altered the mid-day mood from good humoured to mercurial. Having held back within the presence of his sister's friend, once Rose was gone, Charlie made it clear he wasn't a fan of HOOM, and regretted his sister Dina's involvement.

Painting their contemporaries with the same brush, Charlie felt that HOOM members believed they held themselves to a higher standard than some of their adversaries such as Moonies, Hare Krishna's, Scientologists, The Divine Light, Mormons, and others. Citing examples of hypocrisies, Charlie pointed out double standards between men and women and spoke of dissention among the group. Alcohol was permitted, drugs weren't. Charlie lamented how his sister had devolved from an intelligent and empathetic, outgoing human being into an abyss of regulations and convention masked as spiritual freedom. In Charlie's mind, Dina's pursuit, to command supernatural supremacy promised to her by the organization had accomplished little more than a lifetime subscription to a ball and chain. Poking fun at some of the Brothers and Sisters he'd gotten to know through his sister, Charlie began making crude jokes. I asked his opinion of Rose. Charlie liked Rose well enough, but kept his distance.

In Charlie's eyes it was a case of us and them. Rose was the enemy.

Uneasy about these revelations, I didn't let on other than making the initial inquiry about Rose and a couple of the others. Against my better judgment, I joined in on the occasional put down as I might have done in elementary school when some poor kid was being mocked without just cause. Not about to contradict Charlie or demean his right to his opinion, this wasn't grade school. To be fair, through Dina, Charlie did have firsthand knowledge of The Holy Order, and therefore felt entitled to cast disparaging remarks. An even greater reason to be incensed, in his heart, Charlie believed he'd lost his sister forever.

I liked Charlie. He was considerate. A straight shooter. All things being equal, Charlie wasn't coming from a position of objectivity. I couldn't accept what he'd divulged without a smidgen of salt. When push came to shove, I relied upon my intuition. Up until that point, personal dealings with everybody at HOOM were non-threatening. Above board. If anything, I felt validated about my own questions regarding God and other spiritual matters. It nagged at me how Jan joined in on the digs a little too mercilessly. Uncertain if she genuinely yielded to Doug's views or was fearful of her own feelings of attraction, my friend hadn't told me as much, but I'd guessed that she, too, considered joining the Sisterhood.

What a shame if it was all a sham. People resent being made out to be fools. It's the ultimate ego killer.

Leaving the beach, a young woman pressed a fistful of purple wildflowers into my hands. Since arriving in California, flowers had become the window dressing of our daily lives. "Flowers, not guns." That was the sentiment in the sixties. San Francisco, 1976, it still applied.

Later, arranging the bouquet into a clay vase and setting it in the living room, my eyes happened upon Teddy playing hopscotch with a group of children at Duboce Park. Dancing around like Pied Piper, several kids gathered around his waist, I'd never seen him so lighthearted.

Chinatown, San Francisco.

CHAPTER 38

Chinatown, City Lights, Checkmate

"Live, travel, adventure, bless, and don't be sorry."
JACK KEROUAC

Our food supply needed replenishing. Jan and I set out for Safeway to pick up more of what had kept us going since leaving home. Across the street, Teddy swept the front steps of the manse. If not for his scalped head and green kangaroo jacket overtop a black shirt and pants, you'd swear he'd been part of HOOM forever.

One of The Holy Order's hard and fast policies prevented non-novices from visiting trainees inside their place of residence. Our only chance of connecting with Teddy was to seize an opportunity such as this one. Rushing back into the dorm, opening my knapsack, I grabbed the poem and cross I'd picked out at Meadowlark, bounced down the porch steps and crossed the road diagonally toward the manse. Barely containing her excitement, Jan followed a few paces behind.

Unsuspecting, Teddy continued his work. When I erupted into a short coughing stint, he couldn't help but pay attention. From behind my back, I produced two small offerings; a guise of encouragement for the sacred path Teddy had recently chosen. Safeguarding against letdown, expectations were next to nil.

"These are for you. From Meadowlark."

Intrigued when he saw we'd come bearing gifts, Teddy stood the broom against the wood-sided enclosure and assessed both our faces. His blue, translucent eyes adopting a gentle quality, reaching down to accept the items, the Good Samaritan exclaimed, "Wow! Wow! Wow!"

Fixated on the schema of the cross, Teddy lifted his head, eyes gleaming. "I be*lieve* it! Son of a *gun!* You girls are *terrific!*"

Claiming to be unaccustomed to receiving presents or souvenirs, Teddy raked one skinny hand across his head, confessed his embarrassment and thanked us profusely. Gusts of wind rolling in from off the bay proved difficult for him to hold the paper still on which the poem was printed. Promising to cherish the words alone in his room once his daily tasks were completed, the Good Samaritan tucked the little cross and poem protectively inside a shirt pocket.

What happened next took us both by surprise.

Deducing that he had an estimated one week to go before given the boot, Teddy fired a missive about his latest infractions studying under The Holy Order's counsel. "Whenever I ask questions, I get yelled at," he complained. "The Brothers say I'm dubious and stubborn. They call me a blasphemy. Tell me to let go and accept."

Unsure how to react or respond to this confession, rebounding for a moment, I asked Teddy how long he'd been interested in religion.

"I'm not." Clearly amused by our matching stunned expressions and the irony of his own retort, Teddy started to chuckle. Convinced there must be some deeper meaning behind his answer, I truly didn't know what that meaning was. Without question, joining The Holy Order wasn't what Teddy had expected to do with his life. In my own confusion, I dared to put forth another question. "Have you ever felt emotional about your decision to become a novice?"

The Good Samaritan paused, dreamlike, as if recalling a fond memory.

"Of course," he admitted softly. "I've cried many times. This hasn't been easy for me."

Teddy appeared as if he might add something more. Instead, silence hung expectant in the air, and our novice friend awkwardly begged off. Collecting the broom and dustpan, pushing open the door to the manse, he beheld us from his platform. "Hey, will you two be around for a while longer?"

Brushing specks of gravel from her sandals to decoy, Jan said nothing.

"About a week," I shrugged. "Then we'll start making our way back to Canada."

"Great." Teddy flashed a mouth full of white teeth. "Thanks again for the poem. I'll look forward to reading it later."

That evening, we listened to Rod Stewart's *Every Picture Tells a Story* and played cards to pass time. Distracted by the events of the day, I did my best to put on a happy face. Music, even at its most raucous, routinely had a capitulating effect. Now, I felt at loose ends. My stomach, the first body part to cave whenever something troubled me, twisted into knots. Because of the influx of hostellers visiting HOOM, Jan and I forfeited our beds and unrolled our sleeping bags along the floor of the women's dorm. It hardly seemed right that we should have first dibs, particularly since becoming regulars.

Lying inside of my bag fighting off sleep and the tenderness in my throat, I recounted our conversation with Teddy. If indeed there ever was one, it would seem the honeymoon phase of his relationship with HOOM had ended. Having endured a perilous life until that point, I couldn't imagine where his unstructured lifestyle would guide him next. In the span of one day, Teddy *and* Charlie had both pointed out how HOOM was flawed, punitive, and castigatory. *Not unlike most spiritually based organizations*, I thought. Two independent individuals were quick to pan The Holy Order.

Perhaps it was a warning to take stock.

Before talking with Teddy, I'd had it in my head that for the most part, Charlie's negative comments about HOOM were brought on because of his belief that Dina had fallen lost to the herd. On the other hand, Teddy was directly caught up. Possessing no ulterior motive to malign the people involved or the group itself, he'd twice spoken of feeling persecuted and being under the thumb. What he *hadn't* said was he would willingly *leave*.

Before my flirtation with a decision that may collide not only with my freedom but also with the rest of my life took root, I hoped to find resolution.

It had become a simple matter of taking a dump or getting off the pot.

Wednesday morning was overcast and damp. Five days and counting now, Jan and I were back at HOOM with no clear-cut course of action. Surmising that she loved the place as much as I did, I sensed we were both procrastinating to avoid facing the inevitable: *What were we going to do once we returned home?* Maybe only one of us would be returning home.

Another question nagged. Was I was more attracted to Teddy than I was to The Holy Order? How excruciating if it boils down to this plain, niggling truth.

Romantic designs on Teddy were a dead-end street. Entrenched in his own frantic world, one that rotated around hustling and survival, as far as I could tell, the Good Samaritan hardly had spare change for an eighteen-year-old cling-on. If he did happen to put me on the clock, how would I react? I was a girl, a *virgin* nonetheless, one who'd had next to zilch physical encounters with boys. What right did I have to an attraction to a 28-year-old *man* — an individual with one disastrous marriage under his belt, barely scraping through a life utterly converse to my own? To entertain the idea that feelings might be mutual was presumptuous, even laughable. I was a teenager, with little to offer in the way of worldly experiences — sexually, intellectually, and *especially* monetarily. Putting all of that aside, I couldn't deny my feelings. In every imaginable way, I was treading in deep shit.

Despite my emotional unrest, health-wise, I felt mildly better than the day before. My cough sounded worse than I looked, and felt. With zero room for recuperation, this was one saving grace. Recently, Jan had developed a hack as well. Considering our constant close quarters, sickness was to be expected.

At breakfast, we ate the regular day-olds and drank tar coffee. Brother James assigned a couple of the others to dishes duty. A hosteller from Dublin, John Gailey, joined Jan, Charlie, and me on a day trip that began with a quick jaunt to the bank followed by a ride on BART to Fremont just for the hell of it. Taking in Chinatown, the Transamerica Pyramid Building and City Lights Bookstore, the Pyramid Building was scarcely worth the effort. Chinatown and City Lights on the other hand, were fabulous.

The oldest integrated Chinese district throughout North America, San Francisco's Chinatown contains the second largest Chinese population in the world. With its huge incursion of Hong Kong Chinese immigrants flooding the city in the 1960s, founded in 1848, Chinatown spans 24 city blocks and is located between Telegraph Hill and North Beach. Limitless restaurants, flamboyant pagoda-tiled roofs, herbal shops, live fish markets, annual parades, and extraordinary alleyways garner Chinatown one of the most preeminent tourist attractions in all of San Francisco and along the West Coast of the United States. One of Chinatown's historic zones, Portsmouth Square, is where visitors and inhabitants gather to observe Tai Chi devotees performing their daily ritual, and watch elder Chinese chess specialists engage in taut competition. Situated on Grant Avenue (famous for Rodgers and Hammerstein's *Flower Drum Song*, 1961), welcoming visitors to the enclave at Chinatown's entranceway, is the ornate and arresting Dragon Gate. Constructed from stone, wood, and green tile, the elaborate edifice was designed and created in 1970 by three brothers: Clayton Lee, Melvin H. Lee, and Joe Lee.

Because of its beauty, authenticity, eclectic architecture and precipitous terrain, Chinatown and other sectors of San Francisco have served as prime locales for feature film productions such as *San Francisco* (1936), *The Maltese Falcon* (1941), and *Harold and Maude* (1971), among others. During the early to late seventies, San Francisco's lax laws and sexual liberties appealed to the production of adult features, and the windswept city became a bevy of activity for pornographic movies, although arrests were regularly made as officials tried to shut operations down.

In 1973, pioneers Jim and Artie Mitchell shot *Behind the Green Door* starring Marilyn Chambers and Johnny Keyes. Enjoying an extended run at the Mitchell brothers O'Farrell Theater located at 895 O'Farrell Street, the highly successful production encouraged similar subsequent projects. A two-part adaptation of *The Maltese Falcon*, adult pictures *The Jade Pussycat* (1977) and *China Cat* (1978), produced by L.A. based Freeway Films, directed by Bob Chinn and starring legendary porno star John C. Holmes, were shot on location in Chinatown and neighbouring environs.

Chinatown's nearby financial district houses the Transamerica Pyramid, a four-sided, 48-floor skyscraper shaped like a triangular middle finger with a 212-foot pointed spire on top. Formerly headquarters of Transamerica Corporation, in 1976, earthquake proof Transamerica Pyramid had the distinction of being the tallest building in the world.

Riding the elevator to the 27th floor of the Pyramid (Richard, from our maiden voyage to San Francisco with Walter, renamed it "The Ugly Building"), from a staggering perspective, Charlie, John, Jan, and I gawked at the metropolis below. Back on level ground, we started down Columbus Avenue to North Beach, home of City Lights Bookstore.

In 1953, poet Lawrence Ferlinghetti and Peter D. Martin teamed up to create the nation's first all paperback bookstore; a "literary meeting place" designed to attract the influential, politically minded, and revolutionary new writers. Renowned authors, novelists, poets, pioneers, friends and contemporaries such as Jack Kerouac, Allen Ginsberg, and Frank O'Hara were first introduced at City Lights in the 1950s. Expanding over the years to include three main floors, the store also functions as an independent publishing house. Managing to retain its bohemian appeal, intertwining book lovers and tourists seeking to bask in the 'Beat Poet' entrenched culture and artist pedigree, City Lights offers titles by both large and independent publishers.

Tumbling into the emporium mid-afternoon, we discovered that, since first opening its door 23-years earlier, City Lights hadn't likely much changed. Distinguished and beguiling, the main floor's enriching characteristics, evincing faded hardwood, elevated ceilings, muted light, and creaking stairs adding to the store's laid-back milieu, enabled patrons to detach adrift the smells, sights, and soaring shelves stockpiled with novels, textured covers and tomes.

Possessing a wide spectrum of knowledge on cutting edge writers, consisting mainly of hippie-types, City Lights' staff induced customers to sample a vast cross section of works spanning decades, no matter how ambiguous. Deciding to pamper myself, for a five spot, I picked up a copy of author Anne Rice's recently released Gothic horror novel, *Interview with the Vampire.*

Returning to Steiner Street, Brother John appeared to be waiting for us.

"How would you like to go swimming?" No sooner had we accepted, John told us that every Wednesday night, he chaperoned a group of children with intellectual disabilities at Rossi Recreation Center.

Not about to run risk of giving Brother John the impression we had anything personal against "retarded" kids (an acceptable term then), or that we had something better to do, Jan and I went to grab our bathing suits.

Half past six, John, Jan, and I boarded the streetcar to Fifth and Lincoln, making our way to Rossi Center. For the next ninety minutes, we played and applauded the youngsters as they tried to outdo John with outlandish dives, cannon balls, and summersaults producing miniature tidal waves in the chlorine-intoxicated pool. Bright, happy, and outgoing, the kids took to us immediately. When it was time to leave, several children asked if Jan and I could join them again the following week.

"If the girls are still around," John was careful not to promise, "they're more than welcome."

A *lot* could happen in one week.

Joni Mitchell's *Blue* set a solemn tone later that evening while a group of us (including Jan) further dialogued about the spirit world with Brothers Bruce and John.

In April, James, Bruce, and some of the others had hinted about a practice alleged restricted to VIP members of The Holy Order. By altering physical forms into a transformative medium, apparently, advanced participants could transport through walls. In reference to a passage in *The Golden Force* that describes matter particles as a "state of vibration" and physical material and spirit as one succinct unit, admitting he hadn't witnessed this enterprise personally, Bruce proclaimed it to be true.

Thursday, Joanne, one of the female novices, came out to the garden where I had gone to sketch a small patch of cornflowers. Suspicious if she was sent by one of her superiors to try to get inside of my head, I quickly realized I was being paranoid. Outfitted with gardening tools and gloves, Joanne was not there under false pretenses.

A couple of years older than I, Joanne had been raised in a commune in Northern California. Coming from an untraditional upbringing by nomadic parents, joining an alternative religious sect didn't seem an unnatural step for Joanne. She accepted her choice as one might accept an arranged marriage. I came away from our exchange feeling more like a powder puff than an anchor.

In pursuit of a needlepoint kit for Jan (a hobby passed down by her grandmother), on our way through Union Square, we were (pleasantly) accosted by a pair of clean cut Moonies posing as college boys. The matching polyester pants and button-downed shirts fooled us at first, but not for long. Essentially, we were ambushed by two missionaries offering up free dining privileges, lodging, and friendship in exchange for a weekend praying and cavorting at their compound in Berkeley.

A regular barrel of laughs.

Likely, there wouldn't be much cavorting — these guys were a humourless laconic pair. During our travels, we'd heard rumours about weekend rendezvous at Moonie headquarters. Reputedly, the group preyed on aimless teenagers, ridding youths of self-reliance and reducing them to mind-numbed subordinates willing to do whatever was required by leaders — a reverse-suck diversion tactic like the one used by master manipulator Charles Manson.

Isolate. Dominate. Divide.

The unlucky ones don't get away.

It was unanimous. Jan and I would give our walking manikins the brush-off.

Easier said than done. Eyes blazing, expounding passionately about their faith and beliefs while extolling the virtues of Commandant Reverend Sun Myung Moon, the Moonies all but convinced me they were lit up on mescaline or maybe something better. Not that either one of us had anything against mind-altering substances, but the fanatical deportment of these two was more than an excuse to refuse.

It boiled down to a simple case of deduction. Moonies are *freaks*, and not in a good way.

By comparison, HOOM members are innocuous.

Wearing the Green Kangaroo.

CHAPTER 39

Green Kangaroo

"Law, Love, Live. Be in the consciousness of the three L's."
MEADOWLARK — *Valle Vista, CA*

At Steiner Street for exactly one week, time passed quickly. So far, no one made overtures about our leaving. Not wanting to become parasites was one more incentive for making a firm decision to renounce HOOM or remain. Praying for a little more time, an answer would surely arrive soon.

Despite light rain showers, Jan and I invited Charlie to come along with us to Sausalito, *the* place to find something special for his sister Dina's upcoming birthday. Uncertain which direction to head back down to the docks to catch the ferry, waiting on Charlie, Jan and I crossed the street to inquire at the manse.

Sure, there was ulterior motive — the chance that Teddy might answer the door.

One hard knock on the front entry, my wish was granted.

Stepping onto the welcome mat wearing his green kangaroo jacket overtop a crisp, short-sleeved white shirt, Teddy adopted a broad stance. Like a weapon, he clutched a vacuum hose in his right hand; the long plastic neck dangling from his fingers verged on comical. Tentative on the foot of the porch, surveying Teddy from the other side of the mat, it dawned on me, this was the closest we'd ever stood face-to-face.

I related the purpose of our visit.

Teddy asked how many of us were hitchhiking.

"Three."

Puzzled, he looked beyond us to the street where the soft rain had formed puddles in the road.

"You're hitchhiking in the *rain?*"

"Yes sir."

"Do you have any *money?*"

Stalling for a moment, I glanced over at Jan. "Some. We have change. It's enough for the bus if we can't get a ride." Knowing that Jan and I would hesitate to squander our reserves for a short bus trip when we could hitchhike free, I didn't want to come off pitiable. Right then, a croupy cough escaped from my mouth, creating a chain reaction like a yawn. Quietly, Jan hacked into her hand.

"I've been to Sausalito before," Teddy asserted. "But you have *no* money…and in the *rain*? And you're both *coughing!*" The man was completely appalled by our gall.

Jan wore a light blue windbreaker covering her shirt. Teddy asked if I had anything warmer than a sweater. Believing we'd no longer require heavy jackets and coats in spring and summer, our winter clothes were left behind at Vic and Patti's to be shipped home later. Confessing the sorry truth, I admitted we'd dumped our "parkas" in Los Angeles.

"Not even a *raincoat?*"

"Nope."

Carefully, Teddy leaned the vacuum hose against the porch wall, removed his jacket from his scrawny shoulders. Handing the skin over to me, he volunteered. "Here, I want you to use this as long as you need it. You can even keep it for good if you like. It's shrunken a little anyway so it should fit you fine."

Shocked and overjoyed, I was speechless. There was no possible way I could *keep* Teddy's jacket.

From the first time Jan and I'd met him, Teddy had worn a tatty, brown corduroy blazer or green kangaroo jacket over top of a t-shirt, and more recently, over his short-sleeved, white cotton shirt. Additionally, he usually sported his odd-looking pair of two-toned black and green leather shoes — even after making the switch to his novice costume. The jacket was probably one of the few articles of clothing the Good Samaritan owned.

Launching into few words, I expressed how I couldn't borrow the jacket. Quick to argue, Teddy cut me off. "You *can't* run around wearing *only* a sweater in the rain. Especially with a cold."

I caved, mostly because I couldn't come up with anything reasonable to counter his sensible point, not to mention, I was thrilled about the jacket. Searching Teddy's face, I noticed his dark eyebrows forming into a question mark waiting for me to succumb to his offer.

"Thank you." Nonchalant, as if it was an afterthought, I accepted the zippered hoodie from the Good Samaritan's hands. "I appreciate it."

Teddy had loaned to me — the shirt off his back. As far as I was concerned, the kangaroo jacket was on credit. I would take good care of it.

Biting my lip, slipping the fleece-lined cotton over my arms, I imagined being wrapped in a blanket that signified hardship and strength. There was also the inimitable aroma of laundry soap and stale cigarettes.

Skinnier than ever, baring pale arms; the Good Samaritan combed a hand through messy, sheared hair and began gesticulating. Amid arms and fingers waving furiously in the air, Jan and I were provided with clear directions to the ferry docks.

Breaking away, Teddy cautioned from the manse porch. "Watch yourselves down there."

Due to increasing showers, we spent a short time in Sausalito, long enough for Charlie to be suitably impressed though he didn't find the special gift for his sister he was seeking. Afterwards, we headed to Haight Ashbury.

Reminiscent of a bomb shelter, now an austere haven for junkies, the area was a far cry from the mid-sixties when San Francisco was a breeding ground for acid trips and LSD was still legal. In search of something discoverable in one of the miscellaneous shops, Jan and I managed to pop into the Haight switchboard to see if somebody was heading north looking for riders for when or if, we got our act together and decided to leave.

No luck.

Striding through Golden Gate Park frittering away time, keeping out of the wet until the appropriate hour to return to the hostel, we bumped into Richard (aka "Mouth"), the fellow who'd driven with us in Walter's van to the Washington State border when Jan was first turned away. Laughing, we reminisced about our farcical *second* trip with drunken, Quaalude-laden Walter sprawled out along the van floor attempting to grope the females. Jan and I joked that, in Richard's honour, we'd spent part of the previous day in Chinatown touring "The Ugly Building." Leaving Richard and his buddies in the park, we returned to Steiner Street. Some new guests, a couple of men from New York City and two women from Toronto arrived the night before.

Almost a week since Marco had smoked us up; Jan and I were ripe for a night of mini debauchery. Itching to lap up some of San Francisco's nightlife — possibly drinking and dancing at a club — we longed to do *something* other than sit in the hostel one more night. Despite diminishing financial resources and the risk of being turned away at the door, Jan and I were willing to splurge that night. However, it was necessary we be accompanied by at least one legal individual — a group was better, especially when crashing a bar as under-agers.

Disappointingly, nobody was interested in leaving the nest. Like us, everybody was strapped for cash, conserving money for travel, not blowing it in clubs or on the hangover that was guaranteed to follow. We were about to throw in the towel, when one of the new girls, Beth, suggested the three of us pick up a case of beer.

There is nothing better than sweet diversion when you're undecided about something crucial.

Off we trucked to The Island; an inexpensive flavourful Chinese eatery (recommended by Teddy) that also functioned as an unofficial hub for artists and musicians. Next, we walked over to Safeway to pool our money so that 21-year-old Beth could purchase a case of frosty cold Lucky beer from the cooler. Not about to *get* lucky — we all liked the name.

Nestled in the dark amongst cherry trees outlining Duboce Park, the bottles were split between three, and we settled in. An independent and freethinker, not only had Beth seen the Moody Blues *live*, but in the late sixties, she'd attended a Phil Ochs *concert*. At HOOM for one last night before making her way to San Jose, Beth would eventually meet with a friend in Yosemite National Park to go backpacking.

Ambitious to believe that we could polish off the entire case, leaving the remaining bottles in the park, a few hours later, the three of us staggered up to the porch of the hostel. TV blaring on the third floor where the men's dorm was located, I could make out Johnny Carson in typical good humour, riffing through his monologue. Talking louder than they realized, holding on to one another for support, Jan and Beth crept up to the first landing. Figuring it'd be safer remaining on the ground floor close to the women's' dorm *and* bathroom, I desperately needed to get horizontal. Sliding my hands along the wall for guidance, looking toward the kitchen door, I saw Brother John peer out into the hallway. Smiling, he invited me in for tea.

I loved Brother John and enjoyed talking with him, but in no way, could I handle a heavy discussion that night — especially about HOOM. Feeling more vulnerable than usual, my drunken state rendered me unable to rebuff John's gentle proposition.

It's called being a sucker for punishment.

I do not recall, nor did I document the nature of what we discussed that night. I do however; remember the after effects of our mini-party: a tremendous thumping in my head and behind my eyes. Finally peeling off the green kangaroo jacket, tucking it safely next to my face, aimlessly, I fell into my sleeping bag.

What comes crashing down, eventually rises.

Sunshine gleamed through the window at daybreak, ushering a hint of optimism along the way. Following in John Gailey's footsteps, mid-morning, Charlie would be departing for Mexico. The three of us had traded inside jokes and enjoyed one another's company. Watching Charlie pack up his personal effects was a struggle. The vile residuals of a hangover didn't make his leaving any easier.

It's a peculiar feeling when someone walks out of your life, knowing you'll not likely see one another again. To a fault, whenever separating with friends, Jan and I put forth a concerted effort swearing to stay in touch, keep up with one another's activities. The more practiced you become at goodbyes; grim reality has a way of levelling everything out. Making assurances to write and visit is about social etiquette rather than honesty. Verbal contracts are rarely binding.

Before Charlie left, he presented Jan and me with a coconut. A cumbersome item picked up during his stay in Hawaii, Charlie didn't want to tote the souvenir from place to place. Derived from the word "coco" meaning head or skull, it seemed fitting that Charlie had left the coconut behind. A logical and systematic person, Charlie possessed what my mother referred to as horse sense.

Requiring a sledgehammer to crack the shell apart to get to the thin liquid inside, once the coconut was opened, everybody went bananas.

In anticipation of going to San Jose that afternoon, Beth packed up her belongings. Plans to meet at the Golden Gate Park band shell for a free concert prior to her leaving were made. Though we hadn't known one another longer than a half day, since leaving Yvette and the others in Vancouver, Beth had quickly become the closest girlfriend Jan and I had. Moreover, during our beer fest the previous evening, mentioning my thoughts about possibly joining HOOM, Beth had said, "wait."

One word magnified a hundred emotions.

The party at 101 Steiner St. was abandoning ship. Everybody, it seemed, was getting on with the affairs of life. Late next morning, Jan placed a call to the Ride Center to see if anybody was on course for Portland seeking passengers. Assuming a leadership role, my friend had taken it upon herself to see about leaving the hostel before we were thrown out on our asses. Despite trailing on thin ice, not once did Jan hassle me to expedite my decision. I couldn't fault her for ensuring all the bases were covered, particularly should she be travelling back to Canada alone.

Sitting at the base of a statue near a downtown McDonald's, we unpacked bran muffins and milk cartons for lunch. The afternoon had become increasingly warmer, much too warm to wear Teddy's kangaroo jacket. Defiant, I kept it on. Not only did the soft fleece make me feel closer to Teddy, no matter how ludicrous an idea, I anticipated the coat would somehow help channel me in the right direction.

Next to the statue was an emporium where we picked out Father's Day cards for our dads. The longer we were away, the less our families were on our minds. Occasionally, a tinge of melancholy washed over me, and then dissipated. It seemed irrelevant to consult with family about struggles or challenges that Jan and I occasionally encountered. We wrote letters to folks back home when things were going *well*. Anyway, I didn't want to burden anybody with my dilemma about HOOM — a predicament that needed to be discussed face-to-face, not across 3000 miles. I'd made certain not to drag Jan into the minefield of my conflict. My friend had signed up for a six-month road trip, not a circus sideshow.

In fact, Jan gleaned more information about my impasse by what I omitted rather than what I shared. I couldn't say the same about her. An absolute master at keeping people guessing what she was thinking, even those closest to her, the girl could stymie the most persistent. Holding my friend in high esteem for not attempting to push one way or another, in retrospect, Jan might have been muddling through the same madness.

We met with Beth at the band shell and settled in before a three-piece rock group. On weekends, when live music is performed, Golden Gate Park becomes electric. Crawling with freaks, stoners, aging hippies and their families, liquor and hard drugs were ever present. Tripping about in loose, brightly coloured clothing, everybody had a grand old time. Stone cold sober, Jan, Beth, and I observed in awe. When the show ended, we saw Beth off at the bus stop. Excited and envious, I thought how good it must feel to be emotionally free.

Lying on the floor of the girls' dorm that evening, my own coughing prevented me from falling asleep. Rotating my head toward Jan curled up next to me inside her navy shell; I asked if she was awake. Receiving no response, I assumed she was long gone, and cranked my neck around to notice the room steeped in varying shadow shapes. Guessing that it must be past midnight, lowering my lids once more, I turned over on to my left side and tried to sleep. Eyes shut tight; I sensed the presence of white golf balls, the same ones that had invaded my mind a few days before. I watched guardedly as they suddenly began to expand and spin out. Recognizing the effort necessitated to return the balls to the recesses of my brain, unzipping my bag, I decided to get up and make myself a cup of Rose's red zinger tea.

Cloaked inside of the kangaroo jacket covering the top half of my nightgown, tippy-toeing out of the room in bare feet, I entered the hallway. Taking a few paces toward the kitchen, I detected a light on above the stove. Somebody was in the room. Even in the dead of night, it seemed there was always a body awake at Steiner Street.

It was Brother John. Perhaps he too suffered from insomnia. Entering the kitchen, I spoke his name. Rotating his body slowly around as if expecting me, our eyes connected.

John beamed.

For the first few minutes, we made uncomfortable small talk. Plugging in the kettle, I explained how my coughing had kept me awake. John confessed he'd heard my hack from the kitchen.

I started to laugh. Probably, I'd disturbed everybody in the house. Everybody, that is, but Jan.

That was funny.

John didn't hesitate to confide straight away how he'd "felt a whole lot of love" for me the night before. In case he'd forgotten, I reminded him that I was drunk and couldn't remember much about our conversation. It was anyone's guess what kind of bull crap I might have blathered. The answer lay somewhere between Brother John and God.

Looking me dead in the eyes, John said, "I know you're scared."

The rumble of the kettle all but masked John's voice, but I'd heard him all right. Turning away from him, I poured the steaming water into my cup and dropped a cherry coloured tea bag inside. The simple task afforded me a moment to discern if the conversation was preconceived. Perhaps Brother John premeditated it to happen and the words materialized.

That sounded about right.

"You're at a junction in your life," John continued, his voice softening. "Trying to figure out if you want to keep travelling, go to school, work... or...become a trainee."

My back now steadied against the counter, hot mug firmly in my hands, stupefied, I studied the Brother's attractive face.

"Remember," John went on, "the decision is yours. Nobody else can make it for you. In one way or another, don't be influenced or fooled by other people."

That's just it, I reminded myself. If only somebody was willing to tell me what to do, it would be a hell of a lot easier.

Tears welling in my eyes, I confessed. "I don't know what to do. I've been playing it over inside of my head and keep coming up empty." Rather than fearing the consequences of my admission, it was a relief to come clean. A sneak peek at liberation.

Using the sleeve of Teddy's jacket, I attempted to wipe my eyes. Simultaneously, Brother John rose from his chair. Standing tall, he gazed affectionately into my face. Certain that John wanted to hug me, I was thankful when he reached over and drew me close to his chest. Upon his release, caressing the side of my hair, he whispered, "Pray on it some more. Ask for guidance."

Reflecting the small glow of light above the stove, John's illuminated face reminded me of the army of white golf balls populating quietly inside of my head.

Gradually, he raised his right hand in an affected manner. "An answer is waiting out there. Grab a hold of it. Hang on tight."

"Free will." Home of photographer Joel Sussman, California.

CHAPTER 40

Chaos leads to Order

"So we follow our wandering paths, and the very darkness acts as our guide and our doubts serve to reassure us."
JEAN-PIERRE DE CAUSSADE

Another letter arrived. The neatly handwritten return address on the envelope indicated it was from Bruce, our friend from Meadowlark.

Bruce was doing well, still assisting Hal in the organic garden pondering his next move. He wrote that he missed us, and asked that Jan and I consider returning to Meadowlark before going back to Canada.

Spending additional days and nights with Bruce at beautiful Meadowlark didn't seem likely at this stage. Still, it presented a tempting solution. The main impediment continuing to stand in the way of pursuit of opportunity was shortage of cash. Inasmuch as Jan and I had loved it there, like setting a clock to retract time, returning to Meadowlark would be retracing steps.

Craig and Larry hoped we we'd join them at Fisherman's Wharf. Possibly head over to Golden Gate Park. Jan and I were keen, but had promised Brother John and a couple other HOOM members we'd return to Cole Street Community Center for what would undoubtedly be our second and final worship service there. Not that I'd become a church going girl — and this wasn't conventional church by any stretch. With all the commotion my poor stomach endured lately, Cole Street seemed a systematic plan, particularly after my post-midnight chat with Brother John.

Jan confirmed with Craig. We'd meet the guys at the Wharf in the afternoon.

Rolling up our sleeping bags, I stored them in the cupboard as usual in the mornings and told Jan about my short talk with Brother John the night before. As much as I hated to inundate her with my crud, Jan was one of my oldest and dearest pals. With the distinction of being only girls amongst families of boys within our group of friends, in a sense, we were like sisters.

Relating how John had told me resolve would soon come, knowing full well that my fate was also her fate, reassuringly; Jan suggested I ask for help at Cole Street. "It couldn't hurt," she encouraged.

Maybe it was the power of suggestion or a bug had been put in Reverend Patsy's ear. Filling in for Father Allan that morning, the Reverend delivered a message that seemed directed toward me. Lecturing on the energy surrounding language, through her interpretation of specific words, Patsy highlighted the importance of patience.

During her sermon, The Beatles song, "The Word," played around and around my head: "Say the word and you'll be free…Say the word and be like me…Now I've got it, the word is good."

The word *was* good. It was *delay*.

Pretty much what Beth had said during our drunkerama.

Two for two.

Somehow, Jan and I'd gotten our wires crossed with Craig and Larry. Arriving down at the Wharf around two, the guys were nowhere to be found. We searched all along the waterfront, but to no avail. Probably they'd gotten fed up waiting for us to return from Cole Street — not to mention we'd had a bite to eat, withdrew money from the bank, and had to wait for the bus. This effort taking several hours, obviously, Craig and Larry weren't patient boys. It wasn't their fault. As it turned out, they got a better offer and ended up going to a concert.

Back then, when you made plans with somebody to meet, the precision of time and place was imperative. If a party failed to show, you feared there weren't unforeseen circumstances inhibiting someone's ability to be where you'd prearranged. Until you inevitably spoke to that individual, there was no way of knowing *why* they didn't materialize. Living at youth hostels and the homes of strangers for brief intervals created greater reason to be exact when pinpointing locations and hook-up times.

Restless and bored, for a while, Jan and I watched chalk-coloured sailboats chase one another out on the water. Deciding to grab the bus and trolley back to Steiner Street, it would be nearly five by the time I landed in. Jan would catch up later.

Almost telepathically, an underlying need for space had been established. To allow one another room to breathe, it was time to slacken things. Perceptibly and emotionally, my friend sensed it was best to stay at arm's length, at least until I made my decision. In my gut, a shift felt imminent. I simply could not carry on much longer agonizing about what to do about my future.

During services at Cole Street that morning, something hit me. Apart from a measure of familiarity with the Brothers, Sisters, and few of the novices at HOOM, I knew *very* little about The Holy Order of Mans organization. I'd leafed through a copy of *The Golden Force* and yet, the group's practices, procedures and faith origins eluded me. Designed to enlighten, segments of the book were crafted to flatter supporters and impress colleagues, while goading outsiders to believe that HOOM members were part of a private and elite supernatural society. My knowledge of The Order had been shaped mostly by partisan members. This wasn't acceptable. Even Brother John warned not to get sucked in by other people's opinions. Despite this rationalization, mystified by *The Golden Force*, I intended to read it whole.

My pragmatic self resonated. Since all this wavering began, it dawned on me that I might be enlisting for some freakazoid show exactly *like* the Moonies, a group potentially capable and culpable of harvesting brains on loan. In all fairness, the possibility couldn't be disregarded.

I rode the trolley up hill, and then hopped the bus for the final stretch of the ride to Steiner Street. Playing it safe, I dawdled in Duboce Park where Jan, Beth, and I'd held our private party two nights ago. A couple of HOOM novices I hadn't yet met crouched on their hands and knees, working the soil next to the hostel. Spotting me, they meandered over. The female, Rebecca, made a formal introduction. Timidly, Thomas held out a flower picked from a sweet pea plant.

Would I like to have it?

Accepting the gift, I waited.

In recent days, veterans, and new members of The Holy Order seemed to scope the hostel and its hinges like ants. In case there might be reason for it, I kept my ear to the ground. As I'd discovered with Joanne, probably, Rebecca and Thomas were merely being friendly. HOOM folks might be the appendages of a cult. So far, instincts told me they were trustworthy.

A slight, cherub-faced girl with grey-blue eyes, Rebecca's demeanor was gentle, kind. Early into her career as a novice, the eighteen-year-old worked part time at Haven, a fruit shake bar on Clement Street. I couldn't resist asking Rebecca why she'd decided to join The Order, and what her impressions were the first two months under HOOM's command.

Having come from a troubled background, Rebecca admitted she was seeking love and stability in her life. An instinctually spiritual person, Rebecca's close friend had recently become a Sister of the San Francisco chapter. In turn, the friend invited Rebecca to attend some of HOOM's meetings. Upon completing reading *The Golden Force*, Rebecca asserted its message and accounts spoke to her in a way she had never known. Believing that aligning strengths with HOOM was her calling, Rebecca conceded the choice she made wouldn't necessarily be what others might choose.

Thomas and Rebecca soon finished their work in the garden, leaving me alone with my thoughts.

Did a definitive answer really exist in the galaxies somewhere? I felt asinine believing there might be even a remote possibility.

"So…Are you going before the council?"

Swerving my head in the direction of Duboce Park, there stood the Good Samaritan proud as punch, as if he knew something I didn't. For a smartass moment, I thought about sniping, *who wants to know?*

"I don't think so. Why do you ask?"

"I'm psychic."

"Oh…Is that it?" Obviously, my fence sitting was a topic of conversation in a certain neck of the woods. Inspecting my chest, Teddy grinned. "I'm glad to see the jacket is keeping you warm." Casting my eyes down the front of the green kangaroo, feeling the wind kick up as it often did late in the afternoon, I was happy to be zipped inside of the coat.

"Thanks again for letting me use it. It's real cozy. I don't feel right keeping it though. Are you sure I couldn't buy the jacket from you?"

"It's yours."

I began to gripe. Teddy mimicked my complaint. Then, as if remembering something important, without uttering a word, he darted across the street toward the manse and posed precariously on the front porch. Apparent that something was on his mind, turning on one heel, in less than thirty seconds, Teddy zoomed back. Straightforward, he pressed, "So you're *not* going before the council?"

"*The council?* Ah…No, not exactly. Actually…I didn't realize there was a council."

Unsure about sharing the extent of my indecisiveness, and equally wishing that Teddy would say something to convince me to stay, I stated flatly, "We hope to leave here in a couple of days."

As if studying the outcome of a science experiment, Teddy narrowed his eyes. "Have you got a pack and everything?"

I sure did. The thing was starting to weigh like a 100-pound anvil. Uncertain where the conversation was going, I nodded "Yeah."

"So, are you going north?"

"Eventually, yes. Back to Canada…But not *home* right away. Why?"

Firing skinny arms and spider-like hands into the air like a rocket, Teddy raised his eyebrows. "The reason I ask is because I've got a really good pack. I'll give it to you. I know you don't have much in the way of travel necessities."

Staring slack-mouthed at the young man standing across from me, I reevaluated the physical renovation he'd undergone since first laying eyes on him. "Give? As in for *free?*" I blinked hard. "I couldn't accept your backpack...unless you'd consider selling it. Unfortunately, I don't have much money." Before he had a change to argue, I added. "I could write you, an I owe you..."

"Forget it then. I wouldn't *sell* it to you. You can *have* it."

There was positively no way in hell I was going to sponge Teddy's pack, even if the prospect of having the Good Samaritan's backpack for keeps *was* unfathomable. I had seen it once, weeks before. Black and grey, the oval shaped nylon sack had a couple of literary quotes written across it in coloured marker. White gardenias were fastened to the zipper by a bungee cord. Teddy's bag was *amazing.* Jan and I were wholly impressed. Making as if I'd never seen the pack, now up for grabs, I played dumb.

"What's it like, anyway?"

Excited to be regaled with an incredible story attached to the origins of the knapsack, I sat back and waited for Teddy to elucidate about his pack's history. What he divulged wasn't an elaborate tale at all. Instead, in taciturn voice, he contended, "Oh, it's been very good, very loyal."

As if I needed convincing, the Good Samaritan was quick to reassure. "It's a *beautiful* pack. There's not another one like it." Like dew coating a meadow at dawn, past years and memories flashed across wistful blue eyes. Reflectively, Teddy disclosed. "It took ten years for me to build it up to what it is today, you know. I don't give it away lightly."

The emotional attachment to the beloved backpack suggested a parent reticent to let his child loose to the world, yet believing it a necessary measure for personal growth. When we'd first met him, Teddy talked of living out of his backpack for four years after leaving Vietnam and his ex-wife behind, spending weeks surviving in the desert before coming to San Francisco. His knapsack represented friendship, faithfulness, devotion. It was his second skin. What Teddy withheld about the pack was the beef of the story. I'd have to imagine the rest.

"Well, thanks." Feeling my face glow beat red, I added, "I'll definitely think about it."

Falling into an Abbott and Costello sketch, the Good Samaritan push-ing me to accept his pack, my refusal unless I could pay money, struck by the absurdity of going around in circles, we both started to laugh. Before I knew it, the party broke up. Starting toward the manse, the Good Samaritan halted. Turning around, he looked me up and down. "So, you'll be here for another day or so?"

Reaching both hands upward, I pulled my hair to the back of my head, formed it in a ponytail and smiled, flirtatious. "I think so, yeah." Dipping his head in courteous fashion, Teddy broke away and hurried across the street. Reaching the lower steps of the manse porch, he began to perform a light tap dance on each cement block until finally touching down softly on the verandah. Then he vanished through the front door.

I was money in the bank.

Ridding oneself of worldly possessions, a test of worthiness and merit, was one of the unwritten laws of The Order. Rebecca contended that when Teddy first moved into the manse, he'd brought along four plum trees and three oil paintings from The Art Show, where he worked. His ability to unload material belongings, supposedly burdensome and distracting from an individual's relationship with a higher entity, emphasized one truth. The Good Samaritan was a beautiful human being. One that lived up to the nickname Jan and I had given him.

For the duration of the day, I pined about Teddy and the backpack, but in my heart suspected that one day our generous friend would need it more than I would.

That evening we watched *Firecreek* (1968) starring Jimmy Stewart and Henry Fonda, about a sheriff taking a stand against a vigilante group. Jan made popcorn and it burned. Brother James made another batch. Sister Rose put on a pot of water for tea.

This was family.

Hours earlier, after riding the bus and trolley alone from the wharf to Steiner Street, Jan arrived looking as if she'd seen a ghost. Turns out, as she passed by Safeway, some jackass had made lewd remarks. By the time she reached HOOM, Jan was understandably skittish.

At least two blocks in every direction of the hostel danger lurked, there was no question about it. Especially alone. If I hadn't been insistent to leave the wharf when I did, Jan wouldn't likely have run into trouble. Despite our need for privacy, for the first time, we'd broken our rule about sticking together. Reckoning she had wanted to be alone, I apologized for taking off. Jan shrugged off the incident, but it wouldn't happen a second time. This also meant something else. If I chose to remain in San

Francisco and join The Holy Order, Jan would have to travel alone back to Canada by bus or train. Not only that, she'd be cutting her trip short. This hardly seemed fair. To change gears midway would be supremely selfish. We'd talked about this adventure for more than a year. Here I was, potentially ruining everything.

Thinking it over, if I followed through with the inclination to join HOOM, I could do it on my own time, maybe even after returning home in August. I could always find work and get some cash together.

If I wanted *it* bad enough, that's how things might have to be.

Making Jan aware of my thoughts, she appeared happy, comforted. My baggage had become her weight to bear. It felt good to temporarily alleviate her fears.

Details were falling into place. Still, there was unfinished business. Before leaving, I needed to know that returning to Steiner Street was worth *serious* consideration, and not some goofy compulsion. Jan had made rumblings about what we would do if the switchboard at Haight Ashbury notified us about a lift north — a valid point.

It was Sunday. I gave myself two more days to make up my mind.

Deadlines are good.

"Nameless Wanderer"

Monday morning, Craig and Larry left. People were dropping like flies. Washing and drying dishes, Jan and I listened to "Cross My Heart," the first track from the *Pleasures of the Harbor* LP playing on the living room turntable. The song, wherein Ochs cautions about false hope and how it will exact revenge on you in the end, felt oddly meaningful and moving. Grabbing hold of the record sleeve, I slipped into the main bathroom and locked the door. Journal on my lap, I scratched down some of the writings by Ochs that appear on the back of the album jacket. Consistent with many of his lyrical word games, Phil hypothesizes about passion leading to chaos and chaos to order. Placing my marker down for a moment, I looked out the window to Duboce Park. It was still, nothing out of the ordinary except the freshly turned vegetable garden adjacent to the house. Shifting my eyes down the street toward the manse, I saw little activity. Perhaps school was in session.

The joke made me grin.

On a blank page of my book, I wrote a self-directed missive. "People believe it'll help if I ask for an answer. It isn't easy. I want to write to God but can't. The words won't come. There are so many things to consider. It boils down to one basic objective. Stay simple. Don't worry. When you stop worrying, you open yourself up to answers already out there. There is no reason to constantly seek why. Relax, and you shall find your place in space. This is what I need to remember."

Meadowlark continued to ring in my ears. It wasn't much, but it was something.

The temperature soared to 87 degrees; the late morning sky burned a hot hazy blue. No need to wear the green kangaroo, I stored it safely inside of my pack. Jan and I set off to the underground shop and then walked over to the San Francisco Ride Center.

Our visit to the SFRC proved to be a useless effort. We'd each have to pay a $4 registration fee before they'd assist in tracking us a ride.

One fact was steadfast. Without money, vamoosing from San Francisco and heading home through Canada's West Coast wouldn't be easy — not unless we hitchhiked across the border. Sitting in a Chinese restaurant eating 50-cent bowls of steamed white rice, Jan and I volleyed different schemes back and forth. The conversation came back to money. With barely enough cash to get our butts back to Canada, we'd see how far we could make our funds last if work *wasn't* in the forecast. Providing we weren't forking out dough on headhunter fees, I liked our chances. From here on in, jointly, we would *visualize* a ride north of San Francisco.

Starting to feel as if I had a split personality, one side of the divide was about possibly making HOOM my home. The other was excited about going to Alberta with Jan, hanging out with new friends. It was a surreal state of consciousness. Hoping to synthesize my thoughts, with one day remaining on my self-imposed deadline, the pot was about to boil over.

Leaving the Chinese restaurant, we walked over to Hallmark to pick out a couple of birthday cards, one for a friend back home, the other for Marco. Jan planned to mail it to Zurich.

Outside of 101 Steiner Street, busily working in the garden, Joanne asked for assistance. Preferring to spend time with a book at Duboce Park, Jan declined. It occurred to me Jan was hoping that Joanne might help accelerate my decision-making process. Knowing Jan, she'd probably used her extrasensory prowess to consign Joanne to the garden. My friend was beyond capable that way.

Planting alternate rows of white and pink petunias to border the vegetable beds, Joanne and I chatted, mostly about indiscriminate subjects. I noticed Teddy approaching the hostel on his way back from Duboce Park where Jan had gone earlier. Cheerfully addressing me as the "Nameless Wanderer," stopping on the sidewalk out front, the Good Samaritan announced he'd donated his backpack to The Holy Order.

Teddy's action let me off the hook. I supposed what might happen if he decided to leave The Order one day. The backpack being a sentimental object, it seemed a shame for Teddy hand it off.

In my mind, cavalierly.

I told him so.

"We can't hold on to objects forever," he answered sharply. "Our property has no real meaning in our lives. Sure, there was a time when I would chase a guy halfway across the country for my pack. Now, I don't care anymore."

Teddy had started to mimic the Brothers.

"What will you do if you want to go hiking or camping?"

"I'll worry about it when I go."

I understood, sort of, but wasn't sure if I could eradicate everything to which I felt an attachment. Certainly, I couldn't comprehend why it was necessary to donate material belongings to fit in. My collection of favourite novels and Beatles records alone would be the toughest of my personal effects to let go. Unsure how to go about becoming a minimalist, for the right reason, I might be willing to give it a try.

Jan approached the garden. Turning his attention toward her, Teddy asked if she was all right. Eyes to the ground, Jan reported all was well.

I knew she was lying. After Teddy left, Jan spilled the beans. Somebody in the park had bothered her, the same brainless pervert who'd catcalled at her in front of Safeway the day before. Witnessing the man's verbal harassment of Jan, Teddy had entered Duboce Park, told the guy to fuck off and leave her alone.

Asshole beat it the hell out of there.

That's what Good Samaritans do.

HOOM *(Holy Order of MANS) letterhead conveying the San Francisco Youth Hostel logo. May 1976.*

CHAPTER 41

Gold Skies Ahead

"Truth is what the voice within tells you."
GANDHI

We ate something resembling dinner. Afterwards, intent on fine-tuning our preparations, Jan and I returned to Duboce Park. That's where we met Emil, living in a small house located behind the hostel. With the promise of a reunion with Springsteen's *Born to Run*, Emil invited us up to his apartment for tea and a listen to Michael Pinder's new album.

Emil's small living space contained the essentials. Far from extravagant, there was something touchable about the place. It had atmosphere. The short walkup had mood. His futon bed doubling as a couch, funky lime-green throw pillows scattered about, in addition to a couple of barely thriving plants, Emil's apartment made you feel as if you'd been there a hundred times and wanted to keep coming back. Much of that was due to Emil, a friendly, free flowing individual. His surroundings invited the notion how prodigious it might be to live alone.

Emil served chai tea and produced a bit of weed, Panama Red, a welcome surprise. We swapped stories. A Northern California native, having switched programs a couple of times in search of a better fit, Emil was currently enrolled at Berkeley supported by part-time work. As he chewed on about campus life, I marvelled at Emil. He had a good gig going, and wasn't part of an en masse movement to graduate in a designated time frame — a relatively new concept for me. Emil had mastered the role of college junkie.

Parents called it avoidance.

Smoking, listening to the music and Emil, my thoughts decelerated and floated out into the abyss. Pondering more about school, I realized education is obtainable without a punch clock. An individual could progress through studies at her own pace. Back home, people seemed to be on a treadmill, racing to get from A to B as if in a speed relay. Emil called his own shots and didn't care how long it took to reach his goals.

All but passed out from the smoke, around 11 pm, Jan and I decided to call it quits. Thanking Emil for his hospitality, we expected to reconnect before leaving the city.

A fifteen-year-old Canadian girl, Sarah, joined us in the dorm for one night. Jan and she started talking. Wandering out to the living room, I discovered that most of the hostellers had gone out for the evening or were already in bed. Seated in a corner of the room reading, Brother Bruce looked up and smiled. "It's a slow day for a change."

This explained the absence of bodies.

Without hesitation, Bruce shared that Brother John had told him of our conversation in the kitchen a couple of nights before.

I was okay with this. HOOM was a closely-knit, somewhat impenetrable group. Whenever the possibility of a new body coming into the faction, it was newsworthy to the rest of the flock.

Was I any closer to making my decision Bruce wanted to know. In a round-about way, I explained how my heart believed it could be the right thing, only my head kept running interference. What I refrained from saying, before fading into the chasm, possibly never to return — I needed to be confident that joining a spiritual assemblage was the right decision for me.

Inviting me to sit on the floor, Bruce did the same. He asked that I fold my legs beneath my body, close my eyes, and breathe naturally.

Following his instruction, I waited, not knowing what, if anything might happen. Before long, a shock of spiralling energy surfaced, hovering in and around me. A command of light force and atom fragments, barely distinguishable yet present, danced vividly within the black force field inside of my head. Reminiscent of the growing white golf balls I'd witnessed on recent occasions, this flash of illumination was more defined and heady. Culminating in some weird pyrotechnics display — the sheer strength of which was so foreboding, I felt faint. My stomach grew nauseous. It was difficult to breathe. Inexplicably, I felt myself nearing the threshold of what I imagined to be a virtual world. The sensation of loss of control scared the shit out of me.

I opened my eyes.

Though eager for my reaction, Bruce managed to contain piqued curiosity.

Sitting quietly for a moment, trying to catch my breath, I prepared to sort out what had happened, and peered into Bruce's eyes. Was he an actual human being or something foreign taking on human form?

Finally, I uttered few words.

"Did *you* do that?"

Without flinching, Bruce assumed responsibility.

My eyes widened, disbelieving. "But…*How?*"

Placing his hand in front of my face, eyelids contracted, the shaman queried, "What did you feel…Or what do you think you felt?"

Dazed and uncertain if I could respond appropriately, I knew I wasn't high anymore, yet this alien sensation felt like a total mind and body warp. Reluctant to give the wrong answer, one word kept coming to mind. I was afraid to say it out loud. At Bruce's assurance, there were no correct or incorrect reactions.

The noun snuck through my lips. "I don't know…" I sputtered. "God?"

Clamouring to my feet, my legs began to wobble. Arms outstretched, Bruce helped to steady my body until I became stable on my own. Then he took me into his confidence. "God is equipped with the capacity to imprint his omnipotent force anywhere in the universe. We might not understand it to *be* God, but His vibrations can be felt in every one of us."

As far as I could tell, Brother Bruce had pulled off a voodoo scam, not God. Maybe Bruce and God were interlinked; co-conspirators as I'd suspected Fanny and Jan of being back at Evangel Home. Rationalizing that human beings are like God, and that God has gifted each of us with the ability to manifest his work, Bruce began citing examples of supernatural episodes many people take for granted. Somebody he'd known had spent years in seclusion in the mountains, in prayer and meditation. "Like a feather, the man eventually stepped on top of a stream without losing his footing," he said.

The sympathetic Brother upped the ante. "If you can believe that mankind has the power to create — reproduction alone is an example of man's ability to create — then it must also be possible to collapse a body. All of nature's functions are based upon the same scientific principles."

Once again, Bruce had broached the 'walking through walls' subject. Viable or not, no matter how many times the topic was raised, it was a fascinating theory. He went on to say that according to HOOM's spiritual guidebook, *The Golden Force*, this act was accomplished by "dismantling atoms which relates to the Universal Law of the solar system." Members and novices of The Holy Order claimed how appointed folks high up in the chain of command possessed the ability to showcase this matchless feat. As interesting as the deed was, it seemed convenient. At any rate, walking through walls was one stunt I wasn't about to try at home.

Cognizant of losing me, Bruce clammed up. For the next several minutes we made polite conversation until a yawn escaped my mouth — my cue to retreat to the dorm. Emotionally wrecked and physically gutted after receiving all that gratuitous energy, my head felt so heavy I could barely hold it above my neck.

The following morning, chewing on the previous evening's events with Jan and one or two others, privately, I considered Bruce's possible misuse of propriety. Meeting my eyes with an icy stare, Sister Rose stood not ten feet away. Coming from Rose, indignation was not to be taken lightly. When the opportunity presented itself, she took me aside. Clearly, talking about personal spiritual episodes was "an uncool" thing to do. "Sacred enlightenment," she said, "is a gift to be cherished." In other words, divine exposition is trivialized and cheapened when a person goes around blabbering about it.

Not one to keep thoughts or emotions under wraps, especially something *extraordinary*, in my world, Bruce's supercharged energy blitz qualified as BIG news. When Rose quantified my experience as something *special*, I was euphoric. Once paranoia set in however, exhilaration squelched.

Supposing that Rose and Bruce were possibly running a good cop bad cop number on me, I slipped into the girls' dorm. Stewing in my own juices, I took another stab at separating reality from fiction.

Nothing was resolved. For days on end going around in circles, I wasn't any closer to finding truth, or knowing if I belonged with The Order than when leaving HOOM six weeks earlier. Back then, the proposition was a spark that had kept growing like an ugly wart. Needing to put an end to this toxicity once and for all, gathering myself, I headed out of the dorm toward the front door of the house and walked the pathway leading to the garden. Plopping myself on the grass front of the bench, facing street traffic, I suddenly realized I'd forgotten to help Jan with kitchen duty.

Damn.

My bottom lip began to tremble. I started to cry. Tears seeping down my face, I had to face fact. For the past four months, I'd deluded myself into believing I had evolved into a stronger person. A person who could hold it together, fend off immature thoughts and childish habits with an arrogant shrug.

I was still a whimpering baby.

Conceding to the ache in the back of my throat, it felt good to finally let go. Up until this point, nothing else assuaged the emotional torture.

From behind, a firm hand touched my shoulder followed by a familiar voice. "What's wrong?"

For the first time, I was embarrassed to face Teddy. Wiping my wet face hard with both fists until confident that tears were erased from my cheeks, through blurry eyes, I downplayed my emotions.

"Nothing."

Shaking his head resolutely, Teddy didn't buy it. Finding a place on the grass next to me, he sat down.

In midst of sniffling away visible signs of woe, I asked. "Do you have a moment to talk?"

Cocking one ear toward the street, Teddy then turned toward me gently placing a hand on my arm. "I'd love to. I've been waiting for this. You have no idea."

Once he was settled, shifting my body until facing him directly, I asked a plain, simple question. "What made you join The Order? Honestly?"

Looking pensive, his mouth still, I could tell Teddy wanted to be careful how to answer. Likely, a million reasons aligned in his mind. Watching him visibly search through a mental catalogue hunting for the right note, I hoped he would find one to match this saga.

Teddy's eyes suddenly darted off into the street. Mine followed. A long row of vehicles had parked along the shoulder. Summer was only one week away. Already, the thermometer climbed above 89 degrees.

"When I was about seven years old," he began. "I was playing with some kids in a field one day, late August."

Pausing for a moment to study a blue Buick attempting to squeeze between a panel truck and white van, the Good Samaritan suddenly lifted his face toward mine. "The sky turned gold…Seven years later, when I was fourteen, the same thing happened."

I watched Teddy, about to frame his next round of thoughts. This could be my only chance for clarity; I didn't want to screw up.

Folding my hands in silence, poised, I was ready to listen.

"You know, I've been through every other trip in my life." The lines in his forehead slackening, thoughtfully, Teddy continued. "Drugs, sex, Vietnam, marriage, fatherhood, politics, music…I've had fifteen jobs in the last two years. I've been shot at, beaten, imprisoned, chained down, held a boy dying…I've been homeless and scared, and I've been alone. It finally reached a point where God is the only thing left."

Trying to calm my nervous stomach and take everything in, I engaged in a staring contest with a patch of flattened sunburnt grass beneath my feet. Feeling Teddy's eyes boring down on me, slowly, I raised my head.

"A part of me wants to join The Order. You know…the decent part. I think…the good part. Another part of me wants to be free. I feel like a psycho. A complete loser."

Teddy grinned. "Follow how you feel."

"I don't think I want to join."

Letting out a laugh, he chirped. "Then drop it!"

"I *can't*. That's just *it*."

Aware of how scatter-brained I must have sounded, I figured I'd make it crystal clear I knew I wasn't fooling anybody.

"I know. It's all pretty stupid."

"No." Teddy shook his head. "It's not stupid. I honestly feel your heart. I really can."

A small sphere of sunlight surfaced behind the top of Teddy's dark shorn hair. Cupping a hand above my brow, I managed to shield its glare. Then, resting one palm upon my knee, eyes hypnotic, Teddy levelled with me.

"Look, I realize it's hard for you to understand why I gave away my possessions. But do you want to know something? One day you wake up in your life and understand that it's about filling the cavities with what's precious and real. Not shit, that doesn't have any meaning or substance. Right now, God is feeding me. It's where I need to be. All that other crap I thought was important is superfluous. It's trivia. It's trash."

Not knowing the meaning of "superfluous," I behaved as if I did. However, I did get Teddy's meaning. He'd laid it out cleanly, honestly as he could without an encrypted code. One of the characteristics I liked about the Good Samaritan, he had a flair for the dramatic, but gave you the goods straight up and to the point.

I had one more question. "Why do the Brothers and Sisters always look like they're high?"

Laugh lines scrunched like meshing around Teddy's eyes and he started to laugh. "Once you rid yourself of the garbage that fills our bodies and our minds, the light is released from within. It's that spirit flame that lives in the core of everybody."

He had an idea. "I want you to talk to Reverend Mary."

I'd met Reverend Mary when we first arrived at Steiner Street and was intimidated by her. The crème of the crème of the HOOM women, Mary was no-nonsense, practical as they come. She didn't suffer fools. One disapproving glance in my direction would surely wound my already too frail soul.

"Reverend Mary? Oh, no…I don't think I can do that."

Placing a boney hand on my right arm, veins straining the surface of his skin, Teddy avowed, "Sure you can. Trust me. Wait right here. I'll see if I can get her for you."

There was no point arguing with the Good Samaritan. He was already off and running. As much as Reverend Mary freaked me out, I had absolutely nothing to lose. If I wasn't mistaken, she was one of the select few able to trip through walls. If there was a lull in conversation, I could always ask her about that.

Minutes later, materializing in signature pale blue gown, Mary advanced toward the garden. Watching her approaching the bench where I was now seated, I studied her plain facial features, and long, medium-brown hair carefully creased down the middle. I thought how attractive she might be with a hint of eyeliner. A foreigner myself to face paint, I was hardly one to assume the role of cosmetics advisor. It dawned on me nevertheless; mature women are enhanced by a little colour in their faces and around their eyes. Ironically, Mary was decades away from being a *mature* woman.

I had no context.

The Reverend sat next to me on the bench. A Mona Lisa smile curving her lips, Mary got down to business.

"Teddy tells me you're struggling with something this morning."

There was no beating around the bush with Reverend Mary. Teddy had informed her correctly — *This* morning, the morning before, and many mornings before that.

"It's true." I began picking the cuticles on my already raw, red fingers — another disgusting childhood habit.

"I've been seriously considering asking about joining The Order but my head and my heart aren't in sync. That's about the best way to explain how I'm feeling. I'm at a total loss and don't what to do."

Her demeanor softening, Mary replied. "Jill, we'd love to have you join us. You'd be a great addition…. But honey; we couldn't accept you just now."

"You *couldn't?*"

"Not right now, no…" The Reverend did not mince words.

"You're not ready yet. Once you finish this journey with your friend Jan, if you're still interested after your return to Canada, you may get in touch. We'll talk then. You know where to reach us."

A panel of floodlights switched on inside my head and I stared, mouth gaping. All at once, I put it together. I was seeking acceptance or rejection from an *official* source. Reverend Mary was my out. Granting permission to be a quitter for my own good, Mary didn't hesitate to let me know that it was okay to postpone my decision to be a disciple. I was invested, yes, but not nearly enough. That didn't make me a shitty or irreverent person. It meant that I was carefully considering opportunities.

"Wow…I don't know what to say…except thank you."

Already on her feet, a knowing smile crept across Mary's face. I waited for her to tap me on the head with a magical baton and send me on my way.

"Enjoy the rest of your travels. The life you lead can be affected in only one way. Your realization of what exists is *now*. Expand your consciousness to know yourself. Keep your mind sharp, always."

My eyes tearing up, I clung to the Reverend like a long-lost child.

"I'll do my best."

It was over.

Last days in San Francisco, Golden Gate Park.

CHAPTER 42

Ticket to Ride

"Painful though parting is; I bow to you as I see you off to distant clouds."
EMPEROR SAGA

Jan figured something heavy had taken place outside when I reentered the kitchen. What she didn't know was that I had been counselled by Reverend Mary — *Mother* Mary, to be apropos. Without going into details, I whispered, "Everything is okay now," and apologized for being unavailable to help with dishes. Someone else had picked up the slack. A true-blue friend, Jan was cool about everything. My only regret was not having the guts to tell Teddy how I felt about him when I had the chance. The fact I hadn't meant that maybe it wouldn't have been a wise play.

Jan heard a rumour that some of the folks over at the manse were not amused that she and I had become hangers on at HOOM. Our act had worn thin. Our passes finally expired; we were starting to be perceived as a pair of groupies lingering around a dressing room long after the band hit the road. Deciding to make a return visit to the Ride Center on 24th Street, we asked around about people heading up the coast. It was Tuesday, June 15. Providing we found the right driver, we'd be on tap to depart the following day. Neither of us wanted to pay the $4 finder's fee, but there was no sense groaning about it. Jan and I wanted to leave Steiner Street on *good* terms, particularly if we were ever to show our faces around the place again. Recalling our drive through the Blue Mountains of Oregon on our way to California with Walter, we agreed it might be advantageous to revisit the Pacific wonderland before heading north to British Columbia. According to our faithful guidebook, a hostel was located downtown Portland.

Portland would become our next pit stop.

Paying up, Jan and I submitted our legal names to the Ride Center, and then rode the Powell Street cable car over to Geary. Poised to leave the city in less than one day, we wanted to be sure to sample one of the natural fruit shakes Rebecca had raved about, and walked up the street to the Haven to see if she was working.

Up to her eyeballs serving a sizable group, Rebecca had little time to chitchat. Instead, she invited us to stop in at the manse the following day to say goodbye.

Close to three weeks, my emotions had gone through a virtual wood chipper. Now that I'd had the heartening conversation with Reverend Mary, I felt almost blasé about the whole business. Replacing the pinwheel of doubt and dread was a steady beat of excitement. Nevertheless, that didn't eliminate the sting of preparing to leave HOOM, our friends, and San Francisco behind. Beginning to see that *everything* is *connected* in one way or another, Mary's wise words forced me to face facts. Her point about the relevance of living in the *now* was a model I would try to emulate. Particularly when slipping into destructive thought patterns. One thing about *now*, it's all we have. *Now* is smack in front of your face. *Now* is the only tangible in life — much like the dependable old friend Jan had proven to be.

Making what would become our final return to Steiner Street late that afternoon, Jan and I came upon Joanne toiling in the vegetable garden. The heat of the afternoon sun had baked the compact dirt like an overcooked cake, forming long uneven cracks along the exposed earth. Turning on the garden hose, Joanne watered the patch until the dusty loam released steam into the air, letting out a long sigh of relief.

Following a brief interchange, Jan and I broke away. If we were leaving the next day, there was personal business to take care of. Halfway inside the front door of the hostel, Jan paused impeding my entry. Stumbling forward, I bumped into her back.

Hurrying his way down the hallway toward the front entrance rushed Teddy. Judging by the tool belt fastened around his waist; hammer and wrench hanging halfway down his skinny thigh, there were repairs to attend to over at the manse.

Focusing his eyes on the two of us, he cried "Hey! It's my Happies!" Compressing our bodies against the open front door, Jan and I created a narrow opening allowing Teddy to pass. In doing so, he gave us a wink. Once he'd cleared the steps, his backside facing us from the bottom of the front porch, Jan nudged my arm, encouraging me to follow.

I explained to Jan earlier what had happened in the garden, and how my exchange with the Good Samaritan led to the pivotal conversation with Reverend Mary. On the verge of leaving imminently, Jan guessed I'd be anxious to re-connect with Teddy.

Maybe it would be the last time.

Catching up with him on the sidewalk, I forced myself to let the chips fall. "Teddy?"

Speaking Teddy's name out loud to somebody other than Jan sounded foreign to me.

Spinning around, his movement elastic yet controlled, Teddy's nimble motion reminded me of the tap dance he'd done on the manse steps, still vivid in my mind. Before I said anything more, he beat me to the punch. "How'd things go with Reverend Mary this morning?"

Swaying awkwardly, shifting my weight from one foot to the other, I stammered, "Good, actually…Mary was great. Thanks a lot for suggesting I talk to her. It made all the difference in the world." Making known my idea of an inside joke, I kidded, "Reverend Mary told me I wasn't ready to join The Order right now. I guess she has my number all right."

Smiling wide, Teddy showed off straight white teeth. "All right. It worked then. So, did she make you feel better?"

"Yeah. I feel a whole lot better."

I *did* feel better. It was the undeniable truth. Holding one hand over top of my forehead, safeguarding my eyes against the sun, I was determined to be concise. "Anyway…I just wanted to let you know…and say, thanks again."

Sensitively dipping his head up and down, his blue charged eyes quietly measuring my face, Teddy beamed. "Good. She's a righteous lady then."

"She is," I affirmed softly, and gave my hand a wag.

Clicking his heels together, the Good Samaritan saluted.

Early evening, I borrowed a bike belonging to one of the hostellers and went for a spin around the neighbourhood. Giving the pedals a few hard pushes, I was reminded how uncomplicated it is to arrive somewhere in minutes opposed to hours. Wishing to broaden my recharged autonomy, I pedalled over to Safeway to pick up peanut butter and honey for our trip.

A few blocks from headquarters, I rode past a longhaired man in his late twenties pacing the yard of a green and yellow Victorian house. Bejeweled in sheer black negligee, lacey red bikini panties, garter, and fishnet stockings, spotting me, in shrill voice, the man merrily announced, "*Today* is my birthday!" Flashing him two thumbs up, I whirled past, laughing all the way.

A colourful pool of people congregated at the grocery store as usual. Ahead of me in line, I observed a threesome — the likes of which you'd never see in my hometown. Two gay men, age ambiguous, feminine in their dress and demeanor, nattered away like a pair of gossipy sorority girls while meticulously placing an assortment of groceries on the conveyer counter. The female leg of their ensemble, a butch dyke in her early-thirties clad in heavy artillery — black leather jacket, laced combat boots, and men's baggy khakis — whipped out a thick leather wallet chained to her pants' pocket and proceeded to pay the bill for all three.

Imagining their sleeping arrangements, the threesome could have been involved in a symbiotic sexual relationship. Maybe the two men were a couple and the woman a platonic friend. Possibly, one of the men was a friend and the other two a couple. Not that any of it mattered. Since our exposure to San Francisco, the concept of predisposed living agreements constituting a typical family system had gone straight into the crapper.

Returning to Steiner Street, Jan was dancing a happy little jig. Gary had left a phone telegram from Hope, British Columbia, requesting that we meet him during the week of June 19-25 at the Vancouver Youth Hostel where he worked part-time. The possibility of reuniting with Gary in less than a week made severing ties with HOOM somewhat easier to accept.

Aware of our impending departure, Brothers John and Bruce invited us over to the manse to see their printing press operation. Interested to finally tour inside of the three-story domicile, with a couple smaller rooms tacked on the back, we were surprised to discover the manse was practically a mirror image of the hostel. The Brothers' outfit was in one of the ad on rooms.

John and Bruce were responsible for designing and printing weekly newsletters on HOOM stationary, distributed on foot around the city on by members. The two also produced copies of *The Golden Force*, and other HOOM-associated literature and material. As a parting souvenir, Jan and I were each given a yellow 8" x 10" San Francisco Youth Hostel/HOOM letterhead depicting an ink drawing of a narrow winding road leading toward a big round sun. Wedged between a bold mountain range, extending outward from the ball were five transparent rays.

Thanking John and Bruce, we promised to return the following day to say goodbye. Setting foot on the sidewalk leading away from the manse walkway, I realized the letterhead would serve proof of what had transpired at HOOM. Sometimes, it had all felt imaginary.

That night, Sister Rose and I caught the bus to Polk Street where *Cuckoo's Nest* was playing at a second-run theatre. Afterwards, we crossed the street to a diner for a cup of tea and talked about our favourite scenes.

Enjoying the feature as much as I did, Rose regarded the movie a clever commentary on the marginalized in society. I hadn't looked at it that way before, but she was right.

We agreed on one point: *Nobody* played badass better than Nicholson.

Opting to remain behind that night, Jan played board games with Brother Bruce, Father Donald, and three new girls. A rare occasion for Father Donald to show up at the hostel, like the others, Jan found him pleasantly sociable. Quite possibly, everybody was ecstatic about our exodus the following day — providing a solid ride came through.

Pieces were fitting into place.

Wednesday early, a ringing phone jarred me from a deep sleep. Lifting my head, the heat already pervasive, I felt my nightgown soaked in perspiration.

A male's voice followed a knock at the door.

"Jan? Jill?" Father Donald had apparently taken us on as his pet project. I couldn't blame him.

"Are you girls *up?*"

We are now.

Clamouring from my sleeping bag, I hurried to the door, opening it a crack so not to disturb our three sleeping roomies.

"You might have yourselves a ride up the coast this morning," Donald alleged through the door break. "The Ride Center called. A *Russell* is looking for a couple of people to accompany him to Eugene. He stayed here a few nights ago and remembers you two girls."

Then the punch line. "Do you want to *go?*"

Son of a gun. We could hardly stall. I remembered Russell — haggard looking around the edges, yet he had one of those faces that made it tough to discern his age. Not a big talker, Russell was almost too quiet.

Out of her sleeping bag now, Jan stood next to me at the door. We traded apprehensive glances. Eugene was about an hour south of Portland, our proposed next stop. Russell *was* headed in the direction we wanted to go. Though fully intending to leave, neither one of us believed it would happen at the crack of dawn. Funny thing, every day was up for grabs — you never knew what shape it would take until after it had already happened. For the last couple of days, it felt as if we we'd been trapped in Oz long after the wizard floated away in his air balloon.

"When is he supposed to be here?" I asked.

As if gazing into a crystal ball, Donald raised his left wrist and stared at the face of his wristwatch. "Around ten. He'll be driving a white Beetle."

Following a private mini-conference, I assured Donald we'd happily accept the ride. Then Jan closed the door behind him and the two of us went to work. The process was short. Hauling our green and red backpacks out from the closet where they'd been stowed, we took turns showering, and stuffed our belongings into our bags. Mostly, we had summer clothes, and had managed to get our laundry done the day before. Laundry facilities being a hit and miss from place to place, it was a perk if you could leave somewhere with clean clothes before arriving at another.

Carefully, I lay Teddy's kangaroo jacket on the top of my backpack for easy access. The hoodie was one item I swore I would never throw in with dirty laundry. No way. No how. This significant article of clothing would need to be hand washed, if it ever got washed at all. To prevent breakage, my *Pleasures of the Harbor* album, carted around now for weeks, was placed between the green kangaroo and a pair of jeans. Like matching gloves, Teddy's jacket and the Ochs record belonged together. The Santana album for Dee, I arranged in the bottom of my pack above clean underwear.

Dee would never know.

Reconsidering how careless I'd been, travelling with LPs in an unprotected pack, I guessed we might possibly stay somewhere along our route with a turntable like at HOOM. I simply wasn't leaving the records behind.

Packing our belongings was the easy part. Saying farewell to the people and beloved friends who'd factored prominently in our lives for the better part of two and a half months, even when we weren't physically at Steiner Street, would not be so straightforward.

Together in the garden, Rebecca and Joanne were the first two faces Jan and I encountered outside of the hostel. Stockpiling my tears for the toughest goodbyes of all — Brother's John and Bruce, Sister Rose, and hopefully Teddy, I held up best I could throughout Rebecca's gentle embrace. That is until she whispered, "Don't go, Sister." Watching her hold Jan's gaze as if she'd known her all her life, cautioning us not to worry, Rebecca recited an old Irish blessing: "May God grant you always a sunbeam to warm you. A moonbeam to charm you. A sheltering angel, so nothing can harm you." In true exchange of friendship, I imparted a big smile, the most genuine gift I could afford.

With the absence of histrionics, Joanne, the more practical of the two, posed questions pertaining to the nuts and bolts of our impending trip. Satisfied by our answers to the when, where and how, reaching out, Joanne gave each of us a warmhearted hug.

In another time and place perhaps, Jan and I could have been Joanne and Rebecca.

Leaving the girls to tend their garden, returning to the manse, we were invited downstairs to the back room that housed the printing press. Buzzing with the knowledge that we were on our way to Canada, there was no reason to explain to the tribe why we were there.

Spotting us, Brother John jumped up from the press and rushed over. Rebecca suddenly appeared in the room and walked around to join Brother Bruce.

Approaching Jan in a loving, gentle manner, Brother John soothingly received my friend into his arms. Scuffling his way toward me, Bruce reeled my body close to his. Noticing a copy of *The Golden Force* in his hands, I stepped back.

"It's yours." Placing the paperback firmly on top of my two open palms, he insisted. "Read it. And don't forget to write." I gave Bruce another quick hug and then turned toward Brother John, who patiently waited to proffer his good wishes upon me.

Jan and I switched dance partners.

Enclosing me to his chest, I felt John's long arms tighten around my frame. Wrapped within the warmth of his body, and soft, prayerful voice, hairs prickled the back of my neck. Acting on the urge to close my eyes, I soon bore witness to hundreds of swirling white-light energy balls, fusing into one glowing mass that began to swell. The familiar electrified matrix, modulating parameters distinguishing light from dark, left an impression far more powerful than any tonic or mood-modifying hallucinogen. Through the art of his embrace, Brother John had transcended love and peace in its purest form.

Letting go of John, I espied Sister Rose (Rosamonde — we'd since learned Rose's alternate name) standing in the doorway. Of all the female members of HOOM, I felt closest to Rose and knew that she had a soft spot for me. Reminding the two of us to return one day, Rose hugged me first, then Jan, until Bruce cracked a joke, effectively deflating the emotion in the room. As much as I would miss everyone, the longer we remained, I knew that grief would endure. Forcing small talk to help filter tension, Jan and I slowly edged our way toward the door.

Rebecca followed.

Back outside in the daylight, I hedged around about Teddy's whereabouts. Evidently clairvoyant, while Jan and I waited, Rebecca offered to see if he was within reach.

Reappearing minutes later, Rebecca brought a message. "Teddy is in the middle of completing his household tasks, but wishes you both love and luck. He is confident he'll see you again one day, if not in San Francisco, then elsewhere."

Presuming Teddy was not fond of send-offs, I could forgive him. Yet, reading the expression of uncertainty across Rebecca's youthful face revealed everything.

Appealing to Teddy's irregular, attractive features, I *believed* that before our departure we would see the Good Samaritan again. It had to be so.

Outside, waiting for a city cab to pass before crossing the street toward the hostel, I had a notion to turn around. There, on the manse porch, like a shepherd supervising his flock, stood Teddy. Managing to untangle the vacuum hose from his feet, he started down the steps.

Jan and I turned back.

The Good Samaritan placed a thin hand upon the railing. "So…You're going back up to Canada today?"

"It's sure looking that way." Glancing over at Jan, I smirked. "Father Donald hinted it's time we move on. Probably, we should have left days ago."

Offsetting my remark, Teddy was quick to smooth everything over. "That's okay. You didn't have anywhere else to stay. He understands that. Don't worry about it." Proceeding to tell us he'd never travelled to Canada, Teddy anticipated making it an adventure one day. Acknowledging friends living in British Columbia, he subsequently spun off on various tangents, the inflections in his voice accentuating certain syllables made for a striking effect. Somewhere through the stream of narrative, Bob Dylan's name was mentioned.

Teddy's conspicuous Boston accent began to crowd my mind. There was a good chance I would never see him again. Not in this natural life anyway. Sorrow for my impending loss agitated in the pit of my stomach. Possibly, to my own detriment, I hadn't and wouldn't let him know how I felt. Teddy was a great person, but with a personal war to subjugate. I might have been a kid, but I understood the fundamentals of how things worked. To fight the tide of what comes naturally, a girl could set herself up for heartbreak, or worse, stray so far away from home she might never find her way back.

Keeping things in perspective, I needed to surround myself with truth. *Stay real. Live in the now.* Living in the now means *right* now. Not tomorrow or the day after. Obsessing about a lost or broken opportunity is damaging. Whining about *if only* is pointless. A flash in the pan. Everybody knows that. Only one factor could have bearing on any possible outcome. Returning to Steiner Street and registering as a novice-in-training. Now that I'd made the decision to postpone, seedlings of disconnect from HOOM had already fostered.

The Good Samaritan's discourse lulling, I heard my voice break through, "Well, we just wanted to say goodbye."

"There is no such thing as goodbye."

Maybe so, but if we're keeping it real, Brother, this is ciao.

For the first time since we'd known him, Teddy showed restraint. No motion to throw his arms around us as the others had done. No crafty aside. No fancy footwork. No cute maneuvers on the porch steps.

No faux promises to stay in touch.

Clasping two vein-streaked hands together, bowing his head perpendicular to his waist, in Arabic, the Good Samaritan solemnly quoted from a favourite passage. "Allah yusallmak."

He translated: "God be with you both."

Good enough.

It would have to be.

Santa Barbara Mission.

Southern California vista.

Grace and Jude, Steiner Street hostel.

Marco moves on.

Card from San Francisco Ride Centre.

"Jagger."

*Father Donald and Sister Rose on the front steps
of 101 Steiner Street, San Franscisco.*

CHAPTER 43

Into the Mystic,
Mount Shasta

"Travel is great. Learning is constant. Each new person has *something."*
JAN M.

Russell failed to show. Jan contacted the Ride Center to see if we could catch a lift with somebody else. *Anybody* else. After saying goodbye to everyone at HOOM, before certain individuals got prickly, we were anxious to be on our way. Not only that, wringing every drop of emotion from your being, there's nothing worse than sticking around and marinating in it.

Our new buddy Emil, living behind the hostel, stopped by while we were waiting for a reply from the Ride Center. Earlier, we'd gone around to say goodbye only Emil wasn't home. If all else failed, he was prepared to drive us to the freeway entrance.

We took Emil up on his bid.

Shortly after packing our belongings into Emil's truck, the Ride Center called to say that a man named Howard was on his way to Eureka. He'd be along at two to pick us up.

"Cripes." Shaking my head at Jan, I muttered a phrase my mother was fond of saying, "This day is turning into a B movie."

Out came our packs from Emil's car. For the next ninety minutes, we waited on the front steps of the hostel for a phantasm named Howard. As fate would have it, Jan and I were never to meet Howard. Around one, a tarnished white Volkswagen pointing its nose toward 101 Steiner Street, drove up to the curb and parked directly in front of the hostel. Uneasy on his feet after making an unhurried exodus through the small enclosure on the driver's side, Russell, our *ride*, looked sickly. Behind a sweaty face, unkempt hair, silver-rimmed eyeglasses and slovenly duds, he reminded me of a character I knew back home, a mail carrier we'd nicknamed "Johnny Joint" for good reason.

Standing adjacent to his vehicle, half apologetically, Russell lit a fresh Marlboro and muttered something about a ride up to Eugene.

Could we spare $6 to help with the cost of gas?

Staring hard at Russell, I thought the man looked god-awfully wretched, even a bit sad. Something was amiss, of that I was certain. I just couldn't put my finger on it. There was also a weirdly appealing quality about him. This is the reason why, blindly, Jan and I put our trust in Russell. There was no way we could turn the poor bugger down. Russell needed us. Not to mention, Howard had wanted nine bucks.

Placing a final call to the Ride Center, Jan informed the switchboard that Howard's services would no longer be required.

We had our man.

About to set out, a bit of a fanfare erupted around the front steps of the hostel. Sister Rose and Father Donald had come to see us off. Moments before shoving my pack into the car's tiny trunk, I asked if either one minded posing for a photo. They didn't. Borrowing Jan's Brownie camera, I snapped a magic shot of Rose and Donald sitting on the front steps of 101 Steiner Street, smiles wrinkling their faces; a frozen memory of two of HOOM's finest.

Russell pulled the driver seat forward, enabling me access to the back of his VW. Jan situated herself comfortably in the front seat next to Russell. Adopting the deportment of its owner, like a slug, the vehicle lurched from the curb and out on to the street.

Passing Duboce Park one last time, looking out the back window, I waved goodbye to Rose and Donald. In front of the park bench, flat on his back on the grass, Teddy quietly smoked a cigarette. His two-toned, black and green leather shoes crossed over top of one another, aviator sunglasses resting on the bridge of his nose, staring skyward, the Good Samaritan fixed his gaze on bloated white cloud clusters surrounded by a copious field of blue.

Exiting the city onto the freeway ramp, Russell headed north on I-5 toward Eugene. The distance between San Francisco and Eugene being 530 miles, this two-day journey would preclude any discussion about where we would stay once evening came. Presuming there'd be a hostel somewhere along our travels; Jan said she'd check the book once we reached Sacramento outskirts.

It was Wednesday afternoon. Pre-mid-day traffic flowed harmoniously. Vehicles weaved politely in an out of lanes allowing optimal space for neighbouring cars to duly pass or remain in line. For the first hour, the three of us talked little. After the hurried activities of the first part of the day, the quiet calming, I suspected Jan was snoozing in the front seat. Though tired as well, I would catnap later.

From my position in the back seat of the wagon, on a diagonal view, Russell's head and the side of his face were visible. Since leaving the city, the pallor of his skin had become paler. This was mildly disconcerting. I asked if he was feeling all right. Without shifting his focus from the bumper directly in front of him, Russell admitted to feeling a little under the weather. "Otherwise," he mumbled, "I'm fine to drive."

Lacking driver's licenses, if Russell wasn't good to go, Jan and I would hitch the rest of the way to Eugene. We didn't mind hitchhiking; only we wanted to reach Oregon before trying our luck with our thumbs.

Possibly, Russell was hung over from a booze binge in the days leading up to our leaving. I had a hunch it was something else, something worse. Maybe he had a life-threatening illness. How devastating to carry the knowledge of having fallen prey to some horrific malady with two appendages tagging along. Perhaps Russell sought our company in case he needed a shoulder or support.

This was all fantasy and conjecture. I prayed that whatever was ailing Russell would soon wane.

Russell switched on the car radio. Johnny Cash's "I Walk the Line" detonated the airwaves as the Man in Black sang about going to extremes for his one true love. I couldn't say I knew what it was like to be in Cash's shoes — not yet anyway, but hung to a sliver of hope that before our trip finished I would meet somebody exceptional.

Listening to three decades of rock hits on a local radio station, continuing up the interstate through the San Joaquin County also known as the California Grapevine, time moved fluidly. Vines and an undulating palate of jade were striking that afternoon. Along with the poignant sway of beauty, there was hurt in realizing that we were leaving California, the place which had become a symbolic home away from home. I thought of Teddy, happily unwinding on the grass in the sun, and wondered how long I'd be able to hold that picture in my mind before it would wither, as memories often do through the prolongation of age and distance.

I tried to picture Teddy's gold sky.

Nearing Sacramento County, two hours after our departure, Russell announced he needed a break. He wasn't feeling well. Clutching onto the column of the steering wheel with two hands, making a sharp right motion, our ride proceeded to pull off the freeway.

A teenage girl travelling in a mysterious man's vehicle fears this pivotal moment. My neurosis kicked in big time.

Was this the *real* deal? Did Russell forge an illness so that he could machinate some perverse trick? Manufacturing a frightful drive out to some arbitrary dirt road, I envisioned the two of us raped at knifepoint. Seated closest to our anticipated perpetrator, Jan would be the first one assaulted.

Physically, Russell appeared weak. If necessary, there was good chance either one of us could take him. Seated in the back seat, I had an advantage, and estimated we had about two minutes to proactively attack, or devise a defense strategy — whatever the situation called for.

The Volkswagen signaled another right in the direction of a truck stop parking lot. I breathed a sigh of relief. It had been more than a couple of weeks since we'd driven with an unknown. My sanguinity had gone rusty. I had no idea what Jan was thinking in the passenger seat next to ole Russell. If I had to speculate, when he abruptly broke from the program, she likely entertained an even more extreme mutation of a gruesome slaughter drama. It was altogether unfair of me to charge and convict the poor bastard in the span of one minute. Russell hardly looked threatening.

Stay in the now.

Inside a little coffee shop attached to the gas station, Russell bought a bag of ice, smashing it down on the counter with his fist until it broke into smaller chips. Tearing open the plastic, he poured a handful of fragmented ice pieces into the palm of his hand, and began eating the flakes like candy. Soon, Jan and I chewed on the ice too, keeping ourselves occupied while quietly waiting for Russell. Leaving us in a booth, he'd made a trip to the men's room. In his absence, watching his half-smoked Marlboro burn away in the ashtray on the laminate table, exploring different scenarios as to what might be biting him; we couldn't arrive at a definitive conclusion.

Fifteen minutes later, Russell still hadn't reappeared. His cigarette crumbling to ash, the possibility that he was a junkie punctured my mind. Sharing my epiphany with Jan, she wondered why we hadn't thought of it before.

Go figure.

Finally, the door to the restroom opened. Russell's shaggy dark hair still hung limp. To revive his poor state of health, trying to present as normal, he'd splashed cold water on his face. Below the wire-rimmed eyeglasses, a trace of colour surfaced on his cheeks.

Shuffling his way past a waitress busy serving other customers, joining us in the booth, Russell lit another smoke. In the close, muggy afternoon, covering over a white t-shirt, his faded denim jacket remained on. When Jan asked why he didn't remove it, Russell responded he felt "chilled." Mostly, our compadre stared uneasily at his ice bits, avoiding eye contact unless asked a direct question. About the same age as my brother Chris, Russell was far more subdued. I began to contemplate that rather than a terminal disease or otherwise, depression might be the basis for his introversion. It was anybody's guess. For whatever reason, Russell was tight-lipped, almost as if he was embarrassed about something.

The junkie scenario looked more and more likely.

Talking amongst ourselves about our friends at HOOM and seeing Gary in a week, Jan and I were eager to get back on the road. The sun's inescapable passage from east to west indicated it was getting later in the afternoon. During a break in staggered conversation, rubbing the back of his neck, Russell finally made a quiet proclamation. "Let's head out. We'll make Mount Shasta tonight."

Back inside the Volkswagen, Jan and I switched seats. Sitting up front next to Mr. Cheerful, to make sure he didn't nod off at the wheel, I increased the volume on the radio.

Russell didn't seem to notice.

Opening up somewhat, Russell told us what he knew about Mount Shasta.

Located in Siskiyou County containing the fifth highest peak in the state of California, Mount Shasta is one of the tallest base-to-summit rises in the world. Regarded as a stratovolcano, the stand-free mountain is unconnected to any adjoining ranges. Believed to be sacred, The Karuk Indian people refer to Shasta as *Tuiship ada*, "mountain with snow." If we stayed on course, we were scheduled to arrive around nine — at dusk, surely providing sufficient time to find a place to bunk down for the night.

Our little car sped along at a 55- mile-per-hour clip. Much of the road along the upswing of interstate 5 between Sacramento and Mount Shasta was through miles of farmland. Olive groves, tomato and rice fields, waterfalls, and golden eagles espied en route helped us to forget about Russell's precarious state of health for a while. As if matchsticks lined in a row, pistachio, walnut, and almond crops paralleled one another up and down the gently sloping countryside. Rolling the windows all the way down, the aromatic scent of lavender growing on either side of the freeway suffused the car's interior, remaining long after we were miles past. Jan and I shared the little food we'd brought along with Russell — crackers, apples, bits of cheddar cheese. Lacking anything resembling an appetite, likely for our benefit, Russell did his best to stuff a few dry crackers into his mouth. Placing my drowsy head against the headrest, a new parade of rock numbers played on the radio. The DJ announced a "special treat" for listeners. It was the single, "I'm Eighteen," from Alice Cooper's *Love it to Death*, released a few years earlier. Reaching the top-forty Billboard charts, with its repetition of the phrase, "I'm Eighteen and I don't know what I want," the song had evolved into the quintessential courier of the rite of passage linking youth and adulthood.

Glimpsing out the window, a sign alerted motorists to the Woodland/Redding exit, about 50 miles north on the interstate. Russell had mentioned the road to Shasta could be accessed via the Woodland/Redding cut off. Coinciding with when we reckoned we'd reach our destination, I anticipated pulling off soon and tracking down a place to rest.

Puffing on a newly lit Marlboro, still looking like crap, Russell admitted to having about an hour left in his tank.

Entering what is recognized as the Shasta Cascade region of California, bordering Oregon and Nevada and home to several North American Indian tribes, peering out the windshield, Jan and I regarded our crash site for the night. Rising boldly from a mossy green coverlet of trees, shrubs, and brush, snow-capped Mount Shasta stood grandiose and unbound. Verging closer, the showy topping resembled volcanic residue — exactly as Russell had described. A smaller, darker version of its cousin shaped like a pyramid, Black Butte stood proudly before Mount Shasta. Veering into the periphery of Shasta City, we drove along a narrow road leading through town that cut out toward the base of the mountain incline.

There were no listings in our hostel guidebook. Jan had checked earlier. While in town, I asked Russell if he knew of anything resembling a motel or boarding house where we could find cheap lodging for one night. Shrugging his shoulders, he drove on. Not about to pay for sleep, Russell thought we might edge our way onto the mountain base. Park the car somewhere off the beaten path. Suggesting that Jan and I sleep inside the car, Russell would find somewhere outside on the ground. Remembering how chilly Northern California nights could be after sundown, I didn't think sleeping outdoors was prudent or practical, but kept my mouth shut.

Jan tapped my shoulder lightly from the back seat. Swiveling around, she pulled a face. I knew what it meant: *This sucks*. Rolling my eyes, I teasingly stuck out my tongue and shifted in my seat to regard Shasta out the front window.

It wasn't as if we had a choice. Russell was the captain. Anyway, this setting had the markings of a potentially fun adventure — sort of like a Davy Crockett exploit. Thinking that it might be of some use, before we set out, I'd scoffed a full roll of toilet paper from HOOM.

Creeping slowly upward along the sloping road toward to the base of the mountain spine, stones and slushy ice crushed beneath our tires. At a quarter past eight, it was still bright outside. Soon, the pink tinged sky would signal the arrival of sunset resigned to return.

Most nights, since our journey began, sundown was welcome, even revered. The simple act of nature could be counted upon. Often poignant and affecting, dusk also warned of unpredictable weather conditions ahead. Diminishing colours interchanged with black could suggest uncertainty. Yet, as day converted to night, as a guest of Mount Shasta in mid-June, we anticipated a fascinating metamorphosis. Imperative to find a desirable resting spot for the next ten hours, we would draw on star power to channel our way.

Now almost the first day of summer, because of our elevation, remnants of snow loitered on the patchy asphalt and stone textiles. It seemed that with every few feet the Volkswagen climbed, the temperature continued to drop. Wearing nothing other than an old jean jacket on top of a thin t-shirt, Russell would require heavy artillery to withstand a nippy night on partially frozen ground. If he'd packed something more substantial, there was no evidence of it.

Leaving the truck stop hours earlier, I'd started to look at Russell through another vantage point. Unusual and quiet, sure, but he didn't seem to mind our company. For the most part, his middling temperament had made the drive enjoyable. Russell treated us respectfully, the way my brother had done in Los Angeles. Still, I couldn't help worrying about him. Throughout the last hour of the trip, his skin tone alternated from colourless to pasty. Except for few verbal outbursts, Russell was despondent.

On the brighter side, maybe he had good reason for choosing this allegorical, numinous place.

Our little car finally came to a stop next to a line of junipers fringing the locale. Rolling down the window, I stuck out my head. Cold and damp, ice scraps and snow covered portions of ground. A blast of frosty air propelled against my skin, I began to giggle. The mood felt light again. Eager to be free from the car's confines, opening the door a crack, Jan popped her head outside, shivered, and then changed her mind. The view of enigmatic Mount Shasta directly in front of us, a modicum of stars seemed ready to ignite the sky. The night was beautiful. Clear and clean. Once it grew darker, there'd be a militia of stars.

Russell opened the driver's side door, stepped his scuffed white tennis shoe into a pile of mucky slush and cursed. Scouring the ground and area like a coyote on the hunt, he advised us to bring our sleeping bags from the trunk and store them inside the car. One of us would take the front seat, the other one the back.

Hauling a crumpled, light blue sleeping sack from the rear, apparently, Russell hadn't taken pains packing it into the car. Watching him case the barren vicinity looking for dry ground to unfurl his bag, I guessed he was used to sleeping in changeable conditions.

Our mystery man didn't come down with the first rain.

Sketch of spectacular Mount Shasta, California.

CHAPTER 44

Pressing On

"Use spear of mind which is thought — to stop what negativity has been wrought."
THE GOLDEN FORCE

Russell found the enchanted spot to lay his head for the long night ahead — about twenty feet in front of where he'd parked the car. Close to a tangle of undergrowth, sheltered beneath tall firs on top of broken ice and sludge, it wasn't much of a refuge.

Peeling off his denim jacket and jeans, Russell preferred to sleep in his t-shirt. In the few hours since arriving at Mount Shasta, Jan and I were to bear witness to a stream of speedy disappearing acts into the woods, only to observe Russell minutes later resuming thrashing and flailing about, coughing, even vomiting inside and next to his sleeping bag. At one point, I handed him a huge wad of the toilet paper stashed inside of the vehicle earlier so it wouldn't get damp. With a slight lowering of his head, Russell thanked me.

Later that evening, Jan got out of the car and wandered over to where he lay. Swearing he was fine, Russell directed her to return to the Volkswagen. He wasn't fine, but we were at a loss as how to help except sit tight in the car. If he needed anything, we were on standby.

A classmate of Chris's had OD'd in the late sixties. Afterwards, I read in a book at the local library that withdrawal symptoms from opiates such as heroin can vary from a day to a few days, depending upon the amount ingested and an individual's body type. Russell had proven to be a gentle, sweet man. Neither one of us wished him harm. We didn't want our friend to expire overnight.

Swathed in darkness, a throng of stars blanketing the sky, the dominant presence of Mount Shasta bearing her snow-white tiara seemed to magnify how dependent we three were upon one another. There was something corporeal about the mountain, as if quietly, it watched over us in wait. I recalled some of the mysterious stories Russell had told us earlier that afternoon when the sky was still light. He'd spoken of secret tunnels, and talked about rumours of a subterranean city. There existed eyewitness accounts of abnormal spectacles and reverberations at Shasta believed to be phantoms. Onlookers mentioned the existence of little people, faeries, even a Big Foot population, and other odd, immortal creatures inhabiting the mountain, revealing themselves to chosen few. Evidently, Mount Shasta is one of the landing sites for UFOs. It was and still is, considered a cosmic summit on earth.

Inside the car, clutching Teddy's kangaroo jacket around my shoulders, pulling my sleeping bag to my neck, I asked Jan if she was scared. "I wish Russell would feel better soon," she replied. Deciding it wouldn't hurt, we prayed to the mountain, asking it to make Russell healthy again. In the dark, off in the distance, Mount Shasta's sallow face stared down at the two of us bundled inside of our sleeping bags secured within the enclave of Russell's bug. Our subconscious mindscapes linked, an allusion was shared. Mount Shasta was listening.

Within the hour, we both fell asleep.

Throughout the crisp, cool night, periodically, we awakened, taking turns keeping watch. This wasn't a planned act — my friend and I felt compelled to ensure that Russell didn't freeze to death in the cold. Though improbable a person would perish in Northern California climate in June, naïvely, we didn't want to gamble. Due to the frosty temperature and restrictive space inside of the vehicle, it was tough sleeping more than brief intervals anyway. At times, thick condensation layering the windows coupled with the black sky made it difficult to discern Russell's sleeping bag, even amidst the star fire. Every so often, one of us rolled down a window clearing the mist trapped within the car. The final hour before sunrise, our haunted friend slept uninterrupted.

Dawn poured down through a generous helping of sunlight. Opaque skies overhead enabled us to view Russell's figure shifting on the rutted ground almost in punishing manner, as if he was seeking penance for some unforgivable deed. Given the volatile circumstances, ironically, Russell probably had a better night's sleep than we had.

Oozing through the trees, sunshine warmed the air inside and outside of our vehicle. Feeling a strong urge to pee, I opened the car door, walked over to hide behind a nearby bush, unzipped my jeans and crouched down. Off in the distance, branches snapped. Looking up, I spotted Jan wearing her yellow, cable-knit wool sweater seeking cover. Refastening my pants, I glanced across the way to the surface of the partially icy ground and watched the lumpy mass that was Russell move inside of his sleeping bag. All but concealed by his cocoon, the man was still alive; thank god — evident by the cloudy swirl emanating from his head as he sucked on a Marlboro.

I got back inside the car. Jan soon followed. She appeared tired, exactly how I felt and probably looked. Keeping our eyes fixated on Russell, we pondered his next move.

"What do you think?" Craning my neck around toward the backseat, I expected my friend to sum up our present situation. Looking worried, Jan shook her head. "I honestly don't know. I guess we'll have to wait and see how he's feeling. If it takes longer to get to Eugene than we figured, that's fine by me."

Pointing a finger in the direction of Russell's sleeping bag, she drew a single breath. "Hope he's okay."

The distance between Mount Shasta and Eugene was roughly 250 miles — about five hours drive or more depending upon traffic. Neither of us expected Russell to go anywhere unless he was feeling up to it. Depending upon the kind of night he'd had, it could go either way. If he was detoxifying from drugs, it might be a few days before he'd be in shape to drive. I started imagining what it might be like to remain two or three days in the precise location of the Great Spirit and its clandestine sect of highly evolved human beings. There were tales of conduits with the know-how to channel thoughts of supernatural spirit bodies. If indeed they existed, I had no doubt one of them had the sway to negotiate our prayers on Russell's behalf.

Half-past seven, managing to fight his way out of his sleeping bag, wire-rimmed glasses in hand, Russell ambled toward the car. His appearance hadn't improved much from the day before, but for the first time, hair comically sticking out all over like porcupine quills, leaning against the hood of the Volkswagen, Russell managed a smile. Fearful of disturbing the dragon, we didn't dare ask how he'd slept. Lighting up another smoke, Russell talked about getting on the road soon, and mentioned trying to locate a rest area so that we could all take showers.

This was the best pitch I'd heard in a while. At the very least, I could benefit from a sponge bath. Jan looked forward to ridding herself of the clothes she'd (hardly) slept in. Ostensibly, Russell was the poster boy for somebody in need of the kind of complete makeover that only hot water and soap could provide.

Settled in the vehicle, Russell guided the Volkswagen carefully along receding ice patches dispersed along the contours of the path, and down to the laneway directing us out to the main town road. Food rations, left over from the day before, were shared between us. At least it was edible. While Jan and I finished most of the leftover crackers and cheese, Russell munched on a few broken Ritz pieces.

Reaching the town of Mount Shasta nuzzled at the foot of the mountain, we pulled up to a convenience store to purchase some milk. When Russell came outside, half of the two-quart carton was almost emptied. Figuring the milk might help coat Russell's upset stomach, neither one of us knew until much later that milk enhances and mitigates the effects of heroin. Baffled as to whether Russell was using or trying to free himself from the stuff, at least he was beginning to resemble a human being.

A bright and beautiful morning with a temperature already close to 80 degrees, rolling the windows down, we edged toward the on ramp and waited in queue to merge onto the interstate. Keeping a look out for signs denoting rest areas ahead, the first posting indicated a stop about 50 miles north.

Trying not to fall asleep in the front seat in case Russell needed her eyes, in the end, Jan couldn't help herself. Wiped out myself from spending much of the night awake, leaning my head back, I rested my lids. Fifty miles of steady road would provide ample time for a catnap.

A jolt awakened me. Swerving to the right off the interstate, Russell swung the VW into a gas station surrounded by a wooded area. He mumbled something about our location being about a half hour's drive from Ashland, Oregon — north of the terrain bordering California and Oregon. Excited to stay in one of its main drags, I anticipated garnering a better sense of Oregon's countrified state. If our hostel book was accurate, after Russell dropped us in Eugene, we could hitch a ride to Portland. Spend a couple of nights in the downtown core.

The rest area turned out to be a bust. Equipped with an outhouse, there were no showers in sight.

Russell was more disappointed than we were.

Back on the road, the next couple of hours we continued travelling north through mountainous regions such as Medford, Grants Pass, and up toward Roseburg. Two more times, Russell exited off the interstate in hunt of a rest area. Each one offered every amenity but a shower. I'd have been satisfied with a sink, only Jan and I hadn't slept in clothes stained with vomit. Possibly piss, too.

You couldn't fault a person for trying.

Around two in the afternoon, Russell snagged another exit off the free-way burrowing into Eugene's city center, close enough to the interstate access in case we couldn't locate a hostel or YWCA downtown. Exhausted, Jan and I decided it'd be in our best interest to remain in Eugene for one night and head out to Portland first thing in the morning. Not knowing of any hostel listings in Eugene, we would ask around.

Pulling the car next to a parking meter, Russell turned the key counter-clockwise, silencing the engine. Reaching into his glove compartment for a wooden match to fire up another Marlboro, hands shaking, he managed to get the smoke lit. A forlorn expression engraved upon his face, looking dismally at Jan, Russell subsequently glanced into the back seat — telltale signs that we were at the end of the line.

"This is it, I guess." He grimaced. "I sure wish I could drive you further on."

Jan and I wished the same. Despite Russell's erratic and occasionally disquieting mental and physical states, he was solid. Seeing that neither one of us wanted to get out of the car, Russell made the first move.

"Let me get your knapsacks from the trunk."

Cars passed by in slow motion, I watched Russell open the driver's side door and step out onto the street. Assuming an unhurried gait, he headed toward the hatchback removing our packs one at a time, and eased them down on to the curb.

Jan got out behind Russell. Giving the front seat a push forward, I climbed out from the back seat to join Jan and Russell on the sidewalk. Anguished about something, Russell's nervous body language made it obvious. We were still in the dark as to why he'd chosen to come to Eugene. There had been no mention of family or friends living in the city. The day before, Russell had told us he was from Minnesota.

"Are you girls going to be okay? I really hate dropping you like this."

Not wanting to burden the poor fellow with anything other than what he scarcely held together, Jan was the first to assure Russell we would be fine. Motioning my head in agreement, reaching my arms out, I gave him a big hug. Dumbfounded by the unrehearsed display of affection, Russell was doubly pleased when Jan extended a similar show of fondness.

Excusing himself to retrieve a piece of paper from his glove compart-ment, Russell wanted to give us his home address. Much as I'd grown to care for him, I couldn't imagine the three of us becoming pen pal buddies. As always, promising to keep up was a polite formality.

Crawling into his Beetle, Russell handed each of us a torn lined piece of paper, his name and Minnesota address scrawled across it. "Here," he said. "If you need anything, this is where you can get a hold of me." In minutes, our troubled friend would head to a destination in town, location unknown. Waving goodbye, I cautioned him to take care.

Sticking his left hand out the car window, forming a peace sign, Russell pulled away from the meter and then the Beetle rolled toward the intersection. Making a right-hand turn at the red light, the little car zigzagged over into traffic.

Long after Russell's car disappeared, Jan and I stared after him. As irrational as things had sometimes seemed, Russell's leaving was analogous of a close relative passing on. In the span of one day, we'd said final goodbyes to a handful of people. It was becoming harder and harder to accept. One way to annihilate despair is distraction — keep on moving. Turn another uncertain plan into action.

Unfamiliar with the city, we were slow to gauge our surroundings. Talking with a few locals, it became apparent there wasn't anything downtown within walking distance resembling a youth hostel or even a YWCA. A young woman told us she thought there might be a rooming house about a mile away. Not up to putting forth the effort to follow up, especially if the information was inaccurate, we would explore other alternatives. Portland was about two hours away. It was still early in the afternoon. If we were lucky enough to get a single ride, we could make it there before rush hour.

Hoisting our packs onto our backs, Jan and I began walking the half-mile in direction of the highway on ramp, hoping to catch a ride on the I-5 north to Portland. After spending almost six hours cramped inside Russell's vehicle, it felt good to move my legs freely.

I continued to imagine where Russell had gone. What he might be doing that very minute. Was he crashed on a friend's couch somewhere, chasing after a shower, or a green monster?

Luck struck almost immediately. A pleasant man driving a small truck pulled over next to merging traffic. Originally from Michigan, our driver had lived in Oregon six months and was going to Woodburn via Salem — about half the distance to Portland.

It was a short, uneventful trip.

Next, we were picked up by Mickey (translation: an egotistical jerk) driving a blue Triumph TR6. Mickey used to play for the Toronto Marlies, a professional Canadian hockey team (currently in the American Hockey League). Monopolizing conversation that pertained to his income and several other innocuous accomplishments, Mickey thought he knew of a youth hostel in downtown Portland. Accelerating his speed, TR6 cruised into the city center. Failing to navigate an intersection, Mickey drove straight into the back of a black Oldsmobile. No one was hurt, thank god, but police arrived. Personal information was exchanged, delaying us for some time. Finally, TR6 drove us to the hostel in question, a burnt-out building. Not Mickey's fault, but after he finally let us out at the bus terminal, Jan and I were happy to say good riddance.

The next major city along our route was Seattle — farther than we planned to go. Our initial objective, to spend a few days exploring the Portland area where the Willamette and Columbia rivers converge, was amended to skipping the city altogether. Now close to five, we hadn't yet found a place to bunk down for the night. Though reluctant to fast track our trip, our guidebook cited several listings for youth hostels and a Y in downtown Seattle. Essentially, we could take our pick. A good three hours drive north of Portland, Seattle would be close to dark by the time we arrived.

Far from our best after spending much of the previous night babysitting Russell, Jan and I weren't in a mood to screw around. Purchasing two bus tickets for $7.50, we killed an hour at the terminal café counting down minutes until 6 pm.

When it came time to board, we could hardly wait. Not having eaten much at the terminal, a couple of muffins and hot chocolate — the food would have to last until morning. Pulling out of the station, the finality of leaving behind Steiner Street, Meadowlark, and family in Los Angeles dallied on my mind. Following our return to Southern Ontario, irrevocably, I would have to put on my big girl pants. Come to terms with what lay ahead. Not that I had any hard and fast answers. Home, and all that it represented, waited on the periphery.

Soaring along the interstate, the Greyhound brought us farther and farther north. Determined to submerge my mind in Oregon's Tualatin Mountains, its valleys and plains best I could, before crossing into Washington State, I fought the urge to close my eyes. Coming close to joining HOOM, at the very least, I'd taken away an awareness of something greater than what our conscious minds forecasted early into our journey. That felt relevant, yet there was a long way to go. How probable is it for new insights to sustain when they are no longer nurtured or seen?

I appreciated what Sister Rose had meant.

Dusk less than an hour away, I realized I must have dozed off. Meditating on the quiet of the bus, glancing around, most of the riders had succumbed to various stages of sleep. On the aisle, eyes shut, completely relaxed, Jan breathed evenly. Leaning across, I reached out to lower the plastic blind above the sliding glass window to provide shade for the duration of our ride.

Outside, the sky had taken on an appearance of marble. Skeins of gold wove in and out of clouds as the atmosphere readied itself for nightfall. Lightly pressing my fingers against the glass, watching the colours balloon, I harkened back to the recurring cluster of pregnant golf balls observed in San Francisco before falling asleep.

Teddy's gold sky would pilot our way.

Rendition of Paul McCartney from a local newspaper. June 1976.

CHAPTER 45

Jericho Beach

"Peace. It does not mean to be in a place where there is no noise, trouble or hard work. It means to be in the midst of those things and still be calm in your heart."
UNKNOWN

The downtown Seattle YWCA was nothing to write home about, but it was clean, had single beds and hot showers. Even so, we couldn't help cringe at the price for one night's lodging — a rip off at over $6 a head. For that kind of dough, the place should resemble the Taj Mahal. More like a hovel, the Seattle Y was far removed from anything resembling glamour. Edging closer to the Canadian border — and Gary, with minimal time to assess the city, Jan and I felt ambivalent about staying on. Providence might even intervene, enabling us to possibly see Gary in day or so.

I had reservations.

Two months had passed since we'd torn around the streets of San Francisco together. Moving in converse directions, no doubt, we were living in different headspaces. Jan looked forward to spending time with Gary. Mostly for her sake, I hoped a rekindling of friendship would happen. Planning to hitchhike to the Peace Arch border crossing at Blaine Washington in the morning, an approximate three and a half hours from Seattle, we'd find out soon enough what was in store.

Jan and I continued to ruminate about HOOM and all its players, Bruce Flagg, Evarts, even Russell. All that had come before felt acutely purposeful. Like some propagated vision resulting from lack of vitamins or brain food, our recollections were beginning to feel illusory.

I could not allow that to happen.

The following day would be June 18th, two days before Father's Day. June 18th was also Paul McCartney's birthday. At 34 years of age, the pretty Beatle was quickly becoming a ripened old man. Fronting his new band Wings, currently, McCartney was on an international "Wings Over America" tour in support of two hugely successful back-to-back selling albums, *Venus and Mars* and *Wings at the Speed of Sound*. We'd read about McCartney's sold out show in San Diego at the Sports Arena (now the Valley View Casino Center) two days earlier, and continued to hear of additional dates throughout out travels. Not surprisingly, reviews were rave. During high school, we'd often attend two, sometimes three concerts a month. These days, a rock show was out of reach.

One of the girls from the Seattle Y offered to drop us within proximity of the freeway entrance. Barely time to blink, think, shower, pack and dress, shortly after daybreak, Jan and I were back on the on ramp leading to the interstate.

Ken Wills, a middle-aged Seattle resident behind the wheel of an Audi accompanied by an adorable Angus dog, drove us 90 miles to Bellingham. While he gassed up, Jan and I stopped in at a McDonald's for a quick bite. Wills was kind enough to take us to the freeway access and let us off.

Two boys were in line ahead of us.

This time, we didn't have to compete for a lift. A mid-sized truck pulled up alongside our small group, inviting all four of us to hop in. Jan and I sat up front with the driver. The boys snagged the box seat in the back. It was a one-hour straight shot to the Canada/U.S. border crossing. We were dropped off on the American side — as far as the trucker was going.

After that, things got interesting.

Conferring with our two new mates, we concurred it wouldn't be advisable to take our places in lines designated for vehicles. Unaware of alternate ways to cross the border, all of us presumed it would be best to walk through the park and cross over to the Canadian side.

The tactic seemed simple enough, almost too simple.

Off we strode, toward a stretch of green space surrounding several border patrol booths and administrative buildings. Apprehended by border police while entering the park, our group was informed the RCMP was looking for us. For nearly thirty minutes, the cops had their eyes fixed on our party.

This was confusing, at first.

Two officers hauled our asses into the main building and began inter-
rogating us to some degree, demanding why we four had chosen to pull off
a "defiant and blatantly irresponsible" maneuver. Asking that we provide
sufficient identification, the officials demanded to know where we'd come
from and where we were going.

In those days, a birth certificate sufficed, but Jan was understandably
worried. Deemed underage to travel months earlier by officers who'd
threatened to return her home to her parents if she didn't produce proper
documentation, Jan continued to carry the note from her father that had
saved our butts crossing the B.C. border into the United States during
our second outing with Walter. The letter, dated April 1976, granted
her permission *into* the U.S. only. Nothing was mentioned about travel
beyond that point, or back to Canada. If Jan was inclined to produce the
memo, would the bureaucrats accept it?

Stumped as to why the officers were being so pigheaded, we made it
obvious there were no ulterior motives, nothing sinister up our sleeves. We
weren't fugitives, nor did we possess criminal records, drugs or weapons.
Course, Jan and I could only speak for ourselves. We knew absolutely
nothing about our travel companions.

The police separated us into individual rooms, at which point I thought
I might crap my pants. Forcing myself to keep it together, I explained:
"*All four* of us are Canadian citizens. My friend and I have been travelling
in the United States and are now returning to Canada."

Since no one owned a vehicle, *wrongly*, we'd surmised we could hike
across the border. None of us realized we had trespassed or done anything
illegal, that there is a certain protocol to follow.

Young and senseless, there wasn't much more to say.

The officers finished rummaging through our belongings and running
our information through their system. Sanctioning us a "non-threat," the
four of us were discharged. The entire process lasted about an hour. It
had felt like an eternity. In the end, the bastards were malicious about
the whole misunderstanding. Before letting us go, we were informed that
our "act of trespassing" would remain on "permanent government record."
Confirming our Canadian citizenship, I couldn't understand how we were
trespassing on our own soil. One thing I knew for certain, *nobody* was
thrilled about the whole mess. We wanted to get the hell out of there and
never look back.

Safely (so we thought) on Canadian soil, spotting Jan and I hitchhiking near the border crossing, police chastised us again, shouting, "Get
further up the road and out of sight of the border!" Patrol threatened to

fine us for solicitation of a ride which, apparently, was illegal in British Columbia in 1976.[7]

Jogging a good half-mile up the highway, Jan, I, and the two guys got far as we could until completely out of range of RCMP at the borderline. To have an advantage and not terrify a driver, finally, we split up. Though we were all headed to Vancouver, breaking up the party would surely improve everybody's chances.

One hour later, an orange van powered over to the shoulder and idled. The driver, an older man, was headed 50 miles north to downtown Vancouver, exactly where we were going. It had already been decided we'd check in first at 359 West Georgia, the Vancouver Youth Hostel where Gary might be waiting on our arrival.

The van dropped us in the city's center, not quite close enough to the address noted in Gary's last letter. Climbing aboard a bus, we rode the rest of the way from Granville to West Georgia.

The address Gary had provided turned out to be a post office, not a youth hostel. Disappointed, we caught the next bus, rode the loop back to the terminal and called the hostel from a payphone. Instructed to take the Howe Street and 4th Avenue bus, we would be delivered near 1515 Discovery Street where supposedly another hostel was situated. Unable to locate Discovery Street after disembarking, waiting on the next bus, we eventually rode it out to the end of the line stopping at Jericho Hill School.

Jan and I found ourselves back in Kitsilano. According to the woman we'd spoken with, the Vancouver Youth Hostel was located near the beach, ten minutes from the University of Vancouver.

This was not making any sense. Growing more frustrated by every stale-mate, Jan began to question Gary's sincerity. Maybe it was lack of focus. Surely, *we'd* made an error somehow. However, that didn't explain the West Georgia Street address. Categorically, it felt as if we were on a fool's errand.

Turns out, we were *on* Discovery Street and hadn't realized it. A jogger running through Jericho Park next to the Jericho Hill School helped us find our bearings and provided directions to the hostel, a mere ten-minute walk.

7. Many Canadian provinces (particularly British Columbia) and American States, have outlawed hitchhiking, while Cuba and several European countries have not only legalized solicitation of rides but encourage it, as many citizens do not own vehicles and therefore rely on the kindness of commuters and locals for transportation. Factual studies on the dangers of hitchhiking and picking up riders do not exist. Generally, it is believed there is not a disproportionate amount of crimes associated with hitchhiking or rides offered to strangers.

Late afternoon, Jan and I dragged our packs up the front steps of the Jericho Beach Hostel and into the main lobby. Though decent enough looking, the three-tiered brick compound painted silvery white, lacked the uniqueness of Steiner Street or the curious façade of the quaint Victoria hostel we'd visited early April. During registration, I spotted Fujiko, a chatty Japanese girl who'd ridden out to Jericho on the same bus. Fujiko planned to spend a few days at the beachside complex.

Jan made an inquiry about Gary at the front desk only to learn he *had* been at the hostel but was now AWOL. It didn't mean he wouldn't be returning soon, there was no way of knowing. Instincts told me that if Gary got a better offer, he'd seize it. That could range from anything to hooking up with new friends to go travelling, finding work elsewhere, and meeting a new screw buddy — or two. In San Francisco, he'd let it be known he had a voracious sexual appetite and maintained the energy expended during a single male orgasm was equivalent to running a few miles.

Gary had liked to *run* — a lot.

Learning there was no new news on Gary, reading the look of discouragement on Jan's face, I felt bad for her. I liked Gary too, and had looked forward to hanging out in Vancouver — take him to some of the bars we'd frequented in winter.

Coughing up $2 each for a guest pass enabled us the discounted rate of $3 per night. Subsequently, Jan was handed a key to our small room located on the hostel's second floor. Approaching a single flight of stairs, turning around, I looked down the corridor and surveyed a dejected looking girl tailing several yards behind.

Two sets of bunk beds filled most of the 10 x 10 foot room. Down the hall, stationed beyond three other dorm rooms, was a community bathroom. Leaving my backpack on the bed, I clapped across the parquet floor toward our small window. Giving the wand a sharp twist, I opened the vertical blinds to reveal an elegant Rocky Mountain view fronted by a sandy shoreline, a short walk from our location. Lamentably, the attractive scenery wasn't enough to camouflage feelings of loneliness and nostalgia. Our interim home would take some getting used to.

Unpacking a few clothes and toiletries, we were interrupted by a light rapping on the door.

It was Fujiko.

New to Vancouver, the cheerful, 22-year-old had journeyed solo to Canada's West Coast from her homeland, Japan, to explore Vancouver for a couple of weeks.

Separated by water and distance of more than 4600 hundred miles between Japan and southern British Columbia's mainland, laterally, the continents hosting the two locales are practically neighbouring zones. Since the late 1800's, Japanese migrants found work in forestry, farming, fishing, and sawmills within various territories around the city. Specifically, in the areas of Kitsilano, Mount Pleasant, and Powell Street, a strong, sustainable Japanese presence remains in Vancouver.

Looking a little lost, Fujiko had been consigned to a single room on the third floor of the Jericho Beach hostel. Without prior discussion, Jan and I invited the bright-eyed girl to join us for a feed of pizza and spaghetti, an infrequent food fest.

Fujiko was tickled to come along.

View of Burrard Inlet from West Van at dusk.

CHAPTER 46

Mirror, Mirror

"If you are lacking certain things in your life scheme then you have not made the pattern for them, or you blocked it with another, or you did not think that you would have them anyway. So, did you get what you expected — Did you? Yes, I think you did. We have news for you — you do not face the world at any time; the only world you face is the world of your own being — body/soul/mind, and your atmosphere — which is your responsibility. You should prepare then. This is your world and your responsibility."
THE GOLDEN FORCE, *Chapter 3: "Growth" (pages 27 & 28).*

Reading portions of *The Golden Force*, I had hoped to digest the book's message and assimilate it within my own pre-existing belief system — still fuzzy at best. Deceptively taxing reading, the book required a good deal of thought and analysis. In the past, I'd mostly read contemporary and classic literature, biographies, and true crime. Specific passages of HOOM's holy book were not only tricky to understand, but difficult to imagine within the context of my life.

As of late, I'd found myself re-identifying with one of my literary heroes, twenty-year-old Franny Glass, one of the chief characters in J.D. Salinger's immortal novel, *Franny and Zooey*.

As the story unfolds in the Glass family's New York City apartment, taking a sudden exodus from her studies, Franny clings to an anonymously written book of Russian origin, *The Way of a Pilgrim*, as if it's an appendage. Her preoccupation with the book's divine subject matter drives Franny into a paradoxical and spiritually charged emotional state, causing her to question everything she had accepted and taken for granted up until that point, exasperating her mother Bessie and brother Zooey in the process.

Given my incongruous state of being, I was beginning to understand Franny's impasse. The fact *The Way of a Pilgrim* had belonged to Franny's beloved older brother Seymour did not escape me.

Officially Father's Day, after dinner, Jan, Fujiko, and I walked to a Safeway store to place a collect call home.

Reminiscing with Dad about our family trip to Vancouver and San Francisco many years before, conversation flowed easily. Filling Mom in about our recent adventures, I attempted to prime her for what came next. Broaching the subject containing the four-letter-word, H-O-O-M, I intimated that I might consider returning to San Francisco in the fall as a novice-in-training. Although I'd stressed that this was only *one* option of many, by her silence, I knew what my mother was thinking.

"What about St. Lawrence College?" I had to hand it to Mom for putting forth a concerted effort. "I've sent in the $35 registration fee. I thought you'd at least consider it. All your friends will be going off to school."

I hated letting my mom down. "I don't know," I replied. "I'll have to see what happens with HOOM. But I'm not ruling anything out."

Negative propaganda surrounding counter cultures, communal life-styles, spiritual cults, and worse, left wing grass roots guerilla groups employing weaponry to overpower opposition, populated the news in the years leading to our departure. Stories of diabolical and violent masterminds such as Charles Manson, and more recently, the S.L.A. (Symbionese Liberation Army), a subversive group that headlined media following the 1974 kidnapping of Patty Hearst, daughter of newspaper mogul Randolph Hearst, were in the forefront. These reports left a sour taste in the mouth of parents and establishment. Any conciliatory attempt was a tough sell. Convincing my mother there were differences between HOOM and these other groups was veritably hopeless.

Thankfully, this wasn't the occasion to debate the issue. Keeping our call short, we segued into a softer, more palatable topic. I told my mother how much I looked forward to seeing family again in less than two months. This led her to mention Liz, and how they'd recently had a long talk. The best part of returning to Southern Ontario *was* the assurance of seeing old friends again. With everybody headed in different directions in September however, bittersweet reunions would be short-lived.

Hanging up the receiver, something ugly dawned on me. By relating information, I knew would upset my mother, maybe subliminally, I'd wanted to hurt her. If so, that made me a callous bitch. Quite possibly, it also meant I was hoping to seek revenge. Equal some unspecified score. In truth, I hadn't expected my news bulletin to receive a warm reception. Nonetheless, by stressing words such as *if* and *maybe*, I felt my update was delivered in a way that was informal. It's about making a convincing sales pitch. The way in which something is presented is often easier to digest than what is said. In any case, the strategy had accomplished the reverse, harsher effect.

If only I could convince myself. Returning to Steiner Street would depend upon what happened in the coming weeks, if any of it still made sense. HOOM didn't have the same stranglehold on me it'd had one week ago. Still, it was there, persistent.

Riding the bus ride back to Jericho Beach, I felt low. A long, arduous day, Jan and I were both feeling the effects. We'd pretty much given up on reconnecting with Gary, travelling with him to Alberta. To keep perspective, we reminded one other that we'd continue to meet new friends. As the saying goes, putting all eggs in one basket isn't practical. Not that we had. Heading east toward Ontario, Vancouver wasn't exactly out of our way, though neither one of us was overjoyed to remain at Jericho Beach or Vancouver longer than necessary. Indicative of a 'been there, done that' scenario, it wouldn't have felt that way if only Gary had been at Jericho.

Before falling asleep that night, forcing myself to think happy thoughts, I made a mental memo of the few record albums I aimed to purchase sometime before the end of the year — if ever I were to have money again. At the top of my compilation: Phil Ochs's *Rehearsals for Retirement*, Pied Pumpkin, Rolling Stone's *Black and Blue*, and Electric Light Orchestra's *A New World Record*. As of late, the poem, "Desiderata" written by Max Ehrmann in 1927, had become a favourite. I added it to the list. I'd been told "desiderata" is derived from "desideratum" meaning "desired things" in Latin.

May, an excellent student of the classical language would certainly know all about the poem's linguistic origin.

Loud music blasted from some ingrate's radio awakening us early Saturday morning. For late June, it was relatively cool, only 66 degrees — a good excuse to fish Teddy's jacket out of my backpack. Poking my arms into the fleece-lined sleeves, I visualized the Good Samaritan's face as if he were standing next to me, extremities waving erratically in the air, and zipped the coat over my t-shirt. Perhaps Teddy was fulfilling the infinite list of chores as he'd done every day at the manse while studying to find the right fit within the clique at HOOM. It was also plausible he'd packed it in, fucked off to parts unknown — back to the desert to write, or deliberate in some indeterminate setting wearing his two-toned green and black leather shoes — his customized backpack returned to its rightful owner.

Just in case, Jan left a short note for Gary at the front desk, and then she, Fujiko, and I caught the downtown bus in hunt of a cup of dirty black coffee — a semblance of the grimy, daily pick-me-up we'd grown accustomed to at HOOM. Flush with coin, Fujiko convinced us to stop in at the Pacific Shopping Centre, where she purchased a pair of jade earrings and matching necklace. Sliding them into her pocket for later, for old time's sake, Jan purchased raisins at Galloway's on Robson Street.

The last time we'd heard from her, Yvette was still living at the Y on Beatty. Employing the surprise element rather than calling ahead, arriving in the lobby, we learned Yvette was probably at work. At least she hadn't moved. A woman working the front desk supplied us with the forwarding address of our former roommate, Deb. Luckily; Debbie's new place was a short walk from Burrard. Hoping that Deb wasn't also at work, taking a chance, Jan, Fujiko, and I headed over to her building on Nelson Street. Skipping up the front steps, heading inside, we walked down the main corridor and knocked rapidly on unit 16.

No reply.

Since our Vancouver friends were unavailable, I suggested we take the bus out to Cousin Betsy's in West Van. Even if Betsy wasn't around, it would hardly be a waste of time or money. Fujiko would benefit from being ushered around the city by two tour guides who had reasonable knowledge of the municipality.

Moving beyond high forests and lower slopes within the beautiful mountain country, the ride to West Vancouver was pleasantly familiar. Amused by Fujiko's sparkling disposition, I was encouraged to appreciate how good Vancouver had been to us back in the winter, providing work opportunities that enabled Jan and me to travel south of the border for several months. Once the crest of West Van's seawall ultimately came into view, I looked forward to reuniting with my cousin. Since her separation from Tim, I hoped things were going smoothly for Betsy and the boys.

To our astonishment, it wasn't Betsy who met us at the door that afternoon but Tim. Unreservedly, Tim invited our trio to join him and Betsy on their back patio for lunch. Here, we'd planned to land in well in advance of mealtime so that Betsy wouldn't feel obligated to feed us. Hating to give the impression that we were mooches, neutralizing my anxiety, I reminded myself a reasonable amount of time had lapsed since we'd last eaten a complementary meal.

Gladly, I accepted for our small group.

Betsy looked fabulous — rejuvenated, vivacious — courting the youthful blush of a college student. My cousin was fun and gracious as ever. Full of piss and vinegar, Tim pressed Jan and me about our travels. In turn, he regaled us with a few juicy stories about drunken weekends spent with buddies during wine tasting extravaganzas down in Napa and Sonoma Valley. Not appearing to mind her husband commanding the floor, as Tim grew more enlivened with every tale, Betsy good-naturedly chided him on. Whatever differences the couple may have had a few months ago seemed inconsequential now, practically invisible. They had figured out a way to make their marriage work, and certainly weren't putting on a show for our benefit.

Appearing deliriously happy, Betsy deserved the very best.

A tray of egg sandwiches and fresh fruit were passed around for the taking. When Tim offered, each of us accepted a glass of pink blush wine. In recent months, Tim had started making his own rosé and was quite proud of the finished product. Refilling his and Betsy's glasses, excitedly, he expounded on the bottling procedure from start to finish, and crowed about how many bottles the kit had yielded. During the fermentation process, apparently a lighter shade of red is cultivated because the skins of the grapes remain in contact with the juice for a shorter period, propagating a lighter, fruitier, and sweeter variety.

The only other person I knew of at the time who'd tried his hand at wine making was my father. Much to my mom's consternation, one winter, he stored a large, red, stinky vat of the stuff behind our orange-green floral living room couch. At his encouragement, I sampled from the vat only once, and had to spit it out in to the sink. It was disgusting. Mostly, I was disappointed. I had wanted to like the wine as much as the sips of beer he'd let me try as a kid. Dad's brew wasn't revolting because I hadn't yet acquired a taste for alcohol — the wine truly was raunchy gut rot. Probably, in his impatience, my father hadn't allowed it to ferment for the required time. Other family members had tried it too. No one was a fan. Only a veteran drinker wouldn't object to the repulsive, bitter taste.

Mid-afternoon, Betsy drove us down to the sea walk, the extended, concrete footpath along the Pacific coastline where we leafed through a few tacky shops scattered along the promenade. In search of a beach towel, Fujiko couldn't find one to her liking.

Since hooking up with Fujiko, Jan and I'd raved about Lifestream Restaurant in Kitsilano. While in the U.S., oftentimes, we'd get a hankering for their homemade veggie soups and fresh, multi-grained cheddar cheese sandwiches chalked full of bean sprouts. Validating our decision to be fiscally irresponsible by pointing out we'd barely spent a cent voyaging with Russell, I suggested that Lifestream would make a great dinner choice.

Food was always a *big* deal.

Jan, Fujiko, and I caught public transit from the boardwalk, crossed over the Burrard Street Bridge into Kitsilano, and got off a few blocks from Lifestream. In less than a half hour, we were back at our favourite hangout in the city. Familiarity with the indelible setting felt like reconvening with an old acquaintance. Entering the premises, a local folk artist regaled the prevailing hippie patronage on a wooden mandolin. Hanging thick with heady aromas such as lentil soup, fresh baked breads, lemon cakes, blueberry and peach pies, it was sensory overload of the best kind. Amidst the busy restaurant, unflappable, casually dressed male and female staff, delivered to every customer a mysterious gift: simple, eye-popping cuisine.

Finding an empty table by a picture window hosting a grand view of the street, we positioned ourselves to people-watch without being obvious, and anticipated that Fujiko would be transcended by the dining experience in the same way that Jan and I had. Following our lead, Fujiko ordered homemade macaroni and cheese accompanied by fresh garden greens and side of oil and vinegar. Fujiko's attempts to tame the spongy, cheesy noodles — doing everything to avoid her cutlery — made me smile. Concentrated, she trapped a piece of tube pasta forcefully with her fork, took a couple of bites of the foreign matter, and lay her fork down on her plate. Looking across the table, she complained, "It tastes funny."

Beg your pardon?

We assured Fujiko, the more she ate, the more she would enjoy the food. Giving the dish a valiant effort, Fujiko took another small forkful, wrinkled her nose, and stuck out her tongue. Frowning, she reiterated, "Why would anybody ever want to *eat* this stuff? It's gross!" Congenially, Jan and I took turns ribbing Fujiko about her indifference to the pasta. Apologizing for being finicky, Fujiko settled on the soup of the day.

Passing various ordinary storefronts along our way home, we came across a bookshop located behind a benign exterior. Drawn to the sign overtop the front door, "VICTORIA'S LAIR," we were encouraged to peek beyond the matted windows painted in vivid bold colours.

In we went, dawdling at first, talking, reading amongst ourselves. In the back, on the wall above the john somebody had scribbled, "When the power of love replaces the love of power, man will find a new God." Next to the quote was the name of spiritual leader, Sri Chinmoy. This marker wasn't obvious as the yellow sky had been on our way through Washington State to Seattle. All the same, the bathroom writing was a keepsake uniting past, present, and future.

Fujiko picked up a Japanese/English translation book. Though her command of English was nearly flawless, occasionally, she'd become frustrated by a certain word, and had difficulty understanding or pronouncing specific phrases. An astute and highly intelligent individual, even with limited exposure to Vancouver, I didn't doubt Fujiko could become fluent reading and writing English with little effort.

Leaving the shop, our friend mentioned she had learned to read palms in Japan, and asked if either one of us would like her to read ours.

It sounded like fun. Sort of.

Taking ahold of Jan's hand, Fujuko turned it over, extending it outward from the base of her wrist like branches, to reveal the distinct lines in her palm. In short order, she impressively summed up Jan's personal history through time. According to Fujiko, in one of her past lives, Jan had had a serious accident. She would marry between the ages of 20-24 years. The individual columns in her palm indicated Jan was a multi-tasker. Moreover, she had a very good head for numbers.

When it came my turn, I was nervous. I didn't want to learn bad news from my future, or be bought up to speed about unfinished business in past lives. Unfolding my right hand, Fujiko focused on three parallel lines. She then told me I had the tools to be smart, but that I had not been a good student. Furthermore, I was too serious.

Not a deal breaker so far.

Fujiko sweetened the pot. I'd have a chance to marry early, but would marry late, somewhere between 24-28 years of age. In addition, I would remain married to the same person for many years. Childbirth would prove to be difficult, eventually, I'd deliver two children.

Fujiko had pegged me correctly about school and taking things too seriously. Given the right or wrong situation — maybe *too* many situations, I certainly could be a killjoy. Then again, anybody who knew me could probably see those things. If I'd earned a reputation for being a drag, I was also known to be silly. Fujiko had become increasingly familiar with our personalities as we had hers.

Overall, the experience had served as somewhat of an ego booster.

I was careful not to put much credence in future predictions.

Arriving at Jericho Beach around nine, Jan checked in at the desk. Gary had not come by or called. Incensed, Jan called him an "idiot" and left to do our laundry, no doubt to take her mind off Gary. Another girl from Japan was now staying on our floor. She and Fujiko struck a chord and remained in the lobby together to trade notes.

While Jan was down in the laundry room, I returned to our room and flipped open my journal. Negligent about documenting our latest activities, there were a couple of days to catch up on. I'd discovered it was easier to write a lot in one sitting rather than try to be diligent recording the events of each day in chronological order. My journal, a continuing mess of emotional diarrhea, scribbles, song lyrics, sketches and poems, had accumulated a lot of loose paper, mostly addresses from people we'd met, locations of places we'd visited, names of eateries, and few post-cards. Creating a category titled "New Foods," I listed some of my favourites. Homemade granola, sesame seed buns, Keefer cultured milk and yogurt, banana pancakes, Farrell's ice cream, raisin porridge, sour cream, tuna buns, and coffee were all noted the list. Reading over my inventory, I laughed how ordinary my list would appear to onlookers.

Proceeding to write about the last couple of days, I began with our ride north from Seattle the morning before, the nerve-wracked border crossing, and concluded with our second night at Jericho Beach.

Once I finished writing, I composed letters, the first to Bruce at Meadowlark. Thinking about Bruce lately, as well as the others, I wondered if he would eventually move on from the ranch. Capable of accomplishing great things, Bruce had had exposure to some of the finest mentors the world had to offer.

Following my note, I jotted short memos to May, Liz, and Rebecca of HOOM.

At Jericho Beach, at precisely half past eleven, a "lights off" policy was enforced. This occurred every night without warning. No exceptions were made. If you wanted to read or brush your teeth, you were welcome to use a flashlight. If you were in the shower or in the middle of taking a dump, it made little difference. The entire building went from light to dark in a millisecond.

Try wiping your ass in the pitch black without making a mess.

After being caught unaware the first night, Jan and I were ready for bed — *and* in it — at lights out.

Gigantic Redwood at Vancouver's Stanley Park.
COURTESY OF ANDREA NELSON.

CHAPTER 47

Learning to Unfold

"Miracles unfold in mild places."
JILL C. NELSON, *June 1976*

Sunday morning was warm and sunny — an ideal day to return to Stanley Park. A young lawyer driving a champagne painted Peugeot gave us a lift, dropping us off at McDonald's, about a half mile from the park's perimeter. After loading up on black coffee and hash browns, Jan, Fujiko, and I began hiking the park's footpath.

Three months earlier, the natural habitat for wildlife had been charming, with daffodils, tulips and crocuses scattered about the wet grass and loam. The right mix of sun, rain, and fertile soil had taken full effect. Gorging with new blossoms — roses, peonies, irises, lilies and honeysuckle, Stanley Park never looked prettier. Walking along the five-and-a-half-mile shoreline, a pair of blue herons circled above the marsh. In and amongst leaves and tree debris collecting along the path, squirrels and chipmunks scurried around our feet. The regeneration of red cedars, destroyed during windstorms over the past century, was apparent, while other forest trees destructed by squalls and lightning displayed various stages of regrowth and revitalization.

Summer was fully appointed.

Known at the time for its mélange of bird varieties, black bears, wolves, snakes, and monkeys, barring the bird population, today, Stanley Park is no longer home for wild animals. After a referendum in the 1990s, the practice of harbouring animals was abolished. They were transferred to petting zoos and the Greater Vancouver Zoo located in Aldergrove.

Entering Brockton Point, east at the peninsula north of Coal Harbour, home to a 100-year-old lighthouse and several beautifully wooden, hand carved totem poles signifying First Nation art and history, Fujiko marvelled as to how the park managed to remain free and accessible to visitors and residents. While monkeys seduced tourists with extraordinary acts of athleticism in hopes of securing forbidden treats, glancing over at a group of people standing near the fence, I recognized Grace and Jude, our Aussie friends that had driven us from Yosemite to San Francisco.

Jan called out. Eyes wide with surprise, Grace and Jude started in our direction.

Leaving the Steiner Street hostel, a couple of weeks ago, making their way up the coast, Grace and Jude crossed the border into Canada three days earlier. Planning on one night's stay at Jericho Beach, they would continue driving east.

Following Grace and Jude's departure, we found ourselves at Lost Lagoon, a manufactured lake named after a poem written by Pauline Johnston, a Native Canadian writer. One of the most popular sites within the park, Lost Lagoon attracts many returning visitors, day-trippers and locals who quietly break to bird watch, read, find solace from stresses of the day. Surrounding Lost Lagoon, another footpath accommodates a postcard-like view of Vancouver in the background.

Fujiko continued to find many Canadian conventions troublesome and confusing. For example, she was surprised to observe couples, family and friends kissing, demonstrating any display of affection in public either in greeting or parting company. She explained that in her country, despite lovers or comrades having spent several months apart, locking lips and openly embracing was taboo. In one sense, Fujiko admired the playful, carefree amiability exhibited casually between people around us, but had concerns that flaunting of emotions might lead to apathy or detract from individual focus. While Jan and I tried to impress upon her that expressions of warmth and affection are examples of companionship and love rather than offensive acts, Fujiko remained dubious.

Setting out that morning, I'd packed *The Golden Force* into my satchel. Treading further into chapter four, "The Law of Psychic Unfoldment," the divide between medical and scientific advancements and the psychic body of man is outlined. The term "unfoldment" is defined as unification of self with the universe by which an individual can learn to marry the unconscious and conscious minds to communicate with a "Higher Intelligence." Through practice, quiet, and disciplined meditation, the book elucidates how one can facilitate steps toward a merging or "awakening" of our (two) minds. Laid out in successive order are the stages, which I've paraphrased: *Sit calmly. Be at ease. Phrase a simple question emanating from the conscious mind. Clean the mindscape with a mental cloth so that it is free and clear to receive. As it radiates from the subconscious mind to the surface, the answer will be identified. Sometimes it is audible. Other times, it is imparted with fervor.*

For those inclined to entertain racing streams of fragmented thought, this lesson requires effort. Even during sleep, my mind becomes a fantasy playground that rarely finds respite. Intertwining two mental coordinates would take some doing. Nevertheless, the practice interested me. Knowing that humans have the wherewithal to find answers simply by going inward could prove useful. Looking at the yang side of things, *The Golden Force* had potential to fuck up my brain with information I'd probably never use.

Before returning to Jericho Beach, we consumed a light meal at the Pavilion on the park premises. Then a dope-head in a battered blue van offered us a ride. Rebuking his lame moves on us, we were glad to finally climb out of his vehicle. I didn't mind returning to the hostel, I was even starting to warm up to the place. With access to nearby mountains and beach aside, our beds were comfortable. Some blessed soul had chosen to play *Simon and Garfunkel's Greatest Hits* on the record player, their synchronized angelic voices divine.

Still no word on Gary. Jan started to worry. Although he had been at Jericho Beach, the return address on his last letter was Hope located in the Fraser Valley. Maybe Gary had meant that we were to meet him at Hope's Texas Lake Hostel rather than in Vancouver. With or without him, checking out Fraser Valley before heading to Banff held great appeal.

Wednesday, Jan and I would set off for Hope.

The first day of summer was my parents' 32nd wedding anniversary. Another collect call home was out of the question, I would come up with an alternate way to acknowledge their special day. Planning to return to Japan on July 1, Fujiko needed to book her flight. Following a visit to the Tourist Centre to scour train and bus schedules, leaving Jan and Fujiko at Japan Airlines, I made my way around to the Y to see if Yvette was around.

She wasn't.

Regrouping with Jan and Fujiko, rather than waiting for her to get off work, we decided to surprise Deb at the bank.

Engaged with a customer, Deb eventually caught Jan and me out of the corner of her eye. Finishing with her client, she rushed out from behind her post, giving us bear hugs. Deb insisted we stay at her Nelson Street apartment until Wednesday. Having already paid in advance for two more nights at Jericho Beach, Jan and I would need to negotiate a refund. With plenty of travellers seeking rooms, we didn't anticipate a problem. The downside meant saying goodbye to Fujiko earlier than planned.

Lunch was Honey's in Gastown, another favourite haunt from our previous stay in Vancouver. Laying out more cash than expected since leaving San Francisco, however, was a concern. Intending my dollars to flow another six weeks, an adjustment to spending needed to be made. Having decided against thumbing a ride to Hope, two hours east, money for bus fare was required. It occurred to me that Jan might have more money at her disposal than I did. This wasn't a problem, only in the event we weren't able to find jobs in Alberta, I didn't want to leech off her. Recently, we'd revisited the notion of finding work, possibly in Banff or Jasper, two highly popular tourist attractions during summer months.

Honey's served a tomato sandwich on whole grain bread and carrot soup for just over $1. I couldn't resist buying a homemade butter tart for 25 cents to quench my sweet tooth. The entire meal, including water, was under $2 — even McDonald's had a tough time rivaling these prices.

Finally, Fujiko was impressed!

Meandering through shops along the Gastown strand, purchasing beads to make a necklace, Fujiko treated Jan and me to a respectable cup of coffee. It would be our last beverage together. In the interim, I'd popped back at the Y to leave a message for Yvette at the front desk along with Deb's telephone number. We returned to Jericho Beach to pack up our gear for Deb's place.

Administration at Jericho had no issue refunding our money. We thrust our clothes and toiletries into our bags as if they were rabid. Jan left a final written message for Gary with registration, informing him that we would leave Vancouver in two days. If we didn't meet up, we hoped to see Gary in Hope. Frustrated by the cat and mouse game, running down the hostel steps to catch our bus, Jan shouted, "Gary's a bloody idiot!" Half-heartedly, I teased that if she visualized Gary's appearance in Hope, like an optical illusion, perhaps he would be there.

Touched to notice tiny tears on Fujiko's cheeks as we took turns saying farewell, our new friend allowed each of us to embrace her. In an audacious gesture of fondness, Fujiko returned the show of affection.

Fujiko would be fine in our absence, I was confident of that. Maybe now that Jan and I would be out of the picture, she'd branch out. With more than a week to go before flying back to Japan, Fujiko had plans to sign up for a couple of city tours, visit attractions outside of the metropolis.

She didn't need to worry about moving out of Jericho, there was no dead-line there for hostellers. Fujiko would easily make new friends.

Friendships formed on the road within abbreviated time frames continued to be an empowering experience. I thought about this a lot. When you're on the clock, emotions become heightened. Personality flaws are exposed. Knowing that you'll not likely meet someone again can make or break relations. There is less reason for excuses, concealing vulnerabilities, holding up defenses. You are inclined to lay your strengths and weaknesses on the table.

Jan and I arrived at Unit 16 on the main floor of Debbie's Nelson Street apartment just after six. Deb had her own digs. It looked good on her. A modern and tastefully decorated interior, a great red shag carpet occupied most of the living room floor. Circular rice-paper lampshades hovered over bamboo end tables; art deco paintings embellished newly bleached walls. Peeking out from a brand new feathered hairstyle, blonde highlights, silver hoop earrings and $40 sunglasses, our former roommate was totally in vogue, and sophisticated. Even better, on her way home from work, Deb had thought to pick up a case of Labatt 50.

Picking up from where we left off, the three of us laughed, drank, ate pizza, gossiped about the girls we'd known during the weeks at the Y where Jan, Deb, and I'd had shared our L-shaped room. Apart from Yvette, Denna, and one or two others, almost everyone in our group had dispersed mostly to parts unknown. Deb was interested to know if Jan and I had met any eligible young men during the past two months. Save for a couple of sob stories about unreciprocated love and lust, regrettably there wasn't much news in that department. Deb had been there, done that, a hundred times or more.

Over half a case of Labatt's, we commiserated.

Next morning, Deb had to be at the bank before eight. Cool and sunny, a high of 75 degrees was projected for the afternoon. Easy to take. After Deb left, Jan and I returned to the Y in search of Yvette. This time she was home and sleeping. Scheduled to leave Vancouver the following day, there wasn't much time for a reunion. Leaving a message with the front desk, I let Yvette know we'd stop by again in the afternoon.

Over at ABC records, *Rehearsals for Retirement,* the bookend to Phil Ochs's *Pleasures of the Harbor* LP lay in a dusty discounted bin. I knew I couldn't afford it, nor did I have space in my backpack for another bulky album. Even so, between a stack of other half-forgotten recordings, an antiquated photograph of Phil dressed as a soldier pasted on a tombstone showing 1968 as the date of death symbolizing the year of the Chicago riots, the record reminded me of a wallflower hoping for a chance at a high school prom.

Returning to Nelson Street, Jan and I put *Pleasures of the Harbor* on Deb's turntable, our record's debut. Set against Ochs's sinewy, acerbic commentary, the adept mixture of vocals and instrumentation rendered the record a staggering accomplishment. Attuned to artists of high caliber, in every respect, Jan approved of Phil too.

I called Betsy to let her know we were leaving the city the next day. We arranged to meet for lunch at Breadline for a bowl of homespun vegetable broth or chicken noodle soup. Like Fujiko, my cousin had never partaken of the quaint eatery where senior waiters and waitresses tied linen aprons around their generous middles proudly serving delicious homemade fare. My cousin's easy smile immediately indicated her approval of the modest décor, tasty food, and hospitable atmosphere. Out of range of Tim, eyes sparkling above flaming pink cheeks, Betsy confided to have been blessed with love "as if we're newlyweds again." Pleased to know the affection witnessed days earlier at the couple's home was the real deal, when it came time to say goodbye, I told Betsy that whatever spell she was under I hoped it would last.

Jan and I finally linked up with Yvette, waiting for us in the third-floor lounge. Wonderful to see her again, now working as a waitress, Yvette had undergone what she referred to as her "jewelry and make-up trip" — something I found fascinating yet difficult to imagine. Naturally pretty and down-to-earth, in general, Yvette preferred overalls and long flowing hair to anything trendy or novel.

Privately, I was impressed. Wearing augmented face, and feminine clothes, Yvette had bravely stepped onto the real-world stage. Comfortably dressed down in jeans, earth shoes, and plaid flannel shirts, a part of me alleged my wardrobe camouflaged my dread of transitioning to adult-hood — making mature decisions, evaluating what I wanted to do with the rest of my life. My current disguise obstructed risk of stepping beyond the partition of insecurity.

Scorching in the sun for a couple of hours at Granville Square, we returned to Nelson Street. No sooner had I kicked off my sandals, I became violently ill, retching and diarrhea, the full gamut of symptoms. Figuring I'd contracted the stomach flu or worse, food poisoning — if it was the third culprit, too much alcohol the night before, I should recover by morning. Neither one of us could afford to be down for the count — not for one day. Especially, not more than one day. Reverend Mary's words about keeping my head on straight and eyes open rang in my ears.

The only consolation to a nasty hangover is to consider it a body cleansing, a discharge of toxins.

Quality time on the toilet took care of that.

After five pm, Debbie arrived. Abbreviating the distance between me and the toilet, I'd holed myself up in her lavatory. Taking one look at the disaster in her bathroom, Deb insisted I head directly to her bed. Tired and weak, I didn't dare challenge her good sense.

Wallowing in my own misery, keeping my head perfectly still to prevent vertigo, my mind set adrift. As one blurry thought progressed to the next, putting forth effort to focus on any one thing proved difficult.

Around ten, two more friends from the Y arrived. Louise and Cathy Henry had attended Paul McCartney's "Wings Over America" concert in Seattle and raved about the show. As much as I wished I could have joined in, it was great to hear everybody having a good time.

By midnight, the apartment cleared out, all but Yvette, who scrambled to find somebody to cover her shift the following day.

Texas Lake Community & Hostel, Hope, B.C.

COURTESY OF HTTPS://SITES.GOOGLE.COM/SITE/TEXASLAKESITE/

CHAPTER 48

Hope Reigns

"You draw the near things nearer, by making clear things queerer."
PIET HEIN

My condition hadn't much improved by morning, leading me to conclude I *had* caught a bug. Nevertheless, Jan and I headed out in the rain to purchase our $2.95 bus tickets for Hope. Chilled from fever and now damp weather, unsuccessfully, we tried to hitchhike back to Nelson Street and ended up trudging thirty minutes from the terminal in soaking clothes. Waiting at the intersection of Deb's street for traffic to clear, Jan noticed Yvette and her friend Barbie coming out of Debbie's building. We called over. Turning, they waited for us to cross. Forming a short procession in the hallway, Jan turned the key in the door of unit 16 and we fell upon Deb's shag carpet. Somebody put on a pot of herbal tea. In anticipation of winning Yvette and Barbie over as newfound Ochs fans, I slipped *Pleasures of the Harbor* on the turntable. Yvette gobbled it up straight away. Maybe she was being nice. At any rate, nobody was visibly offended by the music.

At one point, Jan left for Galloway's to pick up additional raisins and sunflower seeds for our trip. Not much of a conversationalist that morning, the company of Barbie and Yvette (coddling a sore head of her own) boosted my spirits, particularly when Yvette announced plans to visit Ontario late summer — an unbelievable surprise!

I took a quick bath, gathered up my property and packed. Yvette prepared to leave for work. With the assurance that she would be visiting before long, resolutely, we embraced.

Half past one, destined for Hope through Surrey, Abbotsford, and Deb's hometown of Chilliwack, our bus broke eastbound for Highway 1. Watching out the window at languid green pastures, rolling foothills and rivers snaking through woodlands with hushed domination, feeling unusually upbeat, Jan and I were excited for all that Hope might bring.

Around the halfway point of the trip, reading chapter seven of *The Golden Force*, titled "Universal Law of the Creative Mind," one section described a dynamic life force living within and outside of us. "To harness and develop acceptance of that strength with confidence is integral." The chapter stressed the power of our receptive capacities that opens the door for all things to transpire. Creative unfiltered thought processes bring about materialization.

Same song and dance, I thought — another assertion of the mental imagery technique Brother James had taught us at Steiner Street. Keeping a clear-cut image of what Jan and I'd anticipated, for much of our trip, expectations *had* become apparent. Could it be we weren't aiming high enough? Had we *deluded* ourselves into believing prayers were being answered?

Thinking about the passage some more, I doubted it. Negative thinking works on the same principle as positive revelation. Looking to darkness, shadows befall you. Employing a faithful formula, hope should be the alchemy of all good things.

One could only hope.

Nearing Hope's municipality, large billowing clouds that had supplemented a portion of our drive through serrated mountains, touched the surface of the highway and enfolded our bus, generating a stir of excitement amongst passengers. Surrounded by the Cascade Mountains and thick, secluded wilderness — valleys, streams, and the Fraser River, Hope resembled an absolute dream paradise.

Pulling into the bus terminal just 6 1/2 miles south of the Texas Lake Hostel, climbing down the steps, Jan and I greeted the sunshine. Purchasing blueberry muffins at a country store, we proceeded out to the main road to hitchhike the remaining miles to our destination. For a $2 overnight fee, our guidebook promised a small supper and breakfast. Dinner was too good to be true and most unusual for a hostel. In case of food shortages, we knew from experience to arrive with a semi-full belly.

Standing on the roadside of the TransCanada Highway, petitioning a ride was a cinch. Driving a light brown pick-up truck, a mid-twenties woman, Sharon, pulled to the shoulder. Currently living and working at Texas Lake, Sharon assured us we would fall in love with the hostel and its adjoining co-operative community.

Fixing our eyes on the serenity of the mountainous setting, nearing the hostel next to a lake, rose-coloured pickerelweed fanned restfully over a quickening waterfall. A pretty sight in summer, I envisioned the opposite effect in winter: barren, bleak, desolate.

Approaching the muddy driveway, Sharon slowed the truck, enabling us to observe buildings of differing sizes: cabins for permanent residents, sleeping dorms for guests. There were chicken coops, an enormous vegetable garden, an odd-shaped dome type structure in behind the main (BIG) house, cows, goats, dogs and cats. If *seeing* is to believe, this utopian designation promised a memorable stay.

Originating from a former automobile court in 1972, Texas Lake moved to the current location in 1973. According to Sharon, for almost five years, as another income source, Texas Lake community catered to universal travellers.

Yvette's older brother Luke had lived at Texas Lake nearly six months. Over Easter dinner in Aldergrove, he described the environment as a commune rooted in egalitarianism. Full-time residents put in a full day's worth of labour at the Co-Op. In exchange, they were provided with a cabin, three square meals, and a core commonality shared amongst friends. Impassioned in their collective vision, to serve people and planet, Texas Lake accomplished big and small goals in creative unencumbered ways. According to Luke, the $2 per diem for hostellers was supported by the Federal government to keep costs low and encourage young people (and high school dropouts) to explore Canada. Additionally, providing an income source for inhabitants of the commune, the fee was subsequently divided, garnering permanent residents $1 a day. In winter, the hostel received a subsidy from the local human resources department for every visitor who spent the night. Folks with few resources staying more than three days were often put to work building or gardening, whatever was required. If a wayward individual found his or her way into the midst, the Texas Lake crew designated tasks to perform — raking, tree planting — anything that might help unburden the soul and embellish the collective dream.

The measly amount of coin earned daily by permanent residents might seem wretched today, but a person would have to be hard-hearted not to be seduced by the charm of Texas Lake. A couple of decades away from melding into the technological age, 1970s youths took pride in small prizes. Kids of our generation rode the coattails of a rousing radical era far longer than anyone could have predicted.

Everything changes.

Sharon introduced Jan and me to a cozy, wood-panelled dorm room, our sleeping space for the night. Accustomed to transients arriving at all hours of the day and night, folks behaved as if they expected us. Desensitized to the irregularity of time tables, Texas Lake fixtures quickly adapted to the swooshing of transport trucks tearing down the highway at breakneck speeds. Sadly, many animals belonging to the community lost their lives navigating the dangerous road at night.

In ritualistic fashion, meals in the communal kitchen at Texas Lake were a celebration. Cooked from scratch, food was prepared by a rag-tag gang of hippies who took pains to ensure there was always a healthy supply at hand so that groups of twenty or more could be fed daily. The main course, a sticky basmati rice dish stuffed with fresh veggies topped with bean sprouts, was sprinkled with generous amounts of grated cheddar cheese. Packed into a large clay casserole, the dish sat piping hot on the counter's tile overlay. In anticipation of snagging a chair, like a group of eager kindergarten kids, we rushed to supper.

Surrounding the round, weather-beaten oak table centered in the kitchen, handcrafted pine stools and small structures made of vine complemented a mixture of watercolour and finger paintings, obviously created by young children. To my left, a labyrinth of gentle light straddled the plate glass window, warming our milieu. Once everyone was settled, one of the women, Trish, asked that we take hold of the hand of our next-door neighbour and close our eyes. As we did, Trish sang a short prayer of thanks. Repeating after Trish, "For the food before us, we give thanks," regulars and guests alike concluded with "For love and brotherhood, we give thanks."

Like rice, gratitude at the Texas Lake dinner table was the primary staple.

Everybody reached for a helping of garden salad and scooped from the casserole. Slices of freshly baked oatmeal bread and glasses of water were served on a platter. For dessert, two plates of homemade brownies swollen with whole walnuts, cooled in the makeshift pantry.

There is credence in the theory that food prepared from loving hands is the best kind. Texas Lake prided itself on straightforward, mouthwatering cuisine. Motivated by classical and folk music discharging from a pair of well-worn speakers balancing on top of a rickety wall cabinet, in a washtub-sized bowl, oatmeal and whole wheat bread were prepared daily by one or more of the occupants. Combining a mixture of up to 20 pounds of flour, yeast, and leftovers from the evening meal, placed into several pans, the batter was slid into two huge gas ovens.

A dozen loaves were produced daily.

Fulltime residents of the hostel were not professional chefs, but learned quickly to be thrifty, preparing economical, nutritious meals for varying numbers. Excluding bulk items purchased locally at Fed-Up Food Co-Op, all food was made on site. Cows and goats provided fresh milk. Farm chickens supplied a regular diet of eggs. The macrobiotic organic garden yielded more than enough vegetables to satisfy the needs of rotating customers.

Ongoing projects consumed the tireless energies of the group. The dome, spotted near the big house when Sharon first pulled into the dirt driveway, was in fact a "geodesic" dome used as a craft shop on site. Assembled by several of the Texas Lake crew and friends, the dome was an impressive, smaller replication of an original planetarium-shaped dome designed in the 1920s by engineer Walther Bauersfeld to house his projector. Based on a polyhedron (a three-dimensional solid made up of many flat faces), the modern dome revised by inventor Buckminster Fuller and artist Kenneth Snelson during the mid-1940s to contain a shell-like lattice became the benchmark influencing the construction of Texas Lake's ecological geodesic structure.

It was the first time I'd witnessed this fascinating construction.

On the surface, everything at Texas Lake seemed agreeable, though Jan and I quickly learned that occupants of the commune had their challenges. Not everyone espoused the spiritually oriented leanings. There were other personal differences pertaining to the daily functions of the co-operative. Disengaged individuals moved on and were replaced by enthusiastic new comrades. In general, minor differences were set aside to sustain a cohesive, robust community. As Jan summarized in her diary during our short stay, "Everyone held hands and we sang grace. It was like one, huge, happy family all on the same line of thought."

Concluding the meal, our group assisted clearing the table, packing away salvageable leftovers, washing and drying supper dishes. Not unlike many a night we'd spent at Steiner Street, the remainder of the evening was reserved for musical entertainment for and by hostellers and Texas Lake dwellers that stayed behind.

Looking around, I noticed that several members of the core Texas Lake group were absent. A small collection of men and women had retreated to one of the vacated cabins near the perimeter of the property to congregate. Apparently, it was routine practice. Intrigued by numerology, some of the Texas Lake residents had taken to revising the spelling of their names and even the names of some of the animals — one of the dogs was named Ching — and even household items, to align with symbolic meanings associated with key numbers. There were cassette tapes featuring lectures recorded by Swami Kriyananda, leader of the Ananda community near Nevada City, whose followers believed in the alliance of Eastern and Western worlds. Digesting the uplifting contents of Swami's tapes, together, devotees of the Ananda teachings chanted sacred mantras in the cabin.

Jan and I chatted with JP, a handsome French-Canadian rogue and his Irish buddy, Ted. Suave and quixotic, JP comfortably held the floor, telling impressionable stories of settling down one day on 640 acres of land he'd purchased in Dawson Creek. Holding onto every promising dream, I swore I heard a collective chorus of sighs emanating from the female persuasion in the room. Through the disorder of everything recently: being under the weather, constantly moving, the Good Samaritan, my dilemma about joining HOOM, our memorable night with Russell in Mount Shasta, the constant worry of money and our return to Ontario, I'd all but forgotten about my intrinsic desires of the heart. Playing into our putty hands, JP's renegade swagger brought everything full circle.

As things wrapped for the night, it seemed probable that somebody within our group of permanents and visitors was carrying. Picking up on our obviousness, JP attested that many at Texas Lake smoked weed, but were careful to keep it toned down. Hard drugs were not permitted. In the past, RCMP officers made impromptu visits to the hostel looking to make busts. Residents did not want to risk charges or closure by promoting or participating in illegal activities. Based upon our recent encounter with border patrol, the reality that police might be lurking didn't shock me.

Smokers were encouraged to walk several hundred yards away from the big house.

That night I skipped ahead and delved into chapter ten of *The Golden Force*, titled "The Ocean of Sex; God — Man — Woman." Near the end of the first paragraph, which hinted at properties of the "eternal triangle" and how sexual sensibility requires the function of the psychic body, I gave in and fell asleep.

Breakfast at eight consisted of porridge topped with raisins and coconut accompanied by an orange, coffee, or tea. Planning to hitchhike our way to Kamloops in midst of a cool and rainy start to the morning, Jan and I crossed fingers the forecast would change. Still not feeling up to snuff, damp weather never helped matters.

On their way to Prince Rupert, an approximate two-day road trip, JP and Ted invited us to come along. Flattered, and eager to hang out with JP, I had it in my mind to convince Jan to go along with a ruse that we were also travelling to Prince Rupert. If we didn't have to watch our coin like hawks, I knew she would have been amendable deceiving JP and his Irish pal.

An impromptu trip would take us off course. Then we'd have to figure out how to right our impulsive action. Not to mention, it would be embarrassing reaching Prince Rupert and having to confess we'd told a big fat lie to win the company of two cute guys. Without a doubt, it wasn't the first time JP and his charms had conned a couple of keen girls. We'd heard from some of the other women that routinely, men came to Texas Lake seeking friends with benefits for the winter months.

Mid morning, Jan and I left Texas Lake in style, riding in a lean black Mustang driven by a young business exec. The tailored suit drove us as far as Boston Bar named after the Fraser Canyon Gold Rush days, about 40 miles east along the TransCanada. At that point, a middle-aged couple, Ted and Marion Schultzman, picked us up on their way to a family funeral in Prince George. It was the first time an older couple had given us a lift. The Schultzman's son and his family lived on 1400 acres at Hidden Valley Farm in Dawson Creek. According to the couple, the farm, a "real gentle Christian community" comprised mostly of young people, advocated co-operative living. Hidden Valley sounded like a sanitized version of Texas Lake, on a much grander scale.

The bulk of our drive was wet and dreary, though accompanied by bountiful tributaries and agricultural landscape, a network of mountain patterns and the blue tinged Fraser Valley — its ancient trains and derailed tracks long discarded after the Gold Rush — made for an unexpectedly pleasant trip.

Completing a hearty lunch at Cache Creek, Ted and Marion dropped us off at the junction. Standing at the edge of the road dressed in layers in anticipation (and *expectation*) of a car that would soon emerge and take mercy on us, the light rain, merely a flirt earlier that morning, turned into a stealthy downpour. A blue van driven by a thirty-ish man, a proud owner of a farm in Cache Creek, rescued us from the soggy weather driving us the rest of the way to Kamloops. Happy to be within the vicinity of our next accommodation, approaching the outskirts of town, we still had a way to go. According to our book, Kamloops Hostel was an approximate half hour walk from where the young farmer had let us off.

No reason to get excited — yet.

Low hanging cedar branches provided partial cover from rain, assisting in making the hike semi tolerable as we trudged through the muck — I in hiking boots, Jan in her worn leather shoes. Along the walk, rain changed to drizzle until eventually, detectable in the distance, a translucent sky radiated a soft white glow. Looking forward to getting into some dry clothes, it would soon be time to do laundry again.

A quarter past two, ushered in on the bosom of what had become a brilliant summer afternoon, within a forested area concealed by dense trees and brush, we arrived at Kamloops Hostel's front gate. A young manager, Paul, strode over from a harvest table where another fellow, Jim, and two others were occupied stringing wood beads of varying sizes on thin wire and jute. Paul showed us to our housing for the night, one of a series of tents clustered together in the middle of an open outside area.

It would do fine.

Originally home to fur trading and logging, Kamloops got its name meaning "meeting of the waters" from the Tk'emlúps Indian Band that first established territory in the region in the early 15th century before European settlers arrived in the 1800s. Situated in the pictographic Thompson Valley, also known as the Montane Cordillera Ecozone, the city's interior is positioned between the north and south arms of the Thompson River. Nuzzled within a rain shadow next to the Coast Mountains, Kamloops' seasonal temperatures range from moderately wet to extremely hot, and are contrasted by dry desert-like conditions. Rattlesnakes and Black widow spiders are native to the area, as is vegetation such as prickly pear cactus and large sagebrush, commonly found in arid zones. A transportation artery, Kamloops has links to the TransCanada and Yellowhead Highways (in addition to 5 and 97), making it conducive to travellers and backpackers.

Stowing our packs in one of the small yellow pergolas, Jan and I returned to the front gate to inquire about purchasing groceries. Paul told us we'd find a small supply store not far up the road, but if we could hang in a few hours, dinner was included in our night's stay.

Beds, breakfast — plus dinner — we happily discovered, were part of the deal in most British Columbia hostels. Relieved to have a reasonable meal to look forward to, Jan and I agreed it would be wise to pick up a few staples anyway, just in case.

I reached down for the door handle to exit the office. Placing his hand on the frame to stop me, Paul's mouth curved into an impish grin. Uncurling his fingers, a lone, generous sized marijuana cigarette lay in his flat palm.

"It's Maui Wowie. But don't feel obliged."

Without reservation, Jan and I accepted.

Kamloops pink Sky. June 1976.

CHAPTER 49

Loopy in Kamloops

"The summit of the mountain; the thunder of the sky,
the rhythm of the sea, speaks to me."
CHIEF DAN GEORGE

JP's comment about RCMP officer's tendency to show up at youth hostels unannounced still fresh in our minds, Jan and I were careful to stow Paul's 'gift' in the safety of our tent. Planning to smoke the joint that evening, anticipation would make it that much sweeter. Waiting would also help to side-step an attack of the munchies mid-afternoon.

Fatigued from the first half of the day, we returned to our tent to rest. Jan read. I fell asleep. When I awoke, light drizzle replaced the radiant sunshine that had complemented our arrival. Rummaging inside of my pack for Teddy's green jacket, I zipped the fleece-lined skin up to my neck. Jan dug out her yellow-knitted sweater.

We were ready to go.

The shelves in the shop down the road were not exactly well stocked. Catering mostly to hunters and fishers, we managed to buy few inexpensive pick-me-ups — snack packages containing cheese, crackers, processed meat, and two bottles of orange juice. On our way back to the hostel, munching on our goodies, we talked about hoping to stay with our friend Lorraine from the Y, now living and working in Banff, where we planned to be within the week. Any inkling of hooking up with Gary was pretty much squashed. JP remembered Gary from Hope — confirmation that Gary *had* materialized there for a few days. Where Gary was headed after that was anybody's guess. Along the west coast, folks travelled fluidly between cities, hostels, and campgrounds. It wasn't atypical to encounter the same faces from place to place, reinforcing how unusual it was that *no one* knew of Gary's current whereabouts. The New Zealander's accent and personality alone were two factors you wouldn't likely forget.

Jan and I returned from the store. Paul, Jim, and some of the others (one, a girl we'd met at HOOM) sat at the table crafting wood necklaces. Many of the designs were simple, while others, intricate and ornate. Encouraging us to dig in, Paul suggested we each create a personal piece of jewelry as keepsakes. Taking a place along the bench at the end of the long table, I reached my hand into a jungle of multihued beads, wire, and jute. There were now fourteen of us from diverse parts of Canada, the United States, and Europe. As many different pouches of the planet as there was jute.

Suggestive of a Mad Hatter tea party, downplaying death-defying tales that had occurred while under the influence of chemicals, Paul, Jim, and a couple others crowed about pick-pocketing unsuspecting folks when the going got tough, and bragged about steamy sexual exploits while thumbing rides. With great bravado and a lethal personality, André, one of three Frenchmen from Northern Quebec, was the most extreme of the bunch. Loud, bawdy, and slightly insane, as if he'd learned the words that very day, *"Jesus Christ!"* became the addendum to every specious tale André told. Rapping almost non-stop, André blurted the very first unedited thought that came into his head and got away with it because his Quebecois-speak won the others over. To a lesser degree, the tone of the Kamloops hostel was comparable to Texas Lake, only less organized, less self-conscious.

For dinner, Paul and Jim served cheddar cheese, tomato and lettuce on wheat bread, with sides of celery and salami — nearly as tasty as our rice casserole had been the night before. In suspense of our special dessert, which we planned to burn as soon as the kitchen was restored to its natural state, I smiled at Jan from across the table. No doubt, fellow hostellers had been bequeathed herbal offerings from Paul.

Starting out toward the hill behind the property, we espied Paul and a few of the others en route to a local bar to sell and trade necklaces in exchange for money or weed. Others had plans to party. Without beer money there wasn't much point going along for the ride. Lone reefer in hand, continuing to the top of the hill, we lit up. Taking the first drag from the plump cigarette, Jan passed it to me. Inhaling deeply, I felt the familiar buzz work its way from the center of my abdomen and pool throughout my body. Mind soon flooding with a jangle of images and euphoric memory bursts; I started in on a verbal binge yapping about our surroundings, and continued to repeat how *pure* Kamloops was now that the rain had finally stopped.

It was true.

The scope and surfaces of surrounding mountains suggested dusky dry ranges we'd grown accustomed to up and down the California coastline.

Bathed by the summer evening's light, in delicate stillness, cactus flowers probed tiny bobble heads out from behind rocks. Small animals hurried furtively about. Spruce, pines, and Douglas firs populated the hill like a poppy field as the sun stole glances from behind dissipating cumulus clouds dominating skies early evening. For a few minutes, there was absolute silence; unruffled calm intensified by the heightening awareness of the marijuana. Embodied by everything surrounding us, the expression, "Beauts," jabbed at my brain before finally making its way to my lips.

Lingering on the hillside, cross-legged on the grass, recounting the best parts of our day, we talked about Paul, André, and other new characters. Augmenting her lightly tanned skin, Jan showed off her newly fashioned turquoise/orange beaded necklace. Admiring the purple and green band hanging prominently on my own wrist, loose jute dangling on the end, I knew I was on the mend. Come morning, we'd hitch a ride to the Banff hostel, stay with Lorraine while in the vicinity. With luck, we'd been told, travel between Kamloops and Banff is one full day.

Cocooned within the effects of our smoke, we returned to the main house. A couple of hours had passed since Paul and some of the others tore off in somebody's beater, hoping to score. Not everybody remained in town that night. More than a few hung back to socialize, do whatever. Evident by heavy eyelids, languid demeanor, easy laughter, and slack posture, I knew that most of our companions were soaring like kites. According to Paul, dope laws in Alberta were more stringent than British Columbia.

Snapping on my flashlight inside our tent, I resurrected *The Golden Force*. Backtracking about forty pages to chapter six titled "The Marriage in Peace," a few paragraphs in, the chapter cautions the contemporary student's thirst for advanced philosophical knowledge while selectively ignoring intuitive data. Citing the theory of vibration, and how it might apply to New Age ideals, to illustrate a point, the book poses a challenge: *How many of you are able to put the Universal Law into action?*

According to the chapter, the universal law of vibration is used to facilitate passage of thought through the atmosphere. Much the same way that telephone communication between two parties takes place when there is a properly adjusted source and receiver at both ends — thoughts are transmitted toward a desired objective. Predicated upon one's acceptance that all life is integrated, and our intelligence is inextricably tied by an obscured lead giving mobility to thought, through unification of physical and spiritual (or psychic) bodies, mental messages and pictures are sent along an invisible cord between our inner and outer selves.

Following this process, the book points out, love and personal happiness are within reach.

Flat on my sleeping bag ogling upward at the V-shaped peak where the tent sides met, I watched mosquitoes collude the long night ahead. Directly out the west window, the sun began to fold into candy floss pigments of orange and pink. Allowing the book's passage to percolate, something seared a nerve. More than anything in life, I wanted to be happy. Not for passing bursts, but long, undulated periods where emotion could be amassed, the afterglow of happiness preserved.

There is a beautiful narrative in J.D. Salinger's *Raise High the Roofbeam, Carpenters* in which Seymour Glass describes a permanent yellow stain on his right hand, a remaining blemish from brushing against a favourite playmate's buttery dress during childhood. Through recollections and emotions, perhaps symbolically, we have ability to engender the same durable effect. Fishing in a pond of happy memories, possibly, there is the means to train ourselves to summon joy at will, conserve it to provide nourishment during dry spells. If the law of vibration detailed in *The Holy Order of MANS* digest really works, and there was evidence of it through the manifestation of our own basic requests, maybe then, all one truly needs to do is *believe* in happiness.

The rest will take care of itself.

Friday, a few days beyond June 21, the grey morning air felt chillier than the day before, and not a drop of precipitation in sight. Thanking Paul for our stay, half past seven, Jan and I made our way from the Kamloops Hostel out to the highway. Stale sesame seed bagels tucked deep into our packs, we were guaranteed a head start. Other travellers, also moving east, had already packed their gear.

Watching a torrent of cars and transport trucks blow by in haste, loitering on the shoulder of the Trans Canada, we contemplated the trip ahead. Habitually, Jan and I willed a harm free journey. Counting our flight to Vancouver, in four months we'd logged close to 6000 miles. Having been in near constant motion since leaving our jobs at the hotel in March, it hadn't felt like a stretch. The unknown quotient of the remaining weeks of our trip was thrilling. Along with the rush of day-to-day adventure, was a dull ache of anxiety. The yin and yang of confronting a faceless future.

An hour passed slowly. Others from the Kamloops Hostel including the girl we'd met at HOOM collected on the highway, upholding careful distance between one another. Everybody practiced road etiquette. In addition to the girl, two New Yorkers and a man from Toronto stood in wait of a lift. Flying solo, Paul decided to make a two-day round trip to Revelstoke to attend a blues festival where he would try to sell more bracelets. Paul's buddy, Jim, would assume operational duties of the hostel.

Close to nine, a green Pontiac rolled past, then quickly reversed. Once the boat-sized vehicle was adjacent to Jan and me, we watched excitedly as the crisp whitewalls jerked to a dead stop. I glanced behind us. Paul and the girl from HOOM had since hooked up with rides. The only leftovers were the two boys from New York. As we ran to catch the Pontiac, they gave thumbs up.

Our driver, a middle-aged local going as far as Salmon Arm, asked where we were headed. Jan and I cried, "Banff!" to which he replied, "Well, I can get you about a quarter of the way." Tossing our packs into the back seat, we took our places along the leather-covered bench next to the driver.

The owner of the vehicle was Sam.

More gregarious than most of the people that had stopped as of late, Sam amused with stories of his own hitchhiking days while on leave during his service in the Canadian Army, from Vancouver across country to Summerside, Prince Edward Island. "Riding was less of a threat during wartime," Sam was quick to remind us. "Drivers have no qualms picking up soldiers." Smiling ruefully at the memory, through hooded eyes, Sam admitted he felt melancholy for his adventurous days. Losing his wife to cancer five years previous, he'd found single life a difficult adjustment. Three grown children were dispersed between British Columbia and Seattle.

Riding in silence along a drawn-out corridor of the highway, flanked by deep coniferous forests glad-handing with low hanging clouds, through clearings, I glimpsed bottle green water. Hanging tough against wind squalls, high above in subterranean blue, red-tailed hawks sporting outstretched wings circled in hunt of the next meal. Poking my hand inside of my satchel, I liberated a sesame seed bagel. His head moving in a swooping motion, Sam asked, "What do your parents think about you girls hitchhiking?" Tearing my breakfast into bite-sized pieces, I glimpsed over at Jan who replied. "I haven't told them yet."

Pretty smart on her part, I thought. The less shared with our parents the better all round. Repositioning herself between Sam and me, my pal glowered with a self-satisfied smirk on her face.

"My parents know we've done *some* hitchhiking." My voice faltered. "I just haven't told them how much." Sam's eyes remained steadied on the rearview mirror as a transport trailer directly behind our vehicle made a semi-circular sweep around the left side, coming within few feet of the Pontiac.

"How do they feel about it?" Unsure of where the conversation was headed, deliberately choosing my words, I fibbed. "I really don't know. I suppose they wished we wouldn't." Responding to my dropping a few crumbs during a weak moment of correspondence, in her last letter, my mom had underlined stern words of warning in bold, Bic pen. *"No more hitchhiking!"*

My parents were worried something horrible might happen. I couldn't fault them for their restless sleeps. In a way, unless a person has zero connection to immediate family or friends, hitchhiking is a thoughtless act. Calculatedly, Jan hadn't spilled the beans to her mom and dad. No doubt, they knew. Jan's parents were not fools.

"We also travel by bus." Though aware that Sam hadn't judged, here I was, defending our free mode of travel to a stranger. Confessing he'd done the same thing himself when he was younger, now that Sam was older, and a parent, his perspective had changed. He could assess the pros and cons.

We had no point of reference.

Arriving in Salmon Arm thirty minutes later, reaching a hand deep into a denim pocket, Sam disentangled a $10 bill from some loose change. "Here. Have lunch on me."

Dan Thompson, a young man from the rural town of Golden, a community implanted within the Canadian Rocky Mountains, pulled alongside. A cabinetmaker by trade, Dan was returning home after visiting a friend. Assuming we'd settle into the Golden hostel for the night, Jan and I rode 158 miles with Dan.

Pulling into the gravel driveway of the premises, Dan pointed to a sign tacked to one of the front windows. Upon closer inspection, it read, "Closed until July." Slamming his car in reverse, Thompson roared down the laneway to the road, righted his vehicle and made a left on to the Trans Canada. Unless something else could be figured out, Dan would drive us to the bus depot.

Sam's ten spot suddenly loomed large. Saving it to buy a quick lunch, with any luck, there'd be money to spare.

Legs dangling atop a picnic table outside of the Golden depot, Jan tore away at a sliced cheese and lettuce sandwich purchased from a vending machine. In perfunctory mode, we conceived a revamped plan.

It had been our wish to stall for a few days before landing in Banff. Not only was there beautiful country to explore in British Columbia, due to various hit and misses experienced with hostel closures, on top of a dwindling cash flow, we didn't want to rush the last few weeks of our journey.

Stymied, we reckoned what to do next. Facing limited prospects, fundamentally, there was no way around it. We would keep travelling east.

Strapping our packs to our backs, walking from the bus terminal back out to the highway, we found a place to rest on the shoulder of the road. The sun had fully broken through the clouds, inspiring us to peel off our outerwear. Bored and not anxious to go anywhere just yet, counting stray cars, vans, and trucks driving east and west along on the Trans Canada, I thought about the people inside and where they were headed. We made a $1 bet how long it would take to thumb a ride.

A couple of folks at Kamloops had joked about a deserted stretch of road, Highway 17, located in the scenic but small Northern Ontario town of Wawa. Legend alleged that a person could starve to death standing at one spot in Wawa for days in anticipation of a ride that would never come. In the early 1970s, as part of a youth employment initiative, the federal government implemented an archaeological field camp known as the Wawa Drop-In Project, aka the "Big Dig," designed to attract young hitchhikers travelling along Highway 17. After a period, the project became non-operational, no doubt because of a lack of recruits. Everybody had either moved on or packed it in.

Very few people lived in Wawa, with even fewer visitors to the tiny town. *Nobody* picked up riders. As the story goes, if you didn't die from hunger or exposure, you'd perish from black fly bites and be relegated to road kill. According to those who'd done it and survived, Wawa is the most ruthless place on earth to wait on a ride.

As an address, Golden was likeable enough, and quaint. Unless you were from the area however, or had ties, Golden was little more than another sleepy post, one that saw people come and go with no plans to commit. After an hour of lazing, recharged, Jan and I were ready to get on the road.

Eighty miles to go.

We could hardly believe our good fortune when André, the crazy Frenchman from the Kamloops hostel, drove past in a dusty Chevy riding shotgun, one of the first vehicles to emerge after more than a one-hour wait. Having almost given up hope of leaving Golden that afternoon,

Jan and I'd started to suspect we'd fallen under the Wawa curse. Already beyond our location, the Chevy pulled a quick U-turn and eased toward us, slowing to a stop next to our packs. Motioning to pull the handle to get into the car, I was shocked to discover the burly individual behind the wheel who introduced himself as Tim, had a broken left leg. Stretching from his left hip all the way down to his ankle, a cast revealed swollen toes sticking out through a jagged plaster opening. It was the required foot if you're driving a stick.

Tim was driving a stick.

Eyeing Jan warily, I was unsure what to do. Reading our concern, Tim threw back his head and started to laugh uproariously. "I was in a car accident a few weeks ago," he mused. "Don't worry though. The accident wasn't *my* fault." Boasting about his competency as a driver, Tim told us he'd cruised all the way from Vancouver with the broken leg. No trouble.

It wasn't much of an assurance, but the afternoon was wearing on. We didn't want to be stuck in Golden forever. Sensing our reluctance, André suddenly went overboard in praise of Tim's "crackerjack driving skills," and stressed how safe *he* felt under the big man's command. As if it would clinch the deal, André threw in a "Jesus *Christ!*" followed by more laughter. Convinced of having pulled off an affecting sell job, leaning into the back seat, André rearranged his and Tim's packs next to a gargantuan tent, obviously stuffed into the vehicle in a pinch. To make room for our gear, gathering a handful of strewn- about clothes, he went about redistributing the items and tossed some camping paraphernalia into the trunk.

Nervous about the fucked-up situation we might be getting ourselves into, aversely, Jan and I climbed inside the Chevy and yanked on the weighty passenger door. Behind my back, two fingers were crossed.

Sometimes you gnash your teeth. Abolish all reservation.

Banff, Alberta. COURTESY OF ANDREA NELSON.

CHAPTER 50

The Blue Hour

"She's love and hate and death and life, I like her."
FRANKLIN PIERCE ADAMS

True to his word, André's friend was anything but cavalier about helming the road. Notwithstanding his temporary disability, Tim proved to be an exceptional driver. Reminiscent of the fictitious character, Luke Moriarty, the unofficial 'driver' in Jack Kerouac's *On the Road* inspired by Kerouac's real-life pal, wild man Neal Cassady, Tim handled his automobile like a pro, as if gliding a precious vessel over glass. Not once did he compromise the safety of his baby or his cargo.

During the two-hour excursion, we crossed over some tremendous terrain. The first half of the drive through Yoho National Park, snow-chalked Rocky Mountains outlining opposite sides of the TransCanada threw a dark veil across the road. Eventually, the Chevy curved around to Lake Louise, a pristine pea-green glacial lake, one of Western Canada's most beautiful and unblemished wonders. Eventually entering Alberta's Banff National Park, at every hook of the highway, mountain peaks grew proportionately larger, more pervasive.

Without forewarning, finally easing on the break, Tim downshifted until almost at a complete stop.

Summer of 1976, Banff was chief party designation on Canada's West Coast. Surrounded by four distinct mountain ranges, the low-populated heritage town with an elevation of 5350 feet enfolding around Tunnel Mountain has long been a favourite resort attracting skiers, bicyclists, and hikers year-round. During spring and summer, tourists are drawn to the area's natural hot springs. In recent years, developing infrastructure and transportation have grown to accommodate a greater need for services.

Tim had taken us directly to the Banff Youth Hostel listed in our guidebook. Little more than a small camping park, there were no dorms, only trampled grass and litter everywhere. Empty beer bottles, soup cans, cigarette butts, toilet paper — the place was completely trashed. Behind the office building, further into the wooded area, red, green, yellow, and blue canvas tents dotted the forest. Despite its condition, Jan and I were set to stay a couple of nights, only we no longer carried a tent. Perhaps there was something elsewhere, not too far away.

The first of one out of the Chevy to have a look-see was André, who scurried off to track down the site manager. Minutes later, André reappeared, confirming our suspicion. No inside sleeping quarters, camping only. Because he often hooked up with acquaintances, André carried a six-man tent and generously invited Jan and me to share space with him and his buddies, a group of French Canadian males expected to arrive that evening. Including us, André estimated, there would be nearly nineteen crashing in his tent, an incredibly tight squeeze. The disproportionate number between the men and the two of us could pose a dicey situation. Though I'd never participated in one personally, the arrangement could potentially set the stage for an orgy — a gang-bang more likely — not my first choice for losing my virginity. Somehow, I knew Jan would not be game.

Begging off André's bid; we decided to thumb the short drive out to the Banff Springs Hotel. Possibly, we could stay a couple of days with our friend Lorraine, who lived and worked on the premises. André, who also had friends employed at the hotel, looked forward to joining up later.

Waiting in queue behind four guys chatting on the shoulder of the road, all of us were in search of work in Banff.

Scooping up the six of us, a couple driving a van heading to Banff agreed to drop our party at the hotel. Riding along, it crossed my mind that we could talk to Lorraine about applying for work as chambermaids at Banff Springs. Maybe she would even put in a good word on our behalf.

Then again, maybe not. Lorraine had been a far superior maid to either Jan or me. Raised in a family of eight kids, early on, Lorraine had learned to cook, clean, and care for younger siblings. Primed for the necessary job requirements and strong as an ox, Lorraine worked quickly, efficiently. Already into the last week of June, job opportunities for summer work at the Banff Springs Hotel had likely been filled.

Still, it wouldn't hurt to ask.

Carting our packs toward the parking lot located in front of the building, we dropped them onto the hot asphalt and calibrated our surroundings.

This was not your common hostel where thrifty youths paid a nominal fee for a one-night stopover. Set above Bow Falls, the Banff Springs Hotel (today a part of the Fairmont Hotel chain) encircled by the Rocky Mountains and hot springs, is a luxury resort built of concrete and stone. Constructed in the 19th century, in 1976, the elegant, historic hotel, a touchstone of premium lodging, had a going rate of more than $90 a day. Showcasing an unrivalled view from virtually every room, the lofty price for one night's stay was easily substantiated.

Banff Springs Hotel epitomized convention, expectations, protocol. Dragging our backsides and toting miserable possessions, Jan and I weren't about to saunter into the lavish front lobby wearing torn jeans and t-shirts, asking after Lorraine. We had no business being there.

Thankfully, we didn't have to go inside the hotel. Lorraine lived in the annex, a spacious, multi-tiered building adjacent to the hotel that provided lodging for its nearly 125 employees. Picking up our gear, we walked several hundred feet to the employee residence: a mature, moss-covered, brick structure resembling student housing. One quick pull on the front door, in we slid into the downstairs lobby. It was almost half past six. Jan and I hadn't eaten anything to speak of since breakfast. We'd find Lorraine soon or figure out dinner.

Asking around if anyone knew our friend, first go, we struck out. A couple of girls heading toward the exit doors paused so that one of them could fish her hand inside of her purse, providing opportunity to make an inquiry. Not only did the girls know Lorraine, they knew what floor she was on but were unsure of her room number. Pointing toward the stairwell, they warned about visitation regulations. The hotel strongly discouraged friends of employees crashing in the annex. If you were caught, it was curtains — a $100 fine.

We hadn't counted on that.

It was my turn to be the asserter. While Jan waited outside minding our backpacks, approaching the stairs, I made my way to the third floor and began knocking on doors. The first four rooms I tried, there was no answer. People were at work, out, or asleep. Reaching the fifth, I lucked out. Lorraine's next-door neighbour, a narrow faced, eyes glazed over soul, peeped out through his door crack and informed me he thought Lorraine had finished work for the day.

It was Friday night. What were the chances that Lorraine was home?

Stepping a few paces down the hallway, approaching room 302, I knocked hard on the door, twice. Detecting movement in the room, peering through the peephole, I observed a fuzzy shape with long brown hair. Soon enough, one eye looked through the hole from the other side. Then the door flung open wide and there stood Lorraine, wearing a long white T-shirt over bare legs, screaming my name at the top of her lungs. Following her lead, we both began jumping up and down, squealing like a couple of maniacs. Doors opened and closed on either side of the hallway; heads bobbed forward and backward like fish in a bowl at a carnival. Calming down, I explained that Jan was outside, waiting. Insisting we stay in her room, hands pressed against her mouth, Lorraine gasped, "You guys picked the *best* possible time to visit! I've got the weekend off work and my roommate Wendy is away for a couple of days. But," she quietly cautioned, "There are dons on the floor so you don't want to get caught here. They'll kick you out and fine you. You'll have to bring your backpacks up through the fire escape and sneak into my room. I'll keep a look out."

Giving me another squeeze, Lorraine cried, "Holy shit, Jill! I can't believe you guys are actually *here!*"

Carrying our cumbersome loads, minutes later Jan and I traipsed up the narrow metal steps located on the anterior wall. Trying to be discreet in broad daylight, we felt like two bumbling thieves in a bad movie, hoping to skip town without getting jammed — our comeuppance for failing to formulate a better strategy.

This was risky business. We couldn't afford the $200 fine. But if it could be pulled off, the reward of having a couple of fun-filled days in Banff with our friend, and free place to stay awaited.

Nearing the top of the fire escape, Jan leading the way, Lorraine held the door open to the small room lending access to the hallway. She motioned for us to hurry up. We had had no way of knowing when one of the hall monitors would arrive on the scene, and had to work fast. On the landing, crouching low, Jan crab-walked underneath Lorraine's arms and hustled in through the doorway to the vestibule. I followed suit. Authoritatively positioned in front of the door leading to her hallway, Lorraine cued us to break. Endeavoring to creep quietly and slowly along the thirty-foot distance, finally, we were secured inside Lorraine's room and behind the closed door.

It all seemed silly, but Lorraine didn't want to run the risk that one of her neighbours might rat us out. To exit and enter, Jan and I would use the fire escape. At least we could unload our packs for a couple of days, making us less conspicuous in the annex.

Door locked, the fear of getting busted in check, we relived our five-minute comedy sketch and fell about in howls of laugher. Regaining our composure, we talked about the next order of business: Food AND drink.

Fully appreciative of our financial situation, Lorraine promised a great place to eat, Moos. Afterwards, we'd head out to Cascade, a popular drinking establishment where Banff Springs' summer staff liked to decompress.

Draught beer cost 25 cents.

Consensus was, for $1, you could get reasonably oiled.

Jan, Lorraine and I hit up Moos for a quick burger. By 8 pm, comfortably seated in one of the Cascade's slimy booths, we were well on our way through our first pitcher of draught. Mired in smoke in a clammy, wall-to-wall packed space resembling "The Corn," from home, Pink Floyd resounded from every corner. Cigarette embers radiated like Bic lighters at a stoner concert glowing from every speck of available space, while patrons in various stages of inebriation made the schizophrenic, seesaw shift between screams and laughter. Partially concealed by a grey-blue blur of bodies and long hair, I became aware of a person in the crowd that had been at Steiner Street during our recent stay. About to make my way over, somebody shouted my name from across the room. Turning, I recognized three acquaintances from high school — two Nancy's and a Rob. Ambling toward our table, the trio remained long enough to explain they were in Banff seeking summer work. "You and a million others," I joked.

To his credit, Rob *had* found a job as a waiter at the hotel's main dining establishment. Apparently, we'd just missed a couple other friends from school by two days, Alex and Marty. Unsuccessful in obtaining employment in Banff, the friends had migrated to greener pastures in Edmonton.

The notion of asking Lorraine about prospects at the hotel was shelved.

The night staggered on. Alcohol's effects quickly grabbed hold, and the bar din engineered an audible threshold shift. Overcompensating, Jan, Lorraine, and I joined a raucous bunch on the dance floor where people grinded absently against one another. Within the maze of arms and legs, André and some of his boys slipped into the crowd, expressing themselves fervidly to the music. Moving purposefully toward the Frenchman, I gave André a big slack kiss and then fell in with the dancing herd. On the surface, it was good to see Lorraine again and be in Banff. Scanning my eyes over nameless shapes, I couldn't help feeling empty. My heart growing lonesome, I began to miss Teddy, the certainty of the HOOM family. Wishing that he was with us in Banff, affectionately, I recalled Gary and his infantile antics.

Not many weeks before, insecurities would have been smothered by the blitzed-out drink and commotion. Something *had* changed. Feeling transparent, like an aimless performer in a gruesome freak show, encountering familiar faces from our hometown had become a double-edged sword. No matter how many miles we'd racked up over the past months, home, the place that typically conjures up hospitable images, hung on the fringes, waiting to gobble us up like a vacuum.

Within the swarm of sweaty flesh, I managed to locate Jan and Lorraine. *Would they come outside for some fresh air?* Only too happy to take a breather, Jan said she felt unwell. I slurred something to Lorraine about heading back to the annex. Not wanting to forfeit her seat at the table, Lorraine would see us later.

Steadying ourselves using the corridor wall, Jan and I weaved our way out the side door until reaching the front of The Cascade. A few minutes past ten, grateful for the cool of the summer night, remarkably, the sun had barely embarked upon its suave seduction of the moon. Early summer, Banff's daylight hangs on until about half past ten. Twilight happens in the blink of an eye. Completely paranormal, it was a thrill to eyewitness.

I unburdened to Jan how afraid I was about returning home, and how everything would revert to the norm as if we'd never left.

This was the full pendulum swing. Hours earlier, I was the affectionate, kissy-huggy girl. Now, I was the wet blanket, sorry-for-herself, bawling-in-her-drink girl. I could count on one hand the number of times we'd gotten loaded since our travels began, Vancouver being one of the last. Suffice to say, I was out of practice. Making up for lost chances, my friend and I had gone full tilt and hit the skids.

Utilizing the building's brick wall as my brace, crouching down on the sidewalk, head in both hands, I heard a resounding splatter, as if somebody had poured five gallons of water onto the pavement. Struggling to keep my eyes focused, slowly, I looked up.

There was Lorraine, spilling her guts all over the sidewalk.

Tomorrow would be another chance to get it right.

With André and Lorraine, Chateau Lake Louise, Alberta.

CHAPTER 51

Going, Gone

"Count each day as a separate life."
SENECA

The aftermath of the beer binge crushing like a sledgehammer, next day
I cringed at the thought of what I might have said or done — though not
to the point where I couldn't breathe a sigh of relief now that it was over.
Certain that spectators would be willing to fill in the blanks concerning
our theatrics outside of the Cascade, in the end it really didn't matter. Jan
and I had the weekend in Banff before heading out Monday morning for
Mosquito Creek Hostel. As always, we wanted to maximize time.

Pulling open her drapes, Lorraine revealed the ground covered in
snow! After two months of mostly summer-like conditions, it was a shell
shock. Not only that, snow meant that it was cold — certainly bitter
enough to require more than Teddy's kangaroo, or a wool sweater.

Somewhere in the confusion of my drunk and disorderly state the
previous night, depending upon what shape *he* was in, I'd made soft plans
with André to spend the day at Lake Louise. Moving slower than usual,
taking turns using Lorraine's latrine and shower, we got our butts down
to Smitty's Pancake House along the main drag. André was already there,
happily helping himself to the all-day breakfast menu. Surprised to see
that we were mobile, the Frenchman made wisecracks about our inability
to hold our liquor.

André was hardly one to talk.

Splitting blueberry pancake breakfasts and a pot of coffee between us,
we were ready to try our luck thumbing a ride out to Lake Louise, a forty-
minute jaunt down Highway 1. Jan and I told Lorraine and André about
our foolproof method for acquiring a ride. So far, we'd approximated a
ninety percent success rate.

They were eager to try.

Since arriving in Banff, we'd been preoccupied with Lorraine, eating and drinking, leaving little time to appreciate our remarkable surroundings. From the outskirts of town, the visage of the self-effacing rocky monolith peak known as Banff's prominent Cascade Mountain, invoked imaginings of the Swiss Alps. Jan and I'd encountered many daunting mountain ranges. Banff is in a league all its own.

A black Dodge Challenger pulled over. It was occupied by three men resembling the French-Canadian trio that had driven Jan and me home from the Cascade the night before.

Suspicion bred like early morning mist. Though common to encounter the same group hostel-to-hostel and city-to-city, it seemed unusual running into the same people so soon. My disoriented, unreliable mind had again kicked into paranoid overdrive — one of many downsides of overindulging.

Calmly, I hit reset.

Hopping into the jacked-up chassis hoisted at least eight inches higher than necessary, sides emblazoned by yellow hand-painted racing stripes, seven of us folded our bodies together. Within the close quarters, it became apparent. This motley crew *had* driven us to the annex from the Cascade the night before. Frayed around the edges, the guys certainly seemed friendly enough.

Innocent until proven guilty.

Despite being crushed between arms and legs, the drive out to Lake Louise hamlet was smooth and uneventful, when Nick the driver, suddenly slammed on the breaks to prevent from overshooting our drop-off point, bouncing everybody around like kangaroos. The right rear passenger door flew open wide, throwing Jan, seated next to the access, onto the road. There were no broken bones, only bruises but this was getting weird. If bad things happen in threes, there was the risk of a third freak accident.

Disembarking from the Challenger was a relief. Regaining her composure, Jan brushed herself off and we caught another short ride out to Chateau Lake Louise (also part of the Fairmont chain today) located on the eastern shore. Along the stony edge of the emerald blue lake, teasing our eyelashes and noses along their path, delicate white snowflakes began to spot the ground like confetti. Tentative at first, skirting closer to the water's edge, thousands of silver-white flecks parachuted softly on to the earth.

Thick as pancake batter, tinted blue like a peacock's feathers, Lake Louise is disseminated by rock flour carried down from melted glaciers encircling the lake's perimeter, giving the water its luxurious hue. Providing insulation from drafts, directly in front of the Chateau and glacial lake, snow-heavy mountains reflect upon the water's surface. Snow Dome, one of two hydrological apexes in the world whose entire summit is covered by the Columbia ice field, rests in the distance.

The four of us began hiking to the foot of the lake. Periodically stopping along the shoreline, Jan snapped a few photos until eventually; we circled back at the Chateau for a tea break.

Wet and muck sticking to our footwear, tramping into the café, though lighter now, the snow persisted. Excusing himself from the group to investigate another one of the trails, André promised to return soon. Feeding off the hearth's warmth, removing our jackets, we continued to peel off layers. When the server came to take our order, Lorraine requested a round of tea and jam biscuits.

Sipping chamomile from dainty, bone-china teacups, my doubtful speculation about work was confirmed. Banff Springs Hotel already had full-time and part-time staff in place. Looking for summer employment was useless. If only Jan and I'd thought to apply back in winter. This left no alternative. After Mosquito Creek, we'd keep moving east to Edmonton and Calgary — larger cities with greater work potential. If we were able to secure jobs, there was the real possibly of stretching our journey indefinitely.

Returning from wherever he'd disappeared, André pulled up a chair, turned up the dial on the charm meter and chatted up a short, doe-eyed French girl seated alone at an adjacent table. Close to five, that magical hour, the lightweight Casanova finally bummed a few smokes from the girl before tossing some loose change into our pot. To avoid another hit and miss, we decided to split up. Jan and André teamed together. Lorraine and I formed a twosome.

One hour later, no one had made progress. So much for great odds. As a last resort, swearing the signage approach was the preferred way to go; André pulled a magic marker and plaque from his backpack and began printing something on the cardboard.

I had to hand it to the quirky Frenchman. While Lorraine and I continued to play the waiting game, without hesitation, the very next driver waved André and Jan and over.

Back in Banff, we ate a small meal at the snack bar, bought ice cream cones at Hamburger Hut, and returned to the Cascade. This time, we didn't stay longer than an hour, barely time to make donkeys of ourselves, long enough to mix and mingle. Chipping in to split a pitcher of draught, I made a point of *soberly* checking the place out.

Chatting with folks, some travelling through, others employed by the hotel — mostly everybody was coming or going through a revolving door of some sort. People were not only friendly, but in better-than-average spirits.

What a difference one day can make.

Barring the exception, I've always contended there are far more attractive women than men. For some inexplicable reason, on *this* night, an illogical number of good-looking men hunted the nightspot. Considering the size of Banff, this was an astounding scene.

Where did these people come from suddenly? A horde of long wavy hair, plaid work shirts, hiking boots, and lean, sturdy bodies posed at various points within the bar. It was as if a portal had opened and we had front row seats to a superior dimension at work. Soon enough, the cavity would close and poof, away they'd go.

Perhaps this was a top-secret assignment? Part of some 'Handsome Man' competition? Faith that *I* might meet somebody was restored. Though far removed from the slutty type, courting a couple of bottles of courage in my belly, I could be as flirty as the next girl.

With a little practice, seductive.

If I believed it to be true, a kissable, adoring boyfriend was within possibility.

That evening, rather touchingly, André fixed his sleeping bag next to mine on the floor of Lorraine's room. Knowing him only a few days, I'd figured it out that our friend's bluster and over the top, bombastic exclamations of "Jesus *Christ!*" were reflective of a lack of self-confidence. This weak spot made me like the Frenchman even more — as a friend.

Pleasant enough looking, save the beginnings of a goatee — a redeeming add-on — André's sandy brown, messy haircut reminded me of a little boy's. Likable for the most part and surprisingly sweet, André was the kind of person who crossed the line, then grabbed a helping of seconds and thirds. Rather than be irritated by his madcap personality and predilection to con, you couldn't help but laugh.

Anyway, André wasn't my type. Whatever that meant, I was no longer certain.

Dead tired, around 10 pm, the four of us watched out Lorraine's window as the graceful red sphere, motionless in the sky, launched into its elegant dance. As the sun began to fade, the sky got blacker and blacker until a circular pale-yellow outline of a new moon was accentuated. Lasting less than ten minutes, this transient twilight phase, an incisive expression of flawless organic clockwork, was our payday.

Now that the room was dark, goodnights were exchanged among us. Settling into my sleeping bag, I felt a hand reach over for mine. In the shadows, eyes squinting, André smiled. Leaning in, squeezing his fingers tight, I placed a tiny kiss on his lips.

In the morning, the Frenchman, we'd discovered, had risen early and taken his backpack with him. Off to pursue another caper, in remembrance, our friend had left behind a single piece of evidence. Propped up on the chair by Lorraine's desk stood the small piece of cardboard André had used the day before as an appeal to drivers.

Underlined in black marker, a single, capitalized word was written. "PLEASE."

Bow River, Alberta. COURTESY OF ANDREA NELSON.

CHAPTER 52

Mosquito Creek

"Half the fun of travel is the esthetic of lostness."
RAY BRADBURY

Two weeks had passed since leaving Steiner Street. Only three days remained in June. Once July arrived, it would be pointless claiming to having recently stayed in San Francisco. The space between our last hours at HOOM and our impermanent status felt like a giant crater. The same would hold true for what lay ahead.

Most days, usually in the quiet of the morning, or before going to sleep, thoughts strayed to Teddy. My overactive imagination took off like a runaway train. Worried about his state of happiness or unhappiness, I wondered if he left The Holy Order, where his life would take him. The idea that he might return to street drugs, become a desperado, give up or even die entered my mind. Not yet thirty, Teddy had experienced many faces of tragedy, and prevailed. His proclivity for being headstrong was Teddy's saving grace. Given the Good Samaritan's questioning nature, there was also a good chance he'd flee from his internship, never become a fully-fledged Brother. Surely, he'd find a way to prevent from bottoming out.

Still divided about the whole issue of HOOM, leanings pointed toward joining rather than not — mainly because I hadn't come up with enough reasons to resist. I'd yet to figure out if entering The Order was the greater or lesser of my so-called choices. As Reverend Mary rightly pointed out, HOOM isn't going anywhere.

I hoped to go somewhere.

Sunday morning was hot and sunny. On Lorraine's endorsement, the three of us walked the 2 1/2 miles through the forest, along the length of the meadow trail to the far side of Bow River and out to Hoodoos viewpoint. With birds of prey and elk marshalling us along the path, before long, another dreamscape opened.

Behind pea green water, massifs calmed immaculate blue skies. Locating a boulder overlooking the water, we sat down and dipped our bare toes into the riverbed. Over several months, in my journal, I'd tried to communicate innumerable prepossessing settings along our course. One of the drawbacks to imprisoning moments; an ineffectual incarnation can potentially repudiate a setting.

Silence is almighty.

Stopping in for iced-tea at Moos, we met up with Jennifer, a friend of Lorraine. Cheerfully grousing about shitty job prospects, time passed quickly. On the far side of the room, a jukebox parked against the wall. I had an idea. Knitting my way beyond elbows and legs, stopping in front of the machine, I scanned the play list until settling on a number that, in recent months, held special meaning for Jan and me. Dropping a quarter into the slot, leaning against the apparatus, I listened closely as the tender electric piano's introductory bars of "Daddy You're a Fool to Cry" filtered throughout the room. Crooning about his lover on the wrong side of town, Mick Jagger's faux southern twang sliced sharply through the racket. Shifting sideways in her chair, tears fringing dark eyelashes, Jan turned her face toward mine before lowering her head. Though it was not my intention to hurt her, I knew that I had.

I missed Gary too. Reading melancholy upon Jan's face however, it wasn't the same.

Picking up on the faraway look in Jan's eyes, Lorraine announced she planned to treat us to Bumpers, a casual eatery, easy on the pocket book.

A double salad bar set up, Bumpers served raw veggies, soups, breads, cheeses on one side, hot meats and cooked vegetables on the other. The cold section of the buffet was half the price of the hot food. At the end of the buffet on a display table, dessert squares and ice cream beckoned brave souls who'd survived the first course. Happily, we pigged out on soup and salad — it was Lorraine's coin after all. When all was said and done, Jan and I'd procured enough extra cheese and bread to carry us through our travels the next day. In a sense it was stealing, though not in the same way that sneaking food out of Woodworth's in the winter was. Then, we hadn't needed to shoplift. Now, it was about endurance and survival. Banff had cost more than we'd bargained. In case we couldn't find work heading east, it was imperative to preserve funds.

Returning to the annex, huddled together on the floor sipping beer and sharing a cigarette, Lorraine's roommate Wendy and her boyfriend competed at a game of Scrabble while a cut from *Abbey Road* played on the radio. Inducing me to stop in my tracks, the harmonious second track, "Because" sounded flawless as the first time I'd heard the song as a twelve-year-old kid. Following the words, "sky is blue…" in which the richness of Lennon, McCartney, and Harrison's blended vocals begin to elevate, somebody mentioned a diary. Soon, everybody compared notes.

Most teenage girls kept a log at one time or another wherein they could write testimonies, gush about boys, record arguments with friends and family, complain about parents and teachers. Air injustices. The Christmas before Jan and I came away, intuitively; May had given me my first diary. Inside the front cover, she'd written an inscription that included a quote from Kahlil Gibran's *The Prophet*, a favourite book of both of ours.

Discussion about keeping track impelled me to catch up before turning in that evening.

Since day one, it seemed a universal powerhouse had been at our sides, watching out for us, facilitating our senses. Through words, it seemed fitting to ascribe homage to the irrevocable prevailing beauty. On a given day, reflecting upon the pitch of the sky, the kaleidoscope rinse of the sea, silhouetted conifer needles fashioning shapes on the grass late in the afternoon, sights were mesmeric as the events associated with the milieu. Sifting through previous entries, I apologized for repetition of banal words such as "blue," "cool," even "God" more than necessary.

Cussing my inept vocabulary, I vowed to improve clichéd descriptions, and fine-tune tacky pencil sketches.

Next morning, after making a pit stop at the laundromat, Jan and I planned to leave for Jasper. Thankful we hadn't gotten busted for trespassing in the annex; it was good we'd kept our stay brief. Lorraine had to leave early for work. The night before, we'd said our goodbyes. Becoming better practiced at saying so long, my friend and I knew the only way to get through it was to pledge to meet again soon.

Even if it was a lie.

Sidelined by hunger pains, a carryover from overeating at Bumpers, our stomachs weren't used to it. To remedy the situation, we finished up the cheese and raisin bread lifted the night before that was supposed to hold us for the duration of the day. Temporarily sated, we tried our luck hitching to the laundromat and ended up walking the mile and a half. While Jan offered to stay with our jeans and underwear, I shopped for more bread, cheese, a new jar of peanut butter. Already 1 o'clock, we wanted to get moving. There was an A&W in the same plaza. Once everything was folded and rearranged inside our backpacks, we went inside and purchased two cans of pop.

Root beer in hands, we struck up a conversation with Clarke, a young man seated alone at a table. Jan informed Clarke that we were headed "25 miles north of Banff Springs Hotel" on route 93, to Mosquito Creek Hostel. Clarke had a set of wheels and offered to drive us out to the highway. According to the listing, the hostel was a wilderness locale located near the ice fields, providing small cabins for visitors, much like our stay in Yosemite National Park, but at a dirt-cheap rate.

Dropping us in the middle of nowhere along the TransCanada, Clarke continued along his way. Another vehicle pulled over. The driver, a woman, about 35, beckoned us inside.

With the exception of Sharon from Texas Lake and this one, the only other occasion in which a female offered a ride occurred when accompanied by another party. Cheerful and chatty, Pamela was on her way to Lake Louise where she worked part-time as a waitress.

From our drop-off at Lake Louise, Jan and I had a further layover. Blatantly ignoring our hopeful mugs, our noblest incarnation of youth and innocence, vehicles, all shapes and sizes bulleted past without so much as a look, reminding me of the indie races Steve and I'd watched on TV as kids. It was an ongoing puzzle. There seemed no rhyme or reason as to why some folks made the effort to stop while others wouldn't dare. Despite our immaturity and gender, perhaps Jan and I appeared spurious, a common day example of fool's gold.

Playing the waiting game, with some reticence, the conversation we usually tried to avoid — how much longer would remain of our trip, was revisited. It was now June 28. If we couldn't find work in Jasper, unless something catastrophic materialized, we would stick it out at least until the first week of August, and hitchhike east across country as far as we could make it.

A done deal, locking pinkie fingers, I smiled over at my friend. This meant that we could bide our time — more than one month.

Close to half past three, a vehicle finally stopped, taking us half the distance to Mosquito Creek. Able to thumb another ride in quick succession, along with our scant cargo, fifteen minutes before opening, we were delivered to Mosquito Creek Hostel, a relatively obscure location enshrouded within a thick-wooded area.

Happy to discover that a couple of females had turned up, Jan and I were whisked into the fold by Howard, an early-twenties Montreal native. Presenting himself as the hostel overseer, Howard introduced us to a couple of pleasant boys from Portland, Oregon. The more attractive one of the pair, Doug, a long-legged string bean beneath a mop of jet-black curly hair that hung loosely over coffee brown eyes, accompanied by a rusty Jack Nicholson voice, had a most appealing gait. In body type and facial features, Doug's best buddy, Randy, resembled John Belushi.

Showing us to our lodgings, a tiny log cabin in the woods outfitted with its own fireplace, Howard demonstrated (in case we were interested) how to build a proper fire (opposed to our unsuccessful attempts on the California coast using damp wood pieces, a lighter, and bits of toilet paper) to keep us warm throughout the chilly night. Always cooler in the mountains, the impromptu lesson would prove useful. Leaving us alone to unpack, Howard parted with an invitation to join him and the others for food, a couple of beers, and some hashish.

Closing the door behind Howard, making certain that he was a good twenty feet from our cabin, I let out a tiny shriek of joy. Scrunching her feet on the needle bed littering the path alongside our cabin, Jan barely suppressed squeals of her own. We were ecstatic for a couple of reasons.

Directly outside our window, extending the length of the cabin wall like a protracted serpent, a rushing creek twisted its way out of view. With limited accommodations at Mosquito Creek, designation to a little haven next to a flourishing stream was too good to be true. Located at the end of the stretch, our abode was one of the most private. This minor advantage and Howard's offer of beer and hashish were enough cause to celebrate.

Changing clothes, we navigated to the outhouse for a quick pee, and met the others in the main building. Open stubbies of warm beer waited on the kitchen table. Placing one into each of our hands, bending his elbow, Howard made a toast to "inner circles."

We all clinked.

Spreading fruit, bread, raisins, peanut butter, honey, ham slices, and cheese on the table, we laughed to discover that essentially, everybody transported similar repertoire. It was no surprise our staples were typical. Day–to-day hostellers travelled light — in our packs — especially in our wallets.

Immediately following dinner, grabbing the case of beer, Howard suggested we go for a hike.

Lagging a little at first, we eventually ventured into an alley that veered toward a straight path leading up a hill. Having grown up in the Portland area about ninety minutes from the Oregon coast and therefore accustomed to rugged beauty, travelling Western Canada, Doug and Randy were properly impressed. For a time, while Jan kept in step with Howard and Randy, Doug and I walked together, comparing notes about our hometowns and families. In general, other than with Jan, family wasn't discussed. Anything that went down prior to leaving home scarcely came up.

Doug had two older brothers, a sister, a handful of stepbrothers and stepsisters. His mom and dad divorced when he was young. Both parents remarried other people with children. Doug loved his stepparents and his stepsiblings. The two remade families got together to celebrate birthdays and other occasions. It was all very amicable. The step families even lived on the same street.

Comfortable in his own skin, Doug was grounded.

When it came my turn, I told Doug about my parents and two older brothers. No anecdotes or glamourized details about home, just basic facts. Explaining about feeling suffocated in my hometown, I told Doug how I'd felt the pull to escape, and figured out the right way to do it. Staring ahead at the path before us while I chattered away, Doug said nothing, only smiled. Then, following minutes of quiet, he admitted he'd never known a girl to say anything like I had. Most of the young females he'd known wanted marriage and babies. In the mid-late 1970s, with the second wave of feminism already more than ten years old, for many girls out of high school, the end game was to position themselves to meet Mr. Right or Mr. Wrong — whatever the case may be.

Flattered, no doubt, Doug's compliment registered on my face.

We continued to walk.

Sneaking subtle glances, I sized up Doug's wide steps, his wrinkled red and blue plaid shirt hanging loose below a lean waist, and black leather hiking boots worn at the toes. Sun faded or bleached, Doug's jeans were so light they were almost white. The more he talked, the more I craved his 'Jack Nicholson' speak.

Nearing the top of the hill, Howard promised the best "bird's eye view of the mountains for miles around," and brought with him just the right measure, a mix of hashish and tobacco to maximize the experience. Heightening expectations, he made us wait until reaching the crown to light up.

Assembled at the highest point of the trail, Howard rewarded us for our patience. One by one, folding our bodies cross-legged onto the grass, congregating in semi-circle, we breathed in the damp, early night air. As the hash was passed from person to person, another round of brown bottles cracked open. I set my focus on the snow dusting the range of mountains, on a diagonal alliance from our resting place. After a time, Howard stood and walked the few feet to a rivulet, filling his empty beer bottle with clear, ice-cold water. Sipping from the glass, a sign of approval crept across his sparsely bearded face and he encouraged each of us to try.

Doug was the first volunteer. Replicating Howard's actions, he filled his empty bottle to the top with the river water. As if he'd sampled the world's finest champagne, turning toward us, Doug pulled a campy Flip Wilson face.

We all started to laugh.

On our way back toward the cabins, Howard mentioned he had an eight-track machine in his Nova, and was well stocked in tapes.

No need to arm twist. Following out to a vehicle parked sideways behind the main cabin, from inside of his trunk, Howard produced another cluster of cold ones.

You had to hand it to him; Howard knew how to party in refined style.

Van Morrison's *Moondance* kicked off what turned out to be a two-hour concert set. Dylan, Yes, Zeppelin, and Tull all took turns at center stage. It was a highpoint in recent days.

Once the show was over, Jan, Doug, Randy, and I sat up in the main cabin's kitchen until two, drinking tea, matching stories about disastrous high school attempts to fit in. We conferred about music. A dyed-in-the-wool Dylan fan, Doug was keen to learn of my new fascination with Phil Ochs, leading to our comparing musical styles and lyrical approaches between the two artists. The mood and conversation perpetually shifting, more information was traded about our families, neighbourhoods, growing up. In a weak moment, I confessed to Doug his voice reminded me of Nicholson, adding, I had a thing for husky male voices.

Doug beamed.

In due course, he and Randy walked us back to our cabin. It was a given. There were mutual feelings between Doug and me. Possibly even a mushrooming romance in the works.

Inside our habitat, soggy kindling and newspaper sabotaged several attempts to generate heat. I rounded up Howard, still up and about. Employing his flashlight to locate smaller, drier branches beneath one of the pines, Howard stuck around until successfully, Jan encouraged the pieces to catch.

Grateful for his assistance, on his way out the cabin door, we thanked Howard for a great night and climbed into our sleeping bags.

There is more than one way to ignite a flame.

Alberta Rockies. COURTESY OF ANDREA NELSON

CHAPTER 53

Bending Light

"Come and be one of us. Descend and appease your hunger with our bread and quench your thirst with our wine."
KAHLIL GIBRAN, *The Prophet*

Jan and I greeted Doug and Randy at the central cabin for a bowl of cereal topped with leftover bananas, enabling another opportunity to chat before dispersing in opposite directions. The boys planned to spend one more night at Mosquito Creek. After that, they were off to conquer Hope.

Too bad they weren't heading east.

Because of our ages, partly because of common interests, in subtle ways, Doug and I'd discovered our teenage lives mirrored one another. We'd both grown up in middle class neighbourhoods, endured excruciating early teen years, shared common musical tastes, travel experiences, and goals. Essentially, Doug and Randy were male counterparts to Jan and me. Imagining what it might be like to beach in Doug's irrepressible aura, I was excited to consider future possibilities. The nicest part of all, Doug revealed his inside didn't match what he presented on the outside. He was terrified of becoming a grown up.

Two peas.

I'd never had a real boyfriend, and couldn't recall the last time any male looked at me the way that Doug had — mystified, maybe even admiringly. One of the best aspects about leaving high school behind was having the chance to make a new start, peel away uncomfortable worn-out skin. Knowing that Doug found me attractive felt weirdly special. Without presupposing too much, maybe he was a little awestruck that I represented a different idea from what he'd been previously exposed to in girls. Hard to conceal my happiness, I didn't want to jinx the potential for something more by expecting anything to come of our bond.

Nor get a big head.

When it came time to part ways, Doug stalled. It was very cute. Rummaging endlessly in his backpack for a bit of paper delayed the awkward exchange of mailing addresses, prolonging our last few minutes together. Once the duty was fulfilled, catching me unaware, slightly lowering his knees, Doug reached his arms around my waist and kissed me softly on the cheek. A flushed patch that had formed on my neck soon spread to my cheeks, and it dawned on me what the sweet display of affection meant. Doug's kiss was a promise. I could count on hearing from him after returning home. For a moment, I thought about suggesting to Jan that we stay on another night at Mosquito Creek but vetoed the idea. Staying would make things complicated, perhaps even embarrassing.

The easterly direction of Jasper National Park in our midst, Doug and I embraced once more, and then he and Randy walked us out to the highway. Like a pair of good-natured doting fathers, the boys hovered nearby while Jan and I waited to be taken away. A green Volkswagen van driven by two men heading to Peyto Lake dropped us at Bow Summit, the lookout-point along the Icefields Parkway. Climbing out of the van, it was time to push the refresh button.

Combing through brush overlooking the valley that shelters Peyto Lake, Jan and I fixed our eyes on the spectacular aquamarine water. My memory of the lake's serenity and quiet beauty was not faulty; large sections of the Columbia ice fields were still in plain view. Hauling my journal out from my backpack, I jotted down my reaction to our new setting.

"We're really up in the mountains now, in the middle of waterfall strands. Clean, good snow is all around. Peyto Lake is even prettier than Lake Louise. The water is pure, an *honest* greenish blue, no matter the weather. Even the creek is a crisp, luxuriant green, no mucky brown. It is *Beauts!!*

Next, we're on our way to Beauty Creek Youth Hostel. Hope we don't have to wait too long for a ride."

Espying the chalet not far from our locality, Jan suggested we help ourselves to a cup of tea and a biscuit, saving our bread, cheese, and crackers for later. An ardent tea lover, my friend couldn't resist checking out Peyto Lake's villa. I wasn't about to deprive her of life's simple pleasures.

Inside, a fellow traveller joined us at our table. Chatting up the Englishman and his German friend both from Halifax, Jan and I managed to scrounge our next ride.

For reasons unknown, Beauty Creek Youth Hostel was closed. I'd had a sneaking feeling that with a name like Beauty Creek, it'd be too good to be true if it had been open for business. Piling back into the Englishman's green Peugeot, the four of us drove on until finally landing at Athabasca Falls.

The hostel was open for business.

Contained within Jasper National Park not far from Athabasca Falls, Athabasca Falls Youth Hostel was primitive as one could get. There were no indoor toilets or shower facilities. Running water was accessible at the well or stream on site. For a thorough, refreshing cleanse, hostellers were encouraged to make a day trip to the Miette Hot Springs. At a nominal fee, dorm style cabins contained several sets of bunk beds. A community cabin was available for all co-ed guests.

House parents, Jeff and Georgina, sent us to room with a couple of high school girls from Edmonton. Three of the boys from a neighbouring group home were staying in the males' dorm. How or why the boys happened to be there didn't matter. Tossing our bags into our cabin, we quickly split to assess our location.

Eager to wash her hair, Jan had brought along a towel and small bottle of shampoo. Wandering around the thicketed area, we came upon a stream. Sampling the water before making a commitment, Jan dipped a plastic cup into the streambed and took a small sip. Head angled back, my friend's favourable eyes told me all I needed to know.

I followed suit.

Rich with minerals, the sparkling wet cold tasted good, regenerating. Kneeling on the rocks, Jan dunked her head into the water several times before applying shampoo. Sprawled out on the flat, sun burnt ground, rolling up my flannel shirtsleeves, I accrued the white-hot heat on my skin and was reminded how idle, sunlit days give way to a sense of entitlement, to kick back and do nothing. Jan and I'd become specialists in that department, though one could make the case that our free-style caravanning ways were completely productive. Here, we were getting an education. The kind you wouldn't find inside a Cracker Jack's box.

Jan's wet hair combed through, we climbed the rocky embankment toward Athabasca Falls to convene with the thundering muscle of the waterfall's potency — three independent dominant forces driving downward, conjoining as one at the bottom of the cliff.

Unreal.

Back inside our cabin, I completed *The Golden Force*. Rereading the final words, "Peace Cometh, as Peace Is" on the book's closing page, I began another entry in my journal. Focusing on the supernatural exploits of the book, I noted, "Tonight, I finished reading HOOM's bible. Some things are clearer to me. Other things are more confusing. According to the book, God chose Jesus to show people how to know God *inside*. By performing miracles and feats, Jesus demonstrated how each one of us has ability to realize anything we *see*, or *expect* to do. The experience I had with Brother Bruce at Steiner Street proves this could be true. My physical body felt small. God seemed so *big*.

What worries me about having a relationship with God is that humans are counted on to sacrifice personal liberties and objects in exchange for peace and freedom from superficiality. Teddy confirmed this when I asked him about giving up possessions. I don't have much in the way of material items. I'm still not sure if I'm ready to give away the few belongings I have. I'll need to think about this some more."

In a separate entry, I wrote, "I love Alberta. It's easy to understand how people find peace in the mountains and forest. I wish I could steal this happy feeling of harmony somehow. Bring it home with me. Let enlightenment erase old patterns."

Carefully, I read over my first entry, frowning at my barefaced gullibility. Did any of it hold water? A person's mind can convince the heart to believe whatever it wants to believe, whether the desired path is mired in light or dark.

Why did I continue to dwell?

As a young person with zero detrimental life challenges, there were no excuses for a lack of inner peace. Yet, more often than I cared to admit, I felt better acquainted with the threatening regions of my brain, the matter that can sabotage a healthy attitude with a self-directed poison thought. I didn't make it a practice seeking negativity, yet it was always there, hovering like a stale fart. Bathing in luminosity in recent months seemed healing, like invisible armor.

Returning to my journal, I added a few lines to the entry.

"I want to feel safe. Now, I think I'd like a small bible. I can't afford it right now though."

Light holds capacity to dispel ugly thoughts.

At breakfast, Jan and I were served black tea, and assigned kitchen tasks to help pay for our keep. Technically, Athabasca Falls Youth Hostel was not a hostel; but a transient home for troubled teens. Like Evangel Home (excluding amenities and religious practice), aside from two other guests, Marilyn and her young son Keith, Jan and I were the oldest people there.

Late that morning, we prepared to leave for another hostel outside of Jasper, a half hour down highway 93. Marilyn drove us to the Jasper train station where we stored our packs inside two lockers, freeing us to browse the area without carrying freight.

Jan cashed a $20 traveller's cheque. Managing to find an inexpensive breakfast nook in town, we split on a candle for Liz and a hand-blown glass bird for Jen, totalling $5. It hurt, but we were determined to bring souvenirs to friends back home. Old Fort Point, a two-and-a-half-mile mountain hike suggested by one of the locals, appealed to us. With our next destination being a short distance, there were hours to spare before the Jasper hostel opened its doors.

Scaling the top of Old Fort Point was no small potatoes. Because many of the gradients were steep, to undergo the delicate climb beginning on rickety wooden steps at the foundation of the precipice, trekkers had to be in good physical condition. At this stage, Jan and I were old hats at the mountain climbing game and should have (seriously) considered applying for jobs as guides.

Arriving at the highest point, resting at the lookout area, we took in more panoramic sights. Preparing to descend the pitch, I became conscious of somebody shuffling his feet on the grass. Standing alone at the lookout, a young man glanced across the water toward the other side. I remembered him from my childhood. His name was Darcy. Along with my brother Steve, Darcy, and his brother Clive had been in my swim class.

Addressing him by name, I approached. Startled to hear somebody call out to him on a mountain peak at Jasper National Park, Darcy turned, looked directly at me and tried to place my face. "It's Jill," I said, helping his recall. "We took swim lessons together when we were kids." Raising his eyebrows, embarrassed, Darcy replied with formality. "Oh, yes. Hello."

I could it in read his eyes, Darcy barely remembered me if at all. If I hadn't said anything, he would have passed us by. As kids, Darcy had been branded with the stigma, "learning disability." Believed to be slow (according to 1960's educational standards used to measure a child's intelligence), nothing was further from the truth. As far as I could tell, the only factor segregating Darcy from peers was his inability to function in social situations. Unlike many of us, Darcy didn't know how to conceal feelings of timidity and uncertainty using a false front. One could hardly fault him for that.

Darcy and his younger brother Clive were tight as two siblings could be. As children, Clive shadowed Darcy, keeping bullies at bay. Kids, the assholes they often are, were relentless taunting Darcy. The same ages as Steve and me, the two brothers attended classes reserved for the gifted. Intently focused on topics of interest such as history and math, Darcy mastered the subjects with certifiable knowledge. Comparable to a savant, the boy had a brilliant memory for facts.

Working in Jasper for the summer, Darcy liked Alberta a lot. Still living in Burlington, Clive had recently graduated high school. The brothers planned to enter the same university in the fall.

Darcy's report made me happy. Smiling, I told him it was nice to see him in the park.

Jan and I began our descent.

Back on lower turf, returning to town, we stumbled upon Peter and Kyle, another pair of high school acquaintances. Suddenly, we were long lost buddies. Bumping into these two back home, we'd likely have given them the bum rush. There certainly wouldn't be any kind of acknowledgement, from their side or ours. Neutral ground changes the game. It frees you.

Returning to the train station to retrieve our packs and set out for the highway, in no time, a red Honda caught up. Peter was behind the wheel, Kyle in the passenger seat. Jan climbed in next to the packs in the back. I sat up front on Kyle's lap. It was a tight squeeze but worth the inconvenience for the short trip.

A converted ski lodge set in Jasper National Park wrapped in bold blue sky, the big old spread that had been converted to a hostel needed a lot of work but otherwise was quaint and cozy. Augmented by a stone hearth in the middle of the living room, the cedar panelled abode hosted high ceilings, creating the illusion of greater space. Once again, sleeping quarters were dorm style. At $2 for one night's stay, we were on easy street.

An hour after our arrival, others started to accumulate. Including a nurse, a mail sorter, and schoolteacher, there were five women in our dorm. The only other male to join us that evening in addition to Peter and Kyle was 19-year-old "Long Island Ron" from Levittown, New York. As engaging as he was handsome, sandy-eyed Ron preferred to travel alone, and had done a fair amount of it, covering a good portion of the Eastern and Western United States. His first trip to Canada, Ron was completely enamoured by our country and our people.

Peter, Jan, Ron, and I took a walk over to the store to pick up food supplies. Out of reach of Kyle's listening range, Peter complained that so far, their trip had been a bust. Discovering they had less in common than presumed at the outset, the two hometown friends nagged at one another and argued. While Peter appreciated sightseeing and exploring, Kyle's mandate, to non-stop party, left Peter to protest, "If I wanted to get wrecked, I'd have stayed in Ontario."

Listening to Peter chew on, the notion of facing the music gnawed in my gut. Reluctant to reoccupy the rut I'd found myself in prior to leaving for Vancouver — going to the Coronation on the weekend, getting wasted — no longer held appeal. In some ways, my mom was right. I had matured. Shifting focus to things that mattered was evidence of that. I only had to clarify what those things were.

In the evening, whittling away hours, Jan, Ron, Peter, Kyle and I sipped tea by the lit hearth. Reminiscing about his buddies and nights of debauchery back home, eliciting laughs, Kyle was on a roll. Employing a different slant than Kyle's depraved accounts; Peter's interpretations of their antics were even more humorous.

Managing to steer conversation to more relevant topics, Ron took a turn in the limelight. During a visit to Boston in autumn one year before, he was convinced that "New England *is the* prettiest place on earth during fall," and had plans to return to Boston in September. Sensing two suckers for adventure and a sweet-talking guy, smiling gregariously, Long Island Ron suggested that Jan and I might want to consider meeting up.

Looking over at one another, the same thought crossed both our minds.

It *was* possible.

Anything was possible.

The sky remained light until late evening, longer than it had in Banff. Close to eleven, unfalteringly, the sun bowed out. In less than five hours, the fiery ball would levitate. Most of the night, it rained like hell. Periodic flashes of lighting and thunderbolts pelted the ground. The windows of our room rattled so loudly I worried about shattering glass. Come morning, we were surprised to discover the building unscathed and no damage done to the outside property.

With the storm came cooler air inviting rain to linger. Fog camouflaged the mountains. It was Canada Day, July 1, our country's 109th birthday. Feeling as if she had a touch of the flu, Jan remained in bed longer than was customary. Around mid-morning, along with Ron, we thumbed a ride to town. Ron checked his backpack into the CN station, and the three of us gathered to watch a drum band follow a parade of Canadian war veterans as they marched through Jasper Park. The solidarity of their dramatic movement reminded me of the annual Remembrance Day Parade, November 11, in my hometown.

Inside Smitty's Pancake House, steering clear of rain and hollow conversation, over limitless cups of coffee, Jan, Ron, and I became better acquainted.

Conspiring people who might not otherwise associate, some of the closest relationships are established through a mutual interest in music. Centering on provocative writers, Ron preferred contemporary artists with a knack for composing absorbing melodies and lyrics. A musician himself and ardent disciple of Dylan, Leonard Cohen, John Fogerty, Carol King, and Neil Young, Ron was additionally attuned to clean harmonies exemplified by the ilk of Simon and Garfunkel, CSNY, and Peter, Paul and Mary. Regarding the subject of school and status of our lives, for the three of us, travel was *it* right now. There was nothing else.

Outside the restaurant, Jan noticed our friend Howard from Mosquito Creek chatting with a woman. We called over. Joining our group, the four of us headed into a grocery store for dinner ingredients.

Though not much of a cook and seldom did we prepare a hot meal anyway, I was, however, capable of pulling off a feed of "blood sauce and maggots," as Jan and I referred to white rice smothered in tomato sauce. Her stomach still unsettled, my friend doubted she'd have much of an appetite for dinner.

Holding onto a paper bag full of foodstuffs, we found a place outside of the Information Centre and listened attentively to a group of Scottish bagpipers. Cylinders, moaning soft, languid, and low engendered a sweeping layer of resonance, tranquilly carrying through the atmosphere until finally dying out.

The music was sadly beautiful.

Leaving Howard and the bagpipers behind, Jan, Ron, and I returned to the hostel on foot. While Jan headed straight for bed, Ron and I went to work, combining our imperfect skills and basic ingredients to create a tomato-laden rice dish and side of mashed potatoes.

Following dinner, we investigated our surroundings.

From the get go, I liked and trusted Ron. Not in the way that I was attracted to Doug, or even Teddy for that matter. Ron offered something subjective and distinct. His passion for travel infectious, appearing well beyond his years intellectually and emotionally, Ron was quick-witted and sensitive. He wasn't afraid to be alone. Secure and self-regulating, Long Island Ron appropriated himself in a manner I envied.

Fortified by the mood induced by grey light drizzle, I came clean about HOOM. To my surprise, Ron got the picture. He knew exactly where I was coming from.

One year earlier, Ron had joined a new wave religious group in New York City. After weeks of compliance to prayer, organic cleanses, and body dancing, he didn't hesitate to "get out quick." Abstaining from telling me what he thought I should do when I imparted my impasse, Ron had simply reciprocated his own experiences. Cult life wasn't for him. I got the impression that Ron couldn't imagine anybody making that kind of lifelong choice.

Returning to the hostel, cloud cover began to evaporate and the rain stopped, revealing a rainbow band of colours.

The first time the skies had been clear all day, the striped arch was a gift.

A lustrous jewel.

Sketch of Maligne Lake, Alberta. June 1976.

CHAPTER 54
Moon Shadows

"When I let go of what I am, I become what I might be."
LAO TZU

I had another golf ball episode. Nearly as intense as the energy surge in the front room of HOOM with Brother Bruce, I'd started labelling these incidents *goof ball* episodes. This time I wasn't afraid. Mostly, it felt like surreal cognizance — a back and forth game of mind over matter — as if the white balls and I were chess partners.

Delineating the experience was to later draw comparison to Findhorn, a small village in Moray, Scotland that recognizes an invisible world of faeries, spirits, little people, and elves as commonplace proliferations. In the book *The Magic of Findhorn* (which Jan once sent me for my birthday), the Findhorn spiritual community edifies that when the mind is quiet and open, one can visualize the unseen spirit world as if observing one hand in front of your face. Like an incorporeal barrier opening up, the goof ball revelries entitled me to temporarily sense every disguised nuance of consciousness.

Clean. Bright. New.

In the morning, following one of these incidents, watching people move casually about caused me to distrust the existence of the golf balls, whether they had even appeared.

I still didn't know what it meant, if anything at all.

The following day, Jan felt better. We prepared to move on to Maligne Lake Youth Hostel (also Long Island Ron's next layover) within Jasper National Park. Ron had decided to hike at nearby Fort Point. Packing our gear, the three of us retraced the three-mile trek down the hill and out to the highway. The rain returning, in a matter of minutes, we were saturated. One of the park's maintenance trucks stopped to give us a lift, dropping Ron at Fort Point, Jan and me at Maligne Lake. Permitted to leave our packs, it was too early to loiter. Finding a small teahouse not far away, we stopped in for a cup, and then scoured our way round the chasm.

A popular spot for kayaking, canoeing, and fishing, Maligne Lake features the prominent Leah and Samson Mountain peaks. In summer months, bears, caribou, wolves, and moose are known to roam freely around the lake. Deriving its French name from the term "malignant," by an early French settler who regarded the fast-flowing river treacherous and turbulent, the bewitching blue-green body of water is probably one of the most photographed and artistically reproduced of all Canada's lakes.

That morning, Maligne Lake was cold but quietly appealing. Though indeed breathtaking, I did not consider the body of water captivating as what photographs depicted. Because of its exquisite canopy of turquoise green, for me, Peyto Lake outshone the rest.

By noon, we'd logged almost 5 miles on foot. Long ago, I'd forgotten about my sore right heel. It had remedied itself somehow, not without leaving a permanent egg below the back of my ankle. My boot tighter than normal, at least the lump no longer caused pain.

My parents' anniversary now past, I hadn't yet mailed a card. Deciding instead to send a personal memento, in rough pencil sketch, I replicated Maligne Lake best I could. Sealing the picture in an envelope, I would send it home next chance I got.

Talking about Doug and his friend Randy, if the two had made it to Hope, Jan and I expected they were enjoying it as much as we had. Since leaving Mosquito Creek, I toyed with the reality of what might happen if Doug and I were to see one another again. Now that he had some time to reflect, it was altogether possible that Doug no longer wanted to communicate, much less care to see me.

This was another of those compulsive, deprecating thoughts. I had no reason or right to question or expect anything, but anticipated that Doug would follow through in contacting me within a few weeks as promised.

Although the subject had been relegated to the dominion of the great unspoken, I was positive that Jan still liked Gary. Whether we'd run into Gary again was anybody's guess. At Jericho Beach, I would have said no.

Martha and Matthew, a couple we'd met the previous evening, picked us up and drove us back to Maligne Lake Hostel where they were also staying the night. The pair was spending the summer driving across Canada in Matthew's truck. Along route, Matthew pointed out leafy-coloured

Medicine Lake, one of two vanishing lakes in the area that disappears completely in winter. Enjoying the drive, I wondered how different our trip might have been had Jan or I had owned a vehicle.

At the hostel, Ron was joined by 26-year-old New Yorker, Ted Tsamisis. Ted had brought along a guitar and collection of eight-track tape cassettes. Much the same set up as Mosquito Creek, small cabins peppered alongside the creek bed. A few hours in, next to a makeshift fire pit near the cabins, a group of us gathered on tree stumps anticipating the evening's entertainment. Borrowing Ted's instrument, Ron began to play several renditions by Cat Stevens, Neil Young, and The Beatles. Then he performed a superb interpretation of "I Shall Be Released," one of the Good Samaritan's favourites.

Somewhere along the line, I was told I had inherited my mother's ear for harmony. Of the three of us, Brother Steve acquired my father's musical aptitude, playing keyboards, trumpet, and drums like a virtuoso. As kids, we used to enjoy singing harmony together. Joining Ron for "The Wind" and "Moonshadow," two Cat Stevens songs, was great fun.

Next morning, July 4, Jan and I would be on the move again, leaving the quietude of Jasper National Park for Edmonton, Alberta. Planning to ditch Maligne Lake Hostel for Banff, Ron anticipated reuniting with his "lady," a girl he'd met travelling Canada's West Coast. The first we'd heard of any kind of romantic liaison, it made perfect sense. If there was such a thing as a good catch, Ron was indeed a heartbreaker. Grateful to have shared in ephemeral moments, I would surely miss Long Island Ron.

Ted offered us a drive out to Highway 16. While Jan and I packed our belongings into Ted's Firebird, making his own way to the road, with a reminder about a promising autumn reunion in Boston, Ron hugged each of us goodbye.

After Ted dropped us off, an RCMP vehicle came into view. Easing to a stop, the cop parked his cruiser on the shoulder of the road. Emerging from the car somber as hell, the officer asked us to produce I.D. Reaching into bags, Jan and I handed our identification over to the cop. Analyzing our two birth certificates, other than informing us that hitchhiking is illegal "not to mention unsafe for two young ladies," the officer said nothing more. Trading stunned looks with Jan, I managed to mutter, "Thank you, officer."

Returning our credentials, the cop issued one more warning, climbed into his cruiser, and left the scene in a cloud of exhaust dust. His vehicle safely out of view, reestablishing our marks on the shoulder of the highway,

Jan and I raised our right thumbs. In two rides, we journeyed 250 miles to Edmonton, Alberta — a five-and-a-half-hour trip. Seated in the back of a pick-up manned by a couple of homeboys taking us two thirds of the way, the first leg of the trip was a breeze. In the company of three punks driving a Chrysler New Yorker, the second was less than stellar. This was the first occasion riding with strangers in which anything of a sexual nature was seriously suggested.

Hoping we'd be game to pull over into a rest area for a quick "fuck" or "hand-job at the very least," the teenagers were nonplussed when Jan and I flatly refused. Legs firmly closed, arms crossed protectively in front of our chests, seated in the rear of the New Yorker anxiously anticipating our arrival in Edmonton, I realized the back of my shirt was soaked through — from fear. When it became clear they weren't going to score without resistance, the boys soon lost interest and ignored us. In their eyes, we'd obviously failed some stupid contrived test. Sure, we could have insisted they let us out, bide our time, wait for another ride to came along. For whatever reason, asking for a free pass didn't seem realistic. In retrospect, things could have been worse. Probably we'd have survived to tell the tale, but the crest of freewheeling good fortune to which we'd grown accustomed would come to a screeching halt. During those last weeks of our trip, it sometimes felt as if we were teetering. If life is about balance, after a string of luck, debt is inevitable.

We were driven straight to the Convention Inn downtown Edmonton and let out.

No more mischief. No questions asked. Conversation nil.

Spotting a mailbox outside of the Inn, reaching into my pack, I retrieved the envelope containing the drawing of Maligne Lake and slipped it into the metal slot.

Figuring youth hostels were plentiful in Edmonton (Canada's sixth largest metropolitan area situated on the Saskatchewan River), for once, neither Jan nor I had bothered to route our stay in advance. Unwisely, we misjudged. A couple of hostels ago, somebody mentioned there was accommodation for youths near the Convention Inn. Making few inquiries, apparently, we'd been led astray. Over a couple of steaming black javas at the Inn's café, Jan and I thrashed around what to do next. A young couple sitting in a booth directly behind ours happened to pick up on our conversation.

Allan and Ellen shared a house with two other people in the northwest part of Edmonton.

After some discussion, the pair invited us to come stay at their home "at least for one night" until we could figure out an alternative deal. "The couch and floor are for the taking," Ellen had said. According to the two, the relationship between the four friends was platonic, strictly a working and living arrangement. Insisting that we participate in a BBQ with them that very day, Allan courteously offered use of their shower.

Not having had a decent shower since leaving Jericho Beach, this was the ultimate in generosity. Negating the near catastrophe with the wannabe rapists, apparently, our angel had returned and was camped out at the Convention Inn.

Loading our kit into a light green, two-door Maverick sedan parked in the Inn's lot, making light conversation along route, Allan and Ellen proceeded to transport us to their homestead. A few years our senior, hailing from Nova Scotia and Waterloo, Ontario, Allan and Ellen had travelled to the West seeking employment, logic being that wages in Alberta were greater than Ontario.

With her long blonde wavy hair, lively personality and buxom figure, easily fitting the description of barmaid stereotype of the decade, Ellen served drinks at a local pub. Allan had found a retail job at a clothing outlet for men. Fair-haired and self-effacing, he hardly resembled the persona of a sharp-dressed man modelling hip ensemble to young business execs. In truth, Allan tolerated his work, nothing more. Despite his quiet, self-disparaging nature, Jan and I would soon discover that among other peculiarities, Allan had a proclivity to blurt things out that were unintentionally funny.

Exiting into a generic suburban neighbourhood in the north-east part of the city, Allan pulled the Maverick into the driveway of an aluminum-sided, story and a half house located at 145th Street.

Nothing fancy.

Taking stock of Allan and Ellen, I speculated some kind of setup. Reigning in those niggling dark thoughts, I remembered they were taking a chance on us too.

Entering the front hallway of the bungalow, we were directed into a large kitchen. Peter, Allan and Ellen's roommate from Kitchener, barely gave us a look before welcoming Jan and me into the fold. We were pleasantly amazed. Lightly tanned, hosting dark, concentrated eyes that hinted at an Italian heritage, Peter was pre-occupied ravaging cupboards in search of hamburger ingredients. Observing the interaction between the three, it became transparent: Peter was Father, Ellen: Mother, Allan:

Son. Now that two foster siblings had joined the little family, extra food was required.

In a couple of hours, the housemates planned to go out drinking at the Mayfield Inn downtown, and wanted to pre-coat their stomachs with a protein diet. Not wanting to come off as mooches, Jan and I offered to walk to the store to pick up buns and eggs. It was the least we could do.

Crossing arms above a puffed-out chest, Peter's eyes shone with pride. Daddy was pleased.

During our mini-shopping outing, Jan and I ventured into a couple of bookstores. In recent weeks, after wrapping up *The Golden Force*, I'd had it in my mind to read the New Testament, something I'd never done. Only if a Bible happened my way, I wasn't about to hand over a fraction of what was left of my cash. Less than $100 remaining between us, Jan and I'd acceded to begin job hunting in Edmonton early Monday morning.

The first store we entered didn't have one. About to credit some sort of divination or mischievous sprite, we entered a second bookstore. Halfway serious, I asked the clerk if they carried a New Testament. The woman reached a hand beneath the counter. "Here." Plopping the red, leather-bound book next to the cash register, she said, "I was waiting for somebody to come along so I could give it away."

Thanking the clerk, we were quickly out the door.

Peter's beefy burgers (Jan finished everything but the meat) left little room for the super sweet, homemade, peanut butter cookies Ellen had baked for dessert. Adhering to our never turn away food motto, dutifully, Jan and I ate the cookies.

Anxious to get a head start on their evening, Peter and Ellen (we hadn't yet met the forth roommate) got ready quickly, informing Allan (who appeared mildly discontented) they'd see him later. Once Peter and Ellen were gone, Jan and I made our way to the living room where Allan had plunked himself in a paisley upholstered chair, holding onto a half-smoked cigarette.

Approaching tentatively, I asked Allan if he'd be affronted if I put *Pleasures of the Harbor* on the turntable. The mention of Phil Ochs and the album in my possession, Allan's face lit up. Encouraged, I boasted how I'd carried the record in my knapsack faithfully for several weeks without breakage. Truly astonished, Allan countered that his favourite Ochs' songs were "Flower Lady" and "I've Had Her."

Introductory chords to "Flower Lady" satiated the confines of the living room. Apparently roused by the music's mercurial quality, Allan produced a dime-sized bag of weed from his pants pocket, asking, "Do you girls smoke?"

Rolling up a couple of spliffs, Allan acknowledged he smoked a lot of pot and liked to stay high for most of the day, particularly during work. With Allan concentrated on his task, seizing the opportunity, I began to blather about Oregon Doug, Long Island Ron, and the Good Samaritan. Tuning out my drivel, Jan intriguingly studied Allan's handiwork.

Under the marijuana's sway, I couldn't help being overwhelmed by the album's elaborate musical arrangements, Ochs's caustic intellect, vociferous wit, his use of satire, and sorrowful observations. Equally overtaken by its beauty and melancholy, when the album finished playing, solemnly, faultlessly, as if it was the most natural thing in the world, Allan rose from his chair and rotated the LP to the 'A' side. Placing the needle on the outer groove of the record, remarkably, the music had supercharged our new friend's cheerless mood. Unsure whether to feel happy or sad, through our actions, unwittingly, Jan and I had impacted Allan's sour morale.

Sparking up another joint, Allan described how much he hated his job and despised his life in general. Disclosing that his fondness for Ellen extended beyond casual friend, Allan's gut told him the feeling wasn't mutual.

I wondered how often Allan's gut was accurate.

While he talked about how much his life sucked, at the risk of angering him, I smiled at Allan's distinctive choice of expletives used to emphasize his current state of mind. Soon, it was all Jan and I could do to prevent from rolling on the floor in hysterics. Unfazed by our reaction to his tales of woe, strangely, the laughter seemed to energize Allan. Somewhere in the calamity, getting back to Ochs, Allan admitted he could empathize with Phil's depression, to the point of suicide. Though said in passing rather than with gravity, the sobering statement quickly mitigated our juvenile bemusement.

By the time the record completed playing through a second time; three joints had been polished off — more than enough. At the very least, one tends to be absurdly over-analytical when high. Some people refer to it as clarity. At the very most, everything is suddenly, outrageously comical — even when it's not. Turning inward, others play the 'I'm a loser' game as Allan had done.

The weed was beginning to fry our brains. It was time for change of scenery and conversation.

A couple of drinks would do nicely.

Piloting the steering wheel of his Maverick minutes later, Allan directed the vehicle in hot pursuit of the Mayfield Inn, the bar where Ellen and Peter had gone to meet friends.

Setting foot inside the old hotel, the place stunk like stale beer and urine. Dim lighting barely concealed elasticized terry tablecloths, stained and stretched around round wood tables. Across the room, major spillage pooled the floor next to a where a tray of full beer bottles had crashed. Piss drunk patrons, obviously responsible, probably had done it for kicks. Indifferent to the chaos, a middle-aged waiter mopped up the mess. To my left, the culprits laughed their asses off.

This was a nightly routine, no doubt.

Not more than ten feet away, cloistered amongst three males, sat Ellen. Rounding out the group was Peter. Our presence acknowledged, enthusiastically, we were waved over. Slightly drunken, Ellen had her hands full making time with John, one of the men whom purportedly, she'd recently met. Beards in their beer, on the other side of the pair, John's two buddies flashed goofy grins.

Encouraged by Peter (the only sober one) to help ourselves to the tray of draught resting on the small table, Allan scooped up three 16 oz glasses. Passing a couple to Jan and me, he began swigging the third one down. In less than three minutes, pausing to take an occasional breath, Allan drained 32 ounces of liquid. Commanding the attention of everybody around the table, I guessed that Allan's act was wasted on Ellen.

Characteristically, women aren't impressed witnessing (or listening to war stories about) undue alcohol consumption by men — only Allan wasn't out to astound. He merely wanted to get wasted. I was amazed by Allan however, who appeared to be as straight as Peter. Combining the beer and the mountain of dope he'd smoked at home, evidently, managing vices presented few challenges for Allan.

Someone mentioned something about a bash at a friend's house not far from Mayfield Inn. This was an open party, meaning that everybody was welcome.

As our table prepared to abscond, Jan and I finished our drinks. Looking up from the bottom of my empty glass, I saw Allan stalling at the exit door in bodyguard posture. A tiny inferno burned in his eyes.

Mountain goat, Alberta. COURTESY OF ANDREA NELSON.

CHAPTER 55

Excellent Adventures

"The trouble is, you think you have time."
BUDDHA

"Wheels of Fortune," the bouncy cut from The Doobie Brothers' recently released LP, *Takin' it to the Streets*, thumped loose gravel on the dead-end street. Amid ultra-soft air, fisting cold bottles and clenching skinny joints between teeth, teens and young twenties dribbled on to the front lawn.

The party was full throttle.

Simulating a manner unaffected by the heavy scent of grass and nonsensical gut-splitting laughter, expecting to find Ellen and Peter around, Allan, Jan, and I filed unceremoniously into the house. On a sofa in the living room, sweet talking a girl, sat Peter. Markedly absent was Ellen. I guessed that she and John must have sequestered themselves in one of the bedrooms.

Beckoning us over, Peter began telling the girl how his friends had happened to meet Jan and me that "very afternoon," inviting us to stay at their house, no questions asked. Through exaggerated dewy puddles, the young woman marvelled at Peter's pronouncement. Undoubtedly, she would have reacted the exact same way had Peter told her he was a child molester — the girl was into him. Good-looking in a Tony Danza kind of way, and decent, I doubted that Peter needed to rely on the deeds of his housemates as leverage to seduce anybody.

Either way, he had it working.

Interrupting the mood, Allan asked Peter if Ellen was around. Absorbed by his own good fortune, Peter turned his hands over, revealing two empty palms.

Leaving Peter and his conquest to fawn over one another, we helped ourselves to free beer from a couple of well-stocked coolers in the kitchen.

Remembering earlier to pick up a case of Labatt's, Allan unloaded it next to the fridge alongside a couple of 24s. Judging by the posh décor, family heirlooms, and antiquated artifacts throughout, the bungalow was owned by somebody's parents, out for the evening, or away for the weekend. On the brink of disaster, the place would require a full day's clean up and replacement of a couple of damaged items, particularly if the kid hadn't mentioned the party to his or her parents.

This was pretty much a given.

Forcing small talk with the odd girl and guy, Jan, Allan, and I hovered for a while in the kitchen clutching our bottles, watching people come and go while The Doobie Brothers played on a repeating loop. This was a relatively malicious crowd, that threw "fuck you" and other insults at one another like they were getting paid — something close friends back home did not endorse unless there was just cause — leaving me puzzled as to whether the abuse was put on or genuine. For all intents and purposes, I believed these people liked one another.

Irritated by the affronts, Allan set off to tour the house. Passing by other half-baked teenagers, Jan and I followed him down the stairs, into the family room, out to the yard, and back inside. Halting near the landing, Allan deduced that Ellen was not at the house. Assuming she probably wouldn't show up at all, he began to question if the invite was a scam so that Ellen could screw John at an undisclosed location in private.

The con game didn't please him.

Allan's let down turned to concern, worry, and then anger. He ran an alternative edition of the party ploy by us. Believing it wasn't right that somebody would take advantage of Ellen by promising a party and then lure her elsewhere, Allan speculated where he might find Ellen, and fantasized the many ways he'd kick John's ass once he did. No consideration was given to the probability that Ellen had *chosen* to get laid. None whatsoever.

Searching one another's faces for a practicable means of running interference, Jan proposed we head back upstairs where Peter was sighted earlier with his female friend. Regulating his temperament, Allan relented.

In our absence, a rowdy bunch had congregated in the front room, practically smothering Peter and his adoring friend. People became increasingly wound up. Joints passed back and forth like the proverbial wave at a baseball game. Testosterone-fueled war cries echoed off the panelled walls. If the interminable cycle of *Takin' it to the Streets* cranked at deafening volume was intended to underscore a point, it would soon become obvious where this was going.

Following a loud yelp, the room suddenly became eerily quiet. A spontaneous game called *Battle of the Bands* was put forth: The Doobie Brothers versus The Beatles. "*Who* is the better group?" invited Martin, lead alpha male, and probable son of homeowners.

Barely a close contest in *my* mind, inexplicably, the Doobies won by a landslide. Allan, Jan, me, Peter, Peter's girlfriend, and a handful of others were the lone holdouts for the good guys.

Now, I liked The Doobie Brothers and held no ill will toward the band. Nevertheless, in what universe would any *logical* thinking person favour The Doobies over the lovable lads from Liverpool? Leaning against the lip of a fat, tan couch, I listened amazed as the fraternity ranted on about the merits of their idols, relegating The Beatles to little more than a garage band that happened to get lucky. Thinking about adding my two cents, I wasn't quick enough.

Inciting his opponents to bring it on, Allan gleefully took flight. Making an airtight case for *our* side, calmly, he cited taut polished musicianship, complex melodies, carefully crafted lyrics, and defined, layered harmonies.

Allan's evaluation was a succinct and accurate endorsement of the Mop Tops, now to move in for the slam-dunk.

Half-smoked joint nestled between his fingers, eyes narrowed for effect, Allan coolly concluded, "By comparison, The Doobies are dog shit."

As if he'd been right hooked in the nose, visibly recoiling at Allan's indolent demission of his boys, fists pumping wildly in the air, Martin went batty. Buddies backing him all the way, the kid began screaming, "Who in the fuck *are* you? You don't know *shit!*"

Basking in all the fun, squeezing his thumb and forefinger together, with one hand, Allan toked from his smoke, and with the other, drew from his Labatt's.

I was seething. I was drunk. Knowing all too well my adorning love and admiration for The Beatles, glancing nervously in my direction, Jan read me accurately. I wasn't about to let this brainless match continue without an opportunity to have a word — at the very least, to support Allan. Like a nervous kindergarten kid desperately clutching her privates, I waited for a lull. Then, raising one hand, clearing my throat, I opened my mouth to speak. "The Beatles are the best goddamn group in the history of the world. *No* one else has ever come close, nor *will* any group ever come close to their genius in the pop and rock world. Not even The Doobie Brothers, talented as they might be as a band."

To seal the deal, I added. "The Beatles can write and play anything. They are fucking *it*. Period."

My comments were answered with a fusion of anger, ridicule, and protests that finally culminated in "No fuckin' way, *bitch!* That's a crock of bullshit!"

Apparently, I hadn't been convincing enough. While the lead boy dreamed up a refutation that would beat my uppercut, I pondered how out of character it was for me to use "fucking," a surplus word held in reserve to add muscle to an argument. If there ever was an appropriate time to strengthen a point, *this* was it. Suddenly, I feared getting clobbered for being a hothead. Maybe it was impudence. On the positive side, I *had* thrown a morsel, a sweet aside.

A backhanded compliment is better than zero praise.

The freaks didn't see it that way.

Made evident by The Doobie divas' bulbous eyes, I knew we were dead ducks. Persona non-grata. On the surface, anyway, Jan kept her cool. Though she hadn't uttered a single word, surely, she was shivering in her sandals. Guaranteed, my friend wished I hadn't opened my big trap.

Before the unruly crowd grew uglier, beckoning Jan and me, Allan pointed toward the hallway. It was time to leave. In the middle of harangue, trailed by seventeen-year-old string bean, Drew, who'd latched on to Jan at some point during the evening, we slipped out of the room.

Drew asked Allan if he could hang out with us for a while. Shrugging him off, Allan lurched at the front door, stepped outside, and began weaving down the darkened driveway. The Maverick his aim, he turned to ensure that Jan and I were close by. Even in his intoxicated state, Allan didn't want us spoiled.

Stopping quickly to grab a pack of smokes, Drew jogged about five paces behind. Threatening voices gathered in the front yard of the house. I hoped we wouldn't be chased, or annihilated. Crowding into the car, Allan at the wheel, me riding shotgun, Jan and Drew in the back seat, we roared down the cul-de-sac toward a landmark lamp post flickering down over a triangular median.

It was well past one when Allan sewed his way through the neighbourhood and, on impulse, veered into a city park. Though cops were not quite so vigilant in pursuit of drunken offenders in those days, if discovered by police, Allan would have been arrested on site and had his car impounded, leaving us to find our way back to 145th Street — a proposition Jan and I didn't want to face past midnight in the middle of nowhere. Intoxicated ourselves however, for the moment, we didn't give it much play. Smart enough to lay low until the alcohol dissipated, Allan's greater love, marijuana, wouldn't wait.

Lighting up an obscenely large joint in the dark of the car's interior, Allan hauled in the smoke cautiously, as if it would be his last, and passed around the tightly wound tube, its orange ember our only funnelling light.

Recounting our adventures at the party house, the battle of the bands challenge suddenly seemed idiotic.

We busted up laughing.

It had been a strange night all round. Reclining in the driver's seat, happily conciliated by the smoke, returning to the subject of Ellen, Allan asked why she was absent from the party. Wildly evident at this late hour, apparently, Ellen had found something *or someone* better to do.

Listening to Allan reel off possible places that Ellen and her buddy might have gone, I thought how easily I'd forfeit a stupid high school party in lieu of being the center of attention, or make out with a cute boy. I wouldn't forfeit a party for *any*body however. There were certain requirements.

It had to be somebody *extraordinary.*

Like Teddy.

Or Doug.

So, Doug is a close second.

There's nothing wrong with number two. Utility players are often power hitters.

A is excellent.

B is good.

A is out of reach.

B is likely.

Allan started the ignition. Much to Jan's relief, en route to 145th Street, Allan dropped Drew at a corner near his house and then hit the gas hard at the next intersection. In doing so, he lost control of the vehicle. Revolving three full rotations on the pavement, the Maverick made a lot of racket until finally coming to a piercing halt and we found ourselves staring out at a lonely black sky. In a desperate attempt to right the car, Allan set his foot on the accelerator, causing us to flail back and forth like ragdolls. Ricocheting over the curb, the car careened across somebody's front lawn, swiping the tips of boxwood bushes until miraculously slamming to an abrupt stop.

Suddenly, we were idling in front of a stranger's living room window.

Not bothering to check first to make sure that everybody was okay, laughing so hard that my feet flew out against the windshield, straightaway, I saturated the crotch of my jeans. Turning around inside the cramped space, I observed Jan. Beside herself with the hilarity of the scene, her legs and torso had bent in two like a hairpin.

An expression of bafflement creasing his face, frozen in his seat, clearly, the amusement ride had sobered Allan. While the Maverick stood unmoving below the homeowner's front plate glass window, an occupant who might be inclined to call the cops, Jan pointed out a few pieces of living room furniture illuminated by the car's headlights.

A light switched on inside of the house. Activity ensued. Swiftly, Allan shifted the Maverick into reverse. Pirouetting 360 degrees, the heavy metal retraced over tire tracks etched into the lawn until arresting at the threshold of the sidewalk. Like a sea captain trying to tame a ship gone astray, Allan trained the wheels over the concrete and on to the road. Where well-groomed grass had once grown, brake lights shone down to expose a nasty divot imprinted in front of the property, one foot thick and more than a few yards in length.

Returning to the intersection in one piece, following a long period of quiet, Allan gave his head a shake and finally cracked a smile. Whistling through his teeth, he clucked, "Shit. That was a close call, eh?

The nasal timbre of a male voice emanated from the record player. Chanting about hoping to endure despite the decaying world around him, Ochs's distinctive vocal inflection brought my tired eyes into focus. Guessing we'd probably need it, Allan, who likely hadn't slept, left two tall glasses of ice-cold water on the coffee table. Reclining in an armchair smoking a cigarette, he studied the back cover of *Pleasures of the Harbor*. I looked over at Jan. Her eyes were barely open.

Without lifting his head, Allan informed us that Ellen arrived home at nearly four and was still asleep. Peter had gone for a morning jog, his habit most days according to all. Unsure how to respond to Allan's comment, adjusting the conversation, I reiterated how much Ochs's writing had influenced me the last few months.

In accord, Allan raised his eyebrows. In less than two days, remarkably, Ochs's music had reawakened something inside of Allan. Uncertain if the provocation was a lamb or a lion, I felt a little guilty.

Leaving Allan in the company of Ochs, Jan and I got dressed and wandered down the street to corral something to eat. It was Sunday morning. Save for a family diner that opened at noon, there weren't many options. As luck would have it, somebody spotted us outside. The restaurant had opened a few minutes early.

Purchasing a bagel and cup of chamomile, I trusted the tea would help subdue the throbbing on the left side of my face. Thinking some more about the Doobie fiasco, again, I began to feel like an imposter, equally complicit as the partygoers' tendency to become numb, and condescend to outsiders. On the flip side, everybody's capable of going crooked occasionally. Disruption and changeable behavior are part of the process of maturity, so we've been sold.

Filing the consolation in my back pocket, I drained my tea and followed Jan out to the street. It was time to return to the house, pack up our things, and relocate to the hostel. Asking around, we'd discovered the Edmonton Youth Hostel wasn't far from where we believed it to be a day ago.

It figured.

At the house, we chatted with Peter, Allan, and Ellen about the strange scene at the party the night before. Shifty-eyed and jittery, Ellen made up a flimsy excuse about why she never made it to the Doobie Mash. Sizing up his roommate from across the room, Allan squirmed uncomfortably in his chair.

Body language does not belie truth. Ellen got laid. Allan hadn't.

Peter and Ellen departed for the store. While they were gone, during an encore listen to Ochs, Allan smoked us up. Urging us to stay, he confided that we were the only people who *got* him. Though kind of Allan to say, being a full-time guest in his surreptitious world was a heck of lot of responsibility. That said; if Allan had been the sole tenant at the house on 145th Street, things might have been different. Anyway, there was no way of knowing exactly where we'd be within the week, much less one day.

Jan promised Allan we'd visit soon.

It was not disingenuous.

Offering us a drive, Allan made a move for his keys.

The Edmonton Youth Hostel didn't open before seven. With an hour to go, it had started to rain. Arbitrary droplets falling onto the windshield of the Maverick, converted quickly to a heavy downpour. Allan dropped us at a bus shelter outside of the Safeway so that we could stay dry until the doors unlocked.

Several minutes passed. Despite the wet weather, we noticed a few people had started to congregate around the property. Kumio, an irksome Japanese acquaintance from the last couple hostels seemed glad to see us. Shauna from New Zealand arrived next. Adrian, a gorgeous musician from back east donning magnificent blue eyes, fell in with the small army gathering on the walkway. Oblong in shape, Adrian's mesmeric babies provided distraction until the doors opened and we flocked inside.

Settling into our prefab dormitory, Jan and I joined the evening's travellers in the community room. Mulling over what we'd do for food, suddenly, somebody rushed into the room alerting us to the sighting of a double rainbow suspended above the hostel.

Outside, the rain had all but stopped. Sun broke through clouds. One positioned above the other, binary arcs marked the sky, resembling two tight clusters of coloured rubber bands. About forty feet away, I detected a couple of silhouetted figures on the opposite side of the street.

Hitting my arm hard, Jan squealed, "Oh my *god!* There's *Alex!*" Prying my eyes from the rainbow pageantry, peering across the road, I observed two longhairs crossing over a bridge. The boy with the messy white-blonde head and torn denims moved with a slight hobble.

Son of a gun, it was *the* kid himself. Only this homegrown friend was different.

Alex had been the subject of Jan's crush during the final year of high school.

Edmonton, Alberta.

CHAPTER 56

Slow Burn

"If you wish to travel far and fast, travel light, take off all your envies, jealousies, unforgiveness, selfishness, and fears."
GLENN CLARK

Leaving his friend, the blonde-headed boy crossed the road to our side and folded his arms over his chest in a friendly, familiar way. Alex appeared enthused.

Reflecting back to a year before, I remembered being in the mudroom in Jan's basement, waiting for her to join me downstairs. Greeted earlier at the front door by one of her grandmothers, from the front foyer, I heard somebody typing — an activity Jan had recently taken up. Her carefully composed, covert letters to select people that were sometimes mailed, sometimes not, were uniformly anonymous. Without being privy to the exact contents, I *did* know the messages inside conveyed thoughtful, agreeable sentiments. Standing together admiring the evaporating rainbow, I wondered, had Alex ever been the subject of one of those letters? If so, would he bother to mention them now?

My knowledge of Alex limited, I recalled he was frightfully smart. With the exclusion of a few close friends and adherents, Alex was somewhat of a lone wolf. Highly discriminatory in his musical tastes, his vast knowledge of the taxonomy of pop, underground, insubordinate, progressive and glam bands populating the decade was unmatched. T-Rex, Deep Purple, Hawkwind, Roxy Music, Lou Reed, Genesis (Peter Gabriel fronting), Golden Earring, Bowie, early Queen and the New York Dolls — all skimmed the surface of his personal preferences. Alex had garnered respect not only from hippies and hipsters in the making, but pre-punk and anti-mainline music frats.

I understood why Jan fell hard.

Renting an apartment on Jasper Avenue a few blocks away, a space he shared with Lucy, an older girlfriend, Alex didn't hesitate to extend a cordial greeting. "Would you like to get high on some black hash?"

Here we go again.

Setting out on the short distance to a low-rise building Alex and Lucy had moved into on Thursday, I somehow pictured Alex in the country, surrounded by a menagerie of wild animals. I never imagined him living and working in a metropolis like Edmonton.

The *working* part of the equation remained to be seen.

Alex's apartment was ordinary, a good size, and almost completely devoid of anything unnecessary. Boxes overflowing with books and albums were stored on a worn laminate floor beneath a barren living room window. Lucy nowhere in sight, Alex wasn't anxious to get his personal items organized.

Taking his place at a high pine table giving him the appearance of a judge presiding over a courtroom, peering over at Jan and me sitting dumbfounded in two metal chairs about a foot lower than his, Alex began to unscrew the lid of a small black vial. Apparently, the irony of the situation — the three of us together in his Edmonton apartment about to get high, struck Alex's funny bone and he started to giggle. Using a bent paperclip, he dipped the pin precariously inside the cylinder and stirred it around. Lifting the pin, now covered in jet-black goo, a generous dose of oil was spread across a flattened Zigzag paper. Reaching over for a matchbox, Alex removed a smooth black square from inside and placed it on the table. Crumbling a few pieces of the soft substance using his fingertips, the tar was scattered on top of the hash oil strewn along the open cigarette paper. Fishing around inside the table's single drawer, a freezer-sized baggie full of marijuana was withdrawn. Adding several healthy buds to the paper mix, folding the paper over, Alex began to roll up the smoke.

All the while, watching Alex conduct what resembled a well-rehearsed science experiment, we stared, amused. His attention to detail, the minute precision of gestures and pains taken to move through the process in steps, you had the sense that Alex had affection for the ritual much as he did the reward.

Lighting the joint, taking three or four deep drags, Alex choked once before passing it over to Jan.

If it wasn't presented on hot knives (another after-school activity), I tolerated hash. Unfortunately (or fortunately), knives always scorched my throat. To the bewilderment of parents, it seemed that most households in our town had a cutlery drawer containing at least two or three table knives burnt at the tips.

Alex's tandem of hash and weed was different. Delicate and sweet to taste, the intake produced a smooth, mellow effect. A slow burn, the combination of the two ingredients made for an extraordinary high, generating what could only be described as a golden hum.

Cheek hurting grins broke out irrepressibly across our three faces. Worries of the day cleansed away. Looking approvingly at Jan and then me, Alex read us accurately.

His dope was excellent. And he knew it.

Wrapped in the sweet comfort of the buzz, I watched fascinated as Alex rose from his chair, and staggered awkwardly toward the record player. He knew exactly what he was after. Soon we were saturated in Robert Fripp and the viscous whirr of the heady King Crimson LP, *In the Court of the Crimson King.* The swelling instrumental effects pasting us to our chairs, we began dialoguing with one another.

With the notion of earning easy bucks, Alex had come to the West in winter seeking work, and quickly realized a greater profit could be made selling drugs. In the past four months, he'd garnered some enormous scores, acquired and lost ridiculous amounts of money. Laughing it off, Alex couldn't account for what had happened to $900 in small bills. He appeared to care less.

Drugs cost money.

Especially good drugs.

Contributing to the financial elements of the household, Lucy served tables and was at work that evening. In addition to earning her keep, Lucy cooked, provided maternal nurturing, enjoyed getting wasted, and was good in bed, the perfect arrangement, according to Alex.

Like Allan, Alex stayed high from morning until night and preferred it that way. Though he did have an *official* job, Alex didn't mention what kind of work he did. As long as there was money to pay rent, eat, keep the drugs flowing, Alex was happy. So far, there was enough capital to sustain his desired lifestyle. Indifferently, Alex remarked that more cash was spent on drugs than food.

The mention of food reminded him to offer us something to eat. Until that point, I'd kept my cravings discreet, but the tidal wave of hunger pains had been triggered. That morning, before leaving for work, Lucy prepared a pot of chicken noodle soup. Alex excused himself to heat the food, inciting Jan and I to exchange one "Holy shit!" before resuming our everything-is-cool demeanor.

Everything *was* cool as far as I was concerned. Minds totally satiated, we were about to be fed. Eventually, euphoria would leave and our heads would revert to their previous conditions, anxious about money and our immediate futures. At that moment, not wanting anything to change, I longed to know what Jan was *really* thinking. She couldn't have predicted this scenario in a million years.

Running into Alex was nowhere near the same as bumping into other kids from school — particularly, the likes of Peter and Kyle. Having criticized *their* superficiality, on top of other faults, it looked as if I was becoming a snob. Alex's present aspirations weren't any more reputable than other friends back home that chose to remain stagnant. Yet, something impressed me about him. Alex treated us magnanimously, far better than any previous, bogus high school encounter had been. Inherently smart enough to get it together in due course, Alex struck me as somebody who'd eventually utilize his assets and intelligence to the best of his ability. Do things his way. Finding his way didn't mean he'd curb his drug habit. That wasn't our business. We were observers. Participants. Friends.

We weren't his mother.

Carrying two bowls of piping hot soup and a plate of thick white bread slices, Alex placed the items on the table and said he enjoyed being able to give because he could.

The charitable posture had not worn out its welcome.

Dining on Lucy's appetizing cooking; Alex inquired what we'd been up to since leaving home. As Jan and I rifled through experiences, he appeared somewhat doubtful. Listening as we described our road trip with Walter to San Francisco, and Russell to Mount Shasta and some of the other characters who'd given us lifts, Alex suddenly broke into a loud belly laugh. I don't think he expected us to have the courage to strike off the way we had.

Time passed quickly. The hostel closed its doors at eleven. It was getting close. I made a motion to leave. Thankfully, we only had to walk a couple of blocks. On our way out the door, Alex invited us to return another day. Like Allan, he hadn't wanted us to go, and even asked us to consider moving our things over to his place. Jan and I expected to return imminently, though a subsequent trip to Alex's lair was dependent upon how successful we were in finding employment.

Job search was to start next morning.

Moving a quick clip toward the hostel, Jan said she was concerned about Alex's drugs and his dealing, believing his extreme involvement was "ruining his mind."

I didn't think Alex's consumption bothered Jan as much as the reality he could get busted and go to jail for trafficking. As consolation, I offered something to this effect: "If in ten years, Alex is still living in a crappy apartment besieged by a cornucopia of weed, pipes, scales, and other paraphernalia, then there will be cause for concern. Right now, he's just another kid living the dream. Taking risks. Doing his thing."

If we'd been talking about anybody else, I might have said something different.

Fantasy rarely lives up to reality. Now that there was opportunity to hang out with Alex barring filters and impediments, Jan had mixed feelings. Moreover, Alex had a live-in girlfriend.

Nearing the front door of the hostel, as Jan raised her right foot to the porch, accidentally bumping into her, I stepped down on the heel of her sandal breaking the strap. Annoyed, my friend looked as if she might cry.

I felt horrible.

Patience was beginning to wear thin. Sliding quietly inside the front door, I pulled it behind us not a moment too soon.

Next morning, priority was to locate a shoe repair for Jan. Carrying one spare pair of footwear in her pack, they were too hot to wear in the summer's sweltering heat. Finding a shop not six blocks away, an old timer charged $1.50 to fix the sandal on the spot. Upon completion of his competent work, I offered to pay. It was my way of apologizing. No longer angry with me and slightly richer than I, Jan pulled a change purse out of her jeans pocket and paid the man.

We were on our way.

Between the sunlit hours of eight am and seven pm, the two of us made good use of the day marching in and out of restaurants, through department stores, laundromats, hotels, and bakeries filling out job applications.

We applied as dishwashers at Boston Pizza.

They'd recently hired somebody.

Woolworths required us to take a simple math test.

That was funny.

Though reluctant to do so, there was no alternative but to write down the hostel's telephone number on application forms. If indeed managers called, we hoped they wouldn't pry. Discovering or presuming we were transients would be the kiss of death.

Jan and I cut a plan. Once we found something, we'd rent a dorm room at the University of Edmonton. An individual could lease a room there for two-week intervals. Until something better came along, the student dorm would become our permanent place of residence. Not only good for us, the address would alleviate the concerns of potential employers.

At the end of the day, there were no assurances, and few pledges of "We'll give you a call." A courteous way of saying, "Don't bother us."

It was a start.

Returning to the hostel that night with burning feet and grumbling stomachs, an austere reminder we hadn't eaten anything of substance since morning, though hating to admit it, I was starting to grow weary. I knew Jan was getting fed up too. Something good needed to happen and fast. Too tired to hang out with the folks that night, resting on my bunk, I drew a pencil sketch of Joni Mitchell and then picked up the Bible I'd received from the cashier. Bound in red leather, it was the King James Version, with small, capitalized gold letters etched across the cover. Leafing through the first chapter of the New Testament, I struggled to concentrate on the tiny script typed across columns of diminutive pages. With its archaic wording and double-entendre, the book was more difficult to decipher than Shakespeare. Before long, I gave up. Pulling my sleeping bag over my shoulders, eyes shut tight, a cabaret of growing golf balls filed past the black field of vision.

Opening them to slits, I kept my eyes fixed on the darkest crevices of the room until the familiar energy surge returned. Resisting at first as I'd done before, my mind and body soon gave way to rushing. Analogous to the conversion point of The Beatles' song, "A Day in the Life," wherein an out of tune orchestra plays an escalating scale from a low octave and climbs higher and louder until reaching a crescendo, this goofball episode was the great granddaddy of all.

Fatigued to the point of nausea, laying down all thoughts, I surrendered to the void.

CBS trucks and associated personnel infested the hostel like cockroaches come morning. A pair of field reporters doing a piece on travelling youths and hostels wanted to interview several people for a forthcoming TV special. Mostly, stringers asked questions about where we all originated, how long had we been on the road, where did we plan to go next. They filmed us packing up our things before moving on. Some of the people were interviewed extensively. It was good fun. The segment was scheduled to air later that week.

When the last of the crew disappeared, Jan and I set out job-hunting — day two. By mid-morning, Jan scored at the National Bakery located at the corner of 102nd Street and Jasper. Receiving a pay rate of $2.64 per hour, she was to report early the following day, start the afternoon shift.

Except for Christmas baking for family and friends, Jan had zero experience as a professional baker. Willing to give it a shot, she looked forward to on-the-job-training. The best perk, she was promised a real chef's hat!

It was my turn. Retracing steps from the previous day, Jan and I circled the downtown core, keeping a lookout for prospective places of employment we might have missed. Wearing my best clothes: wrap around skirt, navy blue cotton t-shirt with three quarter length sleeves and earth shoes, I hoped they would bring luck.

Traipsing around a few more hours, we ducked in to a coffee shop for a muffin and juice, and then got back at it. Not having the option to bounce back from the day before, continuing in the heat, our feet ached and swelled. Logging miles on concrete is nowhere near close to hiking on spongy loam, or over a soft level surface. As much as I loved them, my second-hand footwear, already well-worn when I'd bought the sling back sandals back in winter, not to mention, a half size too small, had become noticeably painful. Fine for ordinary walking maybe, the sandals weren't equipped for anything serious. I bought them because I thought they looked cool. If only I found a job, I could afford to ride back and forth to work.

How pleasurable would it be, feet extended, to catch up on reading?

I was motivated to get back out there.

About to call it quits, late that afternoon, I walked into a Jolly Angus Restaurant, a downtown pub, and filled out a final application. During his preparation for the dinner crowd, the manager motioned me into his office for a brief interview. It was the first time in two days I'd gotten as much as a sniff.

The interview went well, but there were no assurances. The manager would let me know.

Picking up few groceries, Jan and I took our time walking back to the hostel. Next to a grouping of almond bushes with an overview of the city, we munched on grapes and broken crackers. Though close to being depleted, a little reserve remained in our tanks. Despite one of us having found work, there were other things to consider: food, long-term lodging, transportation, and eventually furnishings. Everything required startup money.

Not about to throw in the towel, the reality of our circumstances couldn't be ignored.

I had $40. Not much by a long shot. We had become skilled at stretching our funds, but truthfully, did I really want to live and work in Edmonton? How would that be any different from what home had to offer? On the other hand, returning to Ontario as originally planned, every measly cent would need to be conserved to cover our eating and sleeping costs for 2000 miles of travel. Jan had a little more cash than I did, but it wasn't anything spectacular.

We were adrift on the same raft. From the looks of things, while we paddled madly upstream, our raft was gradually being sucked into a whirlpool.

Alberta Sunset.

CHAPTER 57

Backwards Travellers

"Knowing yourself is the beginning of all wisdom."
ARISTOTLE

Arriving at the hostel after seven, two pieces of information waited. Alex had come snooping around while we were out job hunting, and the bakery tried to contact Jan. Returning the call immediately, speaking tentatively to her new boss, Jan hung up the receiver looking confused.

"I think I just got fired."

As far as she could tell, Jan's luck was premature. Her new employer didn't want to "rush things" was what he'd said. Management requested that she call back early next morning to confirm her services were still required.

Bummer. If either of us were to start work soon, we needed to prepare. That meant looking like worthy recruits. The hostel was merely a place to sleep and pee, no showers on site. A short hike to the Y revealed they closed at six.

Alex had extended an open-ended invitation. We would soon find out if he was the real deal.

Lucy, an attractive, late-twenties blonde who could easily have been older, invited us inside. Already half-baked, skipping the formalities, Alex motioned his hand toward some honey-brown hashish smoldering on the end of a safety pin. In cave dweller-like speak, he grunted, "Help yourselves."

Positioned at the center of the large, magistrate-sized table next to her boyfriend, scrupulously, Lucy assessed our situation. Presenting pointed questions, she formulated them in a humorous, half-mocking manner, as if we were auditioning for coveted roles in a school play. Lucy was having fun at our expense; there wasn't much to tell. Satisfied by our responses, gratuitously, she offered the latrine to take turns bathing if we so desired.

Drawing back the black shower curtain, peering into the grubby tub, cringing, I closed the curtain. Being high only made the room increasingly inferior. The white pedestal sink was a slight improvement. Almost a week since I'd last washed my hair, I decided I wasn't about to neglect part of my body because of a bit of grime. Leaning over the basin, I turned on the faucets allowing the water to run. Dunking my head several times until soaked through, I poured a capful of shampoo into my hand and began massaging the soap throughout my scalp. Rinsing my hair thoroughly with cold water, pulling on a long strand to hear it squeak, I reached for the cotton towel I'd brought along and wrapped it carefully around my head.

Clean hair was almost better than having a clean body.

Joining Jan, Alex, and Lucy in the front room, we talked and smoked for a while until Lucy left for work. Alex's friend Clive arrived and they walked us back to the hostel.

An enterprising sort, Alex had arranged with our hostel to refinish some old wood doors for payment. Along with a few others, Jan and I gathered on the cement pathway, supervising Alex and Clive while they lugged two heavy doors up the street toward Alex and Lucy's apartment.

"I'll bet Blondie put him up to this," Jan quipped.

Calling the bakery, the next morning as she'd been instructed to do, Jan's intuition was spot on. Having hired a baker, the manager no longer required Jan's services. The disappointing news a setback, my friend was understandably let down.

Already oppressively humid, we left the hostel early for McCauley Mall to purchase our breakfast of champions, muffins and coffee. Returning to the Y to take showers, we were charged 10 cents for the rental of two cardboard bath towels that barely covered our asses. In the end, the skimpy rub was worth watching almost a week's worth of mangy sweat disappear down the drain. Revisiting the bakery crestfallen, Jan handed in her unworn uniform and floppy white chef's hat.

Watching the owner retrieve the pancake hat from Jan's hands made me sad. She would have made an excellent baker in training.

Our financial situation having reached the dire stage, outside the bakery, we scanned a half-torn telephone book at a payphone to find the welfare listing under government yellow pages.

Dropping a dime in the slot, I dialed the number. After four rings, reception answered, transferring me to Counselling Services Department. A grave sounding man recommended the Emergency Crisis Centre and gave me an address. I repeated the digits out loud. Jan scribbled them down.

The Emergency Crisis Centre office wasn't handy. Striding along for more than an hour in cruel heat not saying much, eventually, we reached the bureau. I snatched a numbered ticket from reception. Along with other unfortunates, some with toddlers in tow, all of whom were older; Jan and I settled our butts into two white plastic chairs. On the upside, the place was air-conditioned, had a water fountain and decent selection of entertainment magazines to help pass time. Forty-five minutes later, emerging from one of the rear offices, a counsellor called our number.

During a short conversation, we were informed that when administering money or food stamps, funds were allocated for urgent cases. Addressing the needs of Edmonton residents was top priority. Subsequently, Jan and I were given a stern lecture as to how *we* had *fixed* addresses out of province. What could a couple of hapless hippie girls possibly gain by deflecting money from unwed mothers, people in transition or out of work? To put it bluntly, we'd be *stealing* from those in *real* crisis.

The counsellor advised us to wire our parents for money, return home to our families if we couldn't find employment.

How anticlimactic.

Jan and I had our share of flaws, neither of us was a dummy. We were merely seeking a band-aid fix in the way of a few dollars for a couple of days until finding employment. To date, the trip had been independently financed through work. Borrowing money from parents was not part of the code. Begging, maybe even thieving, was preferable. If I was in serious trouble, Mom and Dad would come through. Otherwise, I didn't plan on bothering them.

Asking for a money wire would have been the simplest, most pragmatic way to motor on while trying to land jobs. There would also be a caveat, at least in my situation. My parents would expect me to return home. Not to mention, the money would be on *loan*, not a hand out. This was not criticism, merely fact. Either way, I'd have to figure out how to pay them back. Already, I was living on credit for a couple of collect telephone calls. Obstinate by nature, unless my hand was forced or we ran out of choices, I didn't want to return to Ontario a single day sooner than expected.

Too stubborn to ask Jan her feelings on the subject, if she disagreed, I counted on her to speak up.

En route to the Edmonton hostel, a pit stop was made at the post office to check General Delivery mail. A nineteen-page novella from Liz couldn't have arrived at a better time. This time, Jan didn't receive mail. Not wanting her to feel bad, I tucked the letter away for nighttime reading. To a fault, we shared news from home with one another anyway.

Scarcely in the mood for job-hunting, we paid Allan a surprise visit at the men's shop where he worked. Appearing alien-like wearing a slick, blue pinstriped suit, at least Allan was employed. It was more than we could say for ourselves. Encouraged that we'd made good on our assurance to keep in touch, Allan extended an invitation to the house later that day.

Returning to our hideaway behind the almond bushes with its first-class view of the city, finishing the rest of our carrot sticks and squished cheese sandwiches prepared that morning, the food wasn't half-bad.

Jan and I walked the short distance from the hostel to Alex and Lucy's apartment. Our mission was simple. Having spent three nights at the Edmonton hostel, our quota met, we needed to be out.

I asked Alex if we could crash on his livingroom floor for a couple of days.

No problem.

Irony is an amusing game. Returning to the hostel to pack our stuff, one of the staff told me the Jolly Angus Restaurant had called. Counteracting with a smart-assed, "Is the restaurant looking to fire me?" — I was urged to return the call ASAP. The owner gave me good news. Not only did the smartass get hired, but how soon could she start? Without first consulting Jan, like an idiot, I told the man I'd have to decline. It didn't make sense to go off to work if Jan didn't have a job. When it was the other way around, I hadn't worried so much.

It was important that Jan found employment first.

In a last-ditch effort, I asked the manager if he'd consider taking a package deal. Unfortunately, Jolly Angus required only one waitress. Reading my let down, the proprietor threw me a flotation device. If I changed my mind within a day or so, I was to give him a call, pronto.

Storing our knapsacks with Alex and Lucy, we caught the bus to 145th Street to pay one final visit to Allan, Ellen, and Peter. Phantom roommate, Margaret, was also there, blending easily into the mix. Everybody was in great spirits. In the company of Ellen, even Allan was on his best behavior. Over a couple of Heidelberg's, Peter told an elaborate, harrowing story about a bike accident he'd had the day before. Riding to work, he was sideswiped by a car and sent flying headfirst into a ditch.

The ground being soft, there were no fractured bones, but the accident made him think twice about driving his bike on the highway again — for about five seconds.

Peter didn't own a helmet. Nobody did.

This was the last hurrah. Motions to retire for the evening were made. Jan and I thanked everybody for putting us up and putting up with us when we had nowhere to go. Afterwards, Allan offered to drop us at Alex and Lucy's.

The last couple of days, I'd let Allan keep *Pleasures of the Harbor.* Sorry to let the record go, Allan acknowledged the music had brought him a renewed measure of happiness. Our departure from 145th Street signified that Jan and I truly were closing in on the end of our adventure.

Drawing Jan and I into a three-way hug, smiling uneasily, Allan averred, "You two are right on."

To exemplify the sweet compliment, touching the tips of his right thumb and finger together to form an 'o,' he repeated, "You girls are *O-Kay.*"

Coming from Allan, it was a very big deal.

Bob Dylan, unfinished.

CHAPTER 58

Go Big or Go Home

"Fairy Tales unbutton truths."
JILL C. NELSON, *July 1976*

Like rapids in a thawing spring stream, time continued to scuttle on. Half-awake on the rock-hard floor in Alex and Lucy's living room, comparable to frames on a film reel, images of our travel history and the folks with whom we'd broken bread and smoked herb flickered in my head. Most of the time, the show had been entertaining.

Awake and up at a quarter past six, Alex and Lucy planned to leave the apartment imminently. Lucy would drop Alex at work at seven, and then spend her off day with a girlfriend. Jan and I were free to use their apartment as needed. Full steam ahead back to Ontario, our next scheduled hostel stop was within the perimeter of Elk Isle National Park at Fort Saskatchewan.

The future remained fuzzy.

Following a strawberry pop-tart breakfast, Alex provided us with a new road map. Lucy packed a lunch. Initiating a final round at the arbitrator's table, Alex took an extended burn through a couple of pipes crammed with fresh homegrown and liberal bits of coal black hashish. Sufficiently high, he was insistent, "If you're ever in the vicinity again, we'd be happy to put you up."

Unconvinced of our ability to take care of business, while Alex expressed concern, Jan assured him we could manage ourselves.

Most pleasing was Alex's parting sentiment, echoing my belief that while credit was generally ascribed to Bob Dylan for his status as a brilliant writer, poet, and proactive protest singer, Ochs was the truer, tenacious radical who cared less if he got roasted for his (sometimes) extremist viewpoints. Even if Alex didn't wholly subscribe to this opinion, it was kind of him to pretend.

Once Alex and Lucy were gone from the apartment, Jan gave our hometown pal the benefit of a doubt. "Edmonton has definitely brought about a positive transformation in Alex."

Admittedly, she was over him. This resignation to reality, the equivalent of finally getting the chance to meet your childhood idol and discovering that he or she farts and does laundry, hanging out with Alex that July was a lot like that.

Having the place to ourselves for a few hours, we took full advantage. I began another draft, a rendering of photographer Paul Till's cover photo of Bob Dylan on the *Blood on the Tracks* LP. Penning letters to Rebecca and Brother Bruce, I asked them both not to write me off just yet. Still flummoxed about what to do, I'd arrived at a concrete compromise. Whether I decided to join The Order or not, I would find myself back in San Francisco someday soon.

Our next layover wasn't far, about 30 miles. Like always, on any given day, you could never predict how easy or difficult soliciting a ride might be. Travelling 30 miles sometimes required a full day's effort. Other days, 150 miles could be had in less than three hours. Despite our new road map, unable to establish the most direct way to get to the edge of town, we ended up taking four buses until reaching Highway 16 East, also known as the Yellowhead Highway.

From that point, rides flowed easily. A peculiar incident occurred along the way. The first driver to pull over, a sixty-ish farmer accompanied by his terrier in a two-seat cabin pick-up returning home from a fishing trip, invited us to climb up to the box on the back. The ride went smoothly until the farmer suddenly jerked the vehicle off the highway and drove straight into a cow field, stopping dead about 100 yards in front of what we'd assumed was his farmhouse. As the little terrier's dark perky eyes peered through the glass that separated us from the cabin, the farmer didn't make a motion to get out of the truck. Worried the man was in distress, we waited for something to happen. Except for a small herd of grazing cows in the field just ahead of the truck, everything was still. Maybe the old farmer was experiencing a stroke, a heart attack, or something else? While the man remained stationary, climbing down, I walked around to the driver's side window to see what was going on. The farmer lifted his palms from the grip of the wheel and held them outside of the truck. Seemingly disoriented, he asked, "Do my hands look green?"

Without letting on how unnerved I was, I assured the farmer his hands appeared quite normal. Still, he remained skeptical. Meeting the man's bewildered gaze, I reached my right hand over my shoulder. "Thanks, anyway, we're going to head back up to the highway."

The farmer failed to try to move. Packs dragging at our sides, hands wiping sweaty brows, Jan and I darted through the field leading to the main road. Turning back minutes later, save for the feeding cows, there was little activity around or near the truck.

Burrowed within the Beaver Hills area of the greater aspen parkland, for more than a century, heavily thicketed Elk Island has played host to a thriving population of free roaming plains bison, elk, deer, and moose. Founded in 1906 when a group from Fort Saskatchewan put up $5000 petitioning the provincial government to dedicate the park as a sanctuary for elk, Elk Island has remained open year-round. It continues to be an alluring retreat for snowshoeing and cross-country skiers.

Landing in at Elk Island Park mid-afternoon, a surprise awaited. The front door of the two-story hostel was locked. Unless we wanted to get back on the highway, catch a ride to another location, we'd find a way to make things work — at least for one night. Believing we'd never miss our tent, once more, it looked as if selling the nylon shelter had been untimely. It was a hot, dry day. With luck, the temperature would remain stable throughout the night. Using our bags to support our heads, if need be, we could sleep outside.

Nothing but time on our hands, Jan and I walked the perimeter of the building, seeking an open door or a window — any reasonable sized gap that would enable entry. To be devoid of swarming travellers seemed out of place for this handsome, hilly location with a nearby lake.

Trying every window, around the back of the building few were unlocked. With some effort, Jan managed to slide a dusty wood frame halfway upright. Alternating turns continuing to be a fundamental policy of our travel arrangement, I volunteered to be the first to sneak inside one of the vacated rooms on the main floor.

Compartmentalizing my 5' 6" body inside the cavity of a 24 x 18-inch window frame proved a challenge. I'd have to get creative. Contorting my shape into an inelegant acrobatic pose, managing to pass through, I tore a gaping hole in my cotton-print Indian blouse — one of my few treasures. Naturally, the window frame gifted me with a bloody scrape along the small of my back.

More importantly, we were in.

Snooping around the corridor of the structure looking for signs of human life, we found none; yet, the place had the presence of having been inhabited. In a couple of dorm rooms and offices, healthy houseplants rested neatly upon windowsills. Shiny mugs were stacked next to a coffee machine on a dry dishtowel in the community kitchen, where a small handwritten sign on the counter warned the water was not safe for drinking. A full carton of milk sat in the refrigerator. Except for the shower, cold *and* hot taps worked. There was a water pump near the premises. The cots had sheets with threadbare blankets folded at the foot of each one. Surely, somebody had to be around.

Completing a search of every room in the building, we concluded there were no house parents or hostellers on site, meaning nobody around to collect payment. Recollecting a conversation with my brother in California in which we'd bandied the proposal of taking an intermission from life, stepping back to realign thoughts and motivations, freedom from having to pay for sleep proposed a golden opportunity.

This was all well and fine. We were getting ahead of ourselves. Rather than settling in at the vacated building that first night, Jan and I dragged our bags down to the beach surrounding Astotin Lake and soldiered through a half-assed sleep. In the morning, we returned to the hostel. Retrieving water from the pump, we encountered Kumio, the talkative, mid-twenties Japanese backpacker who'd stayed at three of the same previous hostels along Canada's West Coast. A pattern of some sort had been established.

Jan and I weren't unhappy to have company, long as Kumio didn't pull any weird shit. Remembering that recently, my friend and I'd been invited to crash at a house with four strangers, I felt shame for being quick to persecute Kumio. At any rate, you learn to read people. You pick up on conspicuous signals. Positive imagery practice had become second nature for Jan and me. Kumio didn't exactly send off warning bells. Still, these were the final days of our trip. There was no room for error or slip-ups. Utilizing our built-in sensor system, we had to watch our backs.

Overall, Kumio turned out to be a good egg. Helping us carry two heavy water jugs back from the bathroom at the golf course we'd discovered behind Astotin Lake, Kumio let it be known this was his *second* day at Elk Island. Here, we were infringing on Kumio's territory, not the other way around. Like a veteran burglar that had already cased the joint, Kumio was the first of us to lay down stakes at Elk Island. What remained of the afternoon was spent near the lake, embracing the sunshine, a merciful pardon from a slew of rainy days.

I finished my sketch of Bob Dylan. Not entirely happy with the outcome, I wondered had I become too hard on Dylan. Though a fan of his music, I no longer perceived him defiant maestro, uniting a generation. In my biased eyes, Dylan had evolved into one of the characters harshly scorned in his songs. Often introspective, Dylan's writing was habitually self-derisive. When I showed the drawing to Jan, she started to laugh. "What happened to his *nose?*" Re-examining the picture, I noticed a booger-like teardrop that was supposed to be the tip of Dylan's snout. No doubt, a subliminal rub.

Turning in that night, Jan and I camped out in one of the vacated rooms next to Kumio. Minutes after shutting off the lights, a slight figure appeared in the doorway, scaring the living shit out of both of us. It was Kumio, pleading sex, with whoever was willing. Our *non*-stalker made it perfectly clear. Either one would do nicely. At least Kumio wasn't picky.

The hourglass was running out on that accord. More and more it looked like the choice males in the world were committed, damaged, horn dogs, or narcissists.

Doug was none of the above. Nor was he ancient history.

Kumio's pathetic play for sex scenario thwarted, Friday, July 9, was business as usual. Cooler than the previous day, anticipating the skies would clear and temperature improve, Jan and I revisited the beach. Before long, we gave up and stopped at a corner store to pick up tomato soup and milk for lunch. Resolving to stay at the hostel until Sunday — three nights rent-free with most of the amenities on site, there was no reason not to hang in. After that was anybody's guess.

In the afternoon, I returned to the golf course to refill our water supply. Edging near the hostel carrying heavy glass jugs, suddenly, the wind kicked up, causing twigs and leaves to skip hurriedly along the prairie grass. Dallying for a moment, allowing the breeze to stroke my cheeks, I soon picked up my pace. Lightning sparks followed thunderclaps. Charcoal-blue sky fire flaring magnificent against a spontaneous darkened atmosphere sent an unyielding warning. We could expect more precipitation.

Back just ahead of the rainstorm, I was greeted by foreign faces — three sisters had arrived at the hostel. That made six people, with no one in charge. This beautiful natural reserve was about to grow larger.

A couple vanloads landed in. A Baptist church group from Edmonton planned to spend one night. Eighteen in all, things were starting to make sense.

Assuming an authoritative presence, the clan took over the reins, lighting a bonfire after the storm, inviting us to join them for hot chocolate, donuts, play-acting in a couple of goofball skits, and a singsong around the campfire. One of the boys, Timothy, had brought along a *gee*tar (one in every crowd it seemed carried an acoustic ax) and proceeded to play a couple songs he'd written for his girlfriend and recently deceased mother. For an encore, he tore into James Taylor's "Sweet Baby James."

When the set was over, Jan and I hung back, yakking to Timothy and some of the others. Grazing the subject of spirituality, that ubiquitous theme during those seminal months, my love/hate affair with HOOM was still at a deadlock. Normally Chatty Kathy, for the entirety of the evening, Kumio barely opened his mouth. Given the circumstances, figuring that he was possibly uncomfortable around the larger group, I began to feel sorry for Kumio.

Sympathies were short-lived.

As the troop broke apart, Kumio leaned over to Timothy, talking loud enough to ensure that everybody caught wind, "Jill thinks you're sexy."

Son of a bitch. This was payback for denying sex, I was certain of that.

Saturday morning, the buttery-cinnamon scent of pancakes cooking on the grill drew several of us out of bed to form a line near the stove. Drizzling sweet maple syrup over a flavourful stack of edibles, I pondered our present circumstances. Failing to negotiate significant headway with our appeal for work, food stamps and temporary funds had left Jan and me at somewhat of a standstill. Yet, here at Elk Island, we'd been granted immunity from worries of the day.

In speaking about life's patterns and the cyclical actions of people, Teddy had pointed out how a noble endeavor makes another good deed possible, and eventually, forms a chain of positive command. Beneath the oak in San Francisco's Duboce Park, he explained why his much-loved backpack no longer held importance. Giving way to virtue, Teddy's priorities had shifted. Nearly six months on the road, this stream of consciousness continued to move fluidly in and around us. Recurring evidence of destiny, and the intrinsic will to give, provided the impetus to try to become better people.

The Baptist group gathered up their property and proceeded to roll out. Brad, one of the squad in his late-twenties with his own set of wheels, stayed behind. Interested in locating elk known to be in the vicinity, and excited to witness the big beasts in their natural habitat, Jan, the three sisters, Kumio, and I crammed into Brad's wagon and drove up to the paddock area of the park.

Beasts they were. Herds of elk and enormous plains bison, more than forty in all, foraging wild and free in the aspen play land, it was an extraordinary scene. Leaving the paddock area on foot, Jan and I spent a couple more hours at Astotin Lake, replenished our water supply at the golf course, and returned to the hostel.

The evening was humid. Sweat and grass debris, leftovers from our park visit, clung to our muggy skin. Earlier in the day, before it had gotten too warm, a few of us opened the windows of the building to air the place out. Because there were no screens, by nightfall, our room swarmed with mosquitoes to such an extreme it was impossible to sleep. Looking ahead to morning, Jan and I were off to Saskatoon, the alleged hometown of Joni Mitchell.

In fact, Mitchell was a native of Fort McLeod, Alberta.

One week prior to leaving for our trip, Jan and I'd met up with our friend Anne. Ten years earlier, Anne's uncle was employed as an art instructor at the Alberta College of Art and Design in Calgary, where Joni Mitchell was an attending student. With a reputation for skipping class in favour of picking out melodies on her guitar, catching her loitering in the college corridor one day, Anne's uncle approached Mitchell, giving her advice. "You need to make a choice between music and painting. It's impossible to divide equal time and energy to both."

Though openly critical of her own artistic ability initially, over the years, Mitchell found a way to successfully assimilate multiple mediums.

A couple hours before dawn, in midst of flattening mosquitoes on my arms and face, I mused on Anne's story.

Everything is up for grabs.

Saskatchewan prairie field.

CHAPTER 59

The Bridge City

"Some people never go crazy. What truly horrible lives they must live."
CHARLES BUKOWSKI, *Barfly (1987)*

Sunday morning, carting our "bloody packs" as Jan had taken to cursing our beefy load, we set out for the highway. Several months on the road, the bags weren't getting any lighter. A Japanese couple camping in the park drove us out to the gate entrance. With a long day ahead and a 300-mile stretch of pavement to eat up, we waited more than an hour before being offered another ride. Perched upon soggy remains of the light morning rain, mostly due to lack of sleep, moods were low. We were heading back East to mine our lives.

Gathering a handful of stones, I began pitching one at a time at a dirt embankment a few yards away. I'd been humming Lennon and McCartney's "Two of Us," a cut from the band's final offering, *Let It Be*, which describes John and Paul's two-week journey home to Liverpool from Hamburg, Germany, with a detour in Paris sandwiched in along the way. It was the cusp of the 1960s. Accompanied by seventeen-year-old George Harrison and the newly acquired "Ringo" (Richard) Starkey, formerly of Rory Storm and the Hurricanes, for several months, the musicians had mashed it out nightly, honing their skills during eight-hour stints in seedy nightclubs along Germany's Reeperbaum district. When it was discovered that Harrison was underage to work in clubs, he was sent back to England, resulting in the group's disbanding. Reflecting on their long way home those many years before, tunefully, Lennon and McCartney recount "chasing paper, going nowhere", "burning matches, lifting latches" — bittersweet memories depicting highs, lows, disillusionment. Somehow, they'd hoped for more. Taking guitar lessons from a local teacher in town one year before, "Two of Us" became one of few pieces May and I'd learned to play and sing together, in harmony. For that reason, the song was special.

Recognizing how John and Paul must have felt, returning home to family, friends, and familiarity after a life-changing extended period away, I'd replayed a similar scenario, particularly during the last week when it became apparent our fate was sealed. At first, I envisioned elation in seeing everybody again — tears of joy, happy embraces, contagious enthusiasm. As with most things, once the polish wears off, the circle game of life resumes. The same would hold true for us.

A brown Mustang pulled over, driving us 30 miles. Fifteen minutes later, a purple Dodge Charger owned by Steve, a mid-thirties rambler, came along.

Steve asked where we were headed. Jan replied, "Saskatoon." Once inside the Charger, despite it being more than *200* miles out of his way, Steve said he'd bring us to Saskatoon. The shock on our faces registered. Backpedalling, Steve made a quick recovery. "It's Sunday. I've got nothing better to do."

Incarcerated within the Charger's cavernous interior, I in the front, Jan in the back, it was too late to change our minds even if we wanted to.

Riding east on the Yellowhead highway, far beyond feral berry bushes, dogwood trees, fishponds, and gorges, taking us into his confidence, Steve bared his horrifying time in the Air Force. Declared "certifiably crazy," he'd received a dishonourable discharge.

Steve's confession accomplished little in the way of instilling trust. Nevertheless, he didn't pull punches. On the surface, Steve seemed to be a stand-up person, so-to-speak. Wasn't the supposition anyway, that crazy people didn't *know* they were crazy? If correct, that meant Steve wasn't crazy. For the next several miles, I did some figuring.

Crazy can mean many things. Ranging from mad, to fanatical, to senseless, to indifferent, to eccentric, and to sociopathic, crazy isn't necessarily synonymous with psychopathic behavior, yet it doesn't disqualify psychopaths either. Crazy is like playing a game of Russian roulette. When the gun fires and it shoots a blank, you hope there isn't another bullet lodged inside the chamber waiting to be triggered.

I was not in the mood for surprises.

From the time we'd nestled into his car, Steve didn't stop talking. Recounting the time served in the Air Force, Steve admitted how difficult it was adjusting to civilian society after his discharge. Starved for social interaction and admitting his desperation for company was one of the reasons he'd opted to take us out of his way, Steve felt inferior associating with people his own age. Humiliated about not being tough enough to withstand, the service had pilfered his zest for life. Like the Good Samaritan, Steve was caught in the fray of unstitching the wreckage of the past several years.

Recalling a Phil Ochs' song, "Rehearsals for Retirement," in which Ochs laments how the war reduces brave men to babies, he wasn't wrong.

Life is not for the faint-hearted. As if born with bulletproof hearts, humans are expected to soldier on, resisting pain, hurt, and disaster. Through our interaction with Allan, as of late, Jan and I had some practice trying to bring cheer. When Allan alluded that his depression sometimes bordered suicidal territory, we listened and said little. Without meaning to trivialize Allan's troubles, compared to Steve's grim prognosis, Allan's head was screwed on straight.

The last notion Steve had on his "crazy" mind was swindling or bludgeoning us — the man longed for somebody to pay attention. This summer Sunday morning, he'd hit the jackpot.

When Jan and I were new into the hitchhiking game, it was often reinforced that drivers pick up riders because it enables them an audience — one that can't leave. Like a priest sitting in a confessional while folks repent and unburden, every ride is like reaching your hand into a cereal box and pulling out a surprise. People have no qualms sharing the most bizarre, personal, even incriminating minutiae of their lives.

Looking straight out the Charger's front window, reading names of provinces and states stamped across various license plates, while Steve rattled away a drawn-out list of pessimistic prognostications, I smiled and lied when warranted. Every so often, Jan rescued me from the full onslaught to remark about something she'd spotted out the window, or shared some other random thought that came to mind. At one point, glancing over at Steve while he was on a verbal rampage, I noticed a couple of tears glistening on his right cheek. Once I knew he knew I'd seen them, it made me feel worse, as if I'd trespassed into private domain.

The Charger growled past the billboard welcoming tourists to the province of Saskatchewan. Instead of flatlands and golden wheat fields, costumed by bands of rolling green grasses and brilliant mixes of yellow, red, and purple wild flowers, we were extended the royal treatment. At about the mid-way point, Steve pulled off the road to refuel and get directions. Raising her voice, Jan reported the hostel's address: 2401 Koyl Avenue located in Saskatoon's north end.

Next to the pump, Steve struck up a conversation with a teenage boy studying a road map. Returning to the car a few minutes later followed by the kid, we were introduced to Ross from Vancouver, also on his way to the Saskatoon hostel. Jan and I exchanged places so that she could take a turn riding in front. Seated next to Ross in the rear, as Steve coerced the Charger out of the parking lot and out onto the highway, a stubborn curl on the back of his dark head glared down at me.

More at ease now that Ross had joined our group, I guessed his presence would help divert focus. As far as general company goes, Ross was okay, though it soon became evident our new passenger was enamoured with himself. Thanks to Steve, Ross didn't get much opportunity to boast. Bringing our new travelling companion up to speed, Steve provided Ross with a categorical narrative of his saga and opinions. Empathizing respectfully, Ross proved a courteous listener.

The road trip wrapped up early evening. Thanking us for our loyal company, Steve didn't ask for a red cent. In exchange for gas and miles logged on the Charger, Jan and I had donated our ears and forfeited emotional hardware — a fair trade.

Moral of the story: There are a lot of lonely, disenfranchised men in the world.

Managed by an Irish couple, Louise and Pete, the Saskatoon hostel was located inside a white-sided, three-story apartment building that didn't feel like a hostel at all. Jan, Ross, and I were greeted by Kumio, who'd arrived ahead of us by about an hour, causing management to assume the four of us were two couples. No one let on. Instead of paying $4 a night, Louise cut our fee in half and established us in adjoining rooms.

More than 300 miles east of Elk Island, once again, we were sharing close quarters with Kumio. This made four encounters in total. Vague that morning about where we were headed next, Jan and I didn't expect to see Kumio again. Certainly, we didn't own the road, but this was over the top.

I asked Louise if there was anywhere on site to make food or purchase something to eat. Kindly, she offered to drive the four of us out to the local McDonald's restaurant. Costing more than Jan and I planned to spend, famished, we accepted.

Tucked deep within the prairie belt, the flat grid known for potash, agriculture and oil, Saskatoon (branded City of Bridges) spreads out over hills and valleys. From our marginal perspective, the city appeared and felt cruel. Monolithic structures made of steel peppering the downtown core restricted space between one another, let alone a breath of fresh air. It would take some getting used to.

That night, we were able to shower — a perk in lieu of a working kitchen. With hit and miss showers being one of the sidebars of cheap travel resulting in an inability to maintain good hygiene; being on your period and having no way of properly taking care of business made things even nastier.

I was one of those unfortunates who flooded monthly monsoons. The cylindrical, digital-style modern day Tampax tampons were not robust enough to absorb the heavy flow of menstruation. It was Stayfree maxi-pads all the way — (though rarely did they *stay* attached to your underwear leaving you feeling anything but *free*) — a real inconvenience that gobbled up valuable space in a backpack. Jan was the lucky one — incredibly; she hadn't *had* a period since leaving home. According to her, *nothing* would intrude upon her good time. Mysteriously, masterfully, she'd willed away the inconvenience early on. Whenever Jan happened to teasingly rub it in, I didn't hesitate to express my indignation.

Uninvited, Kumio and Ross appeared at our door and hung out most of the night. Ross had brought a radio along with him. Always game for music in the evenings, the tape player Jan packed for entertainment during our first weeks in Vancouver had long ago given up the ghost.

The four of us got talking. As initially believed, Ross revealed himself a consummate egomaniac — he was completely stuck up. To make matters worse, much like a parent might do, he didn't hesitate to lay some weird trips.

All about doing the *right* thing, Ross prioritized conformity, compliance, traditional values, especially for women, and was shocked to learn that Jan and I'd been away almost six months. Being of same age and mind with similar goals and backgrounds, Doug and I'd felt an immediate connection and attraction. There was no judgement. No condemnation. More and more, I began to see Doug as an admirable and honourable human being. Imagining what it might be like to be on the receiving end of another one of those kisses, perhaps a little deeper, or even make love if I had the nerve, I would soon write Doug a note, and feel out his plans for the duration of August into September.

Finally, Kumio and Ross left the room. No sooner had they closed the door when Jan and I started in gossiping about the two of them.

Thoroughly unimpressed with his outdated ideas, I decided to rechristen Ross *"Dick*-Ball." It sure got a rise out of Jan.

The expanding white goof balls appeared for what turned out to be the final time that night. Sprouting up eloquently at first across the black space behind my eyes while I lay still, face toward the ceiling, eyes closed, I watched as they suddenly inflated like Jiffy Pop popcorn. Demonstrating modest momentum instead of the usual joie de vivre, soon, the spheres fell slack.

In total, I counted twelve white balls. Having an affinity for even numbers, this was a good sign. And there was something else. For the first time, I could make the balls recede and eventually retire.

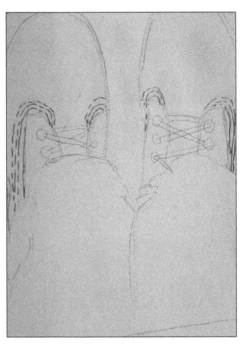

"Self portrait."

CHAPTER 60

Two of Us

"Life is really simple, but we insist on making it complicated."
CONFUCIUS

Next morning, Ross continued to Winnipeg. No sign of Kumio. Louise had some shopping to do downtown and offered Jan and me a lift. Jan withdrew $10 from her bank account, enough to last a few more days. Purchasing a small charm of Saskatchewan's flag, she would add it to a bracelet in her jewellery box back home.

Expecting to be in Ontario by the weekend, it was now a matter of days. Everything seemed to align. For what purpose, I still didn't know.

Walking through the Saskatoon mall, a girl from my high school music class, Chris, and her best friend Natalie headed in our direction.

The two girls were just as surprised as we were. Though I didn't know Natalie well, in the company Chris and a few other students during morning breaks in the high school cafeteria, we'd eat french fries and commiserate about Mr. Martin, our part-time music teacher, full-time taskmaster. Sharing an apartment, both girls worked retail in Saskatoon for the summer, hoping to stick it out long as possible. Jan and I both knew what that meant. After ransacking through a few good yarns, Chris and Natalie drove us back to the hostel in Natalie's car. Handing us a phone number written on the back of a receipt, Natalie asked us to call later about going out drinking that night. Except for the money part, it sounded like a great idea. We'd worry about the specifics later.

Back at the Saskatoon hostel, having spent the afternoon shopping for a new pair of tennis shoes, Kumio hunkered alone in his room taking it easy. The rest of the day was low key. Cocoon mode. Psychologically, Jan and I were in the throes of surrendering to our journey back east. Trying to stay distracted, I sketched a few pictures for family and friends. For Chris, I composed a replica of a postcard picked up in Calabasas where he, Jan, and I'd spent a couple of fun hours. I thought Steve would appreciate a drawing of the Ghosts of the Caribbean, a favourite ride at Disneyland. Drawn on lined paper, for May, I fashioned an interpretation of San Diego by night.

It turned out that Natalie didn't own the car she was driving and was unable to pick us up that night. Though not terribly disappointed, despite having to invent an excuse about money, the evening had potential. It could have been a howl or gone flat.

Jan, Kumio, and I walked over to McDonald's for coffee and conversation. Barring a short dialogue concerning differences between dating customs in North America and Japan, we'd run the full gamut with Kumio. In a surprise twist, Kumio offered Jan something to remember him by, a Japanese coin.

In every which way, examining and reexamining our present status, in my heart, I knew we'd played our final hand. Having removed hitchhiking home from the equation due to a shortage of funds to sustain us, the CN train was leaving out of Winnipeg station Wednesday evening. Jan and I would be on it. Unsure of the cost of one train ticket to Toronto, I doubted I'd be able to scratch together enough dough to cover my share. Having a smidgen more money, once we arrived in Winnipeg, Jan offered to cash advance my ticket. I would pay her back once we were home, a loan that would come from my dad.

Destined for Regina in the morning, there wasn't any point staying up late. Outlining the pros and cons for the final time, beyond reuniting with family and friends, returning home had other advantages. The highlights: eating regular meals, sleeping in our own beds, not having to worry about homicidal freaks. As concerned as I was about uncertainty, when Jan let it drop that she too felt reservation and anticipation, my spirit got a boost.

It wasn't that we'd sat down and had a serious conversation deciding to go home. Because of the inevitability of our condition, returning to Ontario didn't need to be vocalized. Much the way that my desire to leave home back in winter was born out of personal necessity, going east was intuition. Returning to Ontario prematurely, by a couple of weeks wasn't a symptom of weakness or malfunction. On the contrary, we'd had a great time, met amazing people, witnessed beautiful country. We had seasoned.

Then why was I scared?

Next morning, Jan and I were packed and ready to go ahead of schedule. To avoid vying for a ride, also on his way to Regina, Kumio let us get away first. Sunny and warm, after a good night's rest and only 160 miles to travel, it was important we found our way out to Highway 11 South, also known as the Saskatchewan Highway. Hitching a ride into downtown Saskatoon, from there, we took a short bus trip to the city outskirts.

Sure, it was an ass-backward way of doing things. Sometimes, for no justifiable reason, you need to shake it up. With little time left to improvise, why not?

Barely off the bus, and we scored a boon. Spotting us struggling with our knapsacks, Beau, a young trucker from Regina jockeyed his jumbo-sized transport over to the road's shoulder, sprung out of the driver's side and lumbered down the steps to reach the pavement. Hoisting our packs into his sleeper, Beau summoned us to sit alongside him on his bench seat. Without specifying what he was carrying, the trucker admitted to transporting dangerous goods.

If he didn't get reassigned elsewhere, Beau hoped to be able to drive us 470 miles to Winnipeg. That would save us expensing for food *and* a hostel in Regina. A CB radio cradled next to Beau's right thigh blurted a constant stream of mostly incomprehensible static sounding a lot like the muffled speech of Mrs. Donovan, Charlie Brown's teacher. It was cool, something we'd not witnessed before. In response to many of the messages sent and received, Beau quipped, "Breaker, Breaker" or "What's your Twenty?"

Along the dazzling sunshine road, with the added advantage of having the range to survey long, unhindered stretches far ahead on the highway, our first time in a semi, I loved riding high in the cabin. Whistling down the pavement like a sleek featherweight, the monster-sized truck was proof that looks can be deceiving. Twenty miles outside of city limits, Beau barrelled past green distended fields suffused by yellow rapeseed, quilted in alternating patterns along the road.

A fine-looking sight.

Like a standup comic working new material, talking about the countryside, Beau kept us amused. He made cracks about slews, the name given to low lying stagnant ponds of accumulated drainage from groundwater found in ditches at the side of the highway. Every time he pointed one out, we'd howl with laughter, the word "slew" setting us off for no apparent reason. Shy of ninety minutes into our ride, Beau got the call he was waiting for, indicating he might be required to turn his load around for Edmonton instead of motoring on to Winnipeg. Edging closer to noon, Beau informed us he'd need to drop us somewhere, head to his depot for further instruction, and retrace his tracks to retrieve us if he didn't turn around. Either way, he would come back for us.

This news bulletin was disappointing. Jan and I liked Beau, and enjoyed riding in his truck.

Exiting off the highway aimed at a sign pointing to historic downtown Regina, Beau systematically downshifted, swinging his vehicle's hulking mass into a mall parking lot. Close to 1 pm, there was ample time to reach the hostel if need be, though we hedged a bet that Beau would be driving us on to Winnipeg.

Next to the mall, a Dairy Queen adjoined a drycleaner. Since neither of us had eaten, Beau hatched a strategy. "Tell you what. If you girls want to wait while I work things out, I'll buy you each a banana split, then come back to let you know what's happening. I shouldn't be longer than two hours, tops."

Did he say banana split? We weren't about to turn down free ice cream — plus, we could always poke around the mall. The only problem was our backpacks. If Beau didn't come back for a while, we surely didn't want to drag them around a shopping center.

I explained our problem to Beau who had a quick fix. "Don't worry about your packs. I'll keep them stored in my truck and bring them to you when I return."

Jan and I looked at one another questioningly. I was the first to speak up. "Sure…I guess that's okay." Uncertain if it really was the best arrangement, so far, Beau hadn't given any indication he was the thieving type. A hardworking married man and father, about to move into a brand new $100,000 home, his wife expecting another baby any day, Beau had friends camping on the front lawn of his property at night to make sure squatters didn't ransack the premises before he took possession. Only a creditable person would ensure the safety of his house.

We agreed to store our packs with Beau.

Partway through demolishing banana splits draped in gooey chocolate sauce, whipped cream, and maraschino cherries, our two heads followed Beau's truck out the Dairy Queen window until it disappeared. Then something occurred to Jan. Her eyes went wide. "Our purses are inside of our knapsacks!"

Out of sight. Out of our minds.

Fuck.

Keeping belongings together to minimize bulk while travelling, Jan and I had taken to packing our purses into our backpacks, leaving little cash in our jean's pockets. The acquisition of souvenirs the last couple of months was another reason to amass everything in one place.

I didn't have much money. What was left I would desperately need. Not to mention, birth certificates, and other incidentals were stored in our wallets, inside of our purses, inside of Beau's truck — some oddball who'd picked us up on the shoulder of Highway 11.

This is not how I predicted, or expected, the story would end.

"What will we do if Beau doesn't come *back*?" Jan whined, wild-eyed from across the table. Her dessert half-eaten, a touch of chocolate sauce smeared across her right cheek, creating a clean line. Glancing down at my banana split dish, I noticed the vanilla ice cream was almost finished.

Some of the whipped cream I'd saved for last bites.

"Then what?"

To convey confidence, I replied, "Of course he'll come back. All our stuff's inside his truck. He *has* to."

If it wasn't happening to us, I might have found the predicament hilarious. Regrettably, it had happened to us.

Nobody was splitting a gut.

"Dreamscape" watercolour painting by Barbara Mills.
COURTESY OF CARLY MILLS.

CHAPTER 61

Bottomed Out

"Courage is knowing what not to fear."
PLATO

We scraped the last dregs of our ice cream — food that might even have been purchased to throw us off the scent. I started thinking, thinking up a maneuver if Beau didn't return. Not knowing his surname ruled out the idea of calling his house from a payphone, speaking to his expectant wife. He was about to move. Maybe his phone was already disconnected, his new one not yet hooked up. Even if we did have a number, it would be futile to call Beau's house anyway. How would it sound?

"Oh, hello there. You don't know us but your husband picked us up hitchhiking this morning and now he's driven away with all of our stuff!"

Beau's wife might even be angry to learn that her husband was running around giving girls rides when he was supposed to be working. She'd hang up on us for sure. In that case, we'd have to call our parents to wire money home.

That was the last thing I wanted to do.

What if everything Beau told us was bullshit? Maybe he wasn't even married. Maybe he was a loner and fantasized about doing something like this one day. We had no significant cash. It didn't make sense. Beau was a long-distance trucker, a family man with responsibilities. How could he possibly benefit from duping a couple of teenagers?

What about the *slews*? Was that more manufactured crap or the truth?

Running my hands over my face, I had to quiet my head before I went around the bend.

"Well, we'll just have to wait and see if he shows up." Jan's voice was oddly upbeat. "I think he'll come back."

Staring hard at my friend, I didn't dare flinch nor do anything that might neutralize the test pattern on her face. But I had to ask. "Five minutes ago, you didn't sound so sure. What made you change your mind?"

"I don't know." Tilting her head serenely to one side, dream-like, Jan hypothesized, "He seems like a nice person. Anyway, I just meditated on it and imagined his truck pulling back into the parking lot. If we both believe that will happen, then it will. Come on. You do it too."

There are certain people in the world you don't ever want to cross, mock, or contradict. Jan is one of these. Her quiet wisdom and bravery was our one sure bet for climbing out of the sinkhole in which we'd found ourselves. Positive realization focus was all we had left. It was our only chance.

"You're right." A grin snuck up on my face, spreading from cheek to cheek. "It wouldn't hurt." Closing my eyes, I begin visualizing Beau's transport pulling into the parking lot, maintaining a respectable distance from other vehicles. The monster coasts to a slow stop and five fingers on Beau's left hand extend a sharp wave out the driver's side window while he raises his right fist to give the horn a friendly toot, alerting us to his return.

In case somebody of an influential nature was paying attention, I promised that if we got out of this mess, I wouldn't forget.

This time I meant it.

Valiantly, Jan and I wandered up and down mall corridors, trying not to think about how excruciating it would be if Beau decided not to grace us with his jolly presence and our gear. It was tough work, striving not to obsess about our dilemma, only worrying wouldn't help matters. What would Teddy have to say about this? *It's not your fault? Whatever happens will happen? It's getting better all the time?*

When it got close to the two-hour mark, Jan and I returned to the Dairy Queen and waited. At 2:20 pm, there was no sign of Beau. Three o'clock rolled around, still no wisp of a truck signalling into the parking lot followed by a reassuring hand wave and honk of the horn. The second hand on the wall clock crawled down to the bottom of its face. At half past three, nerves frayed, we tried not to let the other one aware. For the next ninety minutes, biding our time, shuffling our feet, we sipped water, talked about friends and our adventures. I'd pretty much given up hope of ever seeing Beau or my green backpack again. It wasn't the end of the world losing a pile of clothes and odds and ends; I just didn't want to go down in flames. The journey overall had been incredible, a sense of real accomplishment. Finally, I was beginning to emerge from my cocoon. Become the person I was supposed to be. My friendship with Jan was solid. We'd proven ourselves to effectively embrace, rebuff, and figure our way in and out of most circumstances.

Except for this mess.

Rechecking her Timex watch, Jan announced it was two minutes past five.

I dropped my head in despair. We'd waited long enough, far more than the two hours Beau told us he'd be gone more than four hours ago.

Excusing myself, rising from my seat, I stepped around a row of empty tables and made my way in the direction of the women's restroom. Gratefully, none of the staff had asked us to leave — yet.

Inside the stall, jeans bunched around my ankles, I thought long and hard about Jan. The last half hour, she had grown frightfully quiet and fidgety. Probably, she was dreading what her mom and dad were going to say when she told them we got ripped off. What about my own parents? They weren't going to be happy, no doubt about it. If only we could reverse time and take another crack, I would certainly do things differently.

Not be so reckless.

Or quick to consent.

Yes sir.

Letting myself out of the cubicle, I pulled up my jeans, stared into the mirror and squeezed a small swirl of soap into the palm of my hand. Fastened neatly into a ponytail earlier in the day, my unkempt hair had fallen loose. Dirty blonde strands wilted around my face. My green plaid flannel shirt had soaked through from humidity. Allowing the ice-cold water to run through my fingers, head hung low, I began to sob. To prevent soap from smearing in my eyes, I rubbed the backs of my hands against my wet cheeks. Wiping my eyes and hands dry with a paper towel, I snapped the copper button on my jeans and pressed on the door handle. Gazing warily out into the restaurant, taking a shallow breath, I hesitated.

There stood Jan, her legs pressed against our table. She was talking with a brown-haired man. Edging closer, his back toward me, I recognized the blue coveralls.

Good god. It couldn't be Beau.

Could it?

Heart pounding, my stomach did a cartwheel as if a kaleidoscope of butterflies had taken flight. Regaining my equilibrium, lurching toward my friend, I slackened next to her like a ragdoll. Obviously mollified by whatever Beau had to say, smiling happily, all concern erased from Jan's face.

"Hi." Beaming a big, apologetic grin, Beau pushed replay. "Hey, I'm really sorry for being a lot longer than I expected. I had to wait for my boss to show up at the depot to find out if I was supposed to be redirected to Edmonton. Turns out, I am. I went home to let my wife know."

Eyes downcast, Beau made another admission. "I was just telling Jan I won't be able to drive you girls to Winnipeg. Wish I could."

Raising and lowering my shaking shoulders, in my mind I'd recited a proposal that had almost been scratched. During my inauspicious trip to the ladies' room, it had likely already been covered by Jan and Beau. "That's alright," I smiled. "We're only a few miles from the Regina hostel. We can stay there overnight and go to Winnipeg tomorrow."

"Great." Turning toward the door, Beau pushed it open allowing us to step ahead of him. "I'll take you there right now."

Sitting next to Beau inside the truck's berth, I turned to notice our backpacks positioned exactly as we'd left them when Beau flung them up there earlier in the day. Relieved to see our personal property intact, leaning back, I managed to enjoy the short drive out to the Regina hostel. The last several hours had been a tidal wave of emotions, and yet everything turned out okay. Inches away from completely losing it, I was wiped out.

Five people were on site when Beau dropped us close to dinnertime. Situated deep within prairie country, the place was buzzing with young men: a pair of French Canadians, a native Canadian, two teenage boys from Santa Barbara and Anaheim, California. Kumio was also on site, complaining of blistering feet from all the miles he'd had to walk in his new tennis shoes.

We weren't the only ones put to the test that day.

The fifth time in nearly two weeks, Jan, Kumio, and I were marooned at the same hostel. As a treaty of friendship and endurance, Kumio bought a round of filet o' fish, fries, and coffee at McDonald's. Thrown together time and time again, strangers become friends or they become enemies. After a fashion, we had become friends.

Bursting with questions, Kumio wanted to know what was in store for us after returning home. Did we have anything *solid* lined up? Would we work or go to school? "What do Canadian girls *do* when they aren't on the road?"

Good question.

Earlier that day, during the fog when Jan and I struggled to put our best faces forward to avoid thoughts of disaster if Beau didn't return; Jan reconsidered Ron's favourable description of Boston. Remembering how beautiful he'd said the city is in autumn, the notion of going there, even on a short trip, possibly with May and Jen, or Liz along for fun, was something worth considering. Moreover, looking ahead to spring, we considered going the opposite direction, to Canada's East Coast, maybe even as far as Prince Edward Island.

Our friendship had withstood minor scratches and dents, yet it was unbroken. Striking off again in the fall might be pushing things. Besides, a break is healthy, a time to retool. Depending whether Doug still had feelings for me or if I had feelings for him once there were no distractions to confuse things, there was the possibility of a long-distance romance.

Of course, there would always be HOOM.

I finished up a couple of rough sketches of Gregg Allman and David Bowie. Picking up the New Testament, I decided to give it another try. From what I'd gathered, and from talking to people, the book held promise of an unsullied start. Representing an opportunity for a second shot at eternal life, the symbolic arrival of Jesus seemed much like being dealt a fresh poker hand in hopes of eradicating mistakes committed during the previous round. Given the way the day had played out, in hindsight, Lady Luck was on our side.

Out of her sleeping bag and gone from our room, next morning, I found Jan in the kitchen eating porridge. An orange lay beside her bowl, a large glass of milk sat on the table. Breakfast cost 30 cents.

One of the friendlier, older guys, Gordy, who'd arrived from British Columbia late the night before, mentioned to somebody he was driving east. Overhearing the conversation, impulsively, I asked for a lift to Winnipeg if Gordy was going that far, and offered to help pay gas. It was a brazen offer. Except for a handful of small bills, I was out of cash and dipping into the imaginary pocket of credit. Pleased to have company along, Gordy expected to get a good start on the 360-mile drive, an approximate nine-hour trip barring any unforeseen interferences. Hurrying through breakfast, we packed up quickly.

Quarter past eight, Jan and I met Gordy in front of the hostel.

Flanking Gordy's white, blacktopped Chrysler, showing off his brand-new pair of tennis shoes, Kumio arrived to bid us a definitive goodbye. Trusting that his footwear would outlast the trip, Kumio planned to continue moving east, though not as far as Toronto, and eventually find work.

My heart went out to Kumio, our pesky, endearing punching bag, friend, and comrade. The next few days, chances of meeting the likes of Kumio, Doug, Gary, Teddy, Marco, Yvette, and Doug from Hemet were nil. Unless something dramatically shifted our course, later that day, Jan and I would be sitting on an eastbound train chewing on our next play.

Gordy hightailed it down Highway 1, manipulating the gears of his Chrysler as if he meant business. From Regina on, the pencil-straight road was unencumbered by much in the way of natural attractions. Enhanced by level lowland, looking infinitely out over the horizon, the pavement ahead fashioned a kind of crude narrowing, culminating in a pointed scale often parodied in Bugs Bunny cartoons. Resplendent doses of sunshine touched down on our vehicle, revealing thick soap streaks on the windshield, a hangover from the Chrysler's last wash. For the first 100 miles, the three of us made casual conversation, the parameter of subjects subtly expanding as the highway continued to lengthen across the plains.

One week before, Gordy returned to Canada following a year travelling Australia and New Zealand, living and working on kibbutzes. Raised in a large family, he'd grown up in a rural area an hour east of Vancouver. Claiming to be the only "normal" one amongst his family, Gordy told us about two older brothers that were currently serving time for drug trafficking in a medium security federal penitentiary in California. His younger sister was a runaway. No trace if she was dead or alive, Gordy's parents were fraught with the horror of waking up one morning to find out she'd been murdered. Two other siblings were estranged from the family. According to Gordy, another sister who resided at home was the only offspring to "turn out straight."

Trying to fathom what could have gone horribly wrong for everything to have turned out so fucked-up, to consistently find yourself at the short end of the stick, there must be justifiable reason. Even on my worst day, I couldn't imagine disconnecting from my family.

Watching grain elevators roost on the prairie pastures, I thought again about San Francisco, our friends at Steiner Street. Recalling the Good Samaritan, the Brothers, the Sisters, even the emotional commotion that had skulked on the sidelines almost from day one, I wouldn't trade any of it. Crashing at Meadowlark for one week had been a far greater education than labouring in school for a four-month term. Those crucial junctures marking our surroundings, the various people, their circumstances, and the scope of everything that had actuated the rhythm of things; remembrances, music, the revelation of Phil Ochs, would persevere long after our return.

Crossing between Saskatchewan and Manitoba was indiscernible. The Chrysler roamed onward to the farming community of Virden, a cute little town situated in the Southwestern part of the province. Once we'd passed through, my stomach began to snarl. Gordy pulled into a truck stop where we purchased a couple of bags of potato chips and pop from a vending machine. Following a quick pee and refill, our vehicle was back on the Trans Canada, one hour this side of Brandon making great time.

In three hours, Jan and I were due to arrive at the CN railway station in Winnipeg.

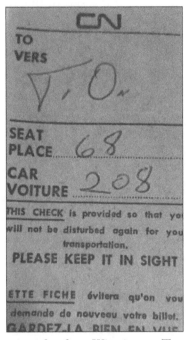

CN train ticket from Winnipeg to Toronto.

CHAPTER 62

All Aboard

"My hopes and dreams assemble like a huge tear. Sliding down the trembling face of time, it lingers for an instant and disappears."
POEM FOUND IN AN OPEN BOOK *in an antique shop in San Diego, inviting collaborators worldwide to contribute.*

Hustling in and out of Brandon, we proceeded to move through Portage La Prairie, a tiny city occupying land on the Assiniboine River, one of Manitoba's major agricultural centers. Beyond a hiking trail dotting Crescent Lake, Gordy's Chrysler tripped around neatly trimmed rows of cottonwood trees where flocks of Canada geese had gathered. Despite having almost no money, Jan and I got to thinking; there might be way to suspend our travels for at least another week. Once we arrived at the station, we would ask for a ticket to Sault Ste. Marie or Sudbury and stay in another hostel a few days. Neither one of us had been to Northern Ontario. It seemed a fitting place to close the final chapter of our trip, navigating the sticks of our own province in the northerly region, where fresh water lakes and forests are dominated by moose and deer. Maybe we'd even learn to become outdoorswomen, educate ourselves on the finer points of rural survival. If we could catch a train to either town, it'd be close enough to home to get there within a day, yet far enough away to perpetuate the insatiable pull of the highway.

First impressions of the Gateway to the West, also known as Winnipeg, were disappointing and harsh. Flat like prairie country and lacking the appeal of the gold, green and blue topography to which we'd grown accustomed for several months, the grubby streets of Winnipeg felt cold, stifling, and hostile. Gordy told us the city was built on a swamp and had mosquitoes the size of dragonflies.

No guff.

Pulling over to an empty parking spot within the business section, Gordy made an inquiry to a pedestrian about the location of the CN rail station. Directing him down the street to the first intersection, the woman instructed Gordy to turn right at the light on to Main Street, keep driving a couple more blocks to Broadway. That's where we would unearth the finish line.

Would supporters greet us there with hot black coffee and applause?

Anxious and apprehensive, I wished we'd chosen somewhere other than the menacing city of Winnipeg to make our transference to reality. Perhaps there were some pretty parts of the city, or cool hangouts, we wouldn't stay long enough to find out. Ours was an objectionable conclusion. I felt cheated suddenly, as if all along, Jan and I'd been easy bait for some cheap parlour trick.

Parking the car at a temporary drop-off zone, Gordy accompanied us into the train station and across to the ticket booth. Wanting to be certain there was an eastbound train that day; he waited by the wicket while Jan and I spoke to the woman behind the grate. It was a few minutes past six. A train scheduled for Toronto that evening was leaving in a little over an hour. No stops. The notion of a layover in Sault Ste. Marie or Sudbury was immediately wiped out. Worse, tickets cost $110 for two! Jan would cover me thirty bucks until we got home.

A queue started to form. Growing impatient, the young ticket vendor wanted to know if we wished to purchase tickets or "stand there looking ugly?" Without any recourse in mind, Jan and I pooled our funds on the marble countertop inches from the snarky agent's face. In exchange, we were given two one-way ticket vouchers from Winnipeg to Toronto, leaving platform ten at 7:10 pm. Scheduled time of arrival: 9 am Friday morning. That left thirty-six hours to sit upright in a rigid seat tracking 1500 miles.

Turning away from the booth, tickets in hand, Jan and I accompanied Gordy outside to claim our gear for the umpteenth time. Slinging the oblong green sack over both my shoulders, hooking my arms into the handles, I sure wouldn't miss the heft of my backpack. Stripping down to a single purse would be freedom.

Another point tacked on for going home.

Gordy hugged us both, and then watched courteously from the Chrysler as we circled in front of the train station. With almost an hour to wait and a long ride ahead of us, Jan and I walked to the nearby Eaton's store to pick up edibles for the trip.

Equipped with packages of peanut butter, crackers honey, and bread, we returned to the station, leaving plenty of time to stop at a payphone and look up a childhood friend. Bonnie had moved to Winnipeg when we were both nine. We'd since lost touch. Running my index finger down the white pages, there were several listings under Bonnie's surname, too many to try. Anyway, the family probably had an unlisted number or moved away.

Re-entering the train station, no explanation given, Jan and I were frustrated to learn that our train would be delayed *four and a half* hours. Sightseeing through the porthole of a fast-moving conduit sidetracked by unexplored territory is a far cry from vacillating in a foreign city anticipating taking the long ride home to a big fat question mark.

Shit.

The next several hours, loafing in the station, my friend and I had a lot on our minds. The cuticles on my fingers were the first casualty. Despite good intentions and positive motivation, returning to my hometown felt like a decree. A little overdramatic maybe, but it was true. I would be reassuming the same status I'd wanted to dodge. Advised by her parents to apply to a few academic schools prior to leaving home, smartly, Jan had heeded her mom and dad's advice. Accepted at all three, she hadn't yet decided on a plan of action, though the discussion of deferring school until winter had fallen by the wayside. At least there was something tangible, and Jan wasn't inflexible in the way that I was. I admired that about her. Our other friends had all applied at schools and would be entering university come September.

Setting an aim toward higher learning was recommended at our house, though not necessarily as a priority. Most of his life, my father had been an entrepreneur in some capacity, my mom worked part-time in retail. If all else failed, there was St. Lawrence College waiting for me in Kingston.

It wasn't absolution.

Because of my single-minded vision about travel and inability to hack school, I wasn't about to capitulate just yet. In the interim, I'd have to apply for something menial, at least for a time, to save money if I wanted to continue to travel, return to San Francisco, or maybe visit Doug in Oregon. Right now, I couldn't justify applying for a loan. Spend it on some program when I had no concept what I wanted to study — if I wanted to study. At least temporarily, finding work, paying board, living at home — the roughest part — would be my reality. I loved my parents, but after knowing the freedom to thrive and fail, I didn't relish the idea of regression or susceptibility to the same contentious buttons being pushed.

There were a few.

To my left, a man reached down to a newspaper stand. Sliding a quarter in the slot, freeing the Plexiglas door, he removed a copy of the Winnipeg Free Press. Across the aisle, a small, dark-haired child clung to the certainty of her mother's handbag. Through enormous brown eyes, she watched travellers and commuters coming and going, toting handbags, luggage, briefcases. Immersed within the pages of a drugstore paperback, the girl's young mother looked up suddenly to ensure her youngster had not gone astray, then returned to her book. Down the corridor of one of the concourses, knapsacks slung wildly across their backs, teenaged couples rushed to catch a train.

Was this the inauguration of their journey, the intermission, or the windup?

Next to me on the adjoining wood bench, prose precise, focused as always, Jan jotted the latest entry in her diary. Possibly, she was describing our day trip. Jan riding shotgun that afternoon in Gordy's white, black-topped Chrysler, the best seat in the house where one dreams of reticent ghosts with outstretched arms giving rise to elongated shadows proliferating the highway. Pulling out of Brandon that afternoon whistling between wide-open plains, "These Days," the emotionally raw Jackson Browne song recorded a few years earlier, captivated me from the Chrysler's brand new built-in speakers. Interchanging optimism and despair, in similar vein to Ochs, Browne sings about thinking, regret, taking risks, the burden of fault, fear, prospects. The song's propensity to touch every nerve renders the piece poignant and prophetic.

As the horizon of our future loomed closer, I began thinking about "These Days" as an effigy, an incarnation, not only denoting the last six months, but our generation. The emancipating moral of Browne's melancholy presents an offering, an avowal that what lies ahead is a mystery, indispensable as the past.

The road trip with Gordy from Regina to Winnipeg was our own foretelling; the ultimate chance that Jan and I would take on a stranger for a long while, but not for keeps.

Looking toward the oath of another adventure to be revealed, I would determine to keep on moving.

Carry on growing.

Flow Steady. Look around. Pick a place.

Dream small. Feel big.

Mind sharp always.

Believe in new possibilities.

In any case, it's getting better all the time.

The End

The Final Word

Over dinner recently, a good friend of mine said, "I think you should write an epilogue."

An epilogue is something I hadn't considered, yet the more I thought about it, I decided it would give proper closure to the book, and provide a brief update for readers who might be curious about the fate of some of the story's friends and acquaintances.

A few weeks after arriving home early August, Jan and I reunited with our hometown friends congregated in Liz's den in a wonderful celebration that exceeded expectations. That September, including Jan, everybody went off to university. Living at home for four months, I found work in a factory assembling windshield wiper parts before entering Guelph University in the winter semester. Leaving school in spring 1977, Jan and I travelled to Prince Edward Island and spent several months living in the country with friends before Jan returned to Ontario in December. Remaining behind, I continued to live on the island for nearly three years where I connected with my husband. In 2018, we will celebrate our 40th anniversary, and have raised two amazing children. During her visit to our apartment in Charlottetown the summer of 1979, Jan was introduced to my brother-in-law. Eventually, the couple moved to Vancouver Island where they lived and worked for several years before returning to Ontario. In 1990 they were married, and have two beautiful daughters.

Prior to returning to their respective homes in Christchurch, New Zealand, and Albany, Oregon, August 1976, Gary and Doug visited Jan and me (though not together!) spending a few fun-filled weeks. The last Jan heard in 2012, Gary and his wife owned and operated a hostel in New Zealand. In the 1980s, while living in British Columbia, Jan received a surprise visit from Marco who is now a surgeon in Switzerland.

Contact with our former roommate, Debbie, and our friend Lorraine from Vancouver's YWCA has been lost.

A few years following my Vancouver Cousin Betsy's divorce, she happily remarried a caring man. The couple resides on B.C.'s Salt Spring Island.

Los Angeles cousins Vic and Patti also divorced. Unexpectedly, Vic passed away a couple of years ago. Through his two grown children and four grandchildren, his lively spirit lives on.

Along with his second wife of almost twenty-five years, Cousin Mark lives and thrives in Northern California. Together, they breed and show dogs.

In spring 1992, my brother Chris died tragically in a horseback riding accident. Remembering him often, I am grateful he was doing something he loved when he passed, and that we could share many memorable times together, especially in California, and later, at his homes in Millgrove, and Lynden, Ontario.

Spring 2014, I returned to Hemet, California, and the location of the former Meadowlark ranch and health spa owned and overseen by Dr. Evarts Loomis. Over past decades, the property has been sold several times, and unfortunately, many of the original buildings have fallen into disrepair. Loomis died in 2003, at 93-years of age. His life's work and legacy continues. For a time, through letters, Jan and I kept up with our friend and polarity healer in the making, Bruce Flagg, but no longer know of his whereabouts.

Through the advent of the internet and social media sites, I have been able to trace some of the other people featured throughout the memoir. In 2016, I corresponded with Ellen from Edmonton, and found Allan who appeared jovial in photos. Russell, who drove Jan and me to Eugene, Oregon through Mount Shasta, is alive, well, and living in Wisconsin along with his partner of thirty-five years. On his Facebook page, there is a sweet photo of Russell and his wife wearing bike helmets standing at a lookout point under sunny skies.

In 2014, I joined HOOM's Facebook group and communicate occasionally with former members. Some of the folks from the original San Francisco chapter are known, or familiar to the group. A year after our journey, Father Donald and Sister Rose married and raised three children before separating several years ago. Now retired from his career as a Mental Health Therapist and Public Health Educator, Donald and his partner of seventeen years have an Airbnb in Portland, and enjoy travel year-round. Though HOOM no longer functions under its initial name, many of its core teachings and original practices have been preserved under the name, Science of Man. Donald continues his faith under the new charter.

Evangel Home continues to function as a hospice for women, families, and children in Fresno, California.

I've exchanged emails with two people formerly of Texas Lake Community and hostel in Hope, B.C. They both look forward to reading the finished book.

For approximately five years, Jan, Yvette and I continued to write letters to one another before falling off. In the winter of 2014, I searched Yvette online and we resumed communication. That summer, my husband and I met Yvette and her partner for pizza outside of Boston. We had a terrific time that evening, laughing, and recapping our experiences. Sadly, her brother Luke passed away from Leukemia in 2002. Yvette and her husband are currently renovating a lovely home they own in the country.

Saving the best for last, or perhaps, the person, who had the greatest impact on my frame of mind during that precarious phase of my life, Teddy/the "Good Samaritan," now in his late sixties, resides in Massachusetts. At some point, Teddy left HOOM, finished college, and in 1981, married a nurse. Retired from a satisfying career in social justice, today, Teddy takes great joy in his stepchildren and grandchildren. He paints, enjoys music, composes poetry, and writes, "I have a wonderful life."

I know these things to be true not from personal experience, but because I have read them. After more than 40 years, still hesitant to burst the bubble, I am heartened that Teddy's life (and my own) turned out far better than I expected, but perhaps exactly as he did.

JILL C. NELSON

Acknowledgements

Tapes from California: Teenage Road Tripping, 1976 would not have been possible without the help of key people who were instrumental in making this book become a reality. For sharing her personal diary, her memories, a cornucopia of photos and memorabilia gathered during our six-month travels, I would like to extend sincere gratitude and love to my sister-in-law, Jan. Special thanks and credit to David Barker for contributing the book's beautiful foreword, to my dear friend Lyn Lawrence for proofing this project with wisdom and heart, to my good friend at JSV Designs for the book's stylish cover design, to David Craig for assisting with the restoration of specific photos, the late William Margold for suggesting "Teenage Road Tripping" as the book's subtitle, Brian Pearce for skillfully crafting the completed book, my wonderful editor, Brian Tedesco, and my steadfast publisher Ben Ohmart.

I would also like to acknowledge my daughter, Andrea, for sharing select photos from her very own August 2015 'Tapes from California' journey, friends Joel Sussman and Carly Mills for allowing the use of special photographs and paintings, and other resources such as *http://evangelhome.org/*; Wikipedia; *https://sites.google.com/site/texaslakesite/*; *The Golden Force*, and *The Meadowlark Cookbook*.

Thank you Hud, Corey, Andrea, my mom, and Brother Steve for your enduring love and devotion, and to my beloved family and friends for your ongoing support and encouragement.

Last, but not least, much appreciation to my Canadian and American relatives that opened their homes to us those many years ago, to the folks we encountered, and friends made throughout our journey.

Peace.

Bear Manor Media 🐼

ALSO STARRING...
FORTY BIOGRAPHICAL ESSAYS ON THE GREATEST CHARACTER ACTORS OF HOLLYWOOD'S GOLDEN ERA, 1930-1965
CYNTHIA and SARA BRIDESON

Affectionately Jayne Mansfield
RICHARD KOPER

Jill C. Nelson

25 legendary women of classic erotic cinema 1968 - 1985

GOLDEN GODDESSES

With over 300 photos, & film highlights

Featuring: Seka, Marilyn Chambers, Serena, Kay Parker, Ginger Lynn, Amber Lynn, Juliet Anderson, Rhonda Jo Petty, Veronica Hart, Kelly Nichols, Annie Sprinkle, Georgina Spelvin, Gloria Leonard, Candida Royalle, Sharon Mitchell, Nina Hartley, Christy Canyon, Laurie Holmes, and many, many more

Foreword by Jennifer Sugar

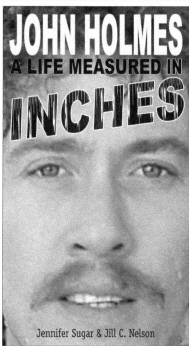

JOHN HOLMES
A LIFE MEASURED IN
INCHES

Jennifer Sugar & Jill C. Nelson

Classic Cinema.
Timeless TV.
Retro Radio.

WWW.BEARMANORMEDIA.COM

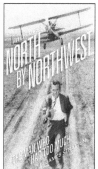

Mel Blanc
THE MAN OF A THOUSAND VOICES
BY BEN OHMART

Dangerous Curves atop Hollywood Heels
The Lives, Careers, and Misfortunes of 14 Hard-Luck Girls of the Silent Screen
by RICHARD A. RUSSELL

NORTH BY NORTHWEST
THE MAN WHO HAD TOO MUCH
JAMES STEWART

VERNON DENT
STOOGE HEAVY
SECOND BANANA TO THE THREE STOOGES AND OTHER FILM COMEDY GREATS BY BILL CASSARA

CPSIA information can be obtained
at www.ICGtesting.com
Printed in the USA
LVHW01s2100220118
563534LV00017B/1885/P